EUROPEAN STATES AND THEIR MUSLIM CITIZENS

This book responds to the often loud debates about the place of Muslims in Western Europe by proposing an analysis based in institutions including schools, courts, hospitals, the military, electoral politics, the labor market, and civic education courses. The contributors consider the way people draw on practical schemas regarding others in their midst who are often categorized as Muslims.

Chapters based on fieldwork and policy analysis across several countries examine how people interact in their everyday work lives, where they construct moral boundaries, and how they formulate policies concerning tolerable diversity, immigration, discrimination, and political representation. Rather than assuming that each country has its own national ideology that explains such interactions, contributors trace diverse pathways along which institutions complicate or disrupt allegedly consistent national ideologies. These studies shed light on how Muslims encounter particular faces and facets of the state as they go about their lives, seeking help and legitimacy as new citizens of a fast-changing Europe.

John R. Bowen is Dunbar–Van Cleve Professor in Arts & Sciences at Washington University in St. Louis, and studies Islam and society in Indonesia and Europe. His most recent books are *A New Anthropology of Islam* (2012) and *Blaming Islam* (2012).

Christophe Bertossi is Director of the Centre for Migrations and Citizenship at the French Institute for International Relations in Paris; his research concerns citizenship and the roles of Muslims in the French military, gendarmerie, and hospitals. His most recent publication is *As Cruzadas da Integraçao na Europa* (2012).

Jan Willem Duyvendak is Professor of Sociology at the University of Amsterdam, and studies questions of belonging, urban sociology, and nativism. His latest books are *The Politics of Home: Nostalgia and Belonging in Western Europe and the United States* (2011) and *Crafting Citizenship: Negotiating Tensions in Modern Society* (2013, with Menno Hurenkamp and Evelien Tonkens).

Mona Lena Krook is Associate Professor of Political Science at Rutgers University. Her research examines electoral gender quotas in cross-national perspective. Her first book, *Quotas for Women in Politics: Gender and Candidate Selection Reform Worldwide* (2009), received the American Political Science Association Victoria Schuck Award for the Best Book on Women and Politics in 2010.

CAMBRIDGE STUDIES IN LAW AND SOCIETY

Cambridge Studies in Law and Society aims to publish the best scholarly work on legal discourse and practice in its social and institutional contexts, combining theoretical insights and empirical research.

The fields that it covers are: studies of law in action; the sociology of law; the anthropology of law; cultural studies of law, including the role of legal discourses in social formations; law and economics; law and politics; and studies of governance. The books consider all forms of legal discourse across societies, rather than being limited to lawyers' discourses alone.

The series editors come from a range of disciplines: academic law; socio-legal studies; sociology; and anthropology. All have been actively involved in teaching and writing about law in context.

Books in the Series

Diseases of the Will
Mariana Valverde

The Politics of Truth and Reconciliation in South Africa: Legitimizing the Post-Apartheid State
Richard A. Wilson

Modernism and the Grounds of Law
Peter Fitzpatrick

Unemployment and Government: Genealogies of the Social
William Walters

Autonomy and Ethnicity: Negotiating Competing Claims in Multi-Ethnic States
Yash Ghai

Constituting Democracy: Law, Globalism and South Africa's Political Reconstruction
Heinz Klug

The Ritual of Rights in Japan: Law, Society, and Health Policy
Eric A. Feldman

(continued after index)

European States and Their Muslim Citizens

The Impact of Institutions on Perceptions and Boundaries

Edited by

JOHN R. BOWEN
Washington University, St. Louis

CHRISTOPHE BERTOSSI
French Institute of International Relations, Center for Migration and Citizenship

JAN WILLEM DUYVENDAK
University of Amsterdam

MONA LENA KROOK
Washington University, St. Louis

CAMBRIDGE
UNIVERSITY PRESS

CAMBRIDGE
UNIVERSITY PRESS

32 Avenue of the Americas, New York NY 10013-2473, USA

Cambridge University Press is part of the University of Cambridge.

It furthers the University's mission by disseminating knowledge in the pursuit of education, learning, and research at the highest international levels of excellence.

www.cambridge.org
Information on this title: www.cambridge.org/9781107038646

First published 2014

Printed in the United States of America

A catalog record for this publication is available from the British Library.

Library of Congress Cataloging in Publication data
European states and their Muslim citizens : the impact of institutions on perceptions and boundaries / edited by John R. Bowen, Washington University, St. Louis; Christophe Bertossi, French Institute of International Relations, Center for Migration and Citizenship; Jan Willem Duyvendak, University of Amsterdam; Mona Lena Krook, Washington University, St. Louis.
p. cm. – (Cambridge studies in law and society)
Includes bibliographical references and index.
ISBN 978-1-107-03864-6 (hardback)
1. Muslims – European Union countries – Social conditions. 2. Muslims – Government policy – European Union countries. 3. Muslims – Legal status, laws, etc. – European Union countries. 4. Muslims – Cultural assimilation – European Union countries. I. Bowen, John R., editor of compilation.
D1056.2.M87E977 2013
305.6'97094–dc23 2013018459

ISBN 978-1-107-03864-6 Hardback

Contents

Contributors *page* ix

1. An Institutional Approach to Framing Muslims in Europe 1
   John R. Bowen, Christophe Bertossi, Jan Willem Duyvendak, and Mona Lena Krook

PART I. PRACTICAL SCHEMAS IN EVERYDAY INSTITUTIONAL LIFE

2. Hospitals as Sites of Cultural Confrontation and Integration in France and Germany 29
   Carolyn Sargent and Susan L. Erikson
3. Schooling and New Religious Diversity across Four European Countries 54
   Thijl Sunier
4. French "Muslim" Soldiers? Social Change and Pragmatism in a Military Institution 73
   Christophe Bertossi
5. Practical Schemas, Conjunctures, and Social Locations: *Laïcité* in French Schools and Hospitals 104
   Christophe Bertossi and John R. Bowen

PART II. INSTITUTIONS AND NATIONAL POLITICAL IDEOLOGIES

6. Juridical Framings of Muslims and Islam in France and Germany 135
   John R. Bowen and Mathias Rohe
7. Legitimizing Host Country Institutions: A Comparative Analysis of the Content of Civic Education Courses in France and Germany 164
   Ines Michalowski
8. Minorities in Electoral Politics: Gender, Race, and Political Inclusion in Sweden, France, and Britain 189
   Mona Lena Krook

9. How Institutional Context Shapes Head Scarf Debates across Scandinavia 216
Birte Siim

10. Populism, Sexual Politics, and the Exclusion of Muslims in the Netherlands 235
Justus Uitermark, Paul Mepschen, and Jan Willem Duyvendak

11. Conclusion 256
John R. Bowen, Christophe Bertossi, Jan Willem Duyvendak, and Mona Lena Krook

Index 273

Contributors

Christophe Bertossi, Director of the Centre for Migrations and Citizenship, French Institute for International Relations, Paris

John R. Bowen, Dunbar–Van Cleve Professor in Arts & Sciences, Washington University in St. Louis

Jan Willem Duyvendak, Professor of Sociology, University of Amsterdam

Susan L. Erikson, Associate Professor, Faculty of Health Sciences, Simon Fraser University

Mona Lena Krook, Associate Professor of Political Science, Rutgers University

Paul Mepschen, Department of Sociology and Anthropology, University of Amsterdam

Ines Michalowski, Senior Researcher, WZB Berlin Social Research Center

Mathias Rohe, Professor of Law, Friedrich-Alexander University, Erlangen-Nürnberg

Carolyn Sargent, Professor of Anthropology and of Women, Gender, and Sexuality Studies, Washington University in St Louis

Birte Siim, Professor of Gender Research in the Social Sciences, Department of Culture and Global Studies, Aalborg University

Thijl Sunier, Professor of Cultural Anthropology, VU University Amsterdam

Justus Uitermark, Associate Professor of Sociology, University of Amsterdam, and Professor of Community Development, Erasmus University Rotterdam

1 An Institutional Approach to Framing Muslims in Europe

John R. Bowen, Christophe Bertossi, Jan Willem Duyvendak, and Mona Lena Krook

Across Western Europe, public discourse has been suffused by claims about Muslims and Islam. These claims are mainly negative. Across a wide political spectrum, public figures denounce Islam for its retrograde values. Some claim that Islam is incompatible with the values of Europe and European states, that Muslims are irreducibly foreign because they will not or cannot abandon pre-Enlightenment ideas. Framing Islam as a set of values intrinsically incompatible with Europe implies that Muslims must choose between abandoning their religion and remaining outside the boundaries of the true European citizenry.

This representation was at the heart, for instance, of the 2004 ban on wearing the Islamic veil in public schools in France. As Joan Scott (2007: 8) argues, "Outlawing the veil … was an attempt to enact a particular version of reality, one which insisted on assimilation as the only way for Muslims to become French." The notion that Islamic moralities and "modern" Europeanness are mutually exclusive has also played a key role in Dutch debates. The highly influential late right-wing populist Pim Fortuyn argued that Islam was a backward religion. Unlike Islam, Fortuyn argued, Judaism and Christianity had been transformed by "the Enlightenment," during which the essential "Western" values such as individual responsibility, the separation of church and state, and the equality of men and women – among others – had developed. Fortuyn described Islam as a backward culture and a threat to his personal way of life: "I refuse to start all over again with the emancipation of women and gays."[1]

[1] *de Volkskrant*, February 9, 2002, http://www.volkskrant.nl/vk/nl/2824/Politiek/article/detail/611698/2002/02/09/De-islam-is-een-achterlijke-cultuur.dhtml. Another example: the Iranian-Dutch professor of law Afshin Ellian published a lecture in 2002 in which he argued against "the relativism of the Dutch state in dealing with Muslim homophobia." Ellian asked: "Do we want to transform Muslims into citizens on the basis of the constitution? Or do we want

Thus the notion of "Muslim citizens" appears as an oxymoron: their presence as citizens would challenge the essential values constitutive of European civilization. We read, nearly every day, stories about Islamic challenges to gender equality, in the form of head scarves in schools or refusals to allow male doctors to examine female patients, or about Muslims weakening civic life either by introducing religion into the public sphere or the opposite, by isolating themselves in religious enclaves.[2]

The response has been varied, and often desperate. Western European states have tried to define national identities as reservoirs of values for citizenship: Dutch values, French *laïcité*, Danish identity, Britishness, or Italian national culture. By doing so they have transformed what had been values of liberal citizenship into values of cultural distinctiveness. To a great and perhaps increasing extent, these nationalist cultural claims are confused with claims about the principles that guide how a particular Western European country works. Some French social scientists use *laïcité* to explain particular laws and policies, writing as if the term had a stable, agreed-on meaning. Others, writing about the Netherlands, argue that "multiculturalism" was once the Dutch national model, and their arguments converge with populist and nationalist uses made of "multiculturalism" in Dutch public debates. Disputes about the future of "British multiculturalism" are structured along similar lines. In these and other instances, it becomes difficult to pry apart national ideologies from analytical models.[3] More often than not, both political and analytical discourses on citizenship share a common concern about the so-called multicultural crisis of European immigration societies and the role played by Islam and Muslims in this crisis. They both identify national idioms of citizenship as the framework of reference at once to assess, explain, and resolve the crisis.[4]

Of course, cross-national differences are real and important. We argue, however, that to understand these variations we must take into account two

them to become citizens of a political Islam which violates human rights?" (*Trouw*, February 2, 2002).

[2] On the claims about enclaving and its supposed cause – multiculturalism – see Bowen (2011a).

[3] On these uses of the notion of national models in the comparative scholarship, see Bertossi and Duyvendak (2012); Bertossi, Duyvendak, and Schain (2012); Bertossi (2011); and Bowen (2007b).

[4] On French *laïcité*, see Baubérot (2004) and Bowen (2012). The Dutch case illustrates the same point, when some authors combine social scientific analysis with normative arguments. On the one hand, they analyze Dutch integration policies as based on a "multiculturalist model" (Joppke 2004: 248; Koopmans 2002: 91; Sniderman and Hagendoorn 2007). On the other hand, they blame these policies for "feelings of homelessness and alienation among native Dutch" (Sniderman and Hagendoorn, 2007; see Koopmans et al. 2005: 143). For a different position on the Dutch case, see Chapter 10.

important sets of dynamics. One is the *relative autonomy* of what takes place in different institutional settings. Each of these locations – for example, the army, the school, or the court – has its own repertoires of "practical schemas" for action, namely complexes of ideas, norms, values, and emotions that are not reducible to a national model or ideology. As such, similar trends can be observed across national borders. At the same time, however, national ideologies do have strong effects of shaping patterns of reasoning and practices. Rather than assuming these effects prior to the analysis, it is essential that such influences be traced and demonstrated, underscoring how they interact with specific institutional logics.

STUDYING INSTITUTIONS

In line with these insights, this book examines both institutional properties and national ideologies, emphasizing one or the other in different analytic moments, in order to accentuate the dual character, national and institutional, of the mechanisms and processes shaping perceptions and boundaries regarding Muslims in Europe. The authors collectively look at schools, courts, hospitals, the military, electoral politics, the labor market, and civic education courses. We analyze representations and policy framings across strategically chosen countries and across institutional locations in order to compare the shaping effects of these particular institutions on the one hand and of national ideologies on the other. Whether institutions provide more or less accommodation to Muslims or, on the contrary, impose negative framings on them cannot be explained by a national ideology about immigrant integration, citizenship, and religious diversity. What we propose here is precisely an analytical framework that emphasizes the different and complex dimensions of this question.

In so doing, we take as our object the relationship of European states to those residents and citizens sometimes viewed as Muslims, and we analyze that relationship through the workings of certain key public institutions, from courts and the military to schools and hospitals. It is through participating in the social life of these institutions that most residents and citizens encounter "the state": as a regulator of citizenship, a provider of services, or a source of employment. It is in these varied and relatively autonomous social contexts that boundaries are created or reaffirmed in ways that have the sanction of the state behind them. It is also in these institutional settings that employees interact both with "clients" (like job seekers, students, litigants) and with the broader political and public settings of state offices, elected officials, and representatives of the media. It is also with regard to these settings that the most visible conflicts have emerged about Muslims and Islam in today's Europe: on clothing in schools and hospitals, ethnic representation in the army or on electoral lists, and challenges from "sharia councils" to the legal system.[5]

These examples should make clear that we do not wish to suggest, either by our title or in our approach, that "the state" and "Muslims" form two homogeneous blocs, facing each other. "Muslims" is used here in the sense of "sociological Muslims" – that is, people whose background and traditions form part of the long history of Muslim civilization, regardless of whether they worship regularly or what they believe. It is very important not to ascribe a uniformity of religious observance to Muslims, but most of them consider themselves to be Muslims, and they are seen as such by others around them. For that reason, we retain "Muslim" as a socially relevant characteristic applying to a broad category of residents and citizens of Europe. But it does not mean that all Muslims always highlight that dimension of their identity in their everyday lives (see Bowen 2010: 11).

Nor do we intend that "citizens" be read in an inordinately literal sense, in terms of the precise requirements for nationality. In this period of increasingly complex and multiple senses of citizenship (Soysal 1994), residents of Europe may be on diverse pathways to permanent status, and, increasingly, they are measured in terms of their potential fitness for citizenship.[6] This "interpellation" of Muslims, their call to present themselves in suitable form for integration, is constitutive both of national imaginaries (can Islam fit into visions of Norway, or France?) and of specific institutions' relationships with Muslims, as Muslims are imagined as components of the army or targeted by citizenship courses and tests. Even those who are recent immigrants, as Sargent and Erikson show in their study of hospitals (Chapter 2) in this volume, are called and measured in this way.

Precisely how specific actors draw on their repertoires of ideas and emotions concerning others – defined in terms of ethnicity, religion, color, origin, or in other ways – is what we wish to uncover, not what we assume. As Glick Schiller, Çağlar, and Guldbrandsen (2006: 613) put it, we are interested in documenting "institutional processes through which ethnic categories and identities are constructed and naturalized." The term "Muslims" is only a starting point, and then it needs to be unpacked and contextualized. For example, although the French media looks for stories about troubles originating from "Islam" and

5 In a few places, as in Chapter 9 by Birte Siim, we also consider the contrasts between private and public institutions (in that case, regarding resolutions of employment discrimination cases).

6 Of course this sense of pathways was endemic to colonial strategies of promotion and status-granting. For an acute recent analysis, among many, see Davidson (2012). In the sentence that follows, we owe the observation on interpellation to James Beckford.

"Muslims" in public hospitals, hospital workers more often draw on schemas concerning the behavior of "Africans," reserving the religious framework for situations when they are faced with specific requests for religious exemptions. German workers in some hospitals are more likely to categorize patients as "Turks" than as "Muslims" (see Sargent and Erikson, this volume; Bertossi and Bowen [Chapter 5], this volume). Along slightly different lines in Sweden, the concept of immigrant replaced the term "foreigner," reflecting a shift in how the state theorized citizens from other countries (and their children).

How does this approach fit into the literatures in politics and sociology on institutions? The institutions studied in this volume shape social life within a broader field of power, but their relative autonomy means that they cannot be *defined* by their roles in distributing power, as is often done in political science for the class of institutions – usually formal political arrangements – on which they focus (see, for example, Moe 2005). A public school, for example, can be located in a broad field of power and accountability, in which ministries, syndicates, and local funding authorities play their role. However, what we take to be the institutional dimensions of a school – ideas and practices about curricula, diversity, responsibility, pedagogy, discipline, play, proper ways of speaking – are not mainly concerned with distributing power, but rather with teaching, producing a certain type of citizenry, and other functions. As Sunier shows in Chapter 4, these features of schools are shaped by shorter- or longer-term historical pathways regarding the place of schools in society.

In this respect, we find ourselves agreeing with those in political science who emphasize the shaping power of institutions, but differing from them in the explanatory role assigned to power and resources, because *our objects differ*. Whereas those scholars ask how national political institutions interact to produce public policy, and therefore focus their studies on the shifting balance of power relations between legislatures, organized interest groups, the electorate, and the judiciary, we look at institutions charged with a wide variety of tasks that include educating, healing, fighting, and judging and examine them only insofar as they structure perceptions and boundaries concerning Muslims and Islam.[7] In some cases, such as elections and the judiciary, our objects overlap, but our focus remains quite different. The chapter by Krook (Chapter 8), for example, explores not the effects of electoral systems per se, but rather the dynamics of electoral competition and how it shapes the initiatives taken by

7 On institutionalist approaches to politics, see Hall and Taylor (1996); Knight (1992); Mahoney and Thelen (2010); March and Olsen (1989); Schmidt (2008); and Steinmo et al. (1992). The chapter by Mona Lena Krook in this volume comes closest to an institutionalist approach in politics, but also with an attention to cultural schemas that moves her analysis toward cultural sociology.

political actors to incorporate particular marginalized groups as candidates. Our questions concern the practical schemas employed by institutional actors – for example, how judges or teachers perceive, justify, and treat others. In this sense, these schemas, rather than policies, constitute our outcomes.

In our approach we might seem closer to institutional analyses in sociology, which employ a broader sense of institutions than those prominent in political science, and train attention on the importance of culturally specific practical schemas.[8] Although economic organizations constitute a central domain for this approach, sociologists also examine schools, professional associations, cultural institutions, and so on. Here again, our questions differ from those that animate most of this work. Because the sociological approaches arose within the study of formal organizations (and in reaction to the assumption that rationality and efficiency explained how these organizations worked), the outcomes of much of this work are explanations of how organizations look and why they function the way they do. One major line of inquiry, for example, concerns how the organizational forms of institutions are reproduced across time and space: why schools, or firms, resemble each other across different countries.[9] We ask different questions; our outputs are not institutional forms, but rather the schemas and boundaries particular to treatment of Muslims and Islam within those institutions.

Our approaches do, however, converge with those adopted by sociologists who seek to combine macro and micro approaches. An important line of sociological inquiry has focused on the flow of everyday social life, and we join with those approaches in looking at everyday ways of classifying soldiers, patients, students, and other actors. Others in sociology have sought to capture the rules and practices underlying an entire domain, whether schools, law courts, or churches.[10] We converge with their concerns, not to explain the forms taken by a school or a hospital, but rather to show how those rules and practices shape the formation of schemas concerning Muslims and Islam. However, because we also ask about the role of institutions in shaping national-level cultural phenomena of racism, Islamophobia, multiculturalist tolerance, and so forth, we pay attention to links between institutional specificities and national discourses. For example, we ask how public intellectuals and journalists have treated particular events in schools, neighborhoods, electoral campaigns,

[8] See Dobbin (1994); Meyer and Rowan (1977); and Stark (2009).

[9] See, for example, Scott and Meyer (1994).

[10] We are inspired by the work of Goffman (1974) for the former emphasis; on the latter, see the formative collection edited by DiMaggio and Powell (1991); for an example of the sociological study of a specific type of organization in terms of its institutional properties and its cultural dimension, see Becker (1999) on religious congregations.

or hospitals as instances of something purportedly nationwide, namely a supposed general threat posed by Islam to social life.

THE ROLE OF NATIONAL IMAGINARIES

The aforementioned relationship between national ideologies or imaginaries, on the one hand, and the social lives of particular institutions, on the other, becomes a key object for our study. We wish to question more centrally the ways in which institutions shape a sense of cultural citizenship, precisely because we wish to move beyond a perspective that sees in national cultures of citizenship and integration the central building blocks of comparative analysis: France as an open and universalist culture versus the "multicultural" cultures of Britain and the Netherlands, so claimed because they organize immigrant inclusion and religious diversity along the idea of "group-based rights" and collective identities, versus Germany's relatively "closed" approach, and so on.

We opt not to follow this approach for two major reasons, perhaps best seen in terms of space and time. First, any approach that seeks to define a single national model tends to *flatten out* the highly complex set of institutions and public actors within any one country, such that they are seen as simply implementing a consensual model: French people execute *laïcité*, Dutch people previously applied multiculturalism but now have seen the light, Germans follow the model of public corporations, Norwegians emphasize social equality, and so forth. In stressing the existence of cross-national differences, this approach may at times provide a useful starting point, but it cannot take account of the highly contested nature of these concepts within each country. For example, in Britain there are powerful voices raised in favor of allowing communities to resolve problems according to their religious values, and equally powerful voices raised against community isolation. Both sets of voices gained strength in the years after the July 2005 bombings. Neither defines a British national model of how to treat religious or ethnic diversity. In Norway there are powerful movements against racism and also powerful movements attacking Muslims as culturally inassimilable – both gaining strength after the 2011 massacre committed by Anders Behring Breivik. The former type of movements draws on Norway's commitments to human rights, whereas the latter type – seen as well in Denmark – views Muslims as posing a threat to widely accepted commitments to gender equality.[11] Neither defines a "Norwegian model" – such a phrase could usefully refer only to a particular form of welfare state nourished by its oilfields.

[11] Breivik himself, however, viewed gender equality as part of the problem of decline of Norwegian society, for which he blamed the Norwegian Labour Party.

Nor can a top-down approach capture the degree to which actors in specific institutions employ specific working models. As Bertossi shows in Chapter 4, the French army does not perceive Muslim recruits as simple citizen-soldiers, as the ideology of republican integration and *laïcité* would predict, but as instrumentally useful because they can appear as Muslims or as Africans to others in French society. As Siim shows for her Scandinavian cases in Chapter 9, it is the specific judicial competences of bodies in Denmark, Norway, and Sweden, and not a national ideology, that best explains outcomes of cases involving women wearing Islamic scarves. Instead of assuming the existence of an unequivocal and stable constellation of meanings in a national context, this institutional complexity must be brought back into the analysis. What we must explain is the capacity of a national imaginary to maintain a moral balance between the given country's most valued principles (e.g., color-blindness, universalism, and *laïcité* in France and other principles elsewhere) and the social and institutional realities of competing values and adaptive responses. This uncertainty and these contradictions are part of the factory of cultural citizenship in a country.

The second limitation of national model approaches has to do with time: that they *telescope* the social, political, and legal history of each country into one or more crucial dates or events, which then are given a pan-historical meaning. For example, rather than tracing the shifting political agendas that gave rise to conflicting French laws and policies on religion during the early twentieth century (as in Baubérot 2004), many French public figures and even some social scientists claim that over the past century, France has followed a single model of *laïcité*, and that this model was implemented by the law of 1905 on separation of churches and state. This claim ignores the long-term practices of regulating religion in France and rests on a law that does not use the term "*laïcité*," was not accepted by the Catholic Church, and was in part superseded by subsequent legislation. It cannot account for the continued highly active support the French state gives to religious institutions, nor can it account for the radically different schemas followed by national actors at different points over the past two centuries. In such ex post reconstructions of institutional national histories, national cultures are seen as stable and all-encompassing.

To summarize, national model approaches may usefully point to important cross-national contrasts, and in this regard we, too, invoke them in this volume as part of an initial level of analysis. In doing so we must take care to distinguish between two quite distinct analytical approaches based on cross-national contrasts. We join in spirit with other authors who seek to base such contrasts on the analysis of specific institutions or policy debates, be it citizenship policy

(Brubaker 1992), juridical traditions and legal debates (Joppke and Torpey 2013), or historical patterns of church-state relationships (Fetzer and Soper 2004). We distinguish this approach from one that takes a national ideology as itself providing a useful analytical model.[12] French approaches to religious governance are indeed based on a very long-term Gallican Church model of supporting and regulating recognized religions, more recently inflected by the twentieth-century legal apparatus often (and incorrectly) glossed as "separation." These approaches can be usefully distinguished at this cross-national level from German forms of decentralized corporatism and from the British tradition of privileging religious communities as bases for education and morality. However, saying this should not then lead us to take the ideological (and "essentially contested") concepts of *laïcité, leitkultur,* or multiculturalism as if they could explain or analyze these cross-national distinctions.

We argue that even the most nonideological analyses of cross-national contrasts cannot adequately account for the practical schemas that shape how particular Swedish, German, or Italian actors, working in specific institutions, perceive and discuss Muslims and Islam. The studies in this volume, by examining in greater depth the dynamics at work in particular institutional settings, allow us to ask how certain elements of national ideologies articulate with representations and practices in institutional contexts. Under what conditions do certain actors working in a public hospital or in a court deploy schemas that reflect national imaginaries? Under what different conditions do these or other actors instead highlight norms and practices linked more directly to the type of institution concerned? If we would see in the former case an instance of top-down shaping by a national ideology, we would need to specify the conditions and mechanisms for such a shaping effect to take hold. If we would see in the latter case an example of the modular argument advanced by John Meyer and his colleagues (Scott and Meyer 1994), namely that types of institutions reproduce their tokens across specific national contexts, we would also need to specify the mechanisms by which those resemblances take on social reality. We note in passing that those practices that tend to be more "accommodative," in the sense advanced in Québec (Bouchard and Taylor 2008), are found across national contexts in schools, hospitals, and armies, where administrators and frontline workers find themselves facing strong pressures to accomplish tasks linked to the specific function of each such institution.

[12] We have in mind work in the comparative study of the integration of immigrants, which seeks to explain national differences in terms of national imaginaries, or ideologies, or ways of thinking about citizenship, rather than in terms of legal or political institutions; see, for example, the references in note 3 to this chapter, and also Favell (1998) and Schain (2009).

CULTURAL DIFFERENCES AND INSTITUTIONAL DIVERSITY

The preceding discussion ought to have made clear that we wish to bring more centrally into our analyses both social imaginaries and the institutions in which actors live and work. When national ideologies have a shaping effect on ideas and practices, they do so in specific contexts of enactment. Take, for example, the matter of Islamic garments worn in schools, which in many ways has been a proxy for debates about tolerable social diversity (see Chapter 3 by Sunier in this volume). The fact that the debate in France concerned students whereas in Britain and Germany it focused on teachers indicates differences in national approaches that do indeed concern national cultures. That the French government decided to ban "ostentatious religious signs" – that is, Muslim headscarves – cannot, however, be understood without looking at lobbying by school heads for the ban. Such lobbying certainly would have been more difficult in Britain, where visible diversity is less likely to be seen as a social issue. Here is where a cross-national contrast provides a starting point. But neither would it have been possible without the efforts of certain school heads to frame the issue as one of protecting schoolgirls from unruly Muslim boys, and a high level of receptivity such arguments received among members of the Stasi Commission. It is noteworthy that prior to 1989, there were girls with scarves in schools, but no one was lobbying against them, for reasons explored elsewhere (Bowen 2007a).

At this general level, there is an obvious interplay between a national repertoire on the one hand (the *laïcité* grammar) and, on the other, a specific belief that the state should protect schools from simple manifestations of religious diversity. At other moments, however, teachers preferred to frame the matter in another way, namely about accommodating in practical fashion the ethnic and religious diversity encountered in the classroom. Similar divergences in practical schemas are found in other settings, such as hospitals and courtrooms (as shown in the contributions by Bertossi and Bowen [Chapter 5], Sargent and Erikson [Chapter 2], and Siim [Chapter 9]).

In the following chapters, we observe interactions, repertoires, symbols, and formal organization within the settings of concrete institutions. But to do that, we must avoid a dual drawback that bringing institutions back to the center stage of comparative sociology of citizenship could cause. The first drawback would be to replace the reified conception of the national with a reified conception of institutional thinking and culture. When we explore how institutions impact boundaries and perceptions, we obviously look for aspects of institutional cultures. However, these cultures are not a single set of dispositions distributed evenly to members of a school, an army, or a law court. For example, if some military sociologists emphasize the role of military socialization in effecting transforming civilians into new and uniform men and women – and thus explain the uniqueness of military people in a large series of attitudes and behaviors (e.g., why and how they divorce, etc.) – others have emphasized the self-selection of those people who decide to enlist and the type of predisposition necessary to opt for a military career.

This question of the institutional habitus concerns all institutions of the state. However, we look at institutions not simply in terms of predispositions but also in terms of contexts of actions. Members of institutions are asked by the state to maintain the normal functioning of these institutions in order to meet their objectives. Members of a school, for example, work to maintain discipline among students as a way to meet the educational objective assigned to the institution by the state, and so do police officers, nurses, judges, and naturalization officers. Members of institutions adapt their repertoires, preferences, and beliefs to the institutional program they believe that they, as institutional actors, must implement in their day-to-day routine.

This is not to understand institutions in a functionalist way, however. The second drawback we want to avoid is to assume that the relative autonomy of institutional dimensions takes the form of an overarching institutional order in which different institutions play their unique role within a single coherent system – a question of particular sensitivity when we address issues of moral and ethnic diversity in modern immigration societies. To respond to this danger, we distinguish our approach from one in institutional sociology that emphasizes the cross-national reproduction of certain specific features of schools, armies, and so forth, and instead draw on another recent current within sociology, one that emphasizes the cultural and moral specificity of structures of justification (Boltanski and Thévenot 2006; Lamont and Thévenot 2000). These latter approaches treat in comparative fashion the moral frontiers in a society, as well as the relationships between those frontiers and institutions. Although their comparative enterprise is pursued in cross-national fashion, these sociologists seek to ground national differences in specific institutional and cultural practices, such as distinct orientations toward and evaluations of "natural environment" (Thévenot, Moody, and Lafaye 2000; Fourcade 2011).

In their North American and French formulations, this approach, perhaps in reaction against an older institutionalism, emphasizes cultural contrasts. For example, in their recent analysis of the interplay between moral visions and institutions of health, Michèle Lamont and Peter Hall (2009) emphasize three dimensions of culture often embodied in institutional forms: symbolic boundaries, status hierarchies, and collective imaginaries. They argue that national cultural understandings of health refract and transform the impact of public policy concerning health, as do Thévenot, Moody, and Lafaye (2000) concerning environment.

We join in that direction of research, but our question is different; it concerns not the cultural distinctiveness of policy outcomes but the ways in which actors draw on specific practical schemas in specific institutional contexts. We are also interested in the impact these institutionally embedded schemas and practices have on the key notions that become projected onto a national canvas and are seized on by politicians and journalists as elements of a national self-understanding regarding religion, ethnicity, and immigration. Our focus is on how, at a more micro level than that of the national canvas, schemas and practices are generated or transformed, and how in certain cases they can have a national impact.

To sum up much of the aforementioned discussion, we situate our approach at the crossroads of two broad orientations in the contemporary social sciences. With those who practice institutionalist approaches in sociology and politics, we share the methodological premise that the social life of institutions is not to be found in organizational rule-books but in patterns of everyday interactions, and in the norms, representations, and practical schemas that inform interactions. With those who have developed comparative sociologies of moral boundaries and social hierarchies, we share the working assumption that norms, representations, and practices are shaped by broadly distributed cultural premises concerning justice, morality, and value. These two approaches are themselves increasingly interpenetrating, as analysts of institutions, for example, emphasize the construction of moral boundaries and the shape of judgments and justifications (Stark 2009).

In our own modest contribution to these literatures, explored in Chapter 11 of this volume, we focus not only on institutions as the source of schemas and practices but on the multiple pressures and motivations within any one institution. Even within a single institution, we do not find a set of global rules, from which we could deduce the practices likely to be observed, say in a school or on a shop floor, but rather a set of relevant practices, specific rules and roles, and grammars of justification (Dewey 1924). As a result, members of different "social locations" within an institution will arrange very differently the interplay between the institutional identities they claim their institution be based on (*the* school system, *the* military, *the* hospital), what they see of their institution's social function in the national society they argue they play (e.g., national integration), and the place the institution offers for the expression of religious or cultural diversity (which can be dissonant with the dominant politics of diversity).

For example, teachers may conceive of a school as neutral with respect to values and identities, but they also must deal with the cultural diversity of the students beyond this neutrality credo. Diversity will not be regulated only according to what principles of *laïcité* or antidiscrimination mean in the general debate and how it is regulated by the law. It will also be dealt with regard to the existing *bricolages* in the schoolyard, or the specific values that teachers or school heads seek to defend – their own understandings, strategic interpretations, various core beliefs, and contradictory practice of *laïcité* or antidiscrimination in general terms (how they see their mission as educators) or in more contingent contexts (the constraints of ordinary life in the class room). In turn, on the basis of how schoolteachers and administrators construct repertoires about the difficulties they may face (or think they face), they can mobilize and shape the public and political debate and make claims about a change in the law. Institutions are not simple receptacles of existing ideas about what they must do, or the passive sponges of national identity principles. They participate in the production of these principles as well.

Consider a second example: the military is seen as an institution that de-emphasizes cultural or ethnic or religious identities; this is how the military is seen as a "total institution" with a total identity (Goffman 1961; Pinto 1975). But it also faces two challenges: to find sufficient manpower and to achieve a proper level of social legitimacy, for example by reflecting the rest of the society and not existing as an insular organization. Minority groups can help the military meet both objectives, by changing the traditional image of the white straight male Christian officer. The institution can be tempted to offer an explicit niche of visibility and expression for diversity through an external communication policy and the advertising of recruitment opportunities targeting specific minority groups, or through (for instance) the provision of halal food in the garrisons and the creation of a Muslim chaplaincy. Such outcomes can be the result of the transformation of the institution itself. For example, the shift from conscription to all-volunteer forces may result in similar readjustments of the military policy irrespective of the dominant national model, be it republican or multiculture-friendly. This is something that belongs specifically to the institution. But what is crucial to observe is how members of the institution construct their interpretations of this transformation, and link it to issues that are debated outside the institution (see Bertossi's contribution to this volume).

In other words, these processes are constructed under the contradictory constraints and facilitations of an institutional structure. But members (say a Muslim noncommissioned officer, nurse, or teacher) and users (the Muslim public who are policed, healed, or taught) are always negotiating what they consider this structure is or should be. That is, institutions shape their own structure of constraints, beliefs, and role assignments, but this structure is always the result of routine interactions among the institutional personnel and its "publics" through which constraints, core beliefs, and role assignment are constantly negotiated, rearranged, and reinvented.

As a result, the fact that institutions play a crucial ordering function in societies is one important dimension of how members of institutions define their roles and social identities. To emphasize this important dimension, our definition of institutions outlines the interplay between objective and subjective dimensions. Institutional actors are engaged in a continual interplay between the constraints and facilities offered by institutional structures, on the one hand, and their ideas of what they want their institution to be, on the other (Lagroye and Offerlé 2010: 17). The belief in an overarching institutional order can have as much of a performative effect as have national ideologies.

PRACTICAL SCHEMAS AND INSTITUTIONAL STRUCTURES

Now we wish to expand on a concept introduced earlier, that of the "practical schemas" used by actors to orient themselves toward their environment, in specific institutional contexts and with respect to specific categories of people. We use this concept to maintain the tension between the individual actor, situated in a particular social location and with a particular set of experiences, and the practical realities of working in a specific institution. We understand schemas as consisting of ideas, evaluations, and ways of speaking that shift in their relative importance or weight as "things happen" in the social world. We see them as practical in that they are deployed without constant reference to theories of why they are important. They are quickly available as guides for living: "marriage ought to look like this or that"; "this is how we do things here"; "religion belongs in the private sphere", "we ought not to disrupt people's lives"; and so forth.

In terms of theories of everyday cognition, schemas are "knowledge structures that represent objects or events and provide default assumptions about their characteristics, relationships, and entailments under conditions of incomplete information" (DiMaggio 1997: 269; see also Fiske and Linville 1980). Schemas process information and guide action (Rumelhart 1980). They contain both relatively fixed ideas and ideas that depend on contextual cues. A schema followed by students in a classroom, for example, would always contain concepts of teachers and examinations and provide "scripts" for answering questions, but these elements would be modified in interaction sequences that are context-sensitive.

DiMaggio (1997) has pointed to the parallel findings of cognitive psychology and sociology concerning the power and attractiveness of typified images and ideas. Schematic organization makes certain ideas particularly accessible to actors (von Hippel et al. 1993) and these are embedded in institutions to the extent that actors take cues from specific contexts as to expected and appropriate ways to act (Meyer and Rowan 1977; see Bruner 1990). If individuals form prototypes of everyday objects as part of carrying out efficient cognition (Rosch 1978), such that typical images of "chair" or "bird" are widely shared within a population, so too, stereotypes organize and even comfort people in situations of uncertainty or unease (Swidler 1986). But these images and ideas are not randomly distributed across societies or characteristic of a "national culture," as we argued earlier; they are shaped by institutions, in what Friedland and Alford (1991: 248–249) call "institutional logics." Here Goffman's (1983) idea of the "interaction order" is relevant, referring to the expectations and tacit forms of knowledge that guide individuals in institutional settings but that are not reducible to the formal rules of an organization.

In the social sciences, cross-cultural comparative research projects have developed what we can recast as schema-oriented approaches to variation. For example, Michèle Lamont (1992, 2000) and her colleagues have highlighted differences in ideas about "worth" across countries, across regions within countries, and across social-class lines. Across these contrasts, differences between individuals can be captured as different weightings of the same bundle of normative qualifiers. All workers value work, for example, but they differ from one place to another in the weightings they give to income, task mastery, and consumption patterns. It is the particular weightings that define that which we often call "the culture."

These comparative sociological studies point to the ways in which schemas are deployed to define one's identity with respect to some other category of people. The diacritic use of schemas about kinds of people draws on the intrinsically negative nature of social schemas. One cannot have a social category schema without distinguishing it from other social categories: one's notions of what upper-class people are like inevitably involve contrasts, positive or negative, with people of other classes (Lamont 1992). In the essays assembled here, actors often employ schemas to construct moral and practical boundaries between themselves and others, distinguished by religion, race, ethnicity, or origin.

An actor's repertoire of such practical schemas may include multiple, sometime conflicting ideas that vary over time in their relative weight – a modification of the approach found in Lamont and Thévenot (2000). For example, a hospital worker may have at her disposal practical schemas about "Muslims," "Africans," "religious people," and "hospital patients," all of which could apply to a particular patient. The worker may draw on one or another of these schemas depending on the cues she receives from the patient, a superior, or a news report heard on her way to work. She also may invoke them strategically in order to justify her actions to specific publics (her superiors, her coworkers, or her family). In her everyday work life she also will take into account the specific range of permissible actions defined by the institution of the hospital (see Sargent and Erickson [Chapter 2] and Bertossi and Bowen [Chapter 5] this volume).[13]

Throughout this volume, we argue that actors' practical schemas develop within institutional contexts, and that institutions present constraints and opportunities that cannot be reduced to a national political culture. Hospital workers must deliver services, schoolteachers must teach, judges must render decisions, each following certain professional and institutional norms, and these norms limit the range of possible actions and justifications. These actors do not simply implement a national model. To some degree, hospital workers or teachers in different countries face similar challenges, and these similarities refract national ideologies through institutional lenses.

Furthermore, different social locations within institutions present actors with quite specific constraints and opportunities. A hospital administrator, for example, with her responsibilities both within the hospital and vis-à-vis other institutions (the press, ministers, university presidents), draws on different schemas in discussing "reasonable accommodations" with religious patients than do first responders and ordinary hospital staff. The same actor might invoke different practical schemas in speaking to different publics. Even in self-consciously secular France, a town councilor repairs the church roof and a nurse works out ways of dealing with patients' religious demands, but the same individuals might speak very differently in public settings, both invoking ideas of neutral public space and church-state separation.

It is in examining justifications that we return to explicit national models. An institutional analysis allows us to recognize the importance of national models as repertoires for public justification of specific actions. The multiple ideas in France about religion-state relations – keeping public space free of religious signs, allowing private citizens to form religious associations, monitoring religious organizations from the Interior Ministry, providing state funding to religious schools – cannot be summed up in any one idea or phrase (and indeed they often clash with each other), nor do they explain actions, but each has a certain legitimacy that allows it to be mobilized for political (or other) purposes. One finds similar coexistent dissonance among British ideas

[13] This multiplicity lies behind our preference for "practical schemas" as our central analytical unit, rather than "frames," which tends to suggest a more stable and encompassing ideational structure; however, we use "framing" throughout the book and do not intend any fixed distinction between the two terms.

about the importance of religious values to construct community, a relatively high tolerance for offensive speech, a concern about community cohesion, and an ideology of English (not British) identity.

In our analysis, the more nationally legitimate schemas about diversity are particularly apt to be mobilized in certain locations with institutions: by the head of a school or hospital, for example, rather than by frontline workers. Furthermore, national ideologies are themselves produced, transformed, and reinforced within specific institutions, such as political meetings, media, and systems of education. At certain points in our chapters, we emphasize the ways institutions contribute to the broader spread of social representations of Muslims. For example, debates about treatment of children in Norway, about schools in France, and about sharia councils in Britain have shaped broader, national representations of Muslims and Islam in those countries. We can thereby better understand some of the microfoundations of large-scale representations and also changes in those representations.

PLAN OF THE BOOK

In the following chapters we do not analyze all institutions across all countries, but carry out strategic comparisons to show how institutions inflect national models: that hospitals, schools, and courts, for example, have their own rules and roles that often are very similar across countries. Focusing on a few cases in depth allows us to show how differently situated actors within an institution find themselves drawing on quite distinct schemas with respect to Muslim colleagues or clients. It also allows us to see whether there exist strong structural similarities across national contexts.

Part I highlights diversities and contradictions within three types of institutions that are defined by their explicit tasks: hospitals, schools, and the military. To varying degrees, tokens of these institutional types also are taken to represent a facet of public life in their country: diversity (or uniformity) and equality (or hierarchy). To analyze institutional life in these settings requires looking at everyday conversations and boundary-setting.

In their study of hospital settings in France and Germany, Carolyn Sargent and Susan L. Erikson document the discrepancies between institutional ideologies and everyday practices. They provide ethnographic material on how hospital personnel represent and discuss patients of African and Turkish origins and chart the ways that the staff define boundaries between French or German people and various kinds of "culturally different" people. Some of these everyday demarcations generalize from specific cases to broad categories of "immigrants" or "Africans," for example regarding language competence.

Others attribute broad behavioral attributes to these categories of patients, such as excessive fertility, and this schema leads some French midwives, for example, to prescribe contraception without discussing the implications with patients. In these hospitals (and, as we see later, in schools), we find highly organized public institutions whose administrators have strong ideas about identity and history. We would expect, and indeed find, efforts to maintain strong boundaries. However, the authors also show how medical settings serve as sites of contestation, where personnel, patients, and others "deploy and negotiate" practical schemas concerning ethnicity and race, religion, and sexuality; these may combine ideas about punctuality, choice of medicines, emotional tendencies, language competency, and so forth. Their study looks at immigrants because of the particular precariousness of their situation; most of the other papers consider immigrants and residents perceived as Muslims.

Thijl Sunier argues that public schools are in many respects the state's main cultural agent, but that they also have specific institutional characteristics, including their role as sites for negotiating national contradictions, such as that between cultural universalism and ethnic identities. He introduces the concept of "civil culture," which refers to the historically particular conventions of how citizens should interact with each other and with the powers that dominate the public sphere, and how they imagine the nation. His study focuses on how, in schools, students pupils are supposed to acquire competencies associated with that culture, and how this works out from school to school. He finds that in practice, the school-specific competencies – for example, how to properly formulate a complaint – work better for students not considered to be "foreign"; their complaints are seen in the Dutch school, for example, as suggesting the presence of discrimination, which would contradict the school leadership's way of presenting Dutch society as tolerant and relatively immune from discrimination. Students in British schools tend to draw on ethnic schemas to frame complaints and to mobilize; such approaches would not be accepted in the German, Dutch, and French schools. Here, national ideology works in indirect fashion to reduce the effective competencies of minority students and to shape their responses to conflicts.

Christophe Bertossi turns to the military, an institution that, as with the school, is taken to operate on universalistic grounds, especially in France where his study is centered. And yet even in the French military, schemas underlying practices of recruitment and everyday interactions come from specific, conjunctural concerns within the military about the practical values of diversity. To think through how and why to expand minority recruitment, the military looked not to other French institutions but to armies elsewhere, on the assumption that those resemblances were more important that national ones in providing ideas and models. Ironically, if the military, and especially its Gendarmerie branch, sees practical value in having visible minorities in its ranks, most of those minorities reject this way of thinking about their value. Bertossi's interview material shows why: non-Muslims continue to treat Muslim recruits, born and raised in France, in terms of anti-Muslim schemas and stereotypes – as drug dealers and unassimilated, owing to their Islamic religion. Muslim recruits thus must negotiate three schemas: color-blind universalism, ethnicity as value, and anti-Islam.

Bertossi and Bowen then compare schools and hospitals in one country, France, in order to underscore a point made earlier in this introduction, namely that within any one institution, the practical schemas actors employ have to do with their social location in the institution and the specific temporal conjuncture where they find themselves. They argue that, in both institutions, directors have a particular exposure to media and to their administrative superiors and that they shape their justifications accordingly, with a particularly heightened attention to national ideologies and political exigencies. Line workers, by contrast, including teachers and medical personnel, face more directly the challenge of negotiating diversity of needs and demands without neglecting the service mission of the school or the hospital. On both levels there is also the temporal dimension: that as the problems change, so do the way that institutional actors conceive of and respond to people they label as "other," and the way they frame the "problem" to be addressed. They examine the extent to which what happens on institutional grounds can result in the public reformulation of a key political concept, as in the example of debates about schools and *laïcité*. They also examine how members of institutions produce schemas about Islam and Muslims through their day-to-day routine practices and through the principles of justice that are specific to each institution, concerning what is good and right for teaching or for delivering care.

Part II of the book approaches our object from a different angle, focusing on the relationships between particular institutions and national political and cultural ideologies. In a series of studies, these contributors examine the schemas and norms that shape judicial decisions, policy outputs, and political rhetoric, and the ways in which those outputs in turn shape national imaginaries.

John R. Bowen and Mathias Rohe argue that judges face specific institutional constraints in how they decide a case and how they justify that decision, and that in doing both they draw on practical schemas that reflect both shared features of European legal discourse and country-specific ideas about public moral order and about the desirability of visible cultural and religious differences. They take the example of legal responses to polygamy to show how courts can differently weigh two ideas about law's function: sending a social and moral message, or regulating relationships among individuals. The former tends to be given greater weight by British, French and Austrian courts, whereas Germany tends to give greater weight to the latter; this example illustrates how schemas may differ in relative weighting across two institutions, not in absolute content. They take the example of laws on Islamic face and head coverings to trace developments with regard to schemas of citizenship and Islamic values, where across Europe the debate on "problems arising from migration" has shifted to a focus on "problems arising from Islam." They trace in detail the shift in French justifications for banning Islamic coverings from 1989 to 2010, particularly the specific institutional sources of the contradictory decisions regarding the constitutionality of a ban on face veils provided by two of France's highest courts. They find iterative relationships between judicial reasoning and culturally dominant schemas. In cases regarding citizenship, dress, and marriage, legal readings using standard judicial frames were followed by cultural framings in which Islam was at issue as a set of values, which were in turn followed by new legal readings that took these cultural schemas into account.

In her analysis of the civic education courses required for access to permanent residence in France and Germany, Ines Michalowski argues that these courses illuminate how citizenship is framed in each country, but also are themselves institutions designed to increase the legitimacy of host country norms among immigrants. Just as public schools are torn between ignoring students' backgrounds in the name of universal ideas, and taking them into account in the name of practical accommodations, these courses and their designers face a dilemma: whether to take a strictly liberal approach that would background immigrants' specific cultural "baggage" or a targeted approach that would seek to remedy "defects" in their cultures – a concern that arises with respect to immigrants from Muslim-majority countries. French and German courses do target Muslims, but in ways designed to hide targeting's traces. French materials, for example, always speak of general principles, but they are chosen to counter an immigrant defect: *laïcité* against overt display of Islam, gender equality against a perceived practice of unequal treatment of women.

Mona Lena Krook asks why it is that across Western Europe, measures to enhance the political representation of women are successful but not the equivalent attempts on behalf of racial, ethnic, and religious minorities. She argues that the answer lies in, first, the institutional dynamics of electoral politics, where political parties seek ways to compete effectively on the electoral market and see the small number of voting minorities as providing insufficient reason for change, and second, the dominant cultural and legal schemas about citizenship and discrimination. It is in the interaction of schemas and electoral strategizing that she finds the best explanation of variation in political representation. For example, schemas concerning race discrimination have a greater depth and salience in Britain than in Sweden, and thus have facilitated attention to minority political representation. In Sweden, schemas concerning class, gender, and indigenous peoples have stronger cultural roots. In all three countries examined – Sweden, Britain, and France – stereotypes about Muslims underlie, at least to some extent, concerns expressed about race- and immigrant-based groups.

In a comparative study of judicial decisions affecting Muslim women, Birte Siim shows that explaining variation in outcomes requires reference to specific judicial mandates. She takes cases involving women wearing Islamic head scarves in public and in private institutions across Denmark, Norway, and Sweden. These three countries have taken relatively accommodating approaches to veiling in public institutions, in spite of differences in migration and integration policies. Given this cross-national similarity, national models are unable to explain the different outcomes. Making a series of two-way contrasts, Siim argues that justifications for judicial decisions are shaped by the kinds of authority actors possess in each setting, as well as the relative weight given to each of several broader principles in each institution. In each case, a number of practical schemas were available to actors: for example, in Norwegian debates about hijab-wearing police officers, actors could and did invoke the neutrality of the state, religious freedom and nondiscrimination, or political Islam to support or oppose the practice. In this and the other cases, outcomes were shaped by the balance of power among various public actors and the norms and schemas characterizing particular institutional settings.

The chapter by Justus Uitermark, Paul Mepschen, and Jan Willem Duyvendak is of a different sort altogether. They trace the rise in the Netherlands of culturalist – or in their terms, "neoculturalist" – schemas concerning Muslims and Islam. They show how the representations and associations introduced by politicians in the 1990s simultaneously referred to Muslims and to the liberal Dutch elite; this linking gave political potency to the culturalist framing and a progressive cultural tone to the political claims. Their analysis situates these specific schemas about Muslims and Islam in a class-based political struggle among Dutch political leaders. Dutch ideologies stand out within Europe for their intense focus on issues of sexual emancipation, by reimagining Europeans as progressive and tolerant by contrast to Muslims, who are framed as homophobic and sexually backward. Although it is particularly evident in the Netherlands, this framing extends to other countries in Europe as well.

In the concluding chapter of this volume, we return to the specific contribution of the approach proposed here, and to some of its broader empirical findings.

BIBLIOGRAPHY

Baubérot, Jean. 2000. *Histoire de la laïcité française*. Paris: Presses Universitaires de France.

——2004. *Laïcité 1905–2005*, entre passion et raison. Paris: Seuil.

Becker, Penny Edgell. 1999. *Congregations in Conflict: Cultural Models of Local Religious Life*. Cambridge: Cambridge University Press.

Bertossi, Christophe. 2011. "National Models of Integration in Europe. A Comparative and Critical Analysis." *American Behavioral Scientist*, **55** (12): 1561–1580.

——2012. "The Performativity of Colour Blindness: Race Politics and Immigrant Integration in France, 1980–2012." *Patterns of Prejudice*, **46** (5): 427–446.

Bertossi, Christophe, Jan Willem Duyvendak, and Martin A. Schain. 2012. "The Problems with National Models of Integration: A Franco-Dutch Comparison." *Comparative European Politics*, **10** (3): 237–375.

Boltanski, Luc, and Laurent Thévenot. 2006. *On Justification: Economies of* Worth (orig. French 1991). Princeton, NJ: Princeton University Press.

Bouchard, Gérard, and Charles Taylor, 2008. "Building the Future: A Time for Reconciliation" (abridged report), http://red.pucp.edu.pe/ridei/wp-content/uploads/biblioteca/buildingthefutureGerardBouchardycharlestaylor.pdf, accessed December 29, 2008.

Bowen, John R. 2007a. *Why the French Don't Like Headscarves: Islam, the State, and Public Space*. Princeton, NJ: Princeton University Press.

——2007b. "A View from France on the Internal Complexity of National Models." *Journal of Ethnic and Migration Studies*, **33** (6): 1003–1016.

——2010. *Can Islam Be French?: Pluralism and Pragmatism in a Secularist State*. Princeton, NJ: Princeton University Press.

——2011a. "Europeans Against Multiculturalism." *Boston Review*, July/August. http://www.bostonreview.net/BR36.4/john_r_bowen_European_multiculturalism_islam.php, accessed 11 May 2013.

——2011b. "How the French State Justifies Controlling Muslim Bodies: From Harm-Based to Values-Based Reasoning." *Social Research*, **78** (2): 1–24.

——2012. "Working Schemas and Normative Models of French Governance of Islam," *Comparative European Politics*, **10** (1): 354–68.

Brubaker, Rogers, 1992. *Citizenship and Nationhood in France and Germany*. Cambridge, MA: Harvard University Press.

Bruner, Jerome. 1990. *Acts of Meaning*. Cambridge, MA: Harvard University Press.

Davidson, Naomi. 2012. *Only Muslim: Embodying Islam in Twentieth-Century France*. Ithaca, NY: Cornell University Press.

Dewey, John. 1924. "Logical Method and the Law." *Cornell Law Quarterly*, **10**: 17–27.

DiMaggio, Paul. 1997. "Culture and Cognition." *Annual Review of Sociology*, **23**: 263–287.

DiMaggio, Paul J., and Walter W. Powell, eds. 1991. *The New Institutionalism in Organizational Analysis*. Chicago: University of Chicago Press.

Dobbin, Frank. 1994. *Forging Industrial Policy*. Cambridge: Cambridge University Press.
Favell, Adrian. 1998. *Philosophies of Integration: Immigration and the Idea of Citizenship in France and Britain*. New York: Palgrave.
Fetzer, Joel S., and J. Christopher Soper. 2004. *Muslims and the State in Britain, France, and Germany*. Cambridge: Cambridge University Press.
Fiske S. T., and P. W. Linville. 1980. "What Does the Schema Concept Buy Us?" *Personality and Social Psychology Bulletin*, 6: 543–557.
Fourcade, Marion. 2011. "Cents and Sensibility: Economic Valuation and the Nature of 'Nature.'" *American Journal of Sociology*, **116**: 1721–1777.
Friedland R., and R. Alford. 1991. "Bringing Society Back in: Symbols, Practices, and Institutional Contradictions." In *The New Institutionalism in Organizational Analysis*, ed. W. W. Powell and P. DiMaggio, pp. 223–262. Chicago: University of Chicago Press.
Gauchet, Marcel. 1985. *Le désenchantement du monde: Une histoire politique de la religion*. Paris: Gallimard.
Goffman, Erving. 1961. *Asylums: Essays on the Social Situation of Mental Patients and Other Inmates*. New York: Anchor.
——1974. *Frame Analysis: An Essay on the Organization of Experience*. Cambridge, MA: Harvard University Press.
——1983. "The Interaction Order." *American Sociological Review*, 48: 1–17.
Hall, Peter A., and Rosemary C. R. Taylor. 1996. "Political Science and the Three New Institutionalisms." *Political Studies*, 44: 952–973.
Joppke, C., 2004. "The Retreat of Multiculturalism in the Liberal State: Theory and Policy." *British Journal of Sociology*, 55 (2): 237–257.
Joppke, C. and John Torpey. 2013. *Legal Integration of Islam: A Transatlantic Comparison*. Cambridge, MA: Harvard University Press.
Knight, Jack. 1992. *Institutions and Social Conflict*. Cambridge: Cambridge University Press.
Koopmans, R. 2002. "Migrant Claim-Making between Transnationalism and National Citizenship." Presented at conference Ethno-Religious Cultures, Identities and Political Philosophies, Amsterdam.
Koopmans, Ruud, Paul Statham, Marco Giugni, and Florence Passy. 2005. *Contested Citizenship. Immigration and Cultural Diversity in Europe*. Minneapolis: University of Minnesota Press.
Lagroye, Jacques, and Michel Offerlé, eds. 2010. *Sociologie de l'institution*. Paris: Belin.
Lamont, Michèle. 1992. *Money, Morals and Manners: The Culture of the French and the American Upper-Middle Class*. Chicago: University of Chicago Press.
——2000. *The Dignity of Working Men: Morality and the Boundaries of Race, Class, and Immigration*. Cambridge, MA: Harvard University Press.
Lamont, Michèle, and Marcel Fournier, eds. 1992. *Cultivating Differences: Symbolic Boundaries and the Making of Inequality*. Chicago: University of Chicago Press.
Lamont, Michèle, and Peter A. Hall, eds. 2009. *Successful Societies: How Institutions and Culture Affect Health*. Cambridge: Cambridge University Press.
Lamont, Michèle, and Laurent Thévenot, eds. 2000. *Rethinking Comparative Cultural Sociology: Repertoires of Evaluation in France and the United States*. Cambridge: Cambridge University Press.
Lijphart, Arend. 1968. *The Politics of Accommodation: Pluralism and Democracy in the Netherlands*. Berkeley: University of California Press.

Mahoney, James, and Kathleen Thelen, eds. 2010. *Explaining Institutional Change: Ambiguity, Agency, and Power.* Cambridge: Cambridge University Press.
March, James, and Johan P. Olsen. 1989. *Rediscovering Institutions: The Organizational Basis of Politics.* New York: Free Press.
Meyer, John W., and Brian Rowan. 1977. "Institutionalized Organizations: Formal Structure as Myth and Ceremony." *American Journal of Sociology*, **83**: 340–363.
Moe, Terry. 2005. "Power and Political Institutions." *Perspectives on Politics*, **3** (2): 215–233.
Pinto, Louis. 1975. "L'armée, le contingent et les classes sociales." *Actes de la Recherche en Sciences Sociales*, **1** (3): 18–40.
Rath, Jan, Rinus Penninx, Kees Groenendijk, and Astrid Meyer. 1999. "The Politics of Recognizing Religious Diversity in Europe: Social Reactions to the Institutionalization of Islam in the Netherlands, Belgium and Great Britain." *Netherlands Journal of Social Sciences*, **35** (1): 53–68.
Rosch, E. 1978. "Principles of Categorization." In *Cognition and Categorization*, E. Rosch and B. Lloyd, eds., pp. 27–48. Hillsdale: Lawrence Erlbaum.
Rumelhart, David E. 1980. "Schemata: The Building Blocks of Cognition." In *Theoretical Issues in Reading Comprehension: Perspectives from Cognitive Psychology, Linguistics, Artificial Intelligence, and Education*, R. J. Spiro, B. C. Bruce, and W. F. Brewer, eds., pp. 33–58, Hillsdale: Lawrence Erlbaum.
Schain, Martin. 2009. *The Politics of Immigration in Britain, France, and the United States.* New York: Palgrave Macmillan.
Schiller, Glick, Nina Ayse Cağlar, and Thaddeus C. Guldbrandsen. 2006. "Beyond the Ethnic Lens: Locality, Globality, and Born-Again Incorporation." *American Ethnologist*, **33**: 612–633.
Schmidt, Vivien. 2008. "Discursive Institutionalism: the Explanatory Power of Ideas and Discourse." *Annual Review of Political Science*, **11**: 303–326.
Scott, Joan Wallach. 2007. *The Politics of the Veil.* Princeton: Princeton University Press.
Scott, W. Richard, John W. Meyer et al. 1994. *Institutional Environments and Organizations.* Thousand Oaks: Sage.
Sniderman, Paul N., and Louk Hagendoorn. 2007. *When Worlds Collide: Multiculturalism and its Discontents in the Netherlands.* Princeton: Princeton University Press.
Soysal, Y. N. 1994. *Limits of Citizenship: Migrants and Posnational Membership in Europe.* Chicago: University of Chicago Press.
——2002. "Citizenship and Identity: Living in Diasporas in Postwar Europe?" In *The Postnational Self*, U. Hedetoft and M. Hjort, eds., pp. 137–151. Minneapolis: University of Minnesota Press.
Stark, David, 2009. *The Sense of Dissonance: Accounts of Worth in Economic Life.* Princeton: Princeton University Press.
Steinmo, Sven, et al. 1992. *Structuring Politics: Historical Institutionalism in Comparative Analysis.* New York: Cambridge University Press.
Swidler A. 1986. "Culture in Action: Symbols and Strategies." *American Sociology Review*, **51**: 273–286.
Thévenot, Laurent, Michael Moody, and Claudette Lafaye, 2000. "Forms of valuing nature: Arguments and modes of justification in French and American environmental disputes." In *Rethinking Comparative Cultural Sociology: Repertoires of Evaluation in France and the United States*, Michèle Lamont and Laurent Thévenot, eds., pp. 229–272. Cambridge: Cambridge University Press.

van Reekum, Rogier, Jan Willem Duyvendak, and Christophe Bertossi. 2012. "National Models of Integration and the Crisis of Multiculturalism: A Critical Comparative Perspective." *Patterns of Prejudice*, 46 (5): 417–26.
Vertovec, Steven, and Susanne Wessendorf, eds. 2009. *The Multiculturalism Backlash: European Discourses, Policies and Practices*. New York: Routledge.
Von Hippel E, J. Jonides, J. L. Hilton, and S. Narayan. 1993. "The Inhibitory Effect of Schematic Processing on Perceptual Encoding." *Journal of Personal and Social Psychology*, 64: 921–935.
Walzer, Michael. 1983. *Spheres of Justice: A Defense of Pluralism and Equality*. New York: Basic Books.

PART I

PRACTICAL SCHEMAS IN EVERYDAY INSTITUTIONAL LIFE

2 Hospitals as Sites of Cultural Confrontation and Integration in France and Germany

Carolyn Sargent and Susan L. Erikson

Hospitals are among the institutions that frame (and reframe) expectations for immigrant's engagement in the everyday life of their host countries. Hospital processes of patient-making coexist with bureaucratic technologies of the state, thus actively initiating migrants in the ways of biomedicine and the institutional arrangements of the public health system. Bureaucratic technologies are not neutral. Completing hospital forms to see a doctor, for example, requires submitting information that the state may not previously possess and which may have implications long after hospital services are needed. Billing addresses may lack permanence, reflecting the realities of living in marginal housing. Absence of a social insurance number may signal to authorities an undocumented resident status, and trigger state mechanisms of surveillance. Accordingly, entering the medical system not only introduces migrants to ideal constructs of the appropriate patient, but in addition, positions them for institutional assessment as social persons in the broader societal context.

This chapter focuses on the institutional configurations, policies, and procedures that immigrants from the West African Senegal River Valley residing in France and the (mostly) Turkish immigrants living in Germany face when they engage with French and German hospitals, respectively.[1] The gendered inculcation of immigrant identities is especially acute in the obstetrical and reproductive scenarios on which we draw, as we compare how German and French hospitals go about constituting and managing state and biomedical compliance in the women patients who seek care.

In this chapter, we analyze cultural confrontation and integration among immigrants, many of whom are Muslim. We are particularly interested in everyday practices of belonging (*intégration*, *Zugehörigkeit*) that signal inclusion

[1] Fieldwork was carried out by Sargent (and collaborators) in Paris and by Erikson in Germany, and the use of first-person singular references should be understood accordingly.

and exclusion in relation to French and German society – and the differences belonging makes. Both France and Germany offer universal health care to citizens and to people with state-registered rights to live and work within their territorialized country boundaries. Both countries generally give medical care even to people who do not have the right to work, live, or vote in the country. This has become more restricted in Germany with recent health care reform. We note the many disconnects between official state discourses of inclusionist human rights to social protection and well-being and immigrants' actual experiences in hospital. We position our work in conversation with others who aim to move discussions of the immigrant "other" beyond the facile use of concepts of ethnic community. We do this by documenting "institutional processes through which ethnic categories and identities are constructed and naturalized" (Schiller, Çağlar, and Guldbrandsen 2006: 613). As anthropologists we collected data on the everyday demarcations of Frenchness and Germanness that inform, bring notice to, and maintain differences between immigrants and people who are identified as culturally French or German. Everyday demarcations fall on a continuum from the seemingly innocuous – bureaucratic practices such as filling out hospital forms – to the more differentiating, such as patients needing language translators. Even with the seemingly commonsense provision of interpreters to accommodate patients' language limitations, we see significant differences in France and Germany, the former provisioning for interpreters, albeit reluctantly and intermittently, whereas the latter does so hardly at all.

It is not unexpected that everyday demarcations of ethnic identity are part of hospital encounters. Hospitals have been the site of several recent ethnographies elucidating cultural habits and value systems (Mol 2002, Kaufman 2006, Joyce 2008, Long, Hunter and van der Geest 2008, Saunders and Farquahr 2009). Our research projects were conducted in public university hospitals, where everyday encounters between people needing health services and biomedical practitioners reveal common tensions and hostilities resulting from the ongoing Pan-European renegotiation of identity at this historical moment.

Scholarly debates about globalization have dislodged the notion of states as bounded economic, political, and social entities, but "the state" as a bureaucratic body interested in self-preservation is far from dead. States as self-interested entities continue to legislate and regulate economic, political, and social life within their territorial borders. The weight of the state, however, is not constant or uniform. Worldwide, there is enormous variation between and within states in the degrees to which the long arm of the state may be experienced in everyday goings-on. Globalizing forces coexist with state-held obligations to provide health, education, and security services to people living within (sometimes heavily policed) national boundaries. This paradox, a worldwide phenomenon, manifests with varying degrees of voracity, but France and Germany are not among those countries in which global forces and influence run unchecked. Both countries possess histories and habits that demonstrably shape what France *is*, what Germany *is* in the global – and local – imagination. Even as nationalist identities are upended and shifting as a result of human migration, even as "new forms of 'noncitizenship'" (Partridge 2008: 1548) emerge in France and Germany, essentialized notions of what it means to be French and German also circulate, simultaneously fortified and enforced through legalities and institutions acting as proxies of the nation-state. Via bureaucratic technologies of citizenship and naturalization, people and institutions operate as if there is still a France and Germany to belong *to*, French and German cultural identities to *become*, even as those identities change and are changing as a result of confrontations and contributions of immigrant populations.

FRAMING "DIFFERENCE" IN FRENCH HOSPITALS

French hospitals are not immune to the implications of the much-debated contradiction between core Enlightenment constructs that identify France as republican, secularist, and universalist and the realities of ethnic and racial identities, conflicts, and inequalities that inform everyday life. As Mestre and Moro (2007) observe, one would be remiss to think that clinical contexts are somehow sheltered from the ambiguities and paradoxes of the broader society. Public hospitals, as state institutions, represent and reproduce widely held assumptions concerning identity. Yet the clinic and clinical practice also serve as sites of contestation, where constructs of culture, ethnicity, nationality, and race are deployed and negotiated among biomedical personnel, interpreters, patients, and families.

Given the normative biomedical premise of the universal suffering body, in which diseases are classified in such texts as the International Classification of Diseases, it is not surprising that one might also find the naturalizing of "difference" in clinical settings (Dewitte 2000: 1). The state's emphasis on the attributes of the Republic, in particular the universal subject, and the biomedical emphasis on the naturalized patient produce a double effect in which cultural difference may be erased. However, the invisibility of cultural, ethnic, and racial differences in the institutional framing of the African migrant patient obscures how "difference" plays out in everyday medical practices.

Kotobi argues that medical professionals produce an emotionally charged, generalizing, and ethnocentric discourse when dealing with migrant patients (Kotobi 2000: 62). Hospital practitioners ascribe specific attributes to migrants, especially to sub-Saharan and North African populations. Such patients, she notes, are above all envisaged as "Other" by virtue of physical characteristics (skin color, clothing), social relations (extended families, polygamy, management of time), beliefs (fatalism, sorcery), or interpretations of misfortune (fate, neglect of social responsibilities, ancestors, etc.). These features are foregrounded when clinicians identify them as problematic in the institutional context of the hospital.

In addition, perceived irregularities such as unreliability in keeping appointments, recourse to ritual practices, and use of local medications purchased in West African shops in Paris or sent from "home" have come to represent characteristics of the challenging patient. For many practitioners, "this type of patient" is understandable only via cultural meanings that are rarely accessible within the institution. Cultural difference, whether denied formal legitimacy by the state or within the public hospital, is thus central to representations of African and other migrant populations. Observations of migrant hospital patients may then be extrapolated to explain why migrants have difficulties in achieving appropriate integration into French society (Kotobi 2000:63). When West African patients or families show limited competence in speaking and reading French, institutional framing of migrants from this region reinforces the premise that they lack even the basic capacity for integration. This is perceived as all the more unacceptable because this population originated in what was formerly "francophone" colonial Africa.

Yet in contrast, for others, the role of doctor, midwife, or social worker places them in the position of state agents guarding French republican values, a role they assume given their status as practitioners of the public hospital system. In the case of public maternity clinics, certain midwives and social workers take on the responsibility of informing African migrant women patients of their rights. Accordingly, a hospital-based discourse of the rights of women relative to their husbands and elders has emerged, couched in the broader framework of the "rights of man" (*les droits de l'homme*). Since 1995, the public hospital system has framed the concept of patient rights in the context of the "*Charte de la personne hospitalisée: des droits pour tous*" (The patient's charter: rights for all). The current charter draws on a 1995 document and has been amended periodically in relation to legislation addressing bioethics, end-of-life issues, and the quality of the health system (Ministère de la Santé, September 16, 2007).

One important directive added to the Charter states that a particular effort has been made to assure the accessibility of the documentation of patient rights, especially for foreigners as well as for the disabled. Accordingly, the Charter is available on the Web site of the Ministry of Health in French and English, and there are plans to make it available in Braille soon. A summary of key points is available in seven languages, including Portuguese, Arabic, and Chinese, but not in any African languages such as Soninke, Bambara, or Wolof.

The question of access to this document detailing patient rights is emblematic of the broader question confronting public hospitals: how to simultaneously represent Republican values of universality while addressing the particular needs of patients from diverse cultural and social backgrounds. In spite of the document's idealistic tenets, assuring a means of translation of vocabulary and concepts remains a vexing and often neglected issue. In an attempt to encourage professional debate, a 2005 conference organized by the *Groupe de Reflexion sur la Prise en Charge des Migrants de l'Hôpital Avicenne*, headed by Prof. Olivier Bouchaud, chief of service for Tropical and Infectious Diseases at Avicenne Hospital, focusing on the theme of "Communication and Migrants: Better Communication for Better Care." The conference was a response to those medical practitioners who are regularly confronted with linguistic and "cultural" difficulties when treating migrant patients.

Hospital personnel (doctors, nurses, midwives, interpreters, and clerical staff) presenting at the conference offered commentaries that indicated the tendency to define patients as "good" or "bad" (IMEA 2005: 2). The good patient was said to correspond to "our" way of experiencing and expressing pain, preventing sickness, eating, washing, and interacting appropriately. The "bad" patient was often defined as "different" in the sense of foreign origin, demonstrating unfamiliar modes of expressing symptoms, and characterized by generalized noncompliance. At the institutional level, diverse forms of mediation, including interpreting services, have been established. However, in three maternity hospitals that served as research sites, practitioners said they had no in-hospital interpreters and rarely or never called Inter-Service Migrants, which provides interpreters by telephone. West African migrant women are framed as "culturally different," and pose "problems of communication." Nonetheless, these problems are often left unresolved. How do practitioners deal with the everyday dilemmas posed by patients of diverse ethnic origins, given the erasure of the "problem of communication"? Midwives and nurses offered the following assertions: all patients speak French, ethnicity/national origin/religion are irrelevant to patient care, to acknowledge ethnic diversity is anti-republican and hence "not done" in hospitals, and hospital personnel have no time to invest in overcoming language barriers.

INTEGRATION AND THE MALIAN MIGRANT PATIENT

Data on French maternity hospitals and their target populations were obtained as part of a larger research project on intersections among Islam, gender, and reproductive health conducted between 2000 and 2007. The patient population in question is primarily from the Senegal River Valley region of West Africa, which includes Mali, Mauritania, and Senegal. The study included historical analysis of immigration policies and politics based on reviews of laws, decrees, circulars, media coverage, political discourse, interviews with hospital authorities (e.g., chiefs of service, head midwives, head nurses), and with government officials such as a high-ranking Paris police figure responsible for migrant surveillance. The research was conducted at four hospitals in the Paris region (two in Paris, two in northern suburbs) and five PMI (maternal and child health clinics), in addition to numerous NGOs (such as the prominent legal aid association GISTI, organizations of cultural mediators, and interpreter associations). Following midwives on rounds in post-partum units and sitting in on prenatal consultations, together with detailed structured interviews with more than two dozen midwives, 200 migrant women in clinical settings, and 50 men in 9 worker hostels generated detailed information on clinical communication and hospital/practitioner representations of migrant patients.

The migrant population reported on in this essay is predominantly Malian and Muslim. The Ministry of the Interior estimates that more than 100,000 Malians currently reside in France, many of whom are undocumented (*Le Monde* 2003: 4). Approximately one-third of the Senegal River Valley population is now women (Barou 2002: 14). The shift in migrant demographics since 1975 from male labor migrants to young families with increasing numbers of children has contributed to the contradictions between formal representations of patients at the institutional level and a much more essentializing set of practices and discourse manifest in patient-practitioner interactions. It is here where we can examine clinicians' practical schemas for interacting with these patients.

Estimates of the number of Muslims in France range as high as 6 million, of whom 250,000 are thought to be of sub-Saharan origin (*Haut Conseil a l'Integration* 2000: 26). For the Malian population, as for many Senegalese and Mauritanians from the same region, Islam plays a significant role in shaping decisions about marriage, family, and reproduction (Sargent 2006: 35). However, in the public hospital system that most migrants rely on, the institutional premise is that religion is a private issue and (theoretically) irrelevant to the practice of medicine. Further, although medical practitioners may assume that North Africans (or those with names that suggest North African origin, those speaking Arabic) are Muslim, they are less likely to recognize the likelihood that Malian and other West African patients may be Muslim as well.

Media coverage of the 2005 and 2007 migrant uprisings accelerated the public process of rethinking sub-Saharan African migrant identities, as journalists analyzed the roots of migrant unrest. These analyses often focused on particular cultural features thought to be associated with West African migrants – especially Malians – such as female genital cutting (FGC) spousal and child abuse, and polygamy, all indicative of a failure to commit to integration. Limited ability to speak French is taken to demonstrate convincingly the lack of integration.

The restrictive immigration policies of the past decade have made it extremely difficult for migrants to obtain residence permits for more than one year at a time. Reaching the ultimate goal of a ten-year residence card now requires evidence of successful integration, or assimilation, into broader French society. Applicants must show their respect for French culture; essential in this endeavor is the demonstrated ability to speak French. According to legislation passed on July 24, 2006, the "foreigner" must demonstrate their "republican integration" in French society, with particular regard to his personal commitment to respect the principles that govern the French Republic, and sufficient knowledge of the French language (Law no. 2006–911, Article L.314–2).

In a speech delivered on November 21, 2007, President Sarkozy underscored the significance of the French language as the defining indicator of integration. He stated that those seeking a *carte de séjour* under the aegis of family reunification must first pass an evaluation of their French language competence. Sarkozy stated that at the heart of French identity is the French language, that it is a culture, a way of thinking, a form of resistance to the homogenization of the world.[2]

In the maternity hospital context, migrant patients' French language skills shape their direct interactions with staff, but also indirectly shape schemas employed by practitioners, schemas that reflect popular representations in the larger society. Increasingly, the imagined African woman in France is framed not only in terms of race (physical and cultural difference traced to colonial period) but as the Muslim (black) female body. In the public imagination, African migrant women are often portrayed as victims, subject to outrageous customs and subordinated to hypersexualized husbands, but are also villainized: analyses of the migrant uprisings can be read as arguing that African women produce excessive numbers of children, and African immigrant children produce violence.

Constructs of the black, Muslim, female body, derived from popular and political discourse, also shape biomedical representations of West African

[2] (*"au Coeur de l'identité française, il y a bien sur la langue française. Le français est un ciment, le français est une culture, une manière de penser, une forme de résistance a l'uniformisation du monde,* Sargent translation, *Quotidien*, April 3, 2007).

women's (hyper)sexuality, (excessive) fertility, and (submissive) marital practices, vis-à-vis which the hospital has responsibilities as an institutional agent of the state. The maternity hospital is thus one site at which the politics of immigration play out in routine practices of practitioners, patients, and family members. One role of the maternity hospital is to disrupt the process of reproducing delinquent African children by encouraging migrants to use contraception and – theoretically – by conveying information, values, and critiques, to West African women. In this way, the maternity hospital and its staff serve as a space for conveying normative behavior and ideal constructs associated with marriage, reproduction, and childrearing.

For Malian women, their husbands, and extended families, biomedical messages are often framed in accordance with or in opposition to Islamic doctrine. Biomedical instructions, interventions, and expectations are reframed in Islamic discourse that has more to do with disruptions in received wisdom concerning gender relations and family structure than with medicine and health care per se.

REPRESENTATIONS OF WEST AFRICAN (MALIAN) MIGRANTS IN HOSPITAL CONTEXTS

How, then, do particular clinicians combine schemas about these women in their workplace contexts? Participating in maternity rounds with midwives, nurses, and doctors offered opportunities to discover how theses schemas reflect or diverge from formal Ministry of Health guidelines, such as those ensuring that information is accessible to patients in general, or that all maternity patients are presented with detailed advice concerning contraception. Midwives, who have the most authoritative interactions with maternity patients, rarely call for interpreters in any of the maternity or child health clinics observed. In the two hospitals with interpreters on staff, the African-languages interpreter complained that she was rarely asked to translate, in spite of the fact that the majority of Malian women speak little French.

One problematic consequence of such communication constraints is that some midwives give women prescriptions for birth control pills without explanation, often in a stack of prescriptions for the new mother and baby (see Sargent and Larchanché 2007). This ethically questionable practice, acknowledged by informants in all research sites to be widespread, reflects diverse schemas among midwives. One is the assumption that it is in migrant women's best interests to have fewer children, thus they should be given the pill whether they know/understand its function and usage or not. Another (for a minority of midwives interviewed) is that "these women" are excessively fertile, having babies every year without self-discipline, "like hens" (using the word *ponde*, as in laying eggs) or rabbits. During discussions about contraception, midwives often contrasted France as exemplifying modernity with Africa as a place of incomprehensible "customs and superstitions." Thus midwives might begin a conversation with a reminder that in France, it is not appropriate to have one baby after another. One must learn how to live in France and take contraceptives, to have fewer children. As the contraceptive implant has been added to the repertoire of contraceptive choices, the limited capacity for direct verbal communication has dramatic consequences when women do not comprehend that the implant is effective for five years, may cause bleeding, and must be removed by a doctor. Reflecting on the lack of rapport and accurate exchanges between practitioners and patients, Marie-Rose Moro, professor of psychiatry and chief of service at two Paris public hospitals, observed: "If we don't have statistics and facts, we will use prejudices" (June 8, 2008, personal communication).

Yet individual practitioners see themselves as advocates for African women. In one maternity service, several midwives approaching retirement called themselves "the team," and worked explicitly to assist pregnant women without papers. One of these midwives is well known among Malian patients, who call her by name and plow through a crowded prenatal consult waiting room to intercept her and ask questions. An active member of the CGT left-wing union, she sees the hospital as her "site of struggle."

Where, one may ask, is Islam in midwives' representations of West African patients and is it a dynamic in therapeutic interactions? For most midwives, Islam is not a central feature in their interactions with patients, as the following remarks suggest:

Virginie is not aware of any reason why Islam is a consideration in dealings with West African patients or North Africans in general. She does not think observant Muslim women might have concerns about Islamic prohibitions regarding contraception. West Africans, she says, are "cool and congenial," but North Africans suffer from a "Mediterranean syndrome" in which they complain excessively.

Naida describes problems of communication and adaptation to France. She had twelve hours of anthropology in her last year of midwifery school and learned that if the patient is Muslim, one should not discuss contraception when the husband is present. As a North African Muslim herself, she thinks modesty is an issue for Muslim women at the maternity hospital, but often it is not possible to find women doctors for these patients. She concludes that Islam is not necessarily a problem; it all depends on level of education of the patient and husband and the country of origin. Moroccans, for example, tend to be more enlightened about family planning, in contrast to West Africans, although both populations are Muslim.

Cecile and Caroline: To them Islam is relevant with regard to the "rule of forty days" (sexual abstinence following delivery), which makes it difficult to explain when to start contraception. Sometimes one finds a miniature Koran in the baby's bed but also an amulet around the baby's waist (surely not a Muslim practice, they note). In general, however, West African women never mention religion; they are "open to everything" (*elles sont ouvertes à tout*; Interview 25, June 2004).

Muriel: West African women have problems with their husbands concerning contraception, so Muriel says "PMI" to indicate that the woman should seek help there (even those who do not speak French know PMI, "except for the Chinese"). Islam or other religious issues have never arisen with African women, but they have numerous social problems.

Sandra: Some Muslim African women talk about the forty days and do not want the pill. She tries to advise them to begin contraception after the forty days; it is a good idea for them because their pregnancies are too numerous and at close intervals and they find themselves in precarious social situations.

Iris: Language is the problem, creating language barriers. One needs sign language or maybe a bit of English. And it is a nightmare to figure out a patient's medical history.

These and other statements reveal that midwives deploy a number of practical schemas concerning West African women, many of them internally contradictory (and often incorrect). These include the following:

- African women have too many children at close intervals.
- African women should be strongly encouraged to use contraception.
- African women are subordinated to their husbands and thus probably will not use contraception.
- African women need to be taught their rights.
- African women are probably Muslim, but this is not relevant to patient care.
- African women probably speak French, as indicated by their congeniality, but if not, pantomime will suffice to explain most medical issues.

Midwives combine these and other schemas to guide their responses to individual woman and their actions. They are characteristic in prioritizing language and "culture" or "social problems" when discussing the African migrant maternity patient. There are visual indicators of religious affiliation (North African and some West African women wear headscarves) and some awareness of "Muslim modesty" or religious icons to protect the new baby.

In general, midwives interviewed are aware that West African migrants are probably Muslim but see this as a relatively insignificant feature of their identity. Thus medical practitioners frame West African women patients drawing on popular representations, personal experience, and political orientation, as well as on assumptions about the meanings associated with immigration, West Africa, and Islam.

CONSTRUCTIONS OF DIFFERENCE IN A GERMAN HOSPITAL

In the German case we find that everyday hospital encounters also reveal discriminations and hostilities resulting from on-going negotiations of identities. The ethnographic data in the German account, however, reveals different tensions and fragmentations than those found in France. Even as the German nation-state works aggressively to promote more expansive categories of citizenship and belonging than ever before, everyday hospital life and the biomedical and epidemiological paradigms informing it generally fail to reflect more inclusive sociopolitical policies. In the university hospitals where the research was conducted, non-German patients were marked in ways consistent with that Partridge has characterized as "exclusionary incorporation" (2008), practices by which noncitizens in Germany are incorporated into the nation-state but only as compromised subjects.

Significant revisions to German citizenship law in 2000 – changes that expanded the long-standing German-by-blood straight gate to citizenship – did indeed create more avenues to *legal* incorporation for non-Germans in Germany. Integration, however, has not been achieved. Even as new citizens and newcomers are producing new forms of Germanness, the cultural shift is far from total or complete. For the women patients I met in German hospitals, different kinds of non-Germanness intersect: "Muslim" cannot be separated out from other forms of categorization and discrimination, subtle and not so, that converge to affect experiences of everyday life: as female, as pregnant, as Turk, as African, as pious or agnostic, as rich or poor, university educated or occupationally trained. As Rottmann and Ferree (2008) articulate in an article about head scarf laws in Germany, women noncitizens living at society's margins may be subjected more as *women* both within ethnic enclaves and in German society, even while at the same time they are marked as "ethnic" and "religious."

The question of which categorization of oppression is more determining is not the point. Lived experiences of oppression and limits on democratic freedoms more typically arise from a convergence of discriminations, fluid, shifting, and temporal. In Germany, at this moment of social and demographic transition, the everyday social engagements that would first frame noncitizens as Turks rather than Muslims or Muslims rather than Turks – that is, categorizations in the first instance as ethnic or religious – are regionally and institutionally variable. For example, recent social science analyses on Muslims in Germany (e.g., Mandel 2008, Yurdakul 2009) draw on research conducted primarily in Berlin. The research described here was conducted at university hospitals in Hesse (former West Germany) and Thuringia (former East Germany), sites almost rural compared to Berlin. The ethnographic data lead to different conclusions about immigrant identity-making in post-9/11 Germany, showing how identity is always mutually constitutive, in-the-making and more unstable than complete.

Officially, about 10 million people (approximately 12 percent of the total population) are considered foreign-born (UN 2006) in Germany. Four million identify as Muslim, the vast majority of whom – almost 3 million – also identify as Turkish, (Spiegel Online 2009). But the numbers alone are not enough to understand the complexities of institutionalized inclusions and exclusions. About half of the Muslim population in Germany are German citizens. More than half belong to German clubs and associations (Spiegel Online 2009). Most are not pious Islamic practitioners. The categorization "Turk" itself is not determinately monolithic in Germany; it includes Kurds and often Arab-speakers from other Middle Eastern countries. And like immigrant populations around the world, within most Muslim-predominant communities in Germany, there are significant social variations within and between the first immigrant generation and the subsequent generations. The generational divide was obvious in the hospital research cohorts.

In the German hospitals where the research was conducted the markers of difference were multiple. Patients from Mediterranean Sea countries and the Middle East were generally labeled Turk, not Muslim. As I traveled back and forth between former East Germany and former West Germany regions, other categorizations and identities also became apparent within the hospitals. Former East German and West German affiliations and differences were commented on many times a week, but only in East Hospital.[3] Additionally, *Aussiedler* (resettlers) – immigrants who are considered German by blood by the state but who may have lived outside Germany for many generations – were often described and treated in the research hospitals settings as "Other" unless they spoke flawless German.

[3] Research supporting this chapter was conducted in one hospital in former West Germany and one hospital in former East Germany, thus we have used toponyms, West Hospital and East Hospital to protect identities. That research project (1998–2008) focused on, among other things, residual effects of Germany's divided medical history.

While "Muslim" likely possesses *social* meaning for the physicians, nurses, and midwives working in the hospital, patient *ethnicity* rather than religion was reinforced more predominately. Everyday hospital and reporting practices featured medical recording and epidemiological risk categorizations that influenced how patients were assessed by their obstetricians. In Germany, these schemas concerned ethnicity more than religion. The epidemiological patient data collected in hospitals for the state (*Länder*) and federal statistics agencies, for example, categorize patients by, first, German and non-German status, and, sometimes by ethnicity data points. One research hospital had only two data categories for *Herkunftsland der Mutter* (mother's country of origin): "Deutschland" (92.9%) and "anderes Land" (7.1%). The other research hospital used these same two categories (73.8% and 24.8%, respectively), and also broke down the "another country" data further using the categories (1) middle and northern Europe, America (11.6%); (2) Mediterranean Sea countries (14.1%); (3) Eastern Europe (19.3%); (4) Middle East and North Africa (47.4%); (5) Asia (6.0%); and (6) Miscellaneous countries (1.6%). Using "social risk" categories to assess prenatal maternal and fetal risk, while not as established in Germany as elsewhere, is increasing becoming a common German obstetrical practice. The point is that hospitals as institutional sites employ all level of personnel trained to look at patients through epidemiological risk categorizations that use ethnicity (and exclude religion) as a significant medical and statistical variable. This is not to say that religious references are never made in hospital, but rather to argue that hospital categorizations do not neatly align with the political, economic, and social categorizations that frame religion in the first instance in other milieus.

"TYPISCHE TURK" AND EXCLUSIONARY INCORPORATIONS[4] IN A GERMAN HOSPITAL

Every day at 4:00 in the afternoon, doctors at West Hospital would stop what ever they were doing and hastily make their way through the hospital corridors en route to the third-floor conference room for the *Besprechung*, the doctors' daily conference. Rushing from the main floor where they attended to women resting with their newborns during *Wochenbett*, the week almost all German women spend in the hospital after giving birth, some doctors would squeeze into the antiquated four-person elevator, the size of an old phone booth, and slowly creak up toward the Besprechung. Other doctors ran the airy stairwells from floors above and below; some came fresh from surgery. Still others

[4] Term used by Partridge (2008) to describe the status of non-German noncitizens in Germany.

ascended in the cavernous stainless-steel elevator from the hospital basement laboratories where doctors stole away hours to conduct research. Quite apart from the hospital suites where the hassles and happiness of new mothers and their babies were everyday fare, the softly lit basement laboratories housed shallow dinner table-sized tanks with rollaway metal tops that peeled away to reveal pregnant sheep suspended in chemical soup, a limbo not quite life, not quite death, but life enough to conduct fetal sheep research. Here in the laboratory suites, doctors studied the effects of oxygen deprivation on fetal sheep blood flow velocities as measureable by ultrasound, research designed for human application. At 4:00 PM, however, everyone made their way to the Besprechung. Attendance was obligatory.

On one level, the Besprechung was a daily logistics meeting. Around an oval table that filled the room, doctors coordinated treatments, reviewed the day's cases, consulted and updated one another, and shared differential diagnoses for various patients' conditions. The Besprechung was show-and-tell time, or, more accurately, tell-and-show time. Each of the various department heads – Labor and Delivery, Ultrasound, Gynecology – would report on the activities in their department that day, with special mention of interesting or unusual cases. Younger and female doctors tended to provide just-the-facts overviews, whereas the older male doctors gave updates notable for their narrative flourishes and, when the director was away, raucous humor. Patient updates, however, were not the only things actively circulated at the Besprechung; these afternoon meetings regularly included "passing of the organs." Recently removed reproductive organs and diseased tissue were circulated around the table in small silver stainless-steel bowls or, if size required it, large white gallon-size plastic buckets. Tucked alongside the diseased bodily detritus lay foot-long surgical tweezers, and while the patient's medical history was verbally relayed as narrative backdrop, the bowl/bucket-of-organ was passed and doctors in turn used the tweezers to poke and pull at tissue, flipping the organ back and forth to better examine in broad daylight the physiological pathologies previously hidden in body cavities. The organs – most frequently cancerous ovaries, mottled grey-black-pink, and uterine tumors often resembling cauliflower – were passed as if they were the patient herself. Offering up the organs to their peers, doctors typically began their narratives with "Here is Frau Bauer[5]..."

On quite another level, the Besprechung was a primary transmission site of hospital culture. It was here that the five or so new medical students who arrived every July were enculturated to their status as German medical doctors and to

[5] All names are pseudonyms.

the knowledge and production of West Hospital culture. Normative hospital culture was actively transmitted during these afternoon sessions. The Besprechung as a reflection of institutional culture also was revealing for the hospital staff who were *not* there. At the time of my research, none of the doctors were Turkish, despite the fact that in West Hospital's small city one in seven residents was categorized *Ausländer* (foreign person) and more than 40 percent of that Ausländer population was Turkish.

The Besprechung was where I first became aware that the comment "*typische Turk*" (typical Turkish person) meant something at West Hospital. During the second week of my fieldwork, one of the older male department heads began describing a patient's labor and delivery. The obstetrician commented that the patient had been extraordinarily noisy during labor, had thrashed and cried, wailed and moaned, all at impressively high decibels. He moaned as he relayed the narrative, generating laughter around the table. But the baby was very healthy and the young mother quickly recovered. "Typische Turk," he tossed in as he concluded to more laughter and head nods from his colleagues.

"Typische Turk," as I learned over time, referred to a collection of behaviors that West Hospital doctors, midwives, and nurses felt they had objectively observed as common to Turkish women who came to West Hospital. These behaviors were deemed decidedly not German. As in the Oberarzt's narrative, they included behaviors assessed as too loud, emotional, and dramatic during labor and delivery, but almost always ending with a healthy woman and infant. She-doth-protest-too-much was a regular feature of this narrative, demarcating "real" and "unreal" patient pain in ways that effectively communicated the idea that "Turkish" expressions of pain could not be trusted in clinical settings. From other comments during the Besprechung and on rounds, I learned that "typische Turk" also included bringing "smelly" (*Geruchsbelästigung*) garlicky foods into the hospital rooms, having large groups of visitors come to the hospital room and stay for hours, as well as having "too many children." "Good" patients, as I learned from West Hospital doctors, midwives, and nurses, were stoic during labor and delivery; able to contain and manage their pain without making noise; had only one or two children; their visitors were few and stayed briefly; and they ate the bland hospital food without complaint and understood that spicy foods meant "spicy" breast milk and gassy babies.

There was much conjecture in the propagation of these Teutonic and Turkish binaries, but subjective as they are, collectively they add up and constitute the everyday habits of "making *Ausländer*."[6] Although Ausländer

6 We borrow this phrase from Mandel (2008) who uses it as a chapter title.

translates in English as "foreigner," the German word possesses little of its linguistic cousin's neutrality; its component parts literally mean "out" (aus) "country" (Land). Mandel (2008: 80) explains, "Ausländer means much more than merely foreigner … it means unintegratable, outsider, alien … apart from the unmarked 'native' citizenry." "Out-lander" – or, more precisely, outlier – characterizes what I observed: Turkish patients received good-quality medical care in hospital, but they were almost always "other."

Analysis of these research data, like those of David et al. (2006) and Reime et al. (2006), does not show statistical differences in perinatal health outcomes between non-German and ethnic German patients.[7] Health outcomes, however, coexist with ethnicity-based characterological demarcations. "Typische Turk" behaviors in West Hospital were mostly tolerated, although usually remarked on and often complained about by staff. To be "typische Turk" in West Hospital was mostly overdetermined; Turks in Germany actively and dialogically shape what post-reunification Germany looks like. Just as Gilroy (2002) has shown for the British case, cultural identity in Germany is not static, but rather develops and changes over time, influencing and influenced by traditions marked "other." Everyday life in hospital indicates that cultural identity in Germany is similarly signified, even as overdetermined characterizations like "typische Turk" remain in circulation.

"WE'RE NOT AN IMMIGRANT NATION"

The schemas shaping hospital life have their counterparts in the broader society. Popular among hospital staff, a television docudrama telecast during one of my fieldwork stays depicted the life of a university professor in Dresden who was fired in 1935 for being Jewish but who ended up living through the war. Based on Victor Klemperer's best-selling diaries, the docudrama portrays a man who describes himself as a "German patriot," a man who felt and thought himself more completely German than Jewish. Episodes chronicled Klemperer's inability to reconcile his Germany of Goethe, Schiller, and Hegel's high-minded secular humanism with National Socialist systems of human extinction, even as he faced everyday discriminations of increasing intensity. In the West Hospital lunchroom during a group discussion of the latest episode, a physician characterized a contemporary tension for my benefit. "Germans are very aware of their history," he said. "We learn every year

7 An important caveat: the German research was not designed to incorporate the likelihood that social frameworks and everyday discriminations affect the ethnicities of people using the hospital, which Casteñada (2008) shows is the case.

in school about the Holocaust. We know that great civilizations can fall, and we must always work against that." Weeks later this same physician, a deeply thoughtful German-born obstetrician who had studied to be a theologian before becoming a doctor, added another layer of complexity to the everyday contradictions of Germany belongingness. Referring to Klemperer when I asked him privately about what I had observed to be selective and automatic HIV testing for patients who were black, he said, "If we Germans could make Germans like Klemperer 'Jews' – he was more German than most Germans – we have no problem [now] making immigrants foreigners." Alluding to an inalienable German predilection to "make others 'other'" struck me as an overly harsh and essentializing explanation of a medical practice, but he was adamant in response to my protestations.

During the fieldwork research stages I conducted in Germany from 1998 to 2008, I heard repeatedly from many different types of people, "We're not an immigrant nation." This is a revealing and significant denial after fifty years of, by almost any definition, immigration to Germany.[8] Implicit in the denial itself is a preference for characterizing the thousands of economic migrants from Turkey as *Gastarbeiter* (guest workers), and nothing more. Today's immigration problem has a history: Germany met its 1960s labor shortage through a "guest worker" program. The German government had formal agreements with Italy, Greece, Turkey, Portugal, and the former Yugoslavia, inviting unskilled workers from those countries to come and work in German factories. The greatest number came from Turkey. When the Gastarbeiter program officially ended in the mid-1970s, the expectation was that the workers would be "good guests" and know that it was time to go home. "We called for labor but people came instead"[9] (Mandel 2008: 51) characterizes what was initially for Germany a no-nonsense plan to meet an economic need that morphed into a human migration dilemma. By the mid-1970s, population pressures were enough for German authorities to mount a family reunification program for Turks who wanted to live in Germany, but this accommodation was only a "right to reside," not the right to full citizenship. Without a path to full citizenship, legal remedies ended up structuring, however inadvertently, second-class citizen status for the majority of Turks living in Germany.

Citizenship law changed in 2000, and immigrants legally residing in Germany for eight years may now become naturalized citizens after demonstrating

8 UN (2006) names Germany as having the world's third-highest numbers of international migrants. Benton-Short et al. 2005 suggest the five-city constellation of Berlin, Munich, Hamburg, Frankfurt, and Düsseldorf, taken collectively, produce this ranking.

9 Mandel's translation of a Max Frisch's (2008: 51) essay title.

German-language fluency, taking a citizenship test, and proving economic independence. But the demarcations in evidence at West Hospital are reflections of everyday German life, and everyday life has not yet caught up with the law. "We're in, but we're not in all the way," *The Economist* (2008) quotes a first-generation Turk living in Germany in an article subtitled: "Germany's Turks do not properly belong. But what is it that they should belong to?"

Citizenship is not now and historically has not been a precondition of health care "deservedness" in Germany. Starting with Bismarck in 1883, health care has long been understood in Germany as "part of the cement that binds a people sharing the same geography into a genuine nation" (Reinhardt 1994: 23). Patients not insured in the typical way – in conjunction with employment – are covered by government-sponsored *Sozialamt* (social assistance). In my East Hospital and West Hospital research cohorts, these patients numbered 2 percent and 3 percent, respectively, of all patients whose prenatal exams I observed.

With the passing of immigration reforms in 2005, however, the legal right-to-reside became a condition of receiving health care in Germany. There has been growing popular interest in tracking undocumented immigrants in the health system and other *öffentliche Stellen* (public facilities), and in some parts of Germany anti-immigrant fervor has even become election fodder. Bureaucratic technologies of the 2005 reforms require the reporting of undocumented residents, criminalizing not only the individuals seeking health care for themselves or their children, but also the professionals who attend to them. The 2005 Residence Act (*Aufenthaltsgesetz*) officially sets up health care professionals in hospitals, clinics, and in private practice (as well as individuals working in other public facilities) as gatekeepers for the nation-state. As such, seeking health care may now result in deportation. This is a significant departure from the days when Germany's postwar commitments to never-again humanitarianism far outpaced interest in tracking Ausländer in Germany or championing anti-immigrant campaigns.

Belonging in Germany has operated as a powerful trope of local village cultures, metropoles, regionalities, and the nation-state (Mandel 2008; Borneman 1992). As long as Turks and others remained Ausländer enough, popular notions of German belonging remained mostly intact. The new citizenship reforms have unsettled these popular understandings, and are further complicated by the fact that the Residence Act does not apply equally to all foreigners in Germany. The English-language page on the Federal Office for Migration and Refugees (*Bundesamt für Migration und Flüchtlinge*) Web site states, albeit somewhat awkwardly:

> The purpose of the Residence Act is to manage and limit access by foreigners to Germany. It facilitates and shapes immigration, taking account of the

> reception and integration capacities, as well as of Germany's economic and labour market interests. At the same time, the Act serves to meet Germany's humanitarian obligations. … The Residence Act does not apply to all foreigners equally. The Act does not apply to certain groups of foreigners (e.g., EU citizens).[10]

EU citizens, while still qualifying as foreigners in Germany, are by degrees not perceived by the nation-state as foreign-enough to require the surveillance "necessary" for more foreign-others.

"WE DIDN'T ASK YOU TO COME" AND OTHER COMPLEXITIES OF CONTEMPORARY BELONGING IN GERMANY

Speeding in 2006 in a dark late-model BMW along a major west-to-east German highway with a university vice president and doctor, the chauffer turned around to me and pointed to an old but well-maintained small wooden house on stilts, encircled by a tumble of barbed wire. In English, he said, "That's an old East German guard station. We've just passed over into East Germany." I noted his use of the present tense and wondered if I was making a translation mistake. It turned out I was not. Further on, when we sought in vain to find an address, the chauffer disdainfully commented on the lack of street signs as proof of *Ossie* (former East Germans) backwardness. A few days later on the return trip, driving east to west, when we passed back over the former border, he exulted rather loudly from the front seat, "Now we're back in Germany again."

In Germany, where belonging has long been a powerful trope of culture and the nation-state (Peck et al. 1997; Herminghouse and Mueller 1997; Hermand and Steakley 1996), German reunification competes with ethnic and religious frames in hospital life. Research data on this point indicate a significant departure from data retrieved primarily from Berlin sources (Mandel 2008; Yurdakul 2009). In East Hospital, more than 90 percent of the patients identified as German-born; the two largest groups of non-German prenatal care patients were Russian *Aussiedler* (resettler) and Vietnamese immigrants. In former East Germany, German identity remains a contested domain, not only because many people thirty years and older continue to feel like second-class citizens within Germany, but also because many feel important social values were lost at reunification. In a casual conversation in the hospital computer room, a West Hospital student nurse in her late twenties who was originally

[10] http://www.bamf.de/nn_432412/SharedDocs/Rechtsgrundlagen/EN/DasBAMF/aufenthg.html?__nnn=true, accessed November 22, 2009.

from former East Germany told me, "Here in Germany I am always Ossie, a second-class citizen. I'm only German when I leave Germany. It's only when I travel and other people see me as German that I feel German." Twenty years after the fall of the Berlin Wall, Germany remains economically and ideologically divided. Unemployment in the former East Germany has hovered around 20 percent since soon after reunification, twice that of former West Germany. Doctors in former East Germany continue to make salaries that are about 80 percent on average that of their colleagues working in former West Germany. In my research I found stark cultural divides between East and West Hospitals' patients: life changed very little after reunification for West Hospital patients, but for East Hospital patients, life after reunification was "completely the other way around" (see Erikson 2005). For East Germans reunification meant "the totality of all they had known disappeared over night. Their world, their state, their lifestyle, their economy, their history, – in short their identity – had been proved wrong" (Mandel 2008:138–139).

At reunification, difference in Germany manifested in new and multiscalar forms; in one, East Germans came to stand in many cases as more "other" than urban Turkish immigrants. Soon after reunification, there was a widely cited joke, first published by Jenny White, which spoke to the antagonisms reunification unleashed. "A Turk is standing on line at [a grocery store] behind two Ossies. One Ossie complains to the other, 'Look at this line. We've been waiting here for hours. I don't know why we came here. It's no different from where we were.' The Turk turns to them and says, 'We didn't ask you to come.' In another version of the joke, the Turk also corrects their grammar in German" (White 1997:761).

German-Turkish antagonisms in former East Germany have different histories and different expressions than in former West Germany. A young female Turkish doctor working at East Hospital impressed upon me during many casual conversations we had in 2000 that she, as a Turk living in former East Germany, experienced very little discrimination. She had always done well in school, was encouraged by her teachers and neighbors, and was well supported throughout medical school and into her early career, she reported. Her tone was markedly changed when I saw her in 2005. "I became a Turk [after the] Muslim terrorist cells in Hamburg" were linked to the September 2001 attacks in New York. She felt that she had had more difficulties at work and her children at their school as a result of a creeping perception that Turks throughout Germany were terrorist sympathizers. The societal shift – from an East German context in which she had been "integrateable" to a reunified German context in which she, and by extension Turks in general, were assumed to be unintegrateable – shocked her. "Not belonging" in reunified

Germany had come to mean not being committed to the social order in the same way as ethnic Germans. She had become suspect, even though she was unchanged and committed to "the German" social order as she had been.

GERMAN AND NOT QUITE "GERMAN"

Even the category "ethnic German" requires further interrogation. With a slight nod of the head, a nurse in West Hospital alerted me to an *Aussiedler* (resettler) patient. This patient, she explained in a whisper, was German but I would not be able to recruit her for my study because she did not speak German. She was Russian, but she was *Volkdeutsche*, which was a way of telling me that she was German by blood and therefore viewed by Germany as German even though her family had lived outside of Germany for decades.

Walking to the market with a neighbor one balmy autumn Saturday, we happened upon a large pile of household effects – chairs, tables, lamps, mattresses – blocking the sidewalk. My neighbor loudly tsked in protest as we moved into the street to pass by. "These people come here," she said. "They know nothing about Germany, but they get to come here, and we pay, we *pay* for them." Confusion must have been evident on my face – there were no people anywhere to be seen – because she continued. "The government pays for their housing and effects, they're moving *in*," she said, pointing to the pile. "And they get a government stipend. They live here for free. They can't even speak German, and they're *Volkdeutsche*." Over the months I lived in this neighborhood, the neighbor continued to provide unbidden updates on the Aussiedler family, using terms that clearly signaled their status as outsiders, despite their legal right to reacquire their German nationality upon request.

Over the ten years of my research, hospital statistics changed with regard to how Aussiedler patients were counted. When I began the research, they were counted in the "ethnic German" category. Their maternal and infant outcomes were indistinguishable from the statistics of women who were born and raised in Germany. More recently, however, as if a symbolic and parallel measure of the perceived challenges immigrants' presence exerts in Germany and on the European Union, state health statistics have been reformed to now to classify Aussiedler separately, as *Osteuropa* (Eastern European) (e.g., 2008 ZQ).

AT THE MOMENT: DESTABILIZED NATIONAL IDENTITY

"Germans really love their Germany," an undocumented Ghanaian woman living in Germany told anthropologist Heide Casteñeda (2008: 349). But who counts as "German" now? German-born and -raised? Second- and third-generation Turks speaking fluent German? Immigrants from around the world who have lived for years in Germany? What of the "not-immigrant other" in Germany: former East Germans still marked Ossie, as well as Aussiedler speaking languages of the former Soviet bloc? With this volume, there is space to ask also: Is being Muslim antithetical to belonging in Germany?

The answer lies in part in the nuances of difference for Muslims and non-German others in contemporary Germany. Consider the young female doctor at East Hospital who was dismayed to discover that in everyday first impressions her Turkish surname had come to trump her status as a well-educated physician, law-abiding citizen, and loving and attentive mother. She became suspect after 9/11 because of a convergence of effects experienced across Europe: fear, ignorance, xenophobia, imagined threat, and real violence. Whether German-born, émigré, or noncitizen, belonging in Germany today is to be part of a destabilized ethnicity, lashed to older and residual notions of state, territoriality, culture, and identity. It is also to be entangled in an uneven and contested social project characterized by cycles of intense legal and bureaucratic activity followed by perfunctory silences that last years as laws settle out into everyday practices, anticipated and surprising, in the hospital and other places.

CONCLUSION

In this discussion of West African immigrants in France and Turkish immigrants in Germany, we have compared how hospitals, as institutions, shape migrant understandings of the ideal patient and the appropriate citizen. At the same time, hospital practitioners engage in practices and discourses that reflect popular and political constructs of immigrants as cultural Others. But they also have become shaped to the particular tasks and interactions in which hospital workers engage. Accordingly, hospitals are among the institutions that frame, reproduce, and reframe migrant identities by means of routinized interactions that signal inclusion and exclusion in the broader society. For migrant women, hospitals participate in the gendered inculcation of immigrant identities, especially in the context of maternal and child health care. In both cases, we analyze social tensions surrounding immigration and cultural "difference," a gloss for multiple categories of identity: religious, ethnic, racial, political, or genealogical.

Germany and France have certain historical similarities with regard to immigration (guest worker populations, family reunification, controversies around concepts of "belonging" and social integration, and an emphasis on demonstrating social personhood through language competence). But we find significant differences as well. In particular, although Turks in Germany and West Africans in France constitute primarily Muslim populations, identification of migrants in terms of religious affiliation is much more salient in France. No doubt France's colonial (and postcolonial) connections to migrant sending societies in North and West Africa have produced unique frameworks for constructing migrant identities and prospects for integration, as has French "republican" political philosophy.

Ethnographic research in Germany reveals different sources of tension and fragmentation than those prevailing in France. In German hospitals, ethnicity is understood as the primary indicator of difference, while other significant identity markers operating within hospitals include former East and West German affiliations, and status as *Aussiedler* (resettlers of German ancestry, from the former Eastern European bloc), in addition to that of "Muslims."

In both countries, however, constructs of culture, ethnicity, religion, nationality, and race are deployed and negotiated among biomedical personnel, interpreters, patients, and families. As we have shown, hospitals are hardly exempt from the broader conflicts and paradoxes of the societies in which they are embedded. Rather, clinical contexts serve as sites of representation and contestation, where widely held assumptions concerning social identities and essentialized constructs of what it means to be French or German play out in everyday "therapeutic" encounters.

BIBLIOGRAPHY

Barou, Jacques. 2002 Les Immigrations Africaines en France au Tournant du Siecle. *Hommes et Migrations* **1239**: 6–19.

Benton-Short, Lisa, Marie D. Price, and Samantha Friedman. 2005 Globalization from Below: The Ranking of Global Immigrant Cities. *International Journal of Urban and Regional Research* **29**(4): 945–959.

Borneman, John. 1992 *Belong to the Two Berlins: Kin, State, Nation*. Cambridge: Cambridge University Press.

Bundesamt für Migration und Flüchtlinge. 2009 Accessed November 22, http://www.bamf.de/nn_432412/SharedDocs/Rechtsgrundlagen/EN/DasBAMF/aufenthg.html?__nnn=true

Casteñeda, Heidi. 2008 Paternity for Sale: Anxieties over "Demographic Theft" and Undocumented Migrant Reproduction in Germany. *Medical Anthropology Quarterly* **22**(4): 340–359.

Comaroff, Jean and John Comaroff. 1991 *Of Revelation and Revolution: Christianity, Colonialism, and Consciousness in South Africa, Volume 1*. Chicago: University of Chicago Press.

David, Matthias, Jürgen Pachaly, and Klaus Vetter. 2006 Perinatal Outcome in Berlin (Germany) among Immigrants from Turkey. *Archives of Gynecology and Obstetrics* **274**(5): 271–278.

Dewitte, Philippe. 2000 Malade Etranger, Etrange Malade? *Hommes & Migrations*. Sante. Le Traitement de la Difference: 1225. 1.
Erikson, Susan L. 2005 "Now It Is Completely the Other Way Around": Political Economies of Fertility in Re-Unified Germany. In *Barren States: The Population Implosion in Europe*. Carrie Douglass, ed. Pp. 49–71. London: Berg Press.
Gilroy, Paul. 2002 *There Ain't No Black in the Union Jack: The Cultural Politics of Race and Nation*. London: Routledge.
Haut Conseil a l'Integration. 2000 *L'Islam dans la Republique*. Paris: Office of the Prime Minister.
Hermand, Jost and James Steakley, eds. 1996 *Heimat, Nation, Fatherland: The German Sense of Belonging*. New York: Peter Lang.
Herminghouse, Patricia and Magda Mueller, eds. 1997 *Gender and Germanness: Cultural Productions of Nation*. Providence: Berghahn Books.
Joyce, Kelly. 2008 *Magnetic Appeal: MRI and the Myth of Transparency*. Ithaca: Cornell University Press.
Kaufman, Sharon R. 2006 *And a Time to Die: How American Hospitals Shape the End of Life*. Chicago: University of Chicago Press.
Kotobi, Laurence. 2000 Le malade dans sa difference : les professionnels et les patients migrants africains à l'hopital. *Hommes et Migrations*. Sante. Le Traitement de la Difference 1225.
Le Monde. 2003 Quelques 120,000 Maliens en France, Don't un Tiers Legalement. February 11: 4.
Long, Hunter and Sjaak van derGeest. 2008 When the Field Is a Ward or a Clinic: Hospital Ethnography, special issue. *Anthropology and Medicine* 15(2): 71–78.
Mandel, Ruth. 2008 *Cosmopolitan Anxieties: Turkish Challenges to Citizenship and Belonging in Germany*. Durham: Duke University Press.
Mestre, Claire and Marie-Rose Moro. 2007 La France Raciste? *L'Autre, Cliniques, cultures et societes* 8(2): 271–277.
Ministere de la Sante et des Sports. 2007 *Charte de la personne hospitalitee: des droits pour tous*. Accessed February 15, 2009. http://www.sante-jeunesse-sports.gouv.fr
Mol, Annemarie. 2002 *The Body Multiple: Ontology in Medical Practice*. Durham: Duke University Press.
Partridge, Damani. 2008 We Were Dancing in the Club, Not on the Berlin Wall: Black Bodies, Street Bureaucrats, and Exclusionary Incorporation into the New Europe. *Cultural Anthropology* **23**(4): 660–687.
Peck, Jeffrey, Mitchel Ash, and Christiane Lemke. 1997 "Natives, Strangers, and Foreigners: Constituting Germans by Constructing Others." In *After Unity: Reconfiguring German Identities*. Konrad H. Jarausch, ed. Pp. 61–102. Oxford: Berghahn Books.
Reime, Birgit, Pamela A. Ratner, Sandra N. Tomaselli-Reime, Ann Kelly, Beate Schuecking, and Paul Wenzlaff. 2006 The Role of Mediating Factors in the Association between Social Deprivation and Low Birth Weight in Germany. *Social Science and Medicine* **62**(7): 1731–1744.
Reinhardt, Uwe. 1994 Germany's Health Care System: It's Not the American Way. *Health Affairs* **13**(4): 22–24.

Rottmann, Susan B. and Myra Marx Ferree. 2008 Citizenship and Intersectionality: German Feminist Debates about Headscarf and Antidiscrimination Laws. *Social Politics* **15**(4): 481–513.
Sargent, Carolyn. 2006 Reproductive Strategies and Islamic Discourse. *Medical Anthropology Quarterly* **20**(1): 31–49.
Sargent, Carolyn and Stephanie Larchanche. 2007 The Muslim Body and the Politics of Immigration in France: Popular and Biomedical Representations of Malian Migrant Women. *Body and Society* **13**(3): 79–102.
Saunders, Barry and Judith Farquahr. 2009 *CT Suite: The Work of Diagnosis in the Age of Noninvasive Cutting*. Durham: Duke University Press.
Schiller, Nina Glick, Ayşe Çağlar, and Thaddeus C. Guldbrandsen. 2006 Beyond the Ethnic Lens: Locality, Globality, and Born-again Incorporation. *American Ethnologist American* **33**(4): 612–633.
Spiegel Online. 2009 *Germany Has 1 Million More Muslims Than Previously Thought.* Accessed December 11, 2009. http://www.spiegel.de/international/germany/0,1518,632290,00.html
United Nations. 2006 Trends in Total Migrant Stock: The 2005 Revision. Department of Economic and Social Affairs, Population Division.
White, Jenny B. 1997 Turks in the New Germany. *American Anthropologist* **99**(4): 754–769.
Yurdakul, Gökçe. 2009 *From Guest Workers into Muslims: The Transformation of Turkish Immigrant Associations in Germany* Newcastle: Cambridge Scholars Press.
ZQ (Zentrum für Qualität und Management im Gesundheitswesen). 2008 Geburtshilfe Jahresauswertung. Einrichtung der Ärztekammer Niedersachsen. Modul 16/1.

3 Schooling and New Religious Diversity across Four European Countries

Thijl Sunier

In recent decades, and as a consequence of processes of globalization and international migration, nation-states have redressed their role as active cultural and social agents in continuously evolving discursive fields (see Geschiere and Meyer 1998). As Rose and Miller (1992: 177) have argued, "It is in this discursive field that "the state" itself emerges as a historically variable linguistic device for conceptualizing and articulating ways of ruling." Most nation-states in Europe have reemphasized their role as a powerful force in cultural processes and a meaningful source of legitimacy in a time when this very legitimacy of nation-states as providers of political meaning is under pressure (Verkaaik 2010; Geschiere 2009). As such, nation-states are cultural projects that present themselves through particular narratives in particular sites. This could be observed first and foremost in the debate about the unification of Europe and the integration of migrants. Nation-states, through different political agents, articulate specific national narratives, concepts of citizenship, and models of integration.[1] But instead of articulating simplistic messages of patriotism or nationalism, their civic and political messages have become far more subtle and sophisticated, concerned with seemingly universal values of democratic participation, supranational inclusiveness, and the peaceful resolution of all conflicts (Baumann 2004; Shils 1994). Nation-states today develop a variety of ways to translate nationalist exclusivism into inclusivist narratives of participation, integration, and identification (Anderson 1991: 6; see Uitermark, Mepschen, and Duyvendak, Chapter 10 in this volume).

Public education is one of the most crucial instruments of nation-states for communicating these narratives (Schiffauer et al. 2004). State-supervised

[1] See, e.g., Brubaker 1992; Duyvendak and Scholten 2012; Favell 1998; Ireland 1994; Koopmans and Statham 1999; Rath 1991; Rath et al. 1996; Schiffauer 1993; Schiffauer et al. 2004; Vermeulen 1997; Walzer 1997; Zolberg and Long 1997.

schooling is the quintessential mechanism by which nation-states turn children into citizens and individuals into political persons. As Baumann puts it: "Without state schools, there would be no nations as we know them in North-Western Europe, no national *conscience collective*, and no effective means of inculcating and rehearsing the conventions of the dominant political culture" (Baumann 2004: 2). The importance of state education for citizenship has long been acknowledged, but since the arrival of migrant children at schools in Western Europe, education has become one of the most crucial instruments of national integration policies. This has become crucial in situations where a relatively high percentage of children come from a Muslim background. The increasing interference of the state in educational matters, its increasing controlling of activities at the expense of the autonomy of schools is a clear indication of this development.

Here we can observe an intriguing paradox. Public education is a prime site of modern cultural statecraft where national narratives are cast in a pedagogical agenda, but it is also a site where controversies and disputes about cultural and religious issues in society are acted out in teaching settings, in daily interaction among students and staff (Schiffauer et al. 2004). However, schools are also institutions with a specific institutional logic and with actors who occupy different social locations within those institutions and within society. This makes the effectiveness of schools as instruments of the state complex and partly unpredictable. As the editors of this volume argue, actors develop practical schemas within institutional contexts that cannot be reduced to simple outcomes of the national models of governance of diversity. Furthermore educational institutions are conditioned by local circumstances, composition of student population, and other factors. Many of these conditions produce situations with respect to educational policies and landscapes, outputs, and institutionalized problematic that show a striking similarity across national borders. We consider schoolteachers at secondary schools as public actors who through their teaching convey messages of all sorts, and do so in a way that is shaped and constrained by the practical tasks and challenges they face *qua* teachers in schools. Although many of the challenges and complexities that national educational systems are confronted with stemming from the growing ethnic diversity at schools are strikingly similar in different countries, and although many of the adopted measurements and policies are also largely similar, the national narratives with which these policies are explained and legitimized do differ considerably. This can be observed especially in state educational institutes. The argument put forward in this chapter is that public education is a field in which framing takes on a very specific form precisely because it is in education where the state's role as a cultural agent becomes particularly manifest.

THE SCHOOL AS A CIVILIZING AGENT

The best way to explore the relation between nationally specific models of governance and the practical schemas and working models operating in public educational institutions is to conduct ethnographic research in schools. This was the main focus of a research project that compared four schools in four different countries: France, the United Kingdom, the Netherlands, and Germany (see Schiffauer et al. 2004; Sunier 2000). In each of the four schools included in the project, one researcher followed school life for more than a year: attending classes, observing students and teachers, participating in activities, and interviewing staff and students. On the basis of the national research reports, compiled through the close cooperation of the four research teams, cross-national analyses were carried out. These analyses were then matched with the initial data and with additional material about education policies and practices in the four countries. We were able, therefore, to trace school-specific practices back to general trends in educational policy. The main conclusion that could be drawn from these data was that although the four schools were facing similar issues with regard to the composition of their students and the specific institutional and local circumstances, in their explanations of these issues they deployed practical schemas that referred to nationally specific modes of public culture. To put it differently, nationally specific modes of public culture provided explanatory and legitimizing repertoires in a variety of daily encounters between actors at the schools.

We were interested in the socializing, disciplining, and integrative mechanisms at work in any process of cultural change as they operate in typical state institutions such as public education and in the legitimizing schemas that undergirded these mechanisms. We therefore introduced the slightly neologistic concept of *civil* culture (Schiffauer et al. 2004). This concept has several advantages over the more common *civic* culture (see Almond and Verba 1980). It first takes on board the relevance of civil society. It is basically through civil society, that "space of uncoerced human association" (Walzer 1997: 89), that migrants integrate into society. The concept of civil culture takes up the normative and disciplining notions of how civil society and civil exchanges should be structured and conventionalized. Secondly, the concept of civil culture refers to the historically particular conventions of how a citizen should interact with the powers that dominate the public sphere, be they institutions of the state itself, judicial institutions or the rule of law, the conjunction of governmental and corporate powers, or civil servants running their bureaucracies. It connects the formal juridical relation between citizens and the state with the idea of civility. Thirdly and most crucially, the concept of civil culture takes on board the idea of a national imaginary as a crucial element in the trajectory to citizenship. Both civil society and civic culture unfold their dynamics in the presence of a state, notably a nation-state. The most effective means to turn a cold and coercive state into a warm and willed nation-state lies in the creation of a national imaginary that imbues its organizational controls with a sense of identification and community (Baumann 2004: 10).

Anderson (1991) and Billig (1995) have provided ample evidence of how this process unfolds. The wide variety of symbolic resources that contribute to this national imaginary can be considered as crucial elements in the making of citizens. From the term "civil culture" it is just one step to the process that is deemed to shape individuals into citizens, what we call "civil enculturation."[2] Once an individual in any given nation-state goes through a process of discursive assimilation or civil enculturation, he or she may be expected to dispose of specific competencies that enable him or her to meet the civic requirements and conventions of that particular nation-state, without rendering "political culture" a "timeless national character" (see Steinmetz 1999: 21).

To sum up: the concept of civil culture fits better in the actor-oriented approach we adopted in the research project than civic culture because it shifts the attention to (civil) *competence*. It criticizes the top-down deterministic underpinnings of the concept of civic culture without ignoring the disciplining mechanisms at work. Civil culture and civil enculturation combine three elements: competence vis-à-vis the workings of a country's civil society; competence vis-à-vis its nationally specific conventions of civic culture and norms of civility; and some familiarity, conformist or critical, with its dominant national imaginary.[3] Civil enculturation is not about conformity or resistance; it is about the competence of arguing for or against an option within a (nationally specific) framework of discursive conventions. One can say "yes" or "no" to any one proposition, but the style of arguing and the phrasing of agreement, difference, or any compromise proposal must be recognizable as a legitimate option by others around the respondent. These methods and discourses are no longer about "who you are," for everyone has the right, at least in normative parlance, to cultural or ethnic difference, but about "how

[2] The term can be specified by adding nothing more than the adjective "civil" to the well-established definition: (civil) enculturation is "the process by which an individual acquires the mental representations (beliefs, knowledge, and so forth) and patterns of behavior required to function as a member of a [civil] culture, [...largely] taking place as part of the process of... education" (Rhum 1997).

[3] We speak of competence comparatively, not competence in, with, or of. The competence we speak of is a capacity to conform to or reject, play along with or undermine, but in socially shareable ways.

one does," for in that respect there must be some similarity of "style" regardless of the variety of "roots." This has fundamental effects on the person thus enculturated into a new civil and/or civic identity. Hence civil identification is a matter of discursive adaptation or discursive assimilation rather than of the formation of new identities.

Civil cultures, then, are primarily, albeit not exclusively, received and absorbed through explicit and implicit curricula at school. Furthermore, civil culture allows for a thorough assessment of the institutional contexts and the practical schemas that operate in daily interactions at schools. Schools provide students with cognitive maps as they are provided in all kind of curricular material, but it should be emphasized that civil culture and framing repertoires are by no means static. As we will see, a crucial aspect of the process of civil enculturation is precisely the contested status of the processes that also undergird educational programs and didactic regimes.

CIVIL CULTURE AT WORK

To analyze these mechanisms, we distinguished two dimensions of civil enculturation as it is practiced and presented at school, each with its respective mechanisms of conveyance. The first dimension is the formal curriculum, and the main question to be asked was how the dominant principles of civil culture are translated into the curriculum and how they are trained, rehearsed, and reproduced. Ideals and narratives of national civil culture are most clearly formulated in explicit curricula.[4] What, however, concerns us here is how these narratives work out in daily school practices and encounters, educational practices, and concepts, for example, frames and modes of teaching. Identifying the differences in frames of teaching in relation to civil culture was one of the more difficult tasks in the research project, but it was important to taking account of the institutional specificity of the school. Schools do not simply reflect national ideologies; to a certain degree they refract them through their school-specific schemas, and to a certain degree they generate them out of school-focused tasks and interactions. Although educational programs as they appeared on paper in each of the schools reflected crucial characteristics of the dominant national civil cultural narrative, to analyze how these traits were interpreted by actors and put across in lessons and extracurricular activities, and how they played out in the school, was one of the more complex aspects of the research. Local circumstances, the location of the school, the composition of students, the image of the school, and the

4 For a discussion of these explicit curricula, see Schiffauer and Sunier 2004

practical schemas on which actors at school drew all contributed to the specific discursive environment of each school. It was, however, the way in which these circumstances were legitimized and explained with principles of civil culture that threw into relief the crucial differences that made these schools unmistakably "Dutch," "French," "German," or "British."

Religion turned out to be one of the most crucial areas of contestation in the production of civil culture at all four schools, but in very dissimilar ways. It is certainly not a coincidence that the legislation in France about "ostentatious signs" in public places, following the report of the Stasi Commission in December 2003, concerns schools first and foremost (Bowen 2007; Bertossi and Bowen, Chapter 5 in this volume). Entering a French state school is entering the republican state. The entrance of the school literally marks the boundary between the "unorganized" society and the "ordered" secular republic. This was certainly the case in the school where the research was conducted. But also in the schools in Berlin, Rotterdam, and London, religion was a sensitive issue that was inextricably linked to the national underpinnings of school identity. The influx of migrants with "new" religious backgrounds has added another dimension to the status of schools as a principal contentious field. However, because the new religious presence is not equally distributed within host countries, specific circumstances in individual schools suggest that each school should be treated as a unique case. Certainly in cases where schools have a relatively great operational autonomy such as in the United Kingdom and the Netherlands, this geographical variety should be taken into account. Nonetheless, distinct national explanations were clearly discernible in each of the schools.

An important question arises about how the school should reflect society. Is the school a part of civil society, or is it an instrument of the state? From a comparative perspective it is crucial to elaborate these arrangements and modes of educational policy because, to a large extent, they set the stage for the status of religion and ethnicity at school. Officials at the school in the Netherlands were very well aware of its social and geographic place on the boundary of two socially distinct neighborhoods. This, according to the school board, rendered the school an important function as a social bridge. Their task reached beyond the school gates. Also the German and British school considered the boundary between school and surrounding society as a highly sensitive and important issue. Closing up the school to the outside (a common practice in the French school) because of problems with young people from outside, was seen as a severe step to take. This attitude on the part of the officials indicates that they see the the school as in and of society rather than as an instrument of the state. In order to fully comprehend the relation between situational factors and principles of civil culture, we thus extensively described the schools as places in their social space.[5]

In the United Kingdom, ideally, the school should reflect the diversity that characterizes society (Skinner 1993; Baumann and Sunier 2004). As a consequence, religious instruction is obligatory in all schools and there should be an emphasis on antiracist education. In most cases, however, religious education is actually Christian in content. This was explicitly formulated in the Education Reform Act of 1988 and is related to the dominant position of the Church of England as a state church. However, the content of religious education is a matter for the local educational authorities, and these authorities reflect the local political and social landscape. As such, there are considerable differences from school to school in the makeup of religious and antiracist education. Schools located in an urban environment with large numbers of migrants actually adopt policies different from those in the countryside. Confessional schools are entitled to apply for so-called voluntary aided status. This status concerns the relative autonomy of the school board as well as the possibilities for state funding. In practice it is hard for a school, especially if founded by "new" religions, to apply for such a status.

In the Netherlands, the educational system is still largely dominated by Article Number 23 of the Constitution, the basis of the so-called pillarization in education.[6] This article stipulates that the organization of education is free in the Netherlands. In addition to that constitutional right, there is supplementary legislation to regulate the financial responsibility of the state in educational matters. This implies that (recognized) confessional schools receive the same funding as state schools.

On the basis of this legislation, Muslims have founded Islamic schools from the mid-1980s onward. At the moment there are some forty Islamic primary schools, two secondary schools, and two Islamic universities in the Netherlands.[7]

5 Schools are real; civil cultures are a heuristic abstraction. What makes them comparable, however, are such factors as their comprehensiveness and thus a socially varied intake – their funding and running as state-financed institutions make them open, in principle at least, to all resident children – and their location in or at the edge of an area of suburban social problems and interethnic tensions. What makes them contrastable, so far as their nation-state and civil-cultural dimensions are concerned, are their different positionings vis-à-vis their local areas, the surrounding civil society at large, and the state conceived of as a nation-state (Baumann and Sunier 2004: 34).

6 Pillars were the politico-ideological blocs that made up Dutch society in the 1920s. Apart from Protestant and Catholic pillars, there were a Socialist, a Liberal, and a Jewish pillar. Although the system lost much of its function, it still forms the basis of the school system and a variety of welfare institutions.

7 These universities are trying to acquire an official status within the system, which is rather difficult under the present circumstances.

The curriculum in state and confessional schools is almost completely the same. The differences lie in the general atmosphere of the schools. Owing to the tendency toward a decline in religious belief and practice in society and post–World War centralization of education policy, the confessional pillars have lost their function, and the differences between confessional and state schools have diminished. The foundation of Islamic schools has invigorated the debate once again (Sunier 2004).

In addition to the religious identity of the school, there is a steady debate in the Netherlands about so-called black schools, the ones with more than the average number of students of foreign background. This debate coincides with that of the confessional schools, but not entirely. Because there is freedom of school choice, "white" parents may contribute by their school choice to "white flight." The choice of schools is a very sensitive and politicized subject in the Netherlands. Presently Islamic schools are under heavy criticism because of poor educational performance and bad results. Discussions about the educational output are easily mixed up with a debate about the general status of Islamic schools.

The German school system is decentralized at the level of the *Länder*, so it is difficult to identify common features in state schools across the country. The code word, *freiheitlich-demokratische Grundordnung*, is taken straight from the German Constitution and counts as the abstract term of reference with respect to the relation between the school and the religious identities present in society. It does not refer to any particular ideal of the Republic, as in the French school, but neither does it engage with any tangible institutions of the state. We observed less "stateness" and objectified citizenship than in the French school, but also less civil society than in the British school.

In practice, schools tend to reflect the religious landscape of the surrounding society. In all four schools we observed that the increase of students with non-Christian (read: Islamic) backgrounds was perceived as a serious challenge to the character of the school as a representation of the dominant civil cultural narrative. In all four schools we reported incidents and negotiations that precisely covered this tension, but with four different ways of interpreting these.

Against the background of these general locations of education, schools, and schooling, practices pertaining to the actual educational process took on specific shapes and trajectories. The issues at stake in each of the schools were strikingly similar and revolved around the question how to manage diversity, but the ways in which they were acted out differed. Religion, national history, and multiculturalism turned out to be the most crucial topics when diversity was at stake. Styles of teaching (knowing versus discussing, frontal versus project teaching), the role of order (discipline versus self-responsibility), the role of extracurricular activities, and the division of tasks may, technically speaking, be the same in each of the schools, but the ways in which these educational strategies were explained and legitimized often demonstrated strong links to national civil culture. Furthermore, the relation between the school and the outside world ("extension or bastion") and the strategies toward the neighborhood were crucial issues where school-specific conditions were connected to the dominant civil narrative. The main differences between the four schools with regard to frames of teaching concerned the extent to which the schools consider themselves as a reflection of (civil) society. Of course, each of the four schools admitted that they have a pedagogical task, but they differed in opinion how far and to what fields this task reaches.

Concepts of discipline and social order turned out to be another central element in structuring implicit curricula in all four cases. It refers not only to common observations of how a practical order is applied in a big social setting like a school, but also to modes of conduct and interaction both inside and outside the classroom. Modes of discipline also turned out to be powerful criteria by which civility and discursive routines and conventions were regulated.[8] In examining these disciplinary modes, we found important differences between the four cases.

At the German school, an explicit code of conduct is not considered genuine if it is an imposed rule. Self-discipline and self-responsibility must come out of one's internalized conviction. Before school, it is a task of the family to install conviction without using authority (which in the form of mere obedience has a checkered history). Non-discipline is a moral failure and is explained by referring to the social class of the family. Contextual evaluation and individual performance of students were always under strong teacher-centered vertical control.

This vertical organization of discipline was also characteristic of the French school; however, it was not extended to the family as much as in the German case, but obviously seen as a public educational task (see Bertossi and Bowen, Chapter 5 in this volume). The fact that children in France are generally sent to day care centers from earlier age and for more hours during the day also contributes to this. Discipline is imposed by the institutions, which represent

[8] As Mannitz has argued: "The concepts of civility aim at social cohesion to activate mutual respect and societal solidarity, they represent codified expectations of adequate conduct and its limits, in the positive norm of suggesting an ideal as to *how* the individual should contribute to the whole, and also in the negative sanctions to recall an expected norm after that it was broken. Neither teachers nor students relate their immediate individual performances in school to the scope of societal reproduction, but school routines of discipline unmistakably reflect and reproduce the ethos of the specific civil culture" (Mannitz 2004: 230).

the neutral, rational project, set up as an objectified system of competition. Thus non-discipline is a failure of living up to these rules, implying a failure of social order.

While in the French and German schools discipline was thus imposed vertically, in both the British and Dutch schools strong bonds of organization on the horizontal level between students were expected to enhance mutual control. Consensus, community, and negotiation were important principles. Horizontally imposed control requires a different form of socialization. In the Dutch case, lack of discipline was often interpreted as a failure to participate in the imagined moral community. In the British case, non-discipline was seen as a failure of loyalty, a lack of respect for the normative multicultural mosaic.

THE ARTICULATION OF IDENTITIES: SCHEMAS AND LEGITIMATING ARGUMENTATION

How did these general institutional constraints work out in actual situations of interaction? How did actors in each of the schools operate in specific situations? To elucidate this, I provide a brief account of three cases of negotiation in the German,[9] British, and Dutch school.

At the German school we observed several incidents that clearly demonstrate the specific procedures to be followed in conflict situations. To understand the cases, we should know that conflicts should ideally be solved individually by going through the official channels. This means appealing to hierarchically organized committees and experts in the matter. In school, to address the "teacher of confidence" who is elected by the students' assembly every year is considered to be the most appropriate channel of negotiation: make up your mind, recollect your arguments, and discuss them with the mediator in charge to check whether they can be regarded as legitimate. If yes, then make use of the mediator to solve the problem. In addition to that, one can consult the students' representative council and utilize them as advocates. A court hearing is conducted when teachers feel the need to solve a problem that concerns a student: all teachers who deal with the particular students come together, the headmaster or head teacher of the grade presides at the hearing, the student's parents are invited to join, and the student in question is also present. The procedure is reminiscent of what in German civic culture and civil service is described as the *Amtsweg*: the ordered sequence of steps from the lower echelons of the administration to the highest. The procedure can thus be regarded as a lesson in civic culture: one is to weigh one's standpoints

[9] The German cases are taken from the report of the fieldwork at the German school.

against one's individual conscience in order to find out whether these standpoints are legitimate arguments for negotiation.

Soon after starting the fieldwork in Berlin, the researcher was invited by some Turkish, German, and Lebanese boys of a ninth-grade group to take part in their lessons. She was invited to watch especially their history and geography lessons. According to the boys, there were regular quarrels in the class, and the teacher, they said, was often insulting students, especially "the foreigners" in the class. The students' class representative (a German boy) even proposed to use the researcher as a witness later on. They had already tried to settle the conflict by applying to the "teacher of confidence," but the accused teacher had denied all of their accusations. The students felt especially offended by remarks about their lack of capacity and intelligence in these procedural matters. They particularly recalled an incident during a geography lesson about the desert. First students had to write down ideas and definitions of the desert, then the teacher ordered a Lebanese student to read aloud a passage from the book, saying, "well that is something for you that part about the camels and all." Although the students had laughed about the "funny" remark of the teacher, they nevertheless understood the message and considered it offensive and discriminatory. The teacher was accused of *Ausländerfeindlichkeit*. The example shows the inherent weakness of the vertically imposed expert procedure. The paternalistic relations at the school made it hard for the students to bring in substantial evidence against the teacher. Therefore, the class representative tried it again by applying for another (external) expert: the researcher. His solution was consistent with the adequate procedure of how such a conflict should be resolved. It bore no fruit, however, and the whole issue petered out without any substantial and further steps taken. There were similar cases where students initially started a protest against alleged insulting behavior but gave up in the course of the procedure.

The cases reveal peculiarities both with respect to how the actual content of the accusations was perceived and with respect to the procedure that should be followed to solve it, but also how these kind of conflicting situations tended to end up. The apparent perception of severe conflicts in these cases was related to a negative attitude toward foreigners (in German: *Ausländerfeindlichkeit*). Minority students often felt treated unfairly when they were pigeonholed as "foreigners," but they never really took issue. In comparison, German students took by far more offense when they felt the need to complain about something or want to discuss a conflict with a teacher. Among "the foreigners," only the "courageous" ones took initiative when they experienced discrimination, but the evaluation of what was a legitimate argument to justify further steps apparently did not create much empathy for them.

The procedure with the teacher of confidence and the council, moreover, functioned as a form of institutionalized clientelism. To be successful in such cases, one must have representatives on one's side who have established positions at the school. Arguments that are put forward must be authorized and approved of by these key persons. These prescribed channels of solving problems with school staff were indeed adequately followed by competent students, irrespective of ethnic background, but in general there seemed to be more restraints and complications in cases where minority students applied for the committee. When the "experts" considered a case not relevant, the students who took issue were silenced. As a result, German students not just made use of the system more easily than Turkish students did; the latter tended to refrain from taking steps altogether. It seemed as if they had "accepted" the fact that they would not succeed anyhow and resigned themselves to the inadequacies of a paternalistic system.

Issues of discrimination and unequal treatment came up at the school in London as well. The principal difference in solving those issues with the German complex procedure is related to sequence of steps likely to be taken. In the German case, students tried to settle the issue by appealing to the court procedure and tried to mobilize the whole class. That was at least the legitimized step to be taken. Although it did not work out, it would be inconceivable to mobilize only the Turkish students in order to render the case an ethnic collective connotation. But this is exactly the viable option for students at the British school, as the following cases demonstrate.

The reported incident took place in a religious education lesson. The topic of the day was the belief in reincarnation in Buddhism. The teacher was explaining that human beings who behaved badly in this life might reincarnate in a different form after their physical existence ceased. She wanted to exemplify this when she pointed to Selim and said: "Selim may become a squirrel in his next life." Although apparently meant as a harmless joke, the statement caused great laughter in the classroom and students started to call the boy "squirrel Selim," making him embarrassed and angry. His classmates continued making fun of him during the break and telling other students that Selim would be a squirrel in his next life. Selim took the issue very seriously and told his parents that the teacher had humiliated him. His parents went to school to make a formal complaint and to ask for an apology. They were assured that it was not a premeditated joke and the teacher did not mean to humiliate him. She randomly chose one of the students. It could have been anyone in the classroom. Although most of the students dropped the joke after a while, there were still few students calling Selim "squirrel" and making him angry. Selim blamed his teacher for this unfair situation and continued to consider it as discriminatory.

We observed similar cases, and whether the teacher deliberately aimed at the Turkish students in these cases remains uncertain, but the example shows high sensitivity about labeling and stereotyping at school. Although the example may sound rather harmless and trivial, it was at the same time the staff of the school themselves who kept students aware all the time of the damaging effect of stereotypes. Even seemingly "ordinary remarks" common among many students referring to ethnic background, like "hey Paki," were taken very seriously by some teachers and made into a principal matter. The net effect was that although conflicting situations were not dealt with in a structured way as in the Berlin case, it was very common that students made their argument by ethnicizing the issue and by trying to mobilize their fellow (ethnic) students. The following rather serious incident clearly elucidates this.

The beginning of the fieldwork at the London school was marked by a violent clash. A Turkish student (Levent) was badly beaten by an English boy (Jim) who hit him with a bottle on the head, whereupon the elderly brother of Levent seriously threatened Jim. Until then the school administration was not involved in solving the conflict and probably not even aware of it. This, however, changed when the conflict escalated, involving more and more relatives and friends on both sides. The police was called to settle the conflict and to separate the parties. The next day Levent brought with him a big knife to school in case he would be attacked by the English group of friends and relatives of Jim who even threatened to kill him. Levent was, however, caught with the knife on the school premises. He was temporarily removed from the school. His dismissal was released in the weekly report published by the school. The incident caused a great deal of concern among Turkish students in the school. When the police arrived at the school, Turkish students had gathered at the front door of the school to support their friends and to protest against the violence against Turkish students. Under the leadership of Salih, a sixteen-year-old Turkish student, a committee was formed that tried to negotiate the issue. After some unsuccessful attempts, they decided to take further steps. Bypassing the year heads, they wanted to talk to the head and deputy head teachers to argue that as long as Jim would stay at school, there would be a feeling of injustice among Turkish students. Again they were unsuccessful. When they failed to get a "just" solution, they decided to organize a collective action.

The next step the committee took was organizing a sit-in protest in the staff corridor one morning. Almost fifty students occupied the corridor where senior teachers and the head teacher have their rooms. Turks, Kurds, and Turkish Cypriots were present. The school's administration had not expected such an extreme action. The students could not be convinced to disperse and go to their classrooms until they had talked with the head teacher. When she appeared, Salih presented her a list of demands and copies of letters to be sent to local newspapers, education authority, and the Secretary of Education. The committee not only demanded Jim to be expelled permanently from the school; they also wanted the removal of the two year heads who had blocked their attempts by not acting as channels to the senior administration. When they were assured that their demand would be looked at, the Turkish students dispersed after half an hour of protest that did not involve any violence or disrespectful behavior.

The reactions of the teachers on the issue, particularly on the ethnic connotations of the whole conflict, were mixed. Some played down the significance by pointing to the troubled behavior of the English student: it had nothing to do with ethnic violence, the boy himself was a problem. They agreed to the Turkish students' demand to expel him. Others held that the conflict indeed showed that disciplinary measures applied to minority students tended to be tougher. In general, however, in such serious cases there was a tendency at the school to play down the ethnic connotations of any conflict because that would provoke even more serious reactions. Yet, given that the principal task of the school is to take into account the sensitivity of ethnic relations in neighborhoods such as the one where the school is located, there is no clear consistency as to how these conflicts must be assessed. There were no principal objections against the ethnic mobilization in the conflict. But the inconsistency in decision making made the Turkish students felt victimized, which created the fertile ground for ethnic mobilization.

The Dutch school was well off at the time of the research, in many respects. It had a low record of serious incidents. It had a relatively low percentage of migrant students, and ethnic issues seemed to be almost nonexistent there. During the research it was hard to collect cases in which differential treatment was involved. Yet there were some demands by Islamic students that allude to ethnic specificities. The most viable strategy when one wanted to achieve something related to ethnic or religious background was to phrase an issue in inclusive terms. The *repas des condamnés*, a tradition at the school in Rotterdam, formed the backdrop for an issue in which special rights were at stake. Several weeks before the beginning of the main final exams, the teachers organize a dinner for the students who will have their final hour (hence the name of the event). The students are asked to dress in their best suits, sit at the table, and generally behave as if they are at a fine dining establishment. Teachers act as their servants. It is a kind of rite of reversal and as such is appreciated by many Dutch students who get to order teachers around with a snap of their fingers. Most of the Turkish students attended the dinner, like the meetings at the end of the year and the end of the term.

Although attendance was voluntary, one was expected to join the *repas* because it was considered to be part of the school life. Most of the students who were interviewed did enjoy these gatherings, possibly because they were actually considered as an extension of the classroom situation, or rather an expression of the relationship between students and teachers.. In the year the research was conducted, the *repas* took place in April, and not long before that, the researcher had an interview with Ugur, a Turkish student in his final year. Ugur is a Muslim, and he complained about the fact that the meat *fondue bourgignonne* to be served was not halal:

> I do not want them to organize something apart for Muslims, but I thought it takes little effort to buy the meat from an Islamic butcher. The meat is not different from other meat and Muslims can sit side by side with other students and participate in the dinner. That is what they want after all. Now we have to sit at the vegetarian table, because they do take vegetarians into account. Why then not Muslims. I asked this to the organizers but they said that it was too late now, they already ordered the meat. The said: maybe next year? But then I am gone from school.

Ugur knew precisely how to phrase this request in the appropriate context. Instead of asking for extra provisions for Muslims, he referred to the principle of equal participation of all students at the school and proposed a practical solution. And instead of consulting Muslim students about this idea to get their support beforehand, he directly addressed the responsible persons. Afterward, in a discussion with some of the organizers, it turned out that they did not seem impressed by it and concluded that going with this suggestion would probably open up a discussion about extra provisions, which was not desired. Some of them even suggested that Ugur had a friend who was a butcher and who might profit from such an arrangement. Some of the Turkish students had heard about Ugur's idea and, although some of them thought it a good idea, most of them did not have any opinion about it. Again they reflected the principles applied at school: If you allow one culturally specific adjustment to a school event, where would you stop? The fact that Muslims comprised only a small number of the Tinbergen student population probably played a role. Most Muslim students were aware of that and chose quiescence over articulation.

The case was typical for many such situations at the school. Although Ugur phrased his argument precisely in the way that is to be expected at the Tinbergen School – low key and inclusive, demanding no separate provisions but rather offering a practical solution – he did not succeed. The reason for that might also be practical (it was made too late, for example). At least none of the teachers who were asked about the case was completely against the idea. If the following year the idea would come up again but earlier, Muslims might very well be able to arrange something to enable them to eat meat as well during the *repas*. But in the reactions we collected among teachers about his demand, there was at the same time a critical undertone to be heard: Why make a fuss about it? There seemed to be a taboo placed on any reference to discrimination at the school. Discrimination seemed to be a very sensitive issue at the school. Anyone who would allude to discriminating behavior would probably be silenced because it is felt to be a very serious accusation. It is not only the Dutch myth that the Netherlands is a tolerant country that counted here. What was essential was the avoidance of making a single incident into a (collective) case.

The most characteristic aspect of handling conflicts at the Dutch school was the low-key approach of every potential source of conflict. There was also a tendency to involve as few persons as possible in a conflict and to treat it as a single case. As in the Berlin case, issues were settled individually, but there existed no official procedure to do that. Although the Dutch member of the research team had access to even sensitive information, the school authorities were very reluctant to give insight into potential sources of conflict. That is reasonable from a general point of view of privacy, but it also showed the policy of the school to treat conflicts as distinct cases and not as instances of more general situations. The school tended to avoid any situation in which groups of students were set apart from others because that would easily create conflicts. As the head of the school put it:

> Every year we receive lots of requests from interest groups. We had representatives here of a Muslim platform who were listing to what extent schools do organize extra provisions for Muslims such as praying rooms etc. Our principal policy is to refuse any such requests. If students themselves ask for a solution, say a day off during important celebrations that can be arranged, not as a principal right but rather as an accommodation for our students ... you know that we do not register ethnic background, or religious background. We very well like to stick to the policy of not putting students apart on the basis of these criteria. For us students are students, just human beings each with his or her personal background and we want them to feel comfortable and at ease at school.

Thus many activities could be organized provided the process remained low key and practical. Even more important, it must not be perceived of as the outcome of a demand based on a collective right to which a specific group or category of students was entitled. Thus in a corner of the library at the Tinbergen, a place had been designated where Muslims are able to pray. This provision was never announced officially or publicly. The place was just there and those who wanted to make use of it could do so. Officials and students appreciated efforts to "de-ethnicize" sources of conflict and to act in conformity with the strong equalizing policy that the school had adopted. Students understood the logic behind it, namely that it de-escalated potential conflicts, but the other side of the coin was that it could in some cases lead to a neglect of actual forms of unequal treatment on the basis of ethnic background.

The cases from the schools described here differ to a large extent from each other with respect to seriousness and impact. Yet they all referred to the same kind of mechanisms of ethnic labeling, discrimination, exclusion, and, last but not least, boundary negotiation. In all schools, any issue that tended to develop into an ethnically inclined conflict was played down as much as possible. None of the school staffs wanted to provoke serious cleavages between students, but the striking differences in the cases show *how* potential sources of conflict were perceived of and how teachers and students dealt with it. These differences are directly related to essential aspects of specific civil culture, as we will see later.

CONCLUSIONS

In this chapter I have presented some of the results of a research project that was carried out in four secondary schools in four Western European countries with a sizable migrant population. I have demonstrated how national projects of citizenship are being inculcated through explicit and implicit educational programs and disciplinary practices as they are applied at the schools. The research was designed to analyze the complex interplay between principles, notions, and imaginaries of national civil culture, the actual interpretation and application of these principles, and the diverse ways in which students take up, alter, or reject these civil requirements. A very general conclusion from the project as a whole would be that those students who are able to handle these requirements adequately are on the whole the more successful ones. Another general conclusion would be that we do indeed see that similar issues are being handled even in similar ways, but the explanations that undergird these practices reflected dominant civil cultural traits and principles.

The complex mechanisms used to translate civil principles into cognitive and disciplinary practices, and how the latter are interpreted and inculcated, clearly show that public schools are at once unique social entities and important settings where principles of dominant civil culture are communicated and reproduced. Schools in their position as prime agents in the making of citizens are crucial locations that must keep the delicate balance between the requirements of national states and the actual developments in societies. In recent years, as a result of the hot debates on the position of

Muslims in European societies, schools are often crucial arenas where delicate issues are played out in an explicit pedagogical format.

With respect to the attitudes of students toward the civil requirements, it should be noted that the nationally specific strategies we distinguished are in no way uncontested. Students, and also staff, may opt in or out of these principles in ways that depend on particular characteristics of schools, and of each set of local histories – what happened the previous year, what this person has done before – and are in no way simple reflections of national ideologies nor of degrees of integration.

BIBLIOGRAPHY

Almond, G. A. and Verba, S. (eds.) 1980. *The Civic Culture Revisited: An Analytic Study*. Boston: Little, Brown.

Anderson, B. 1991. *Imagined Communities*. London: Verso.

Baumann, G. 2004. "Introduction" in Schiffauer, W., G. Baumann, R. Kastoryano, and S. Vertovec (eds.), *Civil Enculturation. Nation-State, School and Ethnic Difference in Four European Countries*. Oxford: Berghahn Books: 1–21.

Baumann, G. and Sunier, T. 2004. "The School as a Space in Its Social Place" in Schiffauer, W., G. Baumann, R. Kastoryano, and S. Vertovec (eds.) *Civil Enculturation. Nation-state, School and Ethnic Difference in Four European Countries*. Oxford: Berghahn Books: 22–36.

Billig, M. 1995. *Banal Nationalism*. London: Sage Publications.

Bowen, J. 2007. "A View from France on the Internal Complexity of National Models," *Journal of Ethnic and Migration Studies* **33**(6): 1003–1016.

Brubaker, R. 1992. *Citizenship and Nationhood in France and Germany*. Cambridge, MA: Harvard University Press.

Duyvendak, J. W. and Scholten, P. 2012. "Deconstructing the Dutch Multicultural Model: A Frame Perspective on Dutch Immigrant Integration Policymaking," *Contemporary European Politics* **10**(3): 266–282.

Favell, A. 1998. *Philosophies of Integration: Immigration and the Idea of Citizenship in France and Britain*. New York: Palgrave.

Geschiere, P. 2009. *The Perils of Belonging*. Chicago: University of Chicago Press.

Geschiere, P. and Meyer, B. 1998. "Globalization and Identity: Dialectic of Flow and Closure" *Development and Change* 29: 601–615.

Ireland, P. 1994. *The Policy Challenge of Ethnic Diversity. Immigrant Politics in France and Switzerland*. Cambridge, MA: Harvard University Press.

Koopmans, R. and Statham, P. 1999. "Challenging the Liberal Nation-State? Postnationalism, Multiculturalism, and the Collective Claims Making of Migrants and Ethnic Minorities in Britain and Germany," *American Journal of Sociology* **105**(3): 652–696.

Mannitz, S. 2004. "The Place of Religion in Four Civil Cultures" in Schiffauer, W., G. Baumann, R. Kastoryano, and S. Vertovec (eds.), *Civil Enculturation. Nation-State, School and Ethnic Difference in Four European Countries*. Oxford: Berghahn Books: 88–119.

Rath, J. 1991. *Minorisering: de sociale constructie van "etnische minderheden"*. Amsterdam: SUA.

——et al. 1996. *Nederland en zijn islam. Een ontzuilende samenleving reageert op het ontstaan van een geloofsgemeenschap*. Reeks Migratie en Etnische Studies 5. Amsterdam: Het Spinhuis.

Rhum, Michael 1997: "Enculturation" in Thomas Barfield (ed.), *The Dictionary of Anthropology*. Oxford: Blackwell, 149.

Rose, N. and Miller, P. 1992. "Political Power beyond the State: Problematics of Government," *The British Journal of Sociology* **43**(2): 173–205.

Schiffauer, W. 1993. "Die civil society und der Fremde" in F. Balke et. al. (eds), *Schwierige Fremdheit. Über Integration und Ausgrenzung in Einwanderungsländern*. Frankfurt/Main: Fischer:185–199. An English translation is available at http://viadrina.euv–frankfurt–o.de/~anthro/veronlI_s.html

Schiffauer, W and Sunier, T. 2004 "Representing the Nation in History Textbooks" in Schiffauer, W., G. Baumann, R. Kastoryano, and S. Vertovec (eds.), *Civil Enculturation. Nation-State, School and Ethnic Difference in Four European Countries*. Oxford: Berghahn Books: 33–60.

Schiffauer, W., G. Baumann, R. Kastoryano, and S. Vertovec (eds.) 2004. *Civil Enculturation. Nation-State, School and Ethnic Difference in Four European Countries*. Oxford: Berghahn Books.

Shils, E. 1994. "Nation, Nationality, Nationalism and Civil Society," *Nations and Nationalism* **1**: 93–118.

Skinner, G. 1993. "Religious Education: Equal but Different?" in Pumfrey, P. D. and Verma, G. K. (eds.), *The Foundation Subjects and Religious Education in Secondary Schools, vol. 1*. London: Falmer Press.: 57–71.

Steinmetz, G. (ed.) 1999. *State/Culture. State Formation after the Cultural Turn*. Ithaca: Cornell University Press.

Sunier, T. (2000) "Civil Enculturation. Nation-State, School and Ethnic Difference in four European Countries" *Journal of International Migration and Integration*, **1**(1): pp. 305–330.

——2004. "Naar een nieuwe schoolstrijd? (Towards a new Schoolstruggle?)," *BMGN* **119**(4): 610–635.

Verkaaik, O. 2010. "The Cachet Dilemma: Ritual and Agency in New Dutch Nationalism," *American Ethnologist* **37**(1): 69–82.

Vermeulen, H. (ed.). 1997. *Immigrant Policy for a Multicultural Society. A Comparative Study of Integration, Language and Religious Policy in Five Western European Countries*. Brussels: Minority Policy Group.

Walzer, M. 1997. *On Toleration*. New Haven: Yale University Press.

Zolberg, A. R. and Long, L.W. 1997. *Why Islam Is like Spanish: Cultural Incorporation in Europe and the United States*. Paper presented at the International Sociological Association's meeting, June 5–7, New York City, revised August 27, 1997 (unpublished).

4 French "Muslim" Soldiers? Social Change and Pragmatism in a Military Institution

Christophe Bertossi

The army provides a clear case of how institutional logics shape schemas concerning Muslims.[1] Armies have relatively clear and explicit missions, and they are governed from the top down, making it relatively clear to see how a particular logic shapes everyday schemas. Here we look at the ways in which Muslims are recruited as such, and how they then perceive this fact. We start from France because, as was the case in the previous chapter, the logics of color-blind citizenship, which should mitigate against religion- or ethnic-based recruitment, are relatively explicit. And yet we see norms emanating from an army at a particular historical moment that drive the construction of schemas about Muslim recruits.

Put differently, why would Muslims be framed as such in the contemporary French military? There are two strong reasons for not asking this question – and for renouncing completely the idea of a chapter addressing the French armed forces in a book on the framing of Muslims in social life. The first reason is that, the military being the military, it de-emphasizes any ethno-cultural, racial, or religious identities of civilians when these civilians become soldiers. This is, after all, what the military does, its raison d'être by comparison to other institutions of the state. The second reason is that the French military is

[1] This chapter is based on the findings of two researches commissioned by the French Defense Ministry in 2003 and 2007. The first project was commissioned by the *Centre d'études en Sciences Sociales de la Défense* (C2SD) on "The French Soldiers From Immigrant Descent". Between October 2003 and July 2005, I conducted 62 in-depth interviews with troopers, non-commissioned officers and officers of the four French armed forces (Army, Navy, Air Force and Gendarmerie). The second project was commissioned by the *Centre de Prospective de la Gendarmerie Nationale* (CPGN). Between February and September 2008, 66 in-depth interviews were carried out with members of the Gendarmerie at all grades who were born to foreign parents or originating from the French Oversea regions (Guadeloupe, Martinique, Réunion). Additional interviews were conducted during both projects with high-level general officers, including the Heads of Staff.

an institution of republican France and, as such, the color-blind principles of France's national self-understanding should govern its functioning. Not only should soldiers have no other identity but that of a fighter, but French soldiers are, by principle, nothing more and nothing less than French citizens wearing a uniform and carrying weapons to defend their nation. In other words, there is nothing more universalistic than a French soldier. However, when we look at the on-the-ground reality, "Islam" and "Muslims" have emerged as major references in various discursive, social, and institutional practices within the French military today. Why is this so?

In this chapter, I argue that we best answer this question if we identify existing repertoires of institutional and social justification used by diverse social agents involved in the military today.[2] The variety of social actors mentioned here ranges from high-level officers who are in charge of the institution's policy to basic troopers with a Muslim background and their non-Muslim comrades.

This perspective differs from at least two other possible approaches. First, instead of addressing the armed forces as a unique structure of "total" socialization, of social control, or of institutional culture (Winslow 2007; Pinto 1975; Janowitz 1991), it suggests we look into details at how social actors involved in the military negotiate and justify their position and the position of others, and draw moral boundaries among them (Lamont 2002). This perspective allows us to see what was not supposed to be seen through the lenses of a homogenous military value and identity system – that is, soldiers actually referring to Islam and ethnicity as an issue that concerns their institution. Nor does this approach presuppose that such references to Islam constitute a deviation within the normal functioning of the military, a challenge to its performance and cohesion, or a failure of its socializing power (cf. Soeters and Van Meulen 2007). My questions are more about how soldiers define their place in the institution and the different values they attach to it, rather than how or whether the institution transforms them into prototyped soldiers and configures them through military norms and values. Such norms and values are viewed here as the outcome of this social activity of justification and moral boundary building, and not as the starting point of the process – and even less as the analytical framework – of what must be explained: ethnicity and references to Islam in the French military.

Second, and for very similar reasons, I do not look at how national public philosophies (Favell 1998), cultural idioms (Brubaker 1992), or national

[2] This approach is directly inspired by the works of Boltanski and Thévenot, 1991 (pragmatic sociology), Lamont, 2002 (cultural sociology) and Bowen, 2009 (anthropology of public reasoning).

models of integration and citizenship (Fetzer and Soper 2005) shape the institutional reasoning about ethnicity and Islam in the armed forces. Of course, the military has played – and probably still does – a crucial role in the interplay between national integration, citizenship, and the creation of loyal assimilated members of the "community of citizens" (Weber 1976; Crépin 2009; Schnapper 1998). The notion of the citizen-soldier has long illustrated this nexus. The values attached to citizenship have been conceived of as providing stylized normative programs for the integration of migrants through institutions, among which the military stands, along with the school system, as one of the most important (Segal 2007: 46; Dubet 2005). More often than not, however, this approach leads some scholars to conclude that claims by certain minority groups (i.e., Muslims) challenge the very values of national citizenship and liberal democracy (Koopmans et al. 2005; Joppke 2009). As a result, any reference to Islam is read as a proof of this challenge, causing concerns about the ability of state institutions to function normally and to deliver national integration (Koopmans and Statham 2005: 156).

Instead of such heavy normative readings (for a detailed criticism of the concept of national models of integration in the literature, see Bowen 2007b; Bertossi 2011), this chapter addresses how individuals end up feeling concerned by questions about "integration" and "identities," the types of answers they reach, the general process through which they reach such answers, the institutional and cultural constraints with which they must deal, the possible contradictions among their conclusions, and finally, their mutual misunderstandings.

MUSLIMS IN THE FRENCH MILITARY: OLD FRAMES FOR NEW QUESTIONS

Among the many social actors involved in the construction of schemas about Muslims in the French military we find – obviously – Muslims.[3] These are

3 As the editors of this book have already emphasized in the introduction, "Muslims" is used here in the sense of "sociological Muslims", "that is, people whose background and traditions form part of the long history of Muslim civilization, regardless of whether they worship regularly or what they believe. It is very important not to ascribe a uniformity of religious observance to Muslims, and most 'sociological Muslims' in France do not take active roles in debates about Islam. But most of them consider themselves to be Muslims, and they are seen as such by others around them. (...) For that reason, (one can) retain 'Muslim' as a socially relevant characteristic applying to a broad category of French residents. But it does not mean that all Muslim always highlight that dimension of their identity in their everyday lives" (Bowen 2009: 11).

French nationals – a strict condition for volunteering into the armed forces.[4] Most of them were born in France. Those who were not, however, were brought up there as young children. All of them are the descendants of postcolonial migrants who arrived in France from the 1960s onward. Most gained French citizenship by birth, while some were naturalized before coming of age. Some are children or grandchildren of "Harkis," the Muslim "indigenous" troopers who fought on the side of France during the Algerian war of independence (Charbit 2006; Crapanzano, 2011). Some are practicing Muslims whereas others are not and only consider Islam as a cultural and family heritage. Finally, they are also dual nationals, a consequence of the principle of "perpetual allegiance" that rules nationality of northern African countries (the Maghreb: Morocco, Algeria, and Tunisia) (Chattou and Belbah 2002).

This ideal type of young French citizens with a postcolonial immigrant origin is not a new one in the French armed forces. Past generations were conscripts before the military became a professional body at the end of the 1990s. As conscripts, they became the focus of public questionings, when their integration into French citizenship entered the public and political agenda in the 1980s. These questionings mainly concerned their identities and habits as Muslims (regardless of their actual beliefs and practices), the conflicting collective memories about colonization and decolonization (regarding mostly Algeria), and their dual nationality as a problem of loyalty and allegiance (Long 1988; see Tribalat 1995: 209). Emblematic of this public perception of Muslim conscripts is the title of an official report commissioned by the French defense ministry: *Armées et populations à problèmes d'intégration: le cas des Français d'origine maghrébine* (Armed forces and populations with problems of integration: the case of French of North African origins) (Biville 1990).[5]

When conscription was suspended in 1996, the shift to all-volunteer armed forces transformed the structural context of the questions but did not change the dominant schemas used to describe these populations. The institution had to find a new source of manpower after the loss of the conscripts. A recruitment strategy was hence decided on that targeted a population for which volunteering constituted at once a valuable professional opportunity and a prospect of social mobility. Recruiters found the reservoir of such manpower in the *banlieues* (the poor outer cities). If the strategy proved to be successful with regard to quantitative objectives, new concerns soon emerged about

[4] This research focuses on the fourth traditional armed forces of the French military (Army, Navy, Air Force, and the Gendarmerie), and does not address the *Légion étrangère* (Foreign Legion).

[5] Or: The Military and Populations with Problems of Integration: The Case of French Nationals Originating from the Maghreb.

the sociocultural profile of the new recruits. The institution had no tools for assessing how many children of "*immigrés*"[6] had entered the military – a consequence of France's prohibition of ethnic categories and monitoring. Because it was impossible to know ultimately "how many Muslims" had been recruited during the first years of professionalization,[7] questions were raised about the "kind of Muslims" who had become professional soldiers.

In the early twenty-first century, as it was already the case ten years before, the framing of Muslims as "*populations à problèmes d'intégration*" dominated this new questioning: Are they assimilated Frenchmen and Frenchwomen, or are they "communalistic" group members? Are they loyal to the French state, or does their second nationality impede their true allegiance to France? Finally, are they "liberal," "communalistic," or "extremist" Muslims? It was precisely to answer these questions, that the institution commissioned two independent studies in 2003 and 2007 (Wihtol de Wenden and Bertossi 2005; Bertossi and Prud'homme 2009).

If the institution imposed these schemas on the researchers when both studies started, the research findings provided a totally different picture of who these so-called Muslims actually were, of their motivations to become soldiers, and of the structure of their value and identity systems. Both researches actually showed that "communalism" (*communautarisme* in French, a heavily normative and pejorative notion) was explicitly condemned by the interviewees and that they did not conceive of their second nationality as a matter of loyalty or allegiance. (Some interviewees even realized they were dual nationals only during the interview we conducted with them.[8]) All expressed their feelings of

6 The term "*immigrés*" (immigrant) is used in public discourse and debates in France to refer to people who are not immigrants at all, but French-born children and grandchildren of immigrants.

7 Despite this impossibility, the institution consistently looked for ways to obtain estimations of the number of Muslims in the armed forces. This was among the reasons for which the Defense Ministry decided to commission our first research in 2003, as reads a 2001 note from the Defense Information and Communication Bureau (DICOD) to the Centre for Defense Social Sciences (C2SD). This objective was also explicitly assigned to us by the Gendarmerie in 2007. In both cases, this was not possible – and the commissioning institutions appeared slightly disappointed.

8 A young female Sergeant in the Air Force explained to me she had had a Moroccan ID Card, which is now out-of-dated because she never renewed it since she was a teen-ager. She became a French national when she turned eighteen. Since then, she has only used her French passport for traveling to Morocco. She then wondered: "I don't know if this is really what you call dual citizenship." To her, the French passport presented more than a formal and legal advantage: "When I'm in Morocco, I can walk hand in hand with my boyfriend [a French citizen from Yugoslavian origin]. If I have a French ID, I can do all I want. Otherwise, they could ask my wedding certificate. Well, so... then yes: that must be dual citizenship, but I didn't realize it was so."

being strongly committed to France as their motherland, and that they were ready to die and kill for it, no less but no more than any other soldiers of their generation (on the attitudes of this new generation of professional soldiers, see Galland and Pfirsch 1998; Porteret and Prévot 2004). Finally, some of the interviewees were practicing Muslims. They all showed anxiety about being visible as such in the institution. They circumscribed their practicing Islam as a private matter, framed within the general principles of French secularism. No sign of "communalistic" Islam could be found (inter alia, see Bertossi and Withol de Wenden 2007: 219–249).[9]

These initial findings are important here, as they give a first account of what type of social actors these French Muslim soldiers are within the military. They do not fit in the sociological type of "Muslim religious innovators" (Bowen 2009: 9), seeking Islamic accommodation within the French society and its institutions (compare with Venel 2004). In other words, the volunteering of "sociological" or practicing Muslims in the French military has not resulted in the emergence of a collective actor making religious claims, as portrayed by Koopmans and his colleagues (Koopmans and Statham 2005; Koopmans et al. 2005).

And yet, in the absence of such a Muslim collective actor, Muslim-related issues have gained increasing visibility in the social, institutional, or discursive practices among French soldiers. For example, the creation of a military Muslim chaplaincy was decided on in 2005. Interestingly enough, this was not judged as an appropriate institutional innovation by a majority of the practicing Muslim soldiers.[10] Fears that "bearded imams" would enter the military and contribute to further stigmatize Muslims were common among the interviewees. If the explicit objective of a Muslim chaplaincy in the military was to better meet religious needs of Muslim soldiers, it was not the outcome of these soldiers' mobilization but a top-down initiative that also took place around the same time in other institutions, such as the French prisons (Beckford, Joly, and Khosrokhavar 2005).

What this example shows in more general terms is that Muslims have had a rather passive role in the process of framing Muslims in the French military. This process is certainly connected to their presence within the institution

[9] The only exception to this conclusion concerned the aircraft carrier *Charles-de-Gaulle*. Concerns about "communalistic practices" among the 150 Muslims on board (out of 2,500 crew members) were raised – up to the Defense Ministry, who asked in 2006 to the newly appointed military Muslim chaplain to address the situation.

[10] The interviewees we met in 2004 (i.e. before the chaplaincy was created) emphasized this. During the second fieldwork (in 2007–8), and after few months of existence, the Muslim chaplaincy was viewed as a relevant and legitimate institutional innovation by Muslim interviewees.

and the institutional questionings this presence created. However, they made no claims as Muslims. Quite the opposite: their strategy was explicitly to disappear behind their uniform, and to be perceived exclusively as "complete French citizens" and "skilled professional soldiers."

This leads us back to our initial question: If Muslim soldiers have not been the main agents in the framing of Islam as an issue of the supposedly colorblind French military, who were those agents and through which mechanisms did they work?

To answer this question, I propose that we now enlarge our analysis to include three different types of actors who, through their interactions, have constructed the matrix used today for the framing of Muslims inside the institution. These three types of actors are: (1) the officers in charge of the manpower policy; (2) the Muslim soldiers as an object of this policy; and (3) the non-Muslim members of the military, who reacted to both the new frames about Islam and ethnicity upheld by the institution's establishment as well as to the silent presence of Muslims in their everyday work setting. The next three sections address these groups and identify their respective structures of schemas.

THE INSTITUTIONAL REFRAMING OF REPUBLICAN INTEGRATION AFTER PROFESSIONALIZATION

General officers who had to rethink the institutional policy after the shift to an all-volunteer force have had a major role in this move. Indeed, the end of conscription not only pushed the military to reorganize itsrecruitment and personnel policy, but also made it urgent to reinvent an overarching narrative about what kind of "institution of the nation" the professional military now was to be.

This was not an easy task. The "armed citizen" (Schnapper 1998), the "peasant soldier" (de Puymège 1997),[11] or the "national conscript" (Weber 1976) had been familiar figures of modern France's identity, celebrated by Victor Hugo in *Les Soldats de l'An II* or by nineteenth-century French historians such as Michelet, among many others (Crépin 2009: 89). The nation as an "imagined community in arms" held a central place in the "print nationalism" of French modern times (cf. Anderson 1991). If this idealized image hardly corresponded to reality for most of the nineteenth century, the military service functioned as an agent of rural emigration, civilization, and acculturation,

[11] The figure of the "peasant soldier", however, had a very complex career. So had the idea of universal conscription.

transforming peasants into Frenchmen from the 1880s onward (Weber 1976). The symbolic construct of citizenship (as an expression of national allegiance demanded of all members of a modern democracy) and of military service (as the institutional site where modern national societies were made) was subsequently lost in the process of professionalization at the end of the 1990s. How to replace it?

The military establishment answered that question by reframing the social dimensions of the new recruitment policy. In doing so, it addressed "immigrés" in a way that went beyond the traditional schema that considered them to be a "population à problèmes d'intégration." A senior official of the Defense Information and Communication Bureau (DICOD) explained this new approach:

> It is true that there are crucial concerns about recruitment... since we shifted to all-volunteer armed forces. In the beginning [i.e., the end of the 1990s], that meant that the institution found an interest in learning more about the young people with an immigrant origin ["*les jeunes issus de l'immigration*"]. This is the question about how the military can best resemble French society. This question concerns women and young people with an immigrant origin. Beyond a purely utilitarian interest – we need them – we are particularly aware that this is also desirable.[12]

This "desirability" of enlisting ethnic and racial minority groups in the French forces had several consequences that put it at odds with the traditional public and institutional reasoning about military-qua-republican integration. A first consequence concerns the policy instruments implied by this new approach to recruitments, and the constraints we already mentioned of the prohibition of "ethnic categories" in France. The same interviewee outlined that military officials "know [they] cannot opt for a recruitment policy targeting" minority groups ("*une politique de recrutement ciblée*").

In the meantime, however, these constraints have also been addressed through a comparison among existing models of professional military in different national contexts (Joana 2004). In this comparison, French officials pointed to Uncle Sam's and Her Majesty's armed forces as major cases of successful military professionalization. The appreciation was that:

> In armed forces that have been professional bodies for a long time, such as in the US and Britain, military recruitment has progressively been diversified, integrating youngsters from immigrant origins through an active policy.

[12] Interview with the author, 23 February 2004.

> In Britain, the underrepresentation of minority groups has become a major cause for concerns and measures were taken to increase their proportion by 1% a year so that it would reach in the end their actual proportion in the British population. The same argument prevails everywhere: it seems preferable that the demographic composition of armed forces globally mirrors the composition of the overall society. This is one of the conditions for harmonious relationships between military and the society, for the acceptance of the military by the population, and this conditions, in turn, the manpower pool.[13]

In other words, while they were seeking guidelines to carry out the professionalization of the French military, French officers looked at foreign past experiences and discovered the notion of military "social representation."[14] This principle, however, was not culturally neutral. It had been particularly salient in institutional narratives of countries historically confronted with sociopolitical dilemmas framed in racial terms (Myrdal 1944; Rose and Deakin 1969). Along with the question of rights of and discrimination against minority groups in the United States and Britain, these dilemmas also raised issues of the underrepresentation of these groups within the institutions of the dominant society or, vice versa, of their overrepresentation, as it was the case in the U.S. military (on the "American Dilemma" in the military, see Moskos 1973; on the U.S. military as a model of racial integration, see Moskos 1966; Moskos and Butler 1996).

French military officials, however, did not understand social representation as a culturally and historically embedded principle. Instead, they saw it as a general rule of the modern all-volunteer armed forces ("the argument prevails everywhere") and a valuable and timely substitute for sociocultural military integration, in the way Eugen Weber described it (1976). This led to a striking paradox. While these French military officials were looking for a way to reframe the republican program of military integration after the end of conscription (Thiéblemont 1997), they started to value an institutional model (U.S. and British military) that was closer to programs implemented in multicultural sociohistorical contexts – the very "Anglo-Saxon communalism" ("*communautarisme*") that had long been viewed in France as the normative anti-model of French integration (Jennings 2000) and used as a frame for the denunciation of the so-called communalistic tendencies among the *population à problèmes d'intégration*.

Of course, this new program of social representation has been addressed in various ways by different actors of the military establishment, sometimes

[13] This is an excerpt of the call for proposals published by the Center for Defense Social Studies (C2SD), which commissioned the first research in 2003. My translation.

[14] "Social representation is the degree to which an armed force represents the population from which it has been drawn" (Armor 2000: 1878).

in an attempt to overcome or euphemize this paradox. The same DICOD senior official defined what he saw as a way forward to a third model, in-between the sociocultural integration through conscription model and the British "multicultural" one:

> Is it possible, he asked, to imagine that France creates a new model of professional military institutions, which is different from the British model? What the French military does is not affirmative action ["*discrimination positive*"]. There are two ways. On the one hand, you ask yourself: don't we need young people with a North African origin? On the other, you say: they [these young people] will automatically enter [the military] if integration works properly. The second way is ours.

Others expressed their opposition to the "social representation" reasoning. The chief of staff of the army, for example, emphasized issues of social mobility and socioeconomic integration over social representation – and went on to challenge the very research the defense ministry had commissioned to us, on the claim that questions about "ethnicity" should not be asked in France. (His successor did not share exactly the same view on the matter). An army marshall in charge of recruitment issues showed a totally different understanding of the "ethnic" question, and mentioned nonofficial figures of the number of French soldiers originating from the Maghreb in the Army (between 10 percent and 20 percent, depending on the type of units and specialization). In the navy, high-ranking officers in charge of the manpower policy clearly emphasized their awareness of the "underrepresentation of Blacks, Jews, and Arabs," using explicit ethnic or racial categories. In contrast to the army and the navy, and because of a structure far less dependent on extensive low-skilled manpower, the air force did not show similar concerns, but the chief of staff of the air forces still declared that ethnicity should not be a question in republican France, because nothing but "the principles of integration govern us."[15]

A distinct mention must be made of the gendarmerie. By contrast to the other French armed forces, the gendarmerie is also a domestic law enforcement force, which operates in rural and semirural areas of metropolitan France and in the French oversea regions. Therefore, social representation is not only an issue of the institution's abstract social legitimacy ("what institution of the nation?") or of manpower pools. It is directly a law enforcement issue. How can one perform law enforcement if the institution does not represent the population it polices? Such a social and racial gap has long been particularly critical in French Guadeloupe,

[15] Interview with the author, 2 March 2004.

Martinique, and Réunion (i.e., a "white institution" policing "black populations"),[16] but gendarmerie officials eventually started to think also about the children of immigrés in the *banlieues* of metropolitan France as well. "Our mission leads us to the use of diversity," the gendarmerie chief of staff told me.[17] Partial evidence shows that, in order to address this question, the gendarmerie tried to implement measures of ethnic and racial monitoring in its recruitment and personnel policy, albeit in very informal ways (mainly on the basis of how foreign the applicants' names sound).

This also seems to be the case in the army and the navy. However, the gendarmerie has probably gone farther than any other French military institution in its attempts to overcome the constraints of the ethnic categories' prohibition. It commissioned a research in 2007 explicitly asking whether or not the notion of "visible minority" could be used as a formal category in its manpower policy (Bertossi and Prud'homme 2009: 11). This questioning was inspired by what officials knew of the British situation, notably through the reading of reports by the Home Office (among the documentation we received from our contact in the gendarmerie were Stone and Tuffin 2000; Miller 2000; Bland et al. 2000). Other institutional reappraisals of this issue included the project of a communication campaign in the oversea departments, based on a poster showing black male and female gendarmes, and aimed at increasing the number of enlisted black French citizens in the force. Another project included a poster showing four young gendarmes, who were clearly intended to be seen as representing four racial phenotypes: a black man, a white woman, an Arab man, and an Asian woman, all young and smiling in their uniforms. The slogan read: "Officer: why not you? A different social trajectory, a common professional future." This project was ultimately abandoned. Eventually, gendarmerie psychologists started to reevaluate the admission tests used in the oversea French regions, under the suspicion these tests were culturally biased and prevented the "black population" from being successful at the entry examination.

All in all, a furtive shift can be seen in the discussion of this section. Our discussion started with a first aspect of the institutional reasoning of French military officials, who found in the notion of social representation a viable replacement to the traditional conception of the military as an agent of sociocultural integration of the nation, after the end of conscription. This concerned primarily what was "not military" in the institution – that is, its social

[16] This racial and ethnic gap was particularly salient in Spring 2009, when the gendarmerie had to do law enforcement during a one-month-and-a-half severe social conflict in Guadeloupe and Martinique, which extended to the Réunion (general strike, street demonstrations gathering tens of thousands of Oversea French citizens, occasional riots).

[17] Interview with the author, 9 November 2007.

function. Covertly, however, a second aspect has shown through this institutional reasoning, which more directly concerns a strict "military" dimension this time. This second aspect repositions ethnic and racial differences far beyond the social program the French military establishment was seeking to reinvent. It frames ethnic and racial difference as an asset for the operational effectiveness of the armed forces.

This leads us back to the specific logic that drove the shift from a universal compulsory military service to all-volunteer armed forces, namely the appreciation that a professional body was more adapted to the new military missions at the end of the twentieth and in the early twenty-first century. These missions include multilateral peacekeeping operations (e.g., Lebanon, Ivory Coast) and engagement in long-distance armed conflicts (e.g., former Yugoslavia, Iraq, Afghanistan). Not only were military professionals (rather than conscripts) perceived to be better adapted to these contexts, but soldiers who could add linguistic or cultural skills to the professional prototyped military were also viewed as a strong asset. The French military was most desirous to find these sociocultural and linguistic skills in the *banlieues*. And so it tried to do. The army opened one additional recruitment center in Seine-Saint-Denis (the region, north of Paris, with the largest concentration of Muslim population in France). The gendarmerie gave priority to Arabic-speaking applicants – or at least, to applicants with a Northern African name, assuming these recruits would speak Arabic. This, however, was hardly the case, and in the end, the gendarmerie had to teach these new recruits Arabic at the Military School of Intelligence and Linguistic Studies in Strasbourg.

MUSLIM SOLDIERS SEEKING MILITARY UNIVERSALISM

Let us turn to the population that is the object of this institutional reframing: the French recruits from postcolonial immigrant origins, the "Muslims." As mentioned earlier, they can be viewed neither as "Muslim normative innovators" nor as a "Muslim collective actor." However, following what was discussed in the last section, a relevant question could certainly be whether or not they actually find in this new institutional reasoning a favorable opportunity structure, offering them a public recognition as Muslims they cannot find in the other French color-blind social institutions. Within this perspective, the military is conceived of as an institutional "model of racial integration," which would emulate other social institutions in societies that have not yet achieved racial equality (on the U.S. context, see Moskos and Butler 1996; Moskos 2007).

As we shall see in this section, however, this question is indisputably at odds with the types of schemas Muslims use for defining their position as members of the French armed forces and, incidentally, with their definition of the military as a specific normative and cultural system. This suggests a discrepancy between the program of minority group incorporation defined by the military establishment and the new recruits' expectations vis-à-vis their enlistment into the armed forces. As we have discussed it so far, the establishment's view superimposes a description of Muslims in terms of *populations à problèmes d'intégration*, a description of the role of the new professional military in terms of social representation, and a description of ethnic and racial differences as a functional asset of organizational effectiveness. I propose we now focus on how Muslim military personnel see these practical schemas.

"Integration is a word that always made me laugh," as a leading seaman put it. "Integration! Just as if we woke up one morning and were told: 'today, you must integrate!' Look. I'm French by birth and I've always considered myself as French." This is probably one of the most shared perceptions among the interviewees, at once in the navy, the army, the air force, and the gendarmerie, and at all ranks, from troopers to noncommissioned officers (NCO) and the few Muslim who became officers, some of whom I met. A female navy ensign expressed the same view:

> People, they talk about integration. First of all, I don't like that people talk to me about integration. ... And they talk to me a lot [about that]: "So, they ask me, what do you think about this and that? And this war in that region? And here [in France], the Islamic veil? ... But, you, they say, you're well integrated." I answer to them: "But, I'm no more integrated than you are! I was born here. I went to school here. We had the same teachers and followed the same curricula. The difference [between you and me] is that I was taught things you don't know." I don't need to be integrated! My parents, maybe, they had to be. But I don't feel I'm more integrated than anyone else!

The complete convergence among the interviewees' perceptions about integration parallels their feelings of alienation because they are constantly questioned by the institution in terms of *populations à problèmes d'intégration*. When I went to an army mountain regiment in March 2004 in the French Alps, I met with an executive officer, a colonel in his fifties, in his office at 7:50 in the morning. He offered me a mug of black filter coffee and asked one of his subordinates to bring the young soldier I planned to interview. When the interviewee finally arrived in the office, the colonel told him: "Now, you! You are integrated, aren't you? This is not a question to be asked in the Army, right? You're a soldier above all, aren't you?" When we walked out the office, the soldier told me: "This is crazy. He obliged me to answer this question about integration, to go along with his line."

Another way to address this issue is to look at the significance the interviewees place on their volunteering into the French military. Regardless whether soldiers are socialized by the institution or whether they volunteered because they already shared military values before enlisting (Cokerham 2003: 502),[18] all interviewees emphasize that their being French soldiers should be taken as a proof of their sociocultural integration. They do not understand why their position in the military would be questioned in sociocultural terms. What is more, they expect that the usual ethnic or racial stigmas they face as Muslims in civilian social interactions will disappear behind the walls of a garrison and the color of the uniform. This is an important line along which interviewees frame their conceptions of the military as a unique institution of the state. While the military establishment reframes this uniqueness through the notion of social representation, Muslims in the military still frame it as what they consider a military cultural and normative exception, and agree on a set of values and norms that are specific to the institution.

Among these values, patriotism, self-sacrifice, commitment, honor, respect, and cohesion are the most often cited. On the one hand, interviewees connect these values to how they see themselves as French nationals, and outline the extent to which their second citizenship is merely a family heritage and not an expression of allegiance to their country of origin. A Franco-Moroccan NCO in the navy, a practicing Muslim, summarizes this view: "I volunteered in the armed forces because I felt I belonged to the [French] state. I considered I formed a part of the French state, that I wasn't Moroccan. I was not brought up in Morocco. I don't have a Moroccan culture. I only have a small part of it, which is a source of personal wealth."

In turn, a Franco-Moroccan female sergeant in the air force remembers:

> When I told [my parents] I successfully passed the [Air Force] exam, my father cried for joy. My parents were born in Morocco. One week later, the entire Marrakesh region knew I had entered the military. A year later, I marched for the 14th of July [on the Champs Elysées Avenue in Paris, before the President of the Republic]. The videotape of the march went on a tour of

[18] Both researches show that most French Muslim soldiers who expressed the strongest military social identity were also those who already had a member of their family or someone they knew in the military. An extensive literature in the US addressed this question of socialization vs. pre-socialization was the object of, right after the 1973 professionalization of the US armed forces, notably through the study of Cadets in military academies: Garnier 1973; Cockerham 1973 and 1978; Bachman et al. 1977. For a review: Cockerham 2003.

Marrakesh. When I go there, everyone knows I'm a Sergeant of the Air Force in Paris. They're hugely proud.

On the other hand, these values and norms are also used to emphasize the moral and cultural dimensions they attach to the military. The institution is framed as a place of "total" socialization. Individuals are transformed into a new role. They are not "individuals anymore, but numbers," as a navy chief petty officer put it. An army trooper originating from a Sub-Saharan country saw the military as "the place for a new birth. We are babies when we arrive here, and the Army is the mother." The uniform concretizes these values. A first sergeant in the army told me: "When we arrived, they gave us the uniform, and all social differences [among us] disappeared at once." Or, as one of his fellows said, "When you take off the uniform, you are nothing anymore." A gendarme is more explicit: "When I take off my military clothes, I pass as a *Maghrébin* like any other." These views held sway over their desire to become soldiers. "You can be a Jew, you can be a Catholic, you can be a Muslim, this is over [here]," an army lieutenant of Algerian origin told me. "From now on, you are nothing anymore. You're just an airborne soldier in the making, and everything must converge towards this ideal. I committed myself totally to this belief."

As already mentioned, this idealization of the military as a unique institution of the state is closely linked to how they imagined and expected the military would enfranchise them from racial and ethnic stigmas. What most of the interviewees had not anticipated, however, is that this strongly idealized military (an institution "legitimated in terms of values and norms, i.e. a purpose transcending individual self-interest" [Moskos 1977: 42]) would, most of the time, be merely an occupation, a "simple job" – "legitimated in terms of the marketplace" (Moskos 1977: 43) and not delineated by clear-cut normative boundaries between the organization they belong to and the rest of society.

Interviewees explain this gap by the move to an all-volunteer force in the 1990s. Of course, they address this evolution in various ways. Some find it a convenient evolution that smoothens the distance between a family and a soldier's life. Most of them, however, fear that professionalization completely dilutes values they placed very high among their reasons for volunteering. As a proof of such a dilution, Muslim military personnel explain at length the problems they find with the newly recruited population in the ranks – that is, very young volunteers who are offered four- or five-year precarious contracts in low-ranking positions. As some put it, "the only objective of these youngsters is money," or "they do not volunteer because they love their country," but for other self-interested (and subsequently irrelevant and illegitimate) reasons. These views eventually draw an additional moral boundary within the institution. However, if Muslims in the military seem here to use the establishment's very own framing of *populations à problèmes d'intégration* – that infuriated them when they were themselves framed this way – their discourse is not aimed at stigmatizing the new generations of troopers.

What they actually talk about here is the institution, how they feel it has transformed in recent years, and how they consider "things went wrong." The emphasis they put on these young "military misfits" is in fact a challenge they address to the recent manpower policy, and a sharp criticism of the notion of social representation and its consequences for the institution. "The Navy had to meet quantitative recruitment objectives," a navy NCO of Maghreb origin told me. "In these populations, there were mainly people from the Maghreb who enlisted massively. They had no military mind at all."

An army officer, in his early thirties and with a Muslim background, added:

> These people, they saw 'the light in the house' [*ils ont vu la lumière*], that's how I call it. They saw a gate outside, and they just came in. They didn't really want to become soldiers. And they bring their [ethnic, racial, or national] origins to the fore. That's a rotten tomato that'll rot all the others. So, a guy who's from the Maghreb and who fucks up, well, here you go: people make generalizations, that's a bit how it happens in the [civilian] society.

We can now come back to the question with which this section began: Do enlisted Muslim men and women find a favorable niche of opportunity in the institutional reasoning that repositions ethnic and racial diversity as an organizational asset? It is not enough to show, as I did, that Muslim French military personnel challenge the *populations à problèmes d'intégration* framing and the social representation principle recently upheld by the military establishment. Of course, these repertoires show that Muslims seek in the military their public recognition as French citizens, and nothing more – that is, not as Muslims. They also view the uniqueness of military social interactions as a resource for getting rid of stigmas they faced, as Muslims, in the civilian society.

But what about the next step? What if the military distributed new forms of social dignity and public recognition to them, as Muslims and skilled professionals – or, more precisely, as skilled professionals and "good citizens" because they are Muslims? Would Muslims not take this "chance" to reframe their place as Muslims in France and its institutions – that is, a chance to reverse the stigma?

All in all, the vast majority of Muslim interviewees consider that ethnicity, race, and religion must remain a "non-issue" in an institutional setting that supposedly de-emphasizes ethnicity and race as much as other social or ideological affiliations. Of course, some of them can regard ethnicity in the armed forces as a normal aspect of a de facto multicultural society and the normal outcome of the French society's transformations in recent decades. Some of them try to fast during Ramadan, try to worship five times a day, try to respect Muslim dietary restrictions – not eating pork, mainly – even if these practices are not easily accepted among the troops. But such practices, they emphasize, do not concern their soldiers' identity, and should not. They do not want to be assimilated to "ethnic" or "Muslim soldiers" and to fall into the trap of ethnicization. An army corporal summarized this conception when he told me that "Frenchmen of foreign descent [*les Français d'origine étrangère*], they are the France of today. One must look beyond their religion or their color. We must look at what they bring to the nation, what they can do." Or, as one private said, "[P]eople don't show their [religious] convictions, because they don't want all the hassle of that." Put differently, the best way to reverse the stigma remains to avoid stigmatization and seek universalistic military roles.[19]

As mentioned earlier, the case of the French gendarmerie is slightly different, and the interviews with Muslims gendarmerie members show this difference. More than any members of the other forces, gendarmes consider that social representation is a relevant principle because of the nature of their missions (Wihtol de Wenden and Bertossi 2005: 117). Consequently, they may conceive of ethnicity and race as an organizational asset. A young gendarme told me in 2004: "As a matter of fact, we, that is, the Gendarmes with a Maghreb origin, we succeed in being really efficient vis-à-vis professional standards, including our ability to have a good relationship with the populations."

Does this mean they endorse the gendarmerie establishment's views on ethnicity and race as formal categories of the institutional manpower policy? In 2007, I directly asked Muslim and black gendarmes how they perceived the eventual use of ethnic and racial categories by the institution in its policy. Some answered they were keen on playing the card of their "origins" to get an interesting and socially relevant job in an unfavorable labor market setting. Others outlined, however, that the gendarmerie misused or even abused their sociocultural and linguistic skills. One NCO said: "I volunteered in the Gendarmerie, but not necessarily because I wanted to work in areas where there are more *Maghrébins* than elsewhere." An officer remembers: "I was

[19] This is certainly the most shared view among the Muslim interviewees, most notably in the Army, but also in the Navy and the Air Force. On the other hand, others dare to eventually confront "all the hassle." I met with a non-commissioned officer in the Navy who connected these two realms of justification (i.e. religion and his military role), showing how both were mutually reinforced by similar values (being righteous and respectful to others).

systematically called for translations [from Arabic…]. Well, after a while, I made them understand that I was fed up, so to speak, with being the Arab on duty [*l'Arabe de service*]. So, I told them: 'Look, I'm not a translator.'" When they were asked about the possible use of ethnic and racial categories in the gendarmerie recruitment policy, answers became sharper.

All the interviewees refused such an innovation. Reasons they gave included the fear of abandoning military criteria in the recruitment, the negative consequences on the composition of the force and its professionalism, the danger of institutionalizing stigmas, the reproduction of moral boundaries along ethnic and racial lines that were so alien to their conception of the military and French citizenship, and their self-identification as French and soldiers (Bertossi and Prud'homme 2009: 115–133). A young cadet at the gendarmerie officer school crystallized these different conceptions, and answered with anger: "To tell you how far I abhor, how far I … it's not even that I despise … how far I'm infuriated, how far … I … am … as a French, I suffer when I hear these terms: 'affirmative action' [discrimination positive], 'visible minorities'… How far that hurts me, how far I'm sore over that. This is exactly the term: I feel sore when I hear these words."

FRAMING MUSLIMS IN ROUTINE MILITARY INTERACTIONS

So far, we have discussed how a new institutional reasoning framed Muslims as an object of manpower and organizational military policies, and how the object of this reasoning – Muslim soldiers – reacted to these framings. The Muslim framing activity in an institutional setting, I argued, can be best understood if we look at the complex interactions among different and contradictory practical schemas used by different members of the institution. In this discussion, however, an important aspect has remained unaddressed: the routine social interactions within the everyday military work setting. Within such a setting, schemas related to Muslims can be found in what non-Muslim soldiers or superiors say about their Muslims comrades or subordinates[20] and, on the other hand, in what Muslims say about their relations with non-Muslim fellows or superiors. This section addresses both ways of this Muslims/non-Muslims

[20] As mentioned, both researches were based on interviews with French members of the armed forces who were born to foreign parents (mostly Sub-Saharan and Maghreb countries' nationals) or who were themselves born foreigners (the 2007 research also included Black Oversea French citizens). Consequently, the view non-Muslims have of Muslims was not part of the initial research questions. However, during the months of both fieldworks, I had the opportunity to engage in informal discussions with members of the institution who were not born to foreign parents but were "white" military members. In this section, I draw from this informal material I could collect in my field notebooks. I also make an extensive use of an interview

relation. It looks at how routine interactions structure a set of practical schemas regarding the three dimensions we have addressed up until now, namely the military-qua-national integration issue, the cultural and normative uniqueness of the institution, and the place of ethnicity and race in a military setting.

If Muslim soldiers react so strongly to the notion of "integration," this is obviously because they are questioned about the issue in more than abstract and general terms by invisible institutional policy makers. Instead, it constantly shows through Muslims'/non-Muslims' routine interpersonal relationships. We already glimpsed this issue in a face-to-face situation involving integration when the mountain regiment colonel enjoined his subordinate to tell me he was "well integrated." More often than not, however, the obverse of integration in these interactions is not "*problèmes d'intégration*" that the military "solves" as a social institution of the nation ("integrating well"). It rather refers to a strict moral and social boundary that goes through units, small teams of soldiers who spend their everyday professional time together. The scale of reference here is micro – that is, the concrete work setting and the "team spirit."[21] At this level, abstract notions of a military social function traditionally attached to integration disappear (Winslow 2007). The question of integration is framed in the terms of an incommensurable social and cultural distance among inmates – a distance that cannot be crossed out and over.

Interviews with Muslim soldiers abound with anecdotes accounting for this social distance they perceive between themselves and their non-Muslim fellows or superiors. Their integration is questioned in the course of discussions with non-Muslims addressing different aspects of their supposed Muslim

I conducted on July 1st, 2004 with a twenty-nine-year-old white French non-commissioned officer in the Navy (in this chapter I call him Franck – which, of course, is not his actual first name). Franck defined himself as a "native French" and "cultural catholic", and wanted to be interviewed because: "The other interviews you'll do [with the young people with a north African origin]... since I know quite well what these youngsters have in their mind... It is necessary that these youngsters do not take this opportunity [of being interviewed by you] to say they are not loved, to tell that we segregate them. [...] Maybe some of them will take the chance [of the interview] to make things change, but along their own lines, for example that, in the military, there should be only Muslims." This three-hour interview was recorded, entirely transcribed and published as the final chapter of Bertossi and Wihtol de Wenden 2005: 271–300.

21 Franck (see previous note) constantly referred to this "team spirit" (*esprit d'équipe*) as the main theme of reference for addressing the integration issue. This concerns, of course, Muslims, but also women and homosexuals in the military. Franck told me: "Because, within this team spirit... We all sleep in the same room. We take our showers together in the same room. If we know there is a queer among us, the first reflex we'll have, is... this is silly, but... if we want to shower, we won't go in the bathroom when he showers. Or, each time we meet him, we have this idea in mind: 'stop fancying me'..."

identity. It can be about religious and cultural practices. As one of the interviewees recalled:

> Sometime, that's really on the borderline. With someone that easily gets pissed off, as I know a lot of people like that who have immigrant origins, it can clash very fast, and get out of hand very fast. Whatever their grade. … Once, it was Christmas time. Someone who wanted to see us getting worked up asked us: "And Christmas, at your place [*chez vous*], how is it?" Hopefully, we were smart enough to be smarter than him. My colleague told him: "At home? In Marseille, you mean? Well, just like in Paris."

Moral judgments are also made about their social behaviors – the music and radio programs they listen to (mainly hip-hop), the drugs they use, their so-called difficulty to speak proper French, and their supposed problems of personal hygiene. These judgments are based on labels used to describe Muslims as "*jeunes des cités*" (youngsters living in the French less favored suburbs) and "*cassos*" (i.e., *cas sociaux* or welfare cases). The image of socially deviant behaviors attributed to Muslims is best shown in what Franck, a twenty-nine-year-old white French NCO in the navy, told me in his interview about what he called the "Algerians":

> Necessarily, in Toulon,[22] the *cités*, that's associated with Algerians. … Algerians are very much committed to … let's say to polygamy, to the place of women in the kitchen, to the idea that women can't command and all that stuff. Then, they're all small chiefs of their tribes, in their *cités*. That's divided up like that. … The problem, it's those [Algerians] who volunteer [in the navy] to find clients, because they find clients for [selling] everything, let's say cannabis, drugs. … And we know that [the Algerian] is inside [the navy] for that, actually. He comes. He specializes in an easy job [*une spécialité tranquille*] … say, mechanics, because he's nifty with his hands and because you don't have to be especially smart. … They come here and they're in touch with lots of youngsters [*jeunes*]. These youngsters, they convert them [sic]. Well, sure, a lot of them already smoked [cannabis]. But they [Algerians] find new clients. … They make their own clans, actually.

Finally, this framing of integration as social closure and moral boundaries comes to question the very allegiance of French Muslim soldiers. Some of Muslim interviewees I met had been sent abroad on duty, for example, on

[22] This interview was made in Toulon, one of the main French military ports, with a huge naval base in the city center.

board military ships sailing to the Middle East. A leading seaman, son of a "Harki," remembered that "when we went to the Gulf, [his colleagues] told [him]: 'hey, you're home!' But, he added, I don't give a shit about these countries." In the aftermath of 9/11 and the Madrid and London bombings, such remarks were commonly made, very often at the mess, by non-Muslims in the presence of their Muslim fellows. A female sergeant in the army recalls that, at the time of the Madrid bombings in 2004, "to me, this was a disaster, what happened [in Madrid]. But it's obvious that, to them, that was my fault."

All in all, Franck probably best crystallized these framings of Muslims' integration, when he told me:

> They were born here but they're not from here, actually. They have not been brought up here, in the French institutions. They have origins that come from there [*là-bas*, that is, the Maghreb]. They don't have the same way to speak, the same way to do things, the same way to live. That's how it is. But, as far as this doesn't make problems for the people around them, that's not a bother. Their only problem, that's this image they have, this image of Muslims, of terrorists, of people who blow everything up in the name of religion, who veil their women. For a Frenchman, it's not normal to veil someone. We're all free and equal in law. Why then would women wear a veil? All these small things make integration impossible, in fact. Because they're not like us! Now, what I say, this is not a critic. I bear no grudge against them because they're not like me! But you can't put different things together and say "that's the same." You can't. ... That's why integration, we can't do it. That's not because we don't want to. Mentalities will probably change. They'll be accepted, more and more. But this difference will always be there. That's for sure. You can't do anything against the fact they're not the same [*pareils*].

After my recording tape ran out, Franck added: "They must integrate to us and we must integrate to them, but the blending is not possible. Since they were kids, they have been told that God is Allah, and that everyone who disagrees with that must be shot in the head. As people say, it's not possible to go against nature. And that's too late [to change them] when we take them [in the navy]."

Not only does this show a striking gap with how the military establishment and Muslim interviewees addressed the question of integration, but it also suggests that the uniqueness of the institution itself is not framed along the schemas we have discussed so far – that is, the social function of representation and the conception of the soldier as member of a unique color-blind value system. When we look at the routine on-the-ground interactions among members of the institution, the military appears neither as a site of sociocultural diversity nor of universalism.

Instead of general principles, the military work setting stages thick cultural conceptions and practices. Through Muslims/non-Muslims relationships, exclusionary boundaries are constructed, notably around the consumption of alcohol at the diverse celebrations that structure military life (as a male Muslim interviewee was once told: "Ice Tea, that's for queers. You're sure you don't want to know how it feels to be drunk?") or pork meat (*saucisson* and *saucisses* at barbeque parties, certainly one of the most structuring rituals of military cohesion). Other issues contested by Muslim interviewees include the access by Muslim (and Jewish) soldiers to meals without pork at the mess,[23] or the ostensive religious practices of some Catholic groups, most peculiarly officers in the navy and the army. Thus at the micro level of ordinary interactions, the "we-feeling" among non-Muslims does not leave much room for Muslim soldiers.

Subsequently, instead of a color-blind institution where no one speaks about politics and religion, Muslims in the armed forces find a setting where everyone talks aloud about these questions, and Islam stands among the most discussed ones. There is a wide variety of situations and ways for discussing Islam, but jokes are certainly the most frequent. Probably in an attempt to reassure me, Franck insisted that "[w]hen [my secretary who is from Algerian descent] was in the office, of course none would have trashed Islam or made a big juicy joke about Muslims. We'd have not done that. That's things you do among Frenchmen."

Most of the time, however, colleagues of the Muslim interviewees showed no such consideration, and not only when it comes to jokes. Comments such as "Muslims must be killed" were heard by some of the interviewees. Some colleagues told them they were members of the Front National, the French extreme-right-wing party, notably when Jean-Marie Le Pen, its leader, reached the second round of the 2002 presidential election. Others ostentatiously left a copy of *Mein Kampf* in the dormitory so that anyone could see it.

In some cases, this construed military culture impacts the formal organization of the institution, and non-Muslim subordinates or colleagues can contest a commandment position held by a Muslim officer or NCO. This is the story I

[23] This issue seems to have lost its salience between 2004 (the time of the first fieldwork) and 2007 (time of the second research). After he was appointed in 2006, the military Muslim chaplain succeeded in organizing the distribution of *halal* meals among the troops. Whereas a circular signed in 1992 by Pierre Joxe, the by-then Minister of Defense, made it mandatory to respect soldiers' religious dietary requirements, the document was "lost" after professionalization. When the Muslim chaplain asked for a copy of the circular, military officials answered they doubted such a document ever existed (my interview with the military Muslim chaplain). Strong indications seem to confirm, however, the document did exist (according to an informal discussion we had with Pierre Joxe, and the 2001 DICOD note to C2SD I mentioned earlier). In any case, the Muslim chaplaincy was successful in resolving what had been a major cause of conflicts between Muslim soldiers and their institution.

was told by an air force sergeant who was born in Algeria and who arrived in France when he was ten after his family fled the 1990s Algerian civil war:

> My first day [on the base], the Warrant Officer with whom I was supposed to work brought me in his office. And he told me straightforward: "Don't you forget you're not at home here [*ici, t'es pas chez toi*]. So, you're going to have to integrate. And that begins with the MTA [ordinary air force soldiers].[24] They're no shit." And the MTA, they clearly told me in the presence of the Warrant Officer: "Maybe you're a Sergeant, but if you try to play your stripes [*si t'essaies de faire péter le galon*], we'll give you all the shit to do. We'll make a complete balls-up of your life.

What normative room do these schemas eventually leave to ethnicity and race in the military setting? The pervasive moral boundaries that crystallize around Islam in military routine interactions constitute a breach of both the notion of "ethnicity as an organizational asset" (as advocated by the establishment) and the "military transcending ethnic and racial cleavages" (as upheld by Muslim interviewees). To the conception of the military as an institution that de-emphasizes ethnic and racial identities, this framing of Muslims makes Islam a most visible dimension of the populations of volunteers from immigrant descent – in the form of an enduring stigma, regardless of the actual religious beliefs or practices of these "Muslims." This certainly hinders any opportunity these Muslims can find for reversing the stigma they tried to be rid of when they enlisted in the armed forces. Conflicts around Islam make the situation even more difficult for practicing Muslims who try to "tinker" with the link between their religious practices and the conception they have of their role as professional soldiers. In some instances, non-Muslims judge the consistence of the Muslims' religious practices, according to how they consider a Muslim should behave if she were a "real Muslim." An interviewee explained that, at the mess, "the cook … kept watching over me. He wanted to know if I drank alcohol, and if I drank, that's clear that he would have served me pork every time. So, in fact, they're here to judge. They wait for us to make a mistake."

On the other hand, this framing is also at odds with the schemas that frame Islam or ethnicity as organizational assets. This, however, creates a paradoxical

[24] MTA stands for "*Militaires Techniciens de l'Air*" (Military Air Technicians). The acronym is also commonly used inside the institution to refer to Muslims in the Air Force, standing for "Moroccans-Tunisians-Algerians"… This superimposition of ethnicity and a low hierarchical position in the organization seems also common in the other armed forces. Franck summarized the situation in the Navy: "Actually, this works this way: you're a guy from the *cités*, you're an ordinary Seaman. You're an average Frenchman [*un Français moyen*], you're an OM or OMS [Navy non-commissioned officers]. You're posh guy [*BCBG*], you're an officer."

situation. While most of the challenge to Islam and Muslims is justified by a homogeneous cultural conception of the armed forces ("they're not like us"), including the historical importance of Catholicism in this identity, non-Muslims sometimes concur in the need to "expurgate" from the military all religions, including Catholicism. This conclusion is supported by a peculiar and ambiguous – but mostly instrumental – definition of French secularism or *laïcité*.[25] During the lunch I had with the colonel who commanded the mountain regiment I already mentioned, he provided a radical solution. "French secularism [*laïcité*]," he told me, "is the smallest common denominator of spirituality. This is a religion of the republic, but that doesn't exist! So, instead of seeing the chapel of the garrison becoming an ecumenical place, I'd rather blow it up! That would prevent religions from entering in the battalion and becoming a problem. Today, who are the proselytists? Not the Catholics, but the Muslims."

This, of course, is far from constituting a homogeneous and dominant conception of Islam among the officers who are in command of Muslims in the field or of all the non-Muslim French soldiers. But this is part of the reality French Muslim soldiers confront. As they kept showing in their interviews, there is not a single prototyped approach to the question of Islam, racism, or diversity among their comrades or superiors, which makes stigmatization or racism "a matter of good or bad luck," depending on the personality of the officers Muslims actually find in their units. And indeed, one week after I left the French Alps for my next fieldwork site – an airborne regiment in the Pyrenees – I had lunch with the colonel who was in command of the regiment. During our discussion, he accounted for a totally different conception of both Islam and French secularism in the military context. He said:

> This question of a military Muslim chaplaincy must be asked. Among the soldiers who die during training exercises [in my regiment], still, we've had no Muslims. But that could happen now with the new populations we have in the Army. The headquarters don't answer this question. So, I had myself to get in touch with people at the city hall [of the town where the regiment is

[25] The context of the 2003–4 research was marked by two events: the vote of the 15 March 2004 Law prohibiting religious signs in public schools (the result of months of public and political debates about Islam and *laïcité*: see Bowen 2007a); the commissioning by the Defense Ministry of a report to Lieutenant-Colonel Aït-Hocine about the possible creation of a Muslim chaplaincy in the armed forces. The months during which I undertook the first research were consequently highly impacted by both distinct but de facto interrelated agendas. While the general principle of French secularism was strongly emphasized outside the military, the military was discussing the prospect of the institutionalization of Islam within the institution. If the establishment framed this reform as the need to meet *laïcité* norms (i.e. equality among all religions), members of the institution rather conceived of it as a breach of the *laïcité* norms (i.e. religious accommodation).

based], and ask them if they knew an Imam in the region who'd be respectable [*fréquentable*].

CONFLICTS AND PRAGMATISM IN AN INSTITUTIONAL SETTING

In this chapter, we did not find one single social meaning of "Muslims" that would inform military social relations, but much contrasted and complex schemas and situations. On the one hand, the French armed forces intend to prove they remain a major social institution of the French republic, able to transform *populations à problèmes d'intégration* into full-fledged French men and women, despite the end of conscription. But to do so, they adopt minority categorizations, which are not consistent with the general principles of France's republicanism. They enlist French Arabic-speaking volunteers but, in turn, these "Arab recruits" do not speak Arabic as the institution imagined they would, and the military finally ends up teaching them a foreign language. Military officials promote a new image of the institution, less focused on sociocultural assimilation and offering new opportunities for Muslims to gain social recognition. However, if these Muslim recruits make claims, it is not on the ground of their ethnic or religious practices or identities, but in the name of a color-blind and complete citizenship. Non-Muslim soldiers may challenge the place Muslims are gaining in "their" institution. But the presence of Muslim soldiers also leads non-Muslim officers to pragmatically regulate Islam among their troops – while others refuse to do so, even when they are placed in the same situation of accommodating Muslim religious needs.

It seems extremely difficult to encapsulate this complexity into binary oppositions used, more often than not, by scholars for analyzing issues of Islam and Muslims in Western European countries – that is, an exclusionary culture of dominant societies' institutions versus institutional models of racial integration, whiteness versus ethnic and racial diversity, Islamophobia versus tolerance, Muslims' normative claims versus the principles of liberal Western democracy, a republican color-blind versus a multicultural model of citizenship and immigrant integration. The French military actually falls on neither side. Quite the opposite. All sides coexist at once in the interactions among French soldiers. Consequently, neither the French citizenship model nor the military institutional model – both understood as coherent and globally distributed sets of values, norms, attitudes, and roles – can account for the variety of schemas that actually shows in the French military setting. None of them answer the question of this chapter: Why would Muslims be framed as such in a color-blind institutional setting?

To overcome this difficulty, I proposed we look at actual institutional, social, and discursive practices in a dynamic way. I suggested that these practices were the result of interactions among various systems of evaluation and justification, upheld by various members of the institution. Within this perspective, three main lines of discussions appear with a peculiar salience, along which a variety of practical schemas related to Muslims and Islam inside the armed forces are produced and deployed. These three main lines are: (1) the place the armed forces hold within France; (2) the uniqueness of the military by comparison to other French social institutions; and (3) the place afforded to ethnicity and race in a military setting.

These lines certainly do not lead to simple questions that could be answered "yes" or "no." They create an intense activity of collective reasoning. In this context, Muslims emerge as a disputed figure of the French military for an apparently simple reason – but this reason is of sociological paramount importance: members always "discuss" the institution they belong to. In doing so, they exchange ideas, images, and conceptions of the world, as well as normative routine theories for justifying their respective positions – what we have proposed to call schemas in this volume. These schemas deal with an infinite range of issues. But all address and reinforce what these social actors share in common: their membership in the institution.

As such a shared "good" (Walzer 1983: 6–10), membership is evaluated through different schemas that give a social meaning to their role as soldiers. These schemas crystallize different dimensions of institutional issues. The place of the military as an institution of the nation concerns its social function. How members consider their institution is unique by comparison to others concerns the normative self-definition of the organization. Issues raised about ethno-cultural and racial diversity concerns the institution's cultural structure. Hence read through these questions, the different schemas concerning one's military membership hold sway for different images of Muslims as soldiers and of the military as an institution. The result is not a continuum of attitudes (ranging from exclusion to inclusion, from conservatism to progressivism, or from homogeneity to fragmentation). But it shows a diffracted mapping of disputes on what institution the military is.

This can be summarized in the following (Table 4.1).

Sometimes these schemas take the form of a coherent set of narratives. For instance, the definition of the institution in terms of a "strict military value system" is consistent with a military cultural structure that views ethnicity and race as a "transcended non-military object." Sometimes they do not. The military social function in terms of "national integration," which is consistent with Eugen Weber's (1976) account of the place held by the military service

TABLE 4.1 *Practical schemas related to Muslims and the military institution*

Disputed Issues	*Practical Schemas about the Institution*	*Practical Schemas about Islam and Muslims*		
"The military is a major social institution of the national society"	Institutional social function	National integration	Completed citizenship	Reproduction of soc
"The military is a unique institution by comparison to the other institutions of the State"	Organizational normative self-understanding	Social representation	Strict military value-system	Cultural exclusionary we-feeling
"The military is a setting for the expression of ethnicity and race"	Institutional cultural structure	Organizational asset	Transcended nonmilitary object	Challenge to normative status quo

in the last third of the nineteenth century, can severely contradict the military cultural structure holding ethnicity and race as an "organizational asset." These sets of schemas are sometimes mutually exclusive (e.g., among the three different ways of addressing the uniqueness of the military as an organization). Sometimes, they apparently converge toward similar conceptions, which actually hide mutual misunderstandings. For example, French secularism or *laïcité* can be formally supported at the same time by the schema of "national integration" (Muslims are transformed into properly integrated Frenchmen and women), "completed citizenship" (Muslims are recognized as full-fledged citizen-soldiers of the French state), "transcended non-military object" (Muslims disappear entirely behind their uniform), and a "challenge to normative status quo" (Muslims disrupt the normal functioning of the institution). However, in each case, the very meaning of the *laïcité* notion will vary, as will perceptions about Muslims.

All these contradictions and misunderstandings could logically result in conflicts within the institution that would make it impossible for the military to function normally. This, however, is not the case. Of course, conflicting issues arise, notably in the form of discrimination against some Muslim members. Accounts of such discriminations are frequent in the interviews, but they rarely result in the decision to leave the military. Most of the time, they are stated as a problem that must be dealt with at the level of interpersonal relations and not be brought to the fore. This does not mean Muslims accept discrimination within an institution they initially idealized as a discrimination-free setting. Nor does this mean that the experience of discrimination does not negatively impact their ideal conception of color-blind armed forces. It only means that the majority of Muslim interviewees assess that the hypothetical cost of complaining would be higher than the actual cost of being discriminated against. Only in some rare instances, interviewees decided to leave the military for this reason. One of them, an NCO in the gendarmerie, finally left the military for a job in a municipal police force. He said:

> I was ready to leave. I even passed the first round of tests for entering the security force of the RATP [the Paris subway]. … By then, I wanted so much to leave that I was ready to take anything, even the job of a prison warden. … I'm glad I was accepted in the municipal police. Well, maybe that's less prestigious than the Gendarmerie. But still, the job is slightly the same.

This gendarme shows the extent to which leaving the military has its own cost – the loss of prestige and social worth attached to the institution. It also suggests that discrimination leads to exit in only a specific situation: when it challenges the membership in the institution so wholly that it becomes impossible to participate in the discussions about the social meaning of being a soldier. In all the other cases, Muslim soldiers declared they simply "dealt with it."

Therefore, beyond the actual problem of discrimination against Muslims, beyond the non-Muslims' actual fear of Islamic proselytism or, on the contrary, the fear expressed by some members of the military establishment that the next "Dreyfus Affair" will involve a Muslim soldier, members of the French armed force deploy theories that justify their membership, but they do so in very pragmatic ways, under the constraints of social life in twenty-first-century France.

BIBLIOGRAPHY

Anderson, Benedict. 1991. *Imagined Communities. Reflections on the Origin and Spread of Nationalism*. London: Verso.

Armor, D. 2000. "Military Sociology." In *Encyclopedia of Sociology*, edited by E. Borgotta and R. Montgomery. New York: Macmillan References: 1875–1883.

Bachman, J.G., J. D. Blair, and D. R. Segal. 1977. *The All-Volunteer Forces*. Ann Arbor: University of Michigan Press.

Becker, Howard. 1963. *Outsiders. Studies in the Sociology of Deviance*. Boulder: The Free Press of Glencoe.

Beckford, James, Joly, Danièle, and Farhad Khosrokhavar. 2005. *Muslims in Prison: Change and Challenge in Britain and France*. Basingstoke: Palgrave-Macmillan.

Benoit-Guilbot, O. and J.-V. Pfirsch. 1998. *La décision d'engagement volontaire des militaires du rang: l'armée de terre*. Paris: Les documents du C2SD.

Bertossi, Christophe. 2011. National Models of Integration in Europe. A Comparative and Critical Analysis. *American Behavioral Scientist* 55 (12): 1561–1580.
Bertossi, Christophe and Catherine Wihtol de Wenden. 2007. *Les couleurs du drapeau: l'armée française face aux discriminations*. Paris: Robert Laffont.
Bertossi, Christophe and Dorothée Prud'homme. 2009. *Mobilité sociale et diversité culturelle dans la gendarmerie nationale: le jeu des identités*. Paris: CPGN.
Biville, Y. 1990. *Armée et populations à problèmes d'intégration. Le cas des jeunes Français d'origine maghrébine*. Paris: Ministère de la Défense.
Bland, Nick, Mundy, Gary, Russel, Jacqueline, and Rachel Tuffin. 1999. *Career Progression of Ethnic Minority Police Officers*. London: Home Office / Police Research Series Paper no. 107.
Boltanski, Luc and Laurent Thévenot. 1991. *De la justification. Les économies de la grandeur*. Paris: Gallimard.
Bowen, John. 2007a. *Why the French Don't Like Headscarves: Islam, the State, and Public Space*. Princeton: Princeton University Press.
——2007b. A View From France on the Internal Complexity of National Models. *Journal of Ethnic and Migration Studies* 33(6): 1003–1016.
——2009. *Can Islam Be French? Pluralism and Pragmatism in a Secularist State*. Princeton: Princeton University Press.
Brubaker, Rogers. 1992. *Citizenship and Nationhood in France and Germany*. Cambridge, MA: Harvard University Press.
Crapanzano, Vincent. 2011. *The Harkis. The Wound That Never Heals*. Chicago: Chicago University Press.
Charbit, Tom. 2006. *Les Harkis*. Paris: La découverte.
Chattou, Zoubir and Mustapha Belbah. 2002. *La double nationalité en question*. Paris: Karthala.
Cockerham, W. C. 1973. Selective Socialization: Airborne Training as a Status Passage. *Journal of Political and Military Sociology* 1: 215–229.
——1978. Self-Selection and Career Orientation among Enlisted U.S. Army Paratroopers. *Journal of Political and Military Sociology* 6: 249–259.
——2003. "The Military Institution." In *Handbook of Symbolic Interationism*, edited by L. T. Reynolds and N. J. Herman-Kinney. Lanham: Alta Mira Press: 491–510.
Crépin, Annie. 2009. *Histoire de la conscription*. Paris: Gallimard.
De Puymège, Gérard. 1997. *Le soldat Chauvin. In Les lieux de mémoire* – 2, edited by Nora, Pierre. Paris: Gallimard: 1699–1727.
Dorman, J.E. 1976. ROTC Cadet attitudes: a product of socialization or self-selection? *Journal of Political and Military Sociology* 4: 203–216.
Dubet, François. 2005. *Le déclin des institutions*. Paris: La découverte.
Favell, Adrian. 1998. *Philosophies of Integration. Immigration and the Idea of Citizenship in France and Britain*. Basingstoke: Palgrave.
Fetzer, Joel and J. C. Soper. 2005. *Muslims and the State in Britain, France and Germany*. Cambridge: Cambridge University Press.
Freidson, Eliot. 1988. *Profession of Medecine. A Study of the Sociology of Applied Knowledge*. Chicago: University of Chicago Press.
Galland, Olivier and J. V. Pfirsch. 1998. *Les jeunes, l'armée et la nation*. Paris: Les documents du C2SD.
Garnier, M. A. 1973. Power and Ideological Conformity: A Case Study. *American Journal of Sociology* 79: 343–363.

Goffman, Erving. 1961. *Asylums*. New York: Doubleday.

Janowitz, Morris. 1991. *On Social Organization and Social Control*. Edited and with an Introduction by Lewis A. Coser. Chicago: Chicago University Press.

Jennings, Jeremy. 2000. Citizenship, Republicanism and Multiculturalism in Contemporary France. *British Journal of Political Science* **30** (4): 575–587.

Joana, Jean. 2004. Les politiques de la ressource humaine des armées en France et en Grande-Bretagne : le sens des réformes. *Revue Française de Science Politique* **54**(5): 811–827.

Joppke, Christian. 2009. Limits of Integration Policy: Britain and her Muslims. *Journal of Ethnic and Migration Studies* **25**(3): 453–472.

Kinnard, D. 1977. *The War Managers*. Hanover: University Press of New England.

Koopmans, Ruud and Paul Statham. 2005. *Multiculturalisme, citoyenneté et conflits culturels: le défi posé par les revendications des groupes musulmans en Grande-Bretagne et aux Pays-Bas. In Les minorités ethniques dans l'Union européenne, edited by Lionel Arnaud*. Paris: La découverte.

Koopmans, Ruud, Paul Statham, Marco Guigni, and Passy Florence. 2005. *Contested Citizenship: Immigration and Cultural Diversity in Europe*. Minneapolis: University of Minnesota Press.

Lamont, Michèle. 2002. *The Dignity of Men. Morality and Boundaries of Race, and Immigration*. Cambridge, MA: Harvard University Press, and New York: Russell Sage Foundation Books.

Lamont, Michèle and Laurent Thévenot (eds.). 2000. *Rethinking Comparative Cultural Sociology. Repertoires of Evaluation in France and the United States*. Cambridge: Cambridge University Press.

Long, Marceau. 1988. *Etre français aujourd'hui et demain. Rapport remis au Premier ministre par Marceau Long, président de la commission de la nationalité*. Paris: La documentation française.

Lundquist, Jennifer. 2004. When Race Makes No Difference: Marriage and the Military. *Social Forces* **83** (2): 1–28.

Miller, Joel. 2000. *Profiling Populations Available for Stops and Searches*. London: Home Office, Police Research Series Paper no. 131.

Moskos, Charles. 1966. Racial Integration in the Armed Forces. *American Journal of Sociology* **72**(2): 132–148.

——1973. The Emergent Military. *Pacific Sociological Review* **16**: 255–279.

——1977. From Institutions to Occupation: Trends in Military Organization. *Armed Forces and Society* **4**: 41–50.

——2007. "Diversity in the Armed forces of the United States." In *Cultural Diversity in the Armed Forces. An International Comparison*, edited by Joseph Soeters and Jan van der Meulen. London: Routledge: 15–29.

Moskos, Charles and John Butler. 1996. *All That We Can Be*. New York: Basic.

Myrdal, Gunnar. 1944. *An American Dilemma*. New York: Harper.

Pinto, Louis. 1975. L'armée, le contingent et les classes sociales. *Actes de la Recherche en Sciences Sociales* **1**(3): 18–40.

Porteret, Vincent and Emmanuelle Prévot. 2004. *Le patriotisme aujourd'hui en France*. Paris: Centre d'études en sciences sociales de la défense, Les Documents du C2SD no. 72.

Rose, E. J. B. and Nicolas Deakin. 1969. *Colour and Citizenship: A Report on British Race Relations*. London: Oxford University Press.
Schnapper, Dominique. 1998. *The Community of Citizens. On the Modern Idea of Nationality*. New Brunswick: Transaction Publishers.
Segal, David. 2007. "Current Development and Trends in Social Research on the Military." In *Social Sciences and the Military. An Interdisciplinary Overview*, edited by Guiseppe Caforio. London: Routledge: 46–66.
Soeters, Joseph and Jan van derMeulen, eds. 2007. *Cultural Diversity in the Armed Forces. An International Comparison*. London: Routledge.
Stone, Vanessa and Rachel Tuffin. 2000. *Attitudes of People from Minority Ethnic Communities Towards a Career in the Police Service*. London: Home Office, Police Research Series Paper no. 136.
Thiéblemont, André. 1997. Les enjeux sociaux et politiques de la suppression du service national. *Les champs de Mars printemps-été*: 27–49.
Tribalat, Michèle. 1995. *Faire-France. Une enquête sur les immigrés et leurs enfants*. Paris: La Découverte.
Venel, Nancy. 2004. *Musulmans et citoyens*. Paris: PUF.
Walzer, Michael. 1983. *Spheres of Justice. A Defense of Pluralism and Equality*. New York: Basic Books.
Weber, Eugen. 1976. *Peasants into Frenchmen. The Modernization of Rural France, 1870–1914*. Stanford: Stanford University Press.
Wihtol de Wenden, Catherine and Christophe Bertossi. 2005. *Les militaires français issus de l'immigration*. Paris: Les documents du C2SD.
Winslow, Donna. 2007. "Military Organization and Culture from Three Perspectives. The Case of the Army." In *Social Sciences and the Military. An Interdisciplinary Overview*, edited by Guiseppe Caforio. London: Routledge.

5 Practical Schemas, Conjunctures, and Social Locations

Laïcité in French Schools and Hospitals

Christophe Bertossi and John R. Bowen

One claim of this book is that we best understand how and why countries develop different frameworks about Islam and Muslims if we look at the practical schemas that actors develop in specific institutions. For example, the way Islam has been described as a challenge to liberal values, and how this challenge has been construed as a problem of the relationship between Muslims and France, arose in great part from debates about Muslim students wearing Islamic headscarves in schools. These debates and their outcomes cannot be understood without analyzing the school as an institution. In all the preceding chapters on institutions, practical schemas found in institutional settings are embedded in popular beliefs, professional representations, organizational issues, and institutional norms and values, and they inform national ideologies about citizenship and boundaries.

In this chapter, we focus in more detail on aspects that have been apparent in the other chapters of the book, but from a different and complementary perspective. If, as we argue in Chapter 1, institutions are contexts of enactment of national ideologies and a place where actors develop practical schemas about Muslims and Islam, these contexts are not homogenous settings, and practical schemas are not only a stable symbiosis between institutional and national repertoires. Moreover, events reshape, sometimes re-weight, the practical schemas these actors employ.

Here, we propose to compare two institutions in the same national context: schools and hospitals in France in the years between 2000 and 2010. During this period, the highly publicized debates on schools and then, almost as a last-minute extension in hopes of raising the level of sensationalism, on hospitals framed a set of problems in terms of how to protect and defend "*la laïcité*" in these two institutions. We propose a different approach, one that considers the ways in which key actors constructed a succession of practical schemas regarding Muslims and Islam, and the ways these processes of construction responded to other national or international events.

We do so to emphasize that as the problems change, so do the way that institutional actors conceive of and respond to people they label as "other," and the way they frame the issues to be addressed. We examine two institutions that have been at the heart of these debates, and so we often come upon these actors as they respond to highly mediatized moments, or, at the very least, as they become aware of the debates around them. We are then interested in how they formulate these same ideological concepts, and in particular those of *laïcité* and such associated notions as *mixité* and *égalité*. We underscore the similarities in how conjuncture and social location shape schemas in schools and hospitals. In Chapter 11, which concludes this volume, we make use of contrasts across institutions to analyze broader institutional processes and mechanisms.

Comparing two different institutions in the same national context allows us to clarify the two hypotheses we presented in Chapter 1. We argued that national ideologies do have a framing power, but this power has to be proven and not assumed ex ante. We also claimed that the social life of institutions enjoys a relative autonomy in the broader political context. The similarities between French schools and French hospitals are not used here to argue that an overarching French national ideology directly imposes ways of thinking and acting on workers and clients. Rather, we propose to see the extent to which what happens on institutional grounds can result in the public reformulation of a key political concept; the example of debates about schools and *laïcité* is particularly revealing. We also look to see how members of institutions produce schemas about Islam and Muslims through their day-to-day routine practices, drawing on prior schemas about what is right and proper for teaching, delivering care, and so forth. The example of hospitals shows most specifically this latter point.

A SUCCESSION OF SCHEMAS ABOUT SCARVES IN SCHOOLS

From the late 1980s, much of France was gripped by a "moral panic" regarding the presence of Islam in public schools, rendered concrete by the presence of a small number of girls wearing Islamic headscarves. We use this case here to show how certain public officials and teachers strategically introduced and deployed a series of distinct practical schemas concerning scarves in schools and the dangers they posed for France. These actors responded to shifting features of international political Islam, domestic politics, and school success.

As we argued in an earlier book (Bowen 2007), political denunciations of girls wearing scarves in schools began in the fall of 1989 because of a conjuncture of several events. Some on the political Left, disillusioned with what they saw as a failure to keep faith with the Republic, and in particular after what some saw as a weak celebration of the Revolution's bicentennial, had already begun to attack multiculturalism and cultural relativism. The Ayatollah Khomeini's death threats against Salmon Rushdie neatly coincided with the formation of the Islamic Salvation Front in Algeria, and together these two events raised the specter of political Islam. The fall of the Berlin Wall left an opening for new targets of denunciation. Political Islam and laxity in Republican thinking fit the bill.

We can see how tied the emergence of this panic over scarves was to the events of the day by looking at the middle school where the 1989 furor began (the Gabriel-Havez middle school near Paris), and noting that in the previous year the class photo showed a girl wearing a head scarf, and no one paid attention. The new set of schemas, around Republican politics and anti-Islam, was necessary for a simple fact to become an "*affaire*." The subsequent ebb and flow of moral panic over scarves supports this thesis: at moments when things heated up in Algeria and about political Islam generally, renewed attention was paid to scarves in schools. Elsewhere (Bowen 2007: 87–97) we identified two such crisis periods: between 1993 and 1994, with increased violence in Algeria, and again from 2001 to 2003, characterized by post-9/11 fears of terrorism and a rising anxiety about malfunctioning public schools and the failure of integration. During 2003, intensive media attention swung public opinion behind the idea of a ban on scarves, and politicians climbed aboard the bandwagon. President Chirac appointed a commission – known as the Stasi Commission after its president, Bernard Stasi – to "reflect on *laïcité*" and, after months of hearings, the commission issued a series of recommendations that included a law banning scarves (and other obvious signs of religious affiliation, to avoid a constitutional challenge) in schools. The law was passed and signed in early 2004.

Religious Freedom versus "Communalism"

Public schools provide a "theatre of integration" for many in France. Perhaps too much is expected of them: they are supposed to create French citizens, erase social inequalities, make everyone accept the same values, and serve as "the only space allowing each individual to live in total freedom of conscience."[1] But the schemas used to think about the presence of Islamic elements (signs,

1 The statement was made by a Paris middle school principal, Louise Arvaud, before the Stasi Commission, on September 9, 2003.

practices) in the schools have been varied. At the start of the "affairs," the State Council, the highest judicial body in the matter, framed the question in terms of individual rights-bearers, whose freedoms to wear scarves were guaranteed by the constitution and by European conventions (see Bowen and Rohe, Chapter 6 in this volume). They contrasted the obligations held by representatives of the state to remain neutral with respect to religion – this was their sense of *laïcité* – with the freedom of the school's clients, private individuals. Objections to scarves in schools on grounds of *laïcité* therefore ran up against the constitutional guarantee of the girls' right to express their religious beliefs. The State Council guaranteed the right to wear Islamic headscarves as long as the wearers did not proselytize or cause disorder. In practice, school heads had to show that girls either had tried to convert classmates or had done something specific to disrupt the normal functioning of the school. It was difficult to prove either of these contentions, and girls who had been expelled and then sued the school nearly always won their cases.

But a second set of schemas then presented itself. One important instrument in raising the level of alarm by reframing the question of Islam was a small book that appeared in September 2002, titled *The Lost Territories of the Republic*, edited by a teacher named Georges Bensoussan who writes under the pseudonym Emmanuel Brenner.[2] The book featured testimonies by middle and high school teachers about acts of "communalism" (*communautarisme*) committed by Muslim students in poor districts in and around Paris. The teachers combined accounts of clearly offensive acts (such as insulting Jewish students), acts that might attest to sheer ignorance (such as contesting a teacher's version of the Shoah), and acts that offend only within a specific logic of *laïcité* in the French school (such as breaking the Ramadan fast on school grounds). The offenders were identified as Muslims, and the authors blamed "Arab Muslim culture" for these communalist actions. This culture, they argued, refuses *mixité* (mixing, between groups and particularly between men and women) and therefore refuses integration into the Republic. *The Lost Territories* appeared just months after public attention turned to the rising number of anti-Semitic acts occurring in France, including desecrations of cemeteries and verbal assaults on Jewish children (a rise that was followed a year or so later by a rise in anti-Muslim acts). Although some of the most flagrant acts turned out to be

[2] Since the publication of *Lost Territories*, Bensoussan has criticized France for ignoring the responsibility of "young men of North African background" for most of the increasing numbers of anti-Semitic acts. Speaking at the Hebrew University of Jerusalem in November 2004 (where he was introduced as "a Polish Jew born in Central Asia"), he contended that the French people are largely silent on the issue because they cannot imagine that Arabs, victims of racism themselves, could be racists (http://www.gafni.co.il/media/sicsa/171104/).

committed by neo-Nazi groups, the initial tendency was to blame Muslims for all such crimes, and this book fed that tendency.

Brenner and his colleagues also claimed that there had been a general "communalist closing-in" (*repli communautaire*) in France. They listed various indices of this process, including the growth in the number of places for Islamic worship, the call by several key Muslim figures for Muslims not to vote for politicians who supported a ban on scarves in schools, and the sympathies of some young Muslims for radical Islamic groups elsewhere in the world. In their analysis, practicing one's religion, playing the French game of electoral politics, and supporting Islamic movements are all evidence of communalist tendencies (Brenner et al. 2002: 43–46).[3]

President Chirac read *The Lost Territories*, cited it publicly during 2003, and worked the title into at least one of his speeches. The book is said to have had a strong influence on his decision to advocate a law against scarves in schools.[4] The importance of the book lies not only in the many examples it provided of objectionable behavior by students, but also because it effectively shifted the argument against the *voile* from a matter of religious freedom to a defense of order in the schools. The authors of *Lost Territories* introduced a new way to think about the problem, via a new set of schemas. They argued that the presence on French soil of Muslim culture leads to the disintegration of order in the schools because it introduces a communalism that divides students among themselves and pits students against teachers. Regardless of what else a student does, in the very act of wearing a sign of her religion she divides and disrupts. Because (according to the State Council) the imperative of preserving order in the school could allow constraints to be placed on religious expression, the Islamic scarf could be banned generically, without having to demonstrate specific instances of disorder.

These new schemas were indispensable to the politicians and public intellectuals who, throughout 2003, regularly denounced communalism in the schools. In February, Education Minister Luc Ferry held a press conference

[3] Ironically, in charging many young Muslim students with communalism, Brenner and his colleagues make generalizations of the sort strongly criticized by many staunch Republicans, who urge France not to single people out in terms of their ethnic backgrounds. For example, they cite (Brenner et al. 2002: 40) polling data that shows the higher rates with which "youth of North African origin" say that Jews have too much influence in government or the media, compared to respondents of long-term French origin. They then infer from these data that this category of people exhibit "anti-Semitism" because of the difference in means between the two groups. They certainly would deny that statements about the undue influence of Muslims in suburbs constitute "anti-Islamic" biases, but it is difficult to see the logical difference.

[4] *Libération*, December 17, 2003.

to denounce the tendency of students to "close themselves off in pseudo-communities." In March, the weekly *L'Express* ran a cover story on teachers who feared turning their backs on their students to write on the blackboard. Prime Minister Raffarin and Interior Minister Sarkozy appeared at the opening ceremony of the French Islamic Council in May, where Raffarin linked the *voile* to communalism, and mentioned cases of students refusing to take an oral exam from someone of the opposite sex and challenging the content of the curriculum.[5] The educators who testified before the Stasi Commission agreed that the visible Muslim presence in public schools posed a communalist danger, even if some opposed the passage of a new law.

Laïcité Brought into Play

By 2003, several distinct schemas about scarves were in play, each resonating with broader fears and philosophies. We have seen two of them. The State Council's position, solidly maintained throughout the furor until the passage of the law in 2004, framed the question in terms of individual rights. The authors of the *Lost Territories* brilliantly countered this "rights" framing by introducing a second set of schemas linking Islamic elements to communalism and disorder. This move reduced the weight of religion and the individual rights-bearing agent in favor of shielding young girls from Islamist threats and thereby shielding France from Islamism.

This "communalism" set of schemas made alliance with a third set, one anchored in the history of struggle between Republican and Catholic schools. Many teachers and not a few politicians emphasized the importance to *laïcité* of maintaining strict boundaries between the school and the world – the sacred temple of the Republic and the profane external world of warring convictions (see Sunier, Chapter 3 in this volume). For many teachers, schooled in the history of combat between secularism and the Church, this distinction was so self-evident that the mere presence of religious elements inside the school building was taken as a transgression. This "secularist" framing represented the prolongation of long-standing ways of viewing the world, with Catholicism as the enemy and the village school as the battleground. Alliance was made with the proponents of the "communalism" framework by arguing that the mere presence of an Islamic element on school grounds – a boy praying, or a girl in a scarf – was a breach in the walls of *laïcité* and also a point of entry for a socially disruptive force. Constitutional objections to

[5] *Le Parisien*, May 4, 2003: 4.

banning the scarves could be downplayed once you saw the problem in this new light.

This secularist framing was well illustrated by one of the more effective school officials in denouncing violations of *laïcité*, the school inspector Alan Seksig. In his testimony to the Stasi Commission he began with a series of "facts" from the world of public school teaching. Seksig considered these stories to be so self-evidently shocking that he did not feel the need to provide commentary or argument. He mentioned a colleague who was asked by a teacher to point out the direction of Mecca. It turned out that a female student was standing in the hall wearing a head scarf. She had been expelled elsewhere but accepted there. She wished to pray and needed to know the right direction. Seksig's colleague gave the teacher a little lesson in *laïcité* then and there. He then told of a primary school principal, herself Jewish, who had wished her Jewish students a good Jewish new year at an assembly. "You can be assured that these are not isolated events," he told the commissioners.

Seksig's testimony also provided the opening clips on a television program that aired on one of France's television channels (France 5) on December 7, 2003, just at the end of the Stasi Commission hearings. Titled *Egalité, Laïcité, Anxiété* (Equality, Secularity, Anxiety), it was structured as a commentary on the hearings. The producers selected several key witnesses, showed a few seconds of each witness's testimony before the commission, and then followed the witness into his or her daily life, deepening the specific argument for a law against the *voile*. In the case of Seksig, we see his first two stories that he told to the commission, and then we see him at work, presiding over a meeting of kindergarten schoolteachers in Pantin, a northeastern suburb of Paris. He speaks about the practice of drawing up lists of the students who do and do not eat pork. He reminds the assembled teachers how such lists have been used "in history" – a reference to the practice under Vichy and the Nazi occupation of posting lists of Jews. This framing of the problem made it clear that Muslims had created the problems, but that a broad statement was important because Jews, too, forget their obligations under *laïcité*.[6]

After the passage of the 2004 law banning "ostentatious" religious signs, some teachers and school principals interpreted particular items of dress through the lens provided by the "secularist" schema. They inspected girls' clothing-related behavior to see whether or not it indicated that they attached

[6] The remaining segments of the program focused on communalist influences coming the Muslim-majority world, the efforts of some secular Muslims to criticize these tendencies, and the hospital segment described later in the chapter.

religious meaning to a scarf, which would make it an infringement on *laïcité*. In the latter case, some allowed scarf-wearing to continue.

Some showed a nuanced sense of how context shapes meaning. As the principal of a *lycée* (high school) in the town of Trappes, south of Paris (which has a large Muslim population), testified before the commission: "What precisely is an ostentatious religious sign? A short beard? A scarf tied behind the head?" She continued with her own interpretation of the word "ostentatious" as having "the notion of something that is perhaps a bit aggressive." But "everything depends on the context. At Trappes we agreed to allow the 'little scarf,' a discrete chignon tied behind the head. In another context than ours this could be judged ostentatious, but here it is not because other young women dress similarly but not with the same meaning, not for religious reasons. So it blends into the background and is no longer ostentatious." But, she added, the situation is different for the keffieh, the red-and-white checked shawl that has become a part of Palestinian male dress and by extension a sign of allegiance to the Palestinian cause. "That strikes me as ostentatious."[7]

This principal's subtle distinctions were based on her sense of whether the overall effect of someone wearing something is to be a bit aggressive or pushy (the French verb *agresser* locates the offense in the act rather than in a character trait). She took careful note of context, of the styles of clothing to which people are accustomed, and the fact that people may or may not make close associations between specific items of clothing and specific meanings. She focused on the effect of wearing clothing in a particular way rather than on the object itself.

In Melun, also south of Paris, principal Ghislaine Hudson (a member of the Stasi Commission) relied on a subjective test when enforcing the law at her *lycée*. She allowed students to wear head coverings, and some girls did wear bandanas in the fall of 2004.

> We have to decide whether or not a scarf has religious meaning. First we see if the girl wears it every day or just sometimes. If she always wears it and it might be religious, then I might talk with her; teachers are instructed not do so lest they differ in what they say. I ask the student whether the scarf is a religious sign or not. Some say it does have religious meaning and then they have to remove it, but we allow her to substitute a bandana.[8]

The Education Ministry took a position on bandanas, saying that they could be accepted if (1) they were worn sporadically, thus not for religious reasons

7 *Libération*, November 29, 2003.
8 Interview, Melun, October 2, 2004.

(in the latter case they would presumably be worn all the time), and (2) they were not unrolled to cover more and more of the hair during the school day.[9]

Here is the analytical importance of schemas: it is not that persons advocating each of these three frameworks (religious freedom, communalism, or secularism) lived on different planets, or refused to recognize the legitimacy of the other two starting positions. The differences lay in the weight given to different schemas. Everyone agreed that French citizens had rights to religious freedom, that the public school was historically defined over and against the religious one, and that schools should protect students from too much family and community influence in the interest of creating like-minded French men and women. Differences lay in how much weight to give each of these precepts, and in whether other schemas were brought into play.

Schemas in Conflict

The multiple schemas came into conflict around specific cases. Late in 2002, a series of new scarf affairs began to appear in the national media, and they illustrate the new combinations of secularist and communalist schemas. They began in Lyon. Lyon has been an important center for new Islamic movements but also for radical activists. The bombs that exploded in the summer of 1995 were set off in Paris and Lyon. The most notorious figure to emerge from the 1990s was Khaled Kelkal, born in France of Algerian origin and living in the Lyon suburb of Vaulx-en-Velin.[10]

In December 2002, a teacher at the La Martinière high school in Lyon, Jean-Claude Santana, complained to the school administration that a sixteen-year-old student named Fatiha was wearing an Islamic head scarf in violation of school policy. The girl had begun to wear a scarf in early December after Ramadan, starting with it rolled up as a "bandana," a dress style that had been allowed, and then gradually unrolling it so that it covered her hair. On December 12, a teacher asked her to remove it. She refused and found herself in the principal's office, where she still refused to remove the scarf and was suspended. She was readmitted when the district superintendent made a phone call to the principal. Later that month one of her cousins joined her in wearing a foulard, leading the teachers at the school to hold a meeting: "they feared a contagion" and a wave of new foulard-wearing students.[11]

9 *Le Figaro*, September 20, 2004. This position was approximately that adopted by the principal Ghislaine Hudson mentioned earlier.

10 Intriguingly, Marseille and the south have contributed relatively little to national fears of Islam, except through the southern strength of the National Front.

11 *Libération*, March 13, 2003.

The teachers asked for the school's disciplinary council to meet (necessary for definitive expulsion), but the superintendent refused, saying that he feared that if they expelled her and were overruled by the State Council (which was likely, given that wearing the scarf was the only accusation made against her) she would be hailed as a victim. And, he continued, her scarves, which were colored and often in floral prints, "are more discrete than the scarves worn by Islamists." The teachers met and issued a statement that "the student considers her scarf to be a sign of her belonging to her community and her religion, thus it is meant to attract attention (it is *ostentatoire*), and our internal rules forbid that." Before the early (February) spring break, they voted to go on strike as soon as they returned from vacation. Upon their return, however, the superintendent urged them to meet with him and with the rector of the Lyon mosque, Kamel Kabtane. They refused, saying that the involvement of the mosque leader was inappropriate. They asked for the disciplinary council hearing and for a clear rule on school dress. Then, on March 13, 80 percent of the teachers went on strike.[12]

Note the different weightings of schemas by different actors. The superintendent drew on the State Council's reasoning and deployed his own fashion sense of what would be a more or less "Islamist" scarf: flowers means less so; black, more so. Teachers drew on personal experiences with Islam to frame the matter as a struggle with a backward religion, but in their official statement highlighted a different set of schemas, concerning the student's inferred intention to attract attention to her particular identities, of community and religion. They highlighted the "communalist" schema to justify their actions, perhaps mindful of the weakness, at that stage, of the "secularist" schema, given the State Council's rulings.

In past cases, including many in Lyon, the education ministry's mediator in these matters, Hanifa Chérifi, had made good use of the "fashion" schemas, observing that flower patterns, practicing a less severe manner of wearing the scarf, and letting some hair show, were taken by some teachers as signaling a more compromising attitude toward religion and the Republic. "The professors all hate the voile," she explained,

[12] *Libération*, March 13, 2003; *Le Monde*, February 24, 2003, March 15, 2003. Chérifi's efforts to calm things down were met with disapproval by many opponents of the law with whom Bowen spoke. Given that her advice to the girls was also that given by many respected Muslim teachers – put your education first, look for compromises – we suspect that reactions by Arabic-speakers were influenced by her own Kabyle-region origins and the notion that some from Kabylia, oppressed culturally and linguistically by the Algerian government, "settle scores" with Arabs in France.

> but less so if the ears and the neck show, so when I talk to girls, first I explain that things will go easier if they do not wear the voile. "Do you really want to continue fighting all the time, through your exams, so that you can be more Muslim than the others?" They may go into public service, which here in France includes everything from a postal carrier to the head of an office, and in all those jobs it is forbidden to wear the *voile*. If they decide to take it off it is better, because then that will take them out of that fundamentalism. But if they cannot do that, then pushing it back to make it smaller will help, and it does.

The difficulty posed in the Lyon case came when the bandana-wearing student told the principal that she would not remove her bandana because she wore it for religious reasons. Once she said that, then the three professors were able to draw on the subjective version of the secularism schema, based on the girl's professed intentions, to agitate for her suspension. Santana also introduced a new schema, one that focused on protecting the girls. In an interview he said: "The school's mission has a liberating ambition: to give citizens-in-becoming the means to free themselves from social, cultural, ethnic, or gendered determinism. You do not attend school as you go to the post office or to another public service."[13]

Here was the basic challenge to the State Council: *laïcité*, claimed Santana, is about protecting students from pressures, and thus requires active intervention by the state against students and families who try to exert such pressure. We are now far beyond the idea of the state's neutrality, far beyond the requirements of the law of 1905 on separating churches and state, and presented with an argument about the freedom of the student to choose: should she be free to dress according to her religion, or should she be set free to explore her convictions without undue family pressure? The grounds had shifted even within the "communalism" framing, with much greater salience given to one particular schema, that of protecting girls who chose not to wear scarves from other young Muslim boys and girls who exerted pressure on them to do so.

This argument was strengthened by an intensive media effort to link violence against women to the character of Muslim boys.[14] The most shocking incidents of this violence are collective rapes, which in the 2000s came to be

[13] Interview with Jean-Claude Santana, September 18, 2003, available at http://www.communautarisme.net.

[14] The specific claim that students, by wearing the scarf, incited young men to put pressure on other girls to wear them, and somehow also provoked aggression against women, will remind U.S. readers of attempts to blame rape victims for their choice of clothing. The broader French claims took a different direction, however, in condemning female modesty, including demands for separate washrooms and exemptions from attending swimming classes.

known as *tournantes*. The public became aware of the *tournantes* through a 2000 film, *La Squale* (*The Shark*), and the 2002 best-selling account by Samira Bellil of her own rape in *Dans l'Enfer des tournantes* (In Gang-rape Hell). The same year, Bellil became the "godmother" of a new movement aimed at attacking this violence, called *Ni Putes ni Soumises* (Neither Whores nor Doormats, NPNS). In October 2002, a man burned to death a young woman named Sohane in a poor housing project. The first anniversary of this event was heavily covered by the national news media, and NPNS made it central to its campaigns. It also coincided with the Stasi Commission's hearings and entered into the debates concerning the law on scarves.

The film, the book, and the activist movement served to keep *tournantes* in the news between 2001 and 2003 (and much less so before or after). Judging from media accounts, the rapes were invented by young men of North African background at the end of the 1990s. But in fact, collective rape dates back at least to activities by nonimmigrant gangs in the 1960s, and the incidence of these rapes has not increased over the past twenty years. According to the sociologist Laurent Mucchielli, what changed recently were not the practices but the claims made about them, specifically attributing them to Arab-Muslim culture rather than to urban social problems.[15]

School personnel were divided on a new law. Many teachers doubted its effectiveness. In December 2003, three of the four major confederations of teachers' unions asked President Chirac not to propose a new law. Some feared that focusing on the scarves would harden positions and make their work more difficult. In the classroom, they look for compromises. But it was mainly school principals and educational administrators who were heard by the Stasi Commission. They encounter scarf issues as legal or potentially legal battles, and they considered a new law likely to make their task of resolving disputes easier because it would not require them to find non-scarf grounds for expulsion or to negotiate a compromise. Administrators look for definitive solutions.

Furthermore, few believe that the teachers and principals who were selected to testify before the Stasi Commission represented the range of positions held by their colleagues in France. The witnesses generally supported a new law. Furthermore, they tended to generalize their experiences to other teachers and schools. A high school teacher from Lyon refers to the many problems

[15] Mucchielli (2005) and *Le Monde*, April 26, 2005. Mucchielli found himself the object of denunciations by Fadela Amara, the leader of NPNS, for "intellectual terrorism" because his findings undermined claims made by Ni Putes Ni Soumises; see his contribution to http://www.oumma.com, May 31, 2005.

told to her by others in the Lyon area; a middle school principal in Paris says that all her colleagues report incidents similar to those she describes; teachers claim that all the other teachers at their school agree with them. The testimonies thus give the impression of a unified sentiment among teachers and principals throughout France.

The commissioners heard stories about pressure placed on girls to wear the *voile*. Several teachers and principals claimed that families pressured girls to wear scarves, usually by inferring this pressure from the girls' ages, or by changes in their behaviors. One teacher recalled how a girl's knowledge of the State Council's ruling led him to wonder whether she had been coerced or trained, leading some on the Commission to shrug their shoulders and give each other knowing looks. A command of the legal framework could have been celebrated as empowerment, but when girls in scarves knew the law, it was assumed to be evidence of coercion. The new "protecting girls" schema began to take hold.

This way of framing the law has become the basis for the most effective arguments put forth by French-speakers in the United States, in particular by historian Patrick Weil and the reporter for the Stasi Commission, Remy Schwartz. Indeed, when Schwartz played the role of defense attorney for France on the public television program *World on Trial*, he argued that many women had come to the Commission, "saying 'save us, save us!'" There were no such pleas recorded on the tapes of the open hearings; closed hearings have not been opened for public scrutiny, and so Schwartz's claim cannot be verified.[16] But more important for our analysis is that these savvy actors saw that this particular set of ideas would play well in an Anglo-American context, appealing as it does to liberal schemas that highlight the state's role in protecting young people from harm.

A final schema also emerged during the 2002–2003 period: that the head scarf was intrinsically anti-women, that it stood for the oppression of Muslim women by Muslim men. The Stasi Commission avoided attributing a meaning to the cloth itself, but others did make these claims, and indeed it became part of the legal rhetoric that rose to prominence in the late 2000s (see Bowen and Rohe, Chapter 6 in this volume). Proponents of a law could then fashion an argument by drawing on a number of schemas that successfully skirted the issue of religious freedom. They claimed that schoolgirls were pressured by men and boys to wear the scarves, that the scarves intrinsically attacked the dignity and the equal status of women, and that, because they did so, they encouraged violence against women living in the poor suburbs (Bowen 2007: 208–242).

[16] The program, including statements by Weil and Schwartz's plea, can be viewed at: http://www.youtube.com/watch?v=Z_cahKQdSIo, accessed November 10, 2012.

That the law was passed in 2004 with overwhelming public and political support, and with scarcely a whisper that it might violate the French Constitution and the European Convention on Human Rights, testifies to the success of the efforts to strategically shift schemas during the late 1990s and early 2000s. As late as 2000, any observer of French affairs would have concluded that the consistent jurisprudential stance of the State Council made it clear that Islamic scarves could not be banned outright, even under the cover of a statute that pretended to address any and all religions (as did the law of 2004). The law of 1905 and the schemas of secularism and communalism had no legal purchase, given the high weight given to the religious freedom of private individuals. It was only when some public officials and school personnel began to argue on new grounds, and the events of 2001–2003 began to convince the public of dangers from Islamism and school disorder (and to link those two dangers), that the campaign for the law could succeed.

SOCIAL LOCATIONS AND PRACTICAL SCHEMAS IN FRENCH HOSPITALS

During the hearings of the Stasi Commission, the world of another institution entered the discussions about fears concerning public order disintegration and religious communalism. Concerns arose about hospitals. The commission's final report emphasized a series of facts that proved religions, and more specifically Islam, to constitute a threat to the institutional order of French hospitals. It pointed to

> refusals by husbands or fathers, on religious grounds, to see their wives or daughters cared for or helped in birthing by male doctors. Women have been deprived of epidurals. Nurses have been rejected because they were said to be of the wrong religion. More generally, some religious preoccupations by patients can disrupt the hospital's functioning, including turning hallways into private places of prayer, and setting up "parallel cafeterias" to serve traditional food in disregard of health rules. These events contradict the bases of public service: principles of equality, continuity of care, and respect for health and sanitation. (Stasi Commission 2003: 92–93)

As in the case of schools, members of the institution alerted the public about what they perceived as a direct attack against the values and the proper functioning of their institution, in this case delivery of professional care. A scenario developed, very similar to the one told in the *Lost Territories*, centered on concerns caused by Islamic claims and the subsequent relevance of *laïcité* as a program of public order within French institutions. Events occurring in several different hospital departments were used to make the arguments about institutional neutrality and gender equality. Most of them had to do with male physicians being refused by Muslim women or by their husbands and brothers. In 2006, the French National Council of Gynecologists and Obstetricians (CNGOF) released a document denouncing the aggression toward a male gynecologist by the husband of a Muslim patient. In the document, the CNGOF declared that the profession had "the obligation to protect women against attacks on their freedom that some would carry out in the name of a religion, poorly understood," and that "thirty years ago, Muslim women came to our hospitals with no worries concerning treatment by male doctors, and there were no problems or violence." The press release concluded: "Why this regression? Should we just let it happen and slip back ourselves? It is up to Islam to adapt to the individual freedom necessary for all in a modern state, and not the other way around."[17]

Soon, public discourses were suffused with perceptions about hospitals becoming the new battlefield of the conflict between Islam and the French state's institutions. Press coverage of issues involving Muslims in hospitals reached a peak of attention during the debates about the interdiction of full-face veiling that led to the Law of 11 October 2010. Essayists and consultants also warned the public about the "religious threats on hospitals," where "the multiplication of communalist and religious demands is more than troubling; French law and hospital rules are ignored. If no one does anything soon, will our health institutions be devoted to healing the sick or to their religious practices?" (Lévy 2011: 21). This attention eventually made the issue into a taken-for-granted dimension of the new politics of *laïcité* and Islam in the 2010s. Claude Guéant, the interior minister, commented: "We know that at the hospital there are a certain number of people who refuse that men provide medical care to women. Now, that is just not acceptable."[18]

When hospitals entered the debates about Islam and French values, how did the social life of the institute shape those debates? Conversely, how has the national debate affected the representations and practices of professionals

[17] Press release of the Collège National des Gynécologues et Obstétriciens Français (CNGOF): "Les gynécologues-obstétriciens défendent les femmes contre l'intégrisme musulman," October 17, 2006: http://www.cngof.asso.fr/D_TELE/compres_integr_17–10–06.pdf, accessed January 20, 2013.

[18] "Signes religieux dans les services publics: nouvelle polémique autour de Claude Guéant", *Le nouvel Observateur*, March 24, 2011: http://tempsreel.nouvelobs.com/politique/20110324.OBS0184/signes-religieux-dans-les-services-publics-nouvelle-polemique-autour-de-gueant.html, accessed January 20, 2013.

who work in hospitals? Recall when, in the debate about schools discussed earlier in the chapter, Jean-Claude Santana said, "You do not attend school as you go to the post office or to another public service." What comparable claims can be found for hospitals, and what are the consequences?

Addressing Religious Neutrality: National Ideology and Institutional Concerns

To an even greater degree than schools, hospitals show a highly complex organization, with members belonging to various professions, status hierarchies, and institutions. Hospitals bring together biomedical professionals, paramedics and their cohorts of "invisible personnel" committed to ancillary jobs (Arborio 2001), social workers, PR professionals, human resource managers, and experts in New Management (Belorgey 2010; see Peneff 1992). While some locations in a hospital are dedicated to the delivery of care, others are places to die and yet others to rest, and the patient's room is very different from the cafeteria where the personnel take their meals, the ER reception desk, and the aisle of the building reserved to the staff. However, all these people agree that they belong to a common sphere of interactions they identify and call a "hospital" – including the patients (Strauss et al. 1982), most particularly when they have to undergo long-term or frequent treatment. Eventually, because of the central place held by patients in these interactions, many aspects of the life organized by hospital professionals are closer to the condition of inmates in "closed" or "total" institutions (Goffman 1961; Pinto 1975) than is usually the case of street-level institutions (Lipsky 1977; Dubois 2003).

All these aspects make the hospital of today a difficult place to hold ideas of strict religious neutrality. For one, the framing of the issue of public sphere neutrality cannot find one simple answer in hospitals because French hospitals are an institution of the state but not in the public sphere all the time or everywhere.[19] The patient's room and what happens there (being ill, healing, or dying) does not belong to the public realm. This uncertainty about the notion of "religious neutrality" related to patients can expand to discussions among the personnel, and most specifically the practicing Muslims, about what locations do belong to the public realm and therefore require "religious neutrality," and what locations do not call for a strict application of religious neutrality. Is, for example, the cafeteria a place where *laïcité* applies and

[19] More precisely, French public hospital agents belong to one of the three bodies of French public institutions: hospitals (the *fonction publique hospitalière*), the public administration (*fonction publique d'Etat*), and local and regional authorities (*fonction territoriale*).

where head scarves must be removed?[20] It is not an accident that the HCI, the gatekeeper of the French republican integration doctrine, based its 2007 report on *laïcité* in public institutions on the distinction between "open" institutions (that is, institutions with "intermittent contact" with the public) and "closed" ones (such as prisons, the military, and hospitals; HCI 2007: 201).

The problem is still more complex in that no one thinks that hospitals can be empty of norms and rules about religion. Patients have the right to refer to their personal beliefs, including religious beliefs, when deciding on treatment, and even when choosing a physician, on condition that this does not impede the normal functioning of the service or the patient's condition (*Code de la Santé Publique* and *Charte de la Personne Hospitalisée*). The idea of neutrality that was paramount to the debates about schools cannot be directly transported into the hospital context (Baubérot and Lioger 2010).

Hospital professionals logically develop practical schemas that give very different weight to these various aspects when they deal with Muslims or with Islam-related issues. Some think spontaneously of the publicly held notion of *laïcité-qua*-neutrality as the relevant framework to address religious claims inside the walls of their institution. In this case, the institution is not thought to make a difference in these matters: *laïcité* is conceived of as applying here as everywhere else. Hospital managers, for example, are prone to share this general notion of *laïcité*. Much in line with the concerns expressed in the Stasi Commission's report, the director of an establishment (a *hôpital public*, funded by the state) in the northern region of Paris emphasized what he viewed as an all-encompassing consensus in his establishment, "a consensus among medical and administrative staff and including the unions in favor of religious and philosophical neutrality." He grounded the necessity of such a consensus on his perception of "a rise in hard-line religious and cultural positions" over the decade and the necessity to face the challenge. His concerns focused less on the relationship between Muslim patients and hospital professionals than on headscarves and Jewish skull caps worn during service by some of his personnel.

[20] The analysis in this section is based on the findings of a research undertook in four hospitals of the Paris region between March 2009 and December 2010. Ninety-six in-depth semi-structured interviews were carried out, among which seventy-six with medical professionals, paramedical workers, and administrative staff in three public funded hospitals (*hôpitaux publics*) and in one private hospital (*clinique privée*). In addition, twenty interviews were conducted with patients. The ninety-six interviews were conducted with practicing Muslims or individuals that self-identified as Muslim, mostly French nationals or immigrants from Maghreb countries, as well as with their non-Muslim coworkers. For details about this research, see Bertossi, C. and D. Prud'homme. 2011. *La "diversité" à l'hôpital. Identités sociales et discriminations raciales dans une institution française. Une étude du Centre Migrations et Citoyennetés de l'Ifri* (unpublished report, 257 pp.). The names of the establishments as well as their locations are kept anonymous in what follows.

He also insisted on the issue of gender equality and mentioned tensions among "Muslim men and French women" (sic), concluding that "we have to stay on this side of a line in terms of taking account of peoples' origins." To him, as to other directors met during this research, the Islamic veil is a "means of resisting *laïcité*." "We resist," he summarized in turn.[21] Some directors have taken direct action to rid the hospital of prayer places.[22]

A second set of schemas exists, however, that put into perspective the idea that neutrality or *laïcité* is the appropriate answer to religious issues on the hospital grounds. For example, a surgeon originating from a North African country – not a practicing Muslim himself – who works in a prestigious hospital in the Paris city center made particularly clear that:

> We could not care less! What sort of *laïcité*? Give me an example! Of course not! A hospital is not secular! Quite clearly so! There is a priest, even an imam who can come. No, it is not a secular hospital. ... But here, it is a public place. Are we to not admit sick people? Or we admit them and stop speaking about that; that's what I mean when I say that no, we don't care at all about *laïcité*![23]

These strikingly contrasted schemas coexist, at the intersection of public fears and institutional concerns and depending on specific contexts. A biomedical professional is more concerned with the extent to which the institution performs care delivery than with how it conforms to "republican principles," unlike the director of a hospital. However, medical and paramedical personnel are also obliged to justify what they do vis-à-vis the existing public concerns about religions, Islam, and *laïcité*. In this context, the practical schemas related to Islam and Muslims emphasize a "professional" critique of the usual public reasoning in terms of *laïcité*, based on specific institutionally based concerns. By contrast to schools, however, this specific framing of the issue highlights the possible conflict with the usual *laïcité* reasoning. The issue is not anymore that "[y]ou do not attend school as you go to the post office or to another public service," but, as a young nurse from the ER department in a hospital north of Paris put it: "If I remember well, *laïque* means the separation of the Church from the State. So, you don't bring in religion. Perhaps you could say that for a school, but not for a hospital."[24]

21 Unrecorded interview on December 9, 2009 with the director of a public hospital in a city close to Clichy-sous-Bois where the 2005 riots started in France.

22 Unrecorded interview with the DRH of a public hospital in the South of the Paris region, June 5, 2009.

23 Interview, December 17, 2010. Other interviewees emphasized a similar view.

24 Interview, March 12, 2010. This nurse is a practicing Catholic of South Asian origin: she was born in Vietnam to parents who were born in Pondicherry, one of the territories of former French India.

In other words, the same process of sacralization of principles perceived as specific to an institution (Douglas 1986) can lead to two opposite outputs when on-the-ground institutional actors frame public concerns: perceptions that *laïcité* is topical and timely in schools but not in hospitals.

The "Limits of the System": Justifying Accommodative Practices

How and to what extent do these different set of schemas affect the practices of institutional actors who disagree about publicly contested topics? Here we look in more detail at the consequences of the tension among the different aspects of practical schemas regarding what is acceptable or not in the hospital setting. While the public reasoning on *laïcité* a priori condemns all forms of "religious communalism," the hospital institutional framing of the issue more often than not leads professionals to tolerate and sometime to support practices otherwise challenged as communalistic.

As a result, there is continuous work of justification and reinterpretation carried out by social actors at the level of on-the-ground interactions with patients. The Stasi Commission had denounced the existence of "parallel cafeterias," referring to practices whereby patients ask relatives or friends to bring food to their rooms rather than eating hospital-provided meals, because these practices violated rules of hygiene. However, physicians and nurses usually justify these improvised "cafeterias" as a consequence of the failure of the institution to accommodate the patients' religious dietary needs. Opposing the schema of hygiene used by the Stasi Commission, they prefer that patients feed themselves than not be fed at all. As a result, they knowingly tolerate halal and kosher food brought in by the patients and their relatives. In this perspective, the practical schemas they deploy are centered on the idea that religious claims, including Muslim ones, are part of the normal functioning of their institution. Islam is construed as an unavoidable dimension of the relationship with patients, and the moral boundary between Islam and the institution is subsequently shifted beyond the narrative of the *Lost Territories of the Republic.*

These accommodative schemas can be based on principled views. These can involve ideas about the moral organization of culturally diverse societies or professional ideologies linking the suffering body to cultural practices (cf. Sargent and Erikson, Chapter 2 this volume; Sargent and Larchanché 2007). More often than not, however, the schemas focusing on accommodation are induced by the practice and the concrete interactions with patients. As a matter of fact, the idea that accommodation is part of the relationship with Muslim patients is not necessarily linked to positive perceptions about Islam. Some social actors in the institution frame their patients' religious practices in a negative way because they find them unsuitable given the patients' condition. Such is the case concerning the fast during the month of Ramadan. Others complain because accommodating religious needs of the patients increases the complexity of the usual interactions of caring and nursing. But even these negative perceptions are grounded on the routine life of the hospital, and take place within the constant, albeit unstable, articulation between institutional prescriptions (ensuring care, medication, and appropriate feeding) and the patients' religious prescriptions (fasting during Ramadan, meeting dietary requirements). Concerns about *laïcité* and French state institutions' neutrality in matters of religions are not part of these practical schemas of accommodation. In some cases, interviewees who admit to personally agreeing with the narrative of the *Lost Territories of the Republic* and denouncing Islam as a breach of the French republican values in the terms used by the public debate (i.e., communalist practices such as collective prayers and backward machismo in the case of husbands refusing their wife be treated by a male physician) also deploy a sophisticated reasoning about why Muslims must be accommodated when received as patients in a hospital.

Practical schemas about Muslims are thus framed by pragmatic judgments related to the importance of "doing the job." However, the intensely politicized values of the French republic and *laïcité* have their own impact on this relationship between hospital professionals and Muslim patients. The formal values of republican color-blindness constitute a web of constraints on the interactions with patients, and push professionals to practical *bricolages* and strategic adaptations. What happens within the institution must be justified to the rest of the society.[25] Despite the formal interdiction of conducting ethnic surveys in France, some nurses and physicians explain they ask their patients about their religion, but "you have to know how to pose the question but you may not write it down."[26] An observation in different hospitals' departments in the Paris region shows that this question has been routinized when new patients arrive in a department. It can take the form of questions about dietary

[25] A physician, head of a department and medical educator at a university hospital in the north of Paris told us the following anecdote: "This is amusing. At the time of the law on visible religious signs, a journalist from the *Figaro Magazine* called me. She said: 'We really want to make a paper on religious signs at hospitals. I imagine that, in your hospital, with all the patients you have, all the Muslims, that must be hell.' I told her: 'Look, you can come if you want but I must tell you that you won't find much to say because, in practice, we have very very few problems.' She became furious. . . . She never believed me; she thought I wanted to cloud the problem, but that's not true. We simply don't have many problems." Interview, December 15, 2010.

[26] Interview with a Franco-Cameroonian physician, born in Cameroon, who works in the ER at a public hospital north of Paris, March 5, 2010.

requirements, which are part of the questionnaire new patients fill out upon arrival. In some instances, the foreign consonance of a family name seems to be used as an indication of the religion of the patients (on similar practices in the French military, see Bertossi, Chapter 4 in this volume).[27]

As a result, justifying what hospital practitioners do when it comes to Muslims and Islam is not an easy task. There is a series of tensions these actors have to negotiate continuously between the popular beliefs about Muslim communalism and the on-the-ground reality. All interviewees insisted that they faced problems very rarely, which stands in sharp contrast to public perceptions. They must negotiate between their own fears of communalism and the accommodative strategies they deploy, between formal norms and values (i.e., the interdiction of ethnic statistics and categories) and the need for informal practices to do the job. As a consequence, it is often difficult to them to know where the moral boundary must lie, what is socially acceptable but institutionally dysfunctional, and what is difficult to accept but useful for a successful delivery of care. This is where limits of such *bricolages* are reached, as a senior nurse in the internal medicine department of a hospital in the Paris city center explained: "I once had a nurse who brought a Qur'an and a small rug and who knows what else for a patient who did not have what was needed to do the prayer. Yeah, that's clearly at the limits of the system."

Can Nurses Be Veiled in a French Hospital?

Until now, we have asked how hospital professionals address issues related to Islam when patients are concerned. The accommodative practical schemas we found show one aspect of the relationship between Islam and the institution. Now we turn to the matter of how members of the institution negotiate the wearing of the head scarf by other members, mostly young French nurses who are practicing Muslims. We are interested as much in the variations in schemas developed on this issue across different social locations as we are in the outcomes of these negotiations. What types of compromises and accommodation are reached in French hospitals when Muslim professionals are concerned?

Let us return to how the directors of establishments framed this issue in terms of a "resistance" to the "rise in hard-line religious and cultural positions." In the name of *laïcité*, they "fight against head scarves and Jewish skull caps"

[27] This was the case systematically in the surgery department of the private hospital we studied.

among the paramedical and medical personnel, as the director of a hospital told us. We already saw that this approach is supported by the need to conform as much as possible to France's self-identification as color-blind in order to protect the normal functioning of the institution. This is exactly the claim made by the Stasi Commission and other actors we already mentioned.

However, hospital managers too are sometimes obliged to shift the weight they give to *laïcité* and to reframe their priority when their personnel is concerned. Such is the case with managers concerned with recruitment and personnel policies in the private and public sectors. The human resource managers we met highlighted a shortage of skilled paramedical professionals, and the consequence this had on the functioning of their hospital. In one public hospital in Seine-Saint-Denis, the director of patient care reported that "we do not worry that much about the religious neutrality of our workers, and what counts on some days here is patient safety. So above all we make sure that the nurse is there, is present, and cares for the patients." A senior male nurse of the ER service of a private hospital in the same area told us a similar story about their director of patient care, who "interviewed a nurse who wore a long veil, from head to toe, and the nurse was hired because she is a good nurse, and she has permission to wear a small cap to work in the patient care area."[28] New schemas are used here. Allowing the presence of a head scarf is seen as "not correct in the sense of managing public civic life, but it's important for internal management, you can't make people feel frustrated."[29] This seems to show an intermediate sphere in the institution, in between the world of directors and the medical departments, in ways not substantially different from what could be found in other institutions of the French state with increased social representation of minority groups (Bertossi, Chapter 4 in this volume). In this case, however, this is not formalized as a recruitment policy but remains an element informally negotiated on the ground.

As a consequence, the general interdiction of religious dress for the personnel is far from an easily applicable norm. This too must be negotiated. These negotiations use different repertoires, among which hygiene is the most frequent. Of course, the advantage of hygiene is that it easily translates the otherwise abstract and politically connoted principle of *laïcité*. The patients' health is the reason for the interdiction of head scarves or long-sleeved blouses. As the patient care director of a public hospital summarizes: "It is a public institution and so there should not be signs. ... And in addition, let me tell you that it is a major problem in terms of hygiene!" The director

[28] Interview with a male head of nurses at the private hospital, June 16, 2010.

[29] Interview with the DRH of the private hospital, May 31, 2010.

of another public hospital shares this view: "The head scarf has become a real concern. We cannot allow it inside the hospital for reasons of hygiene."[30] Hygiene appears here to be an argument capable of supporting the principle of religious neutrality held by the administrators as well as the uniqueness of the practice of care in the services – a way to depoliticize the topic and produce a consensus among all the members of the institution, beyond their respective locations.

This consensus, however, must also be measured against the ability of professionals to assess the practical schema of hygiene. At the time we did our fieldwork, a listserv widely used by professional hygienists working in French hospitals (Nosobase) asked whether professionals may wear a textile fabric headgear inside surgical units. Two different answers were provided. A first answer recalls the principle of *laïcité* and the existing norms. Comments notably emphasized that "we must guard against allowing religious beliefs to damage the quality of care or the rules of hygiene." A second comment, however, framed the question very differently, and addressed the hygienic property of the headgear itself: "In the operating rooms, for several years now we have tried to replace anything woven by non-woven materials in order to reduce the amount of particulate matter. Reintroducing a woven cap [i.e., the head scarf] is inconsistent with this policy."[31] A frequent user of this listserv, a young practicing Muslim public health nurse at the private hospital we studied, argued there was no clear consensus about the issue. She said she had had discussions on the Nosobase listserv, and that her counterparts "especially at the public hospital, because in this network there are lots of public ones, they tell me that there was no problem if heads were covered" – thus excluding the argument of the quality of the fabric used – "so I think that it depends on each director who makes rules as she wishes," she concluded. "In fact, much has to do with the public impression given at the clinic where I work, the '*image de marque*.' So, the director does not want us to wear jeans. We don't wear jeans. I am wearing them today. But for the director, one does not wear them because jeans are for Sundays. And then one either follows the rules or not, applies them or not."

There is yet another way to render consistent wearing an Islamic scarf with the imperatives of professionalism, organizational relations, and public

[30] Unrecorded interview, 15 April 2009.

[31] See http://nosobase.chu-lyon.fr/liste/synthese/9csynthesemars2009.asp (accessed October 17, 2012). Another discussion on this listserv concerned the apparent reluctance of Muslim paramedics to wash their hands with hydroalcoholic gels: http://nosobase.chu-lyon.fr/liste/synthese/10asynthesejanvier2010.asp (accessed October 17, 2012).

concerns in French hospitals. To the paramedical personnel who sometimes claim the right to wear the scarf (as well as in instances where medical professionals wear a Jewish cap) during work hours, local negotiations find in the surgical "mobcap" or bonnet (*charlotte*), a solution relevant to both the service and the individual. We observed such a local compromise in three of the four establishments were we carried out our research, private and public hospitals alike, in the poor outer cities as well as in a very bourgeois district of Paris. In the private hospital, two nurses who are practicing Muslims and wear the Islamic scarf outside the establishment wear the mobcap at work. Azra was the first to use the mobcap as a substitute for her scarf. It did not raise substantial questions among her colleagues because she works in the surgery unit, where professionals ordinarily wear disposable caps and gowns. A neonatal nurse, however, Nayla, was in a different situation. She "wore her own scarf to work, a bandana worn back on the head, with a turtle neck worn under her blouse," Azra told us. When Nayla was sent for by the director of patient care, she was told to dress as Azra did, with a disposable cap and gown. In this case, the compromise worked only within the narrow perimeter of her own unit.

However, when this compromise has become known more widely in the hospital, disputes have emerged and reintroduced other schemas, putting the personnel in question in a position of having to justify themselves. In a hospital in the town of Bassens in the French Alps, a practicing Muslim nurse was allowed by the director to substitute a mobcap for her scarf, but her work led her to move around the entire hospital, making her head covering more widely apparent than in the cases discussed earlier. The hospital workers' union (of the CGT) complained that "unlike traditional hospitals, that of Bassens has no separate operating unit and so no surgeon."[32] In a letter to the director of the hospital, the union delegate wrote, in words redolent of the 2004 law against scarves in schools: "This head covering, original to say the least, and unexpected in the general patient care area [in contrast to surgical units], has not failed to shock some patients and staff. If the mobcap is not the same as the Islamic scarf, it nonetheless does not wipe away the ostensibly (*ostentatoirement*) religious or communalist dimension, if the wearer indeed wears the cap because of those beliefs."[33]

[32] *Le Parisien*, December 3, 2009.

[33] Interestingly enough, the director himself declared that "the mobcap can by no means be interpreted as a religious sign. In my opinion, the principle of *laïcité* is respected (here)" (quoted in *Le Parisien*, December 3, 2009).

Attracting huge attention in the public debates, the problem of Muslim nurses wearing the scarf at work was systematically put into perspective by all the hospital staff we interviewed, including managers in charge of the personnel. They say that actual claims of this type remain relatively rare, sometimes to their own surprise, as said the Personnel Director of a public hospital in the south of Paris. He had only seen one such case during his time there, when an Algerian student was asked to remove her scarf and told she could wear the mobcap instead. "She wore the mobcap for several days and then she grew tired of always having to explain herself on that score, and removed it completely." In other instances, however, the direction of a hospital decides to sanction what is perceived publicly as a breach of *laïcité* and state neutrality principles. But it then becomes sometimes arduous to find the relevant juridical sources for a general interdiction. This was the case of the director of one important public hospital in the north of Paris who sent a circular to staff in February 2010, stating that: "It should be remembered that, according to Law 2004–228 dated 15 march 2004, hospital workers, whatever their grade, are forbidden from wearing religious signs or clothing in public health institutions. You are kindly requested to follow these rules, in consideration of the patients we welcome at the Hospital."[34]

The difficulty in this case is that the juridical reference that is supposed to establish the force of the *laïcité* as a general principle to all members of the institution is in fact the law that was voted for one specific institution: public schools. Instead of reaching an agreed-on meaning on what *laïcité* is and how it should be implemented, the document only further increased the uncertainty of the norms that should be applied in the institution.

CONCLUSION

We saw with the schools and the hospitals that the relationship of practical schemas to national ideologies is highly sensitive to two elements: external conjunctures that transform or re-weight the schemas, and the social location of actors in the institution. Indeed, we can now see that the schemas used by some hospital directors were taken from the circulating schemas produced by the law against scarves in schools. Expressions using "ostensibly" ("ostensibly manifesting religious affiliation") were used in the text of the 2004 law (after much debate in parliament) to target scarves while remaining within the limits of European law. These expressions are awkward in French, and quickly became condensed references, in national, cross-domain circulation, to what

34 Circular of the Director of a public hospital in the north of Paris, February 19, 2010.

many believed were legal instruments against Islamic scarves in other contexts – including that of the hospital. In a few cases, mayors refused to allow women in scarves to attend marriage on the pretext that the 2004 law prohibited scarves in state spaces. Similar attempts were made in university cafeteria and other public services – all with no legal foundation whatsoever. The schema moved from one domain, namely that of public schools, into national discourse, and then was appropriated in other domains, as we saw in the case of one hospital director mentioned earlier in the chapter. But the more one enters into the specific units of the hospitals, the more the staff becomes concerned with ensuring patient care and less with the ideological dimensions of clothing choice. We can thus trace the movement of schemas within and across institutions. They "succeed" because they tap into an element already present in the broad and complex French repertoire of ideas about religion and society. But that is not enough; they also must be mobilized by certain actors at certain moments.

The two institutions illustrate this complex succession and movement of schemas, but not in the same way. The public school debates over students' scarves tapped into long-standing cleavages and worries about Catholicism, schooling, and women's rights. In that sense the French schools are a site always ready and waiting for bitter and divisive public controversy. (In early 2013, for example, debates erupted over whether Catholic schools that enjoy state support could legitimately discuss the views of the Church on gay and lesbian marriage and adoption). Schools are also supposed to guarantee the social realization of Republican philosophy and provide a pathway to success for all. They are thus doubly, or triply, under constant scrutiny. We saw a series of schemas applied to the scarves-in-school question; the school was a site to discuss broader questions of society: about disorder and violence in the poor housing projects, about global Islam, about incivility, about the decline of France! That these issues were debated via the schools has everything to do with the social history of schooling in France. But precisely for that reason the pretext for these debates – that wearing a scarf caused social ills – had very little directly to do with the most pressing everyday problems in the schools.

The hospital resembles the school in its closed nature, but it has a honeycombed quality that supports the implementation of different rules in the inner sanctum of the operating room from those imposed on staff working more in the public eye. It is more internally differentiated and more task-defined than is the school. It was thus more likely that those staff less involved with public relations or public accountability would focus on getting the job done, allowing the mobcap, attending to the dietary or other needs of Muslim patients, and so on. At the same time, the hospital is also more client-focused than the school. Students arrive and are told what to do; parents have an incidental role. Hospitals must admit patients, who come with a wide range of expectations and concerns, and these include demands that touch on such sensitive subjects as gender and religious neutrality. When a few hospital directors said that Muslims had interfered with critical service by asking for female doctors, these claims "played" well in the public sphere – and for that reason were sought out by journalists. (Usually ignored was the inconvenient fact that all patients have this right).

In both institutions, however, we find staff constantly called on by the exigencies of their institutional lives to find ways of accommodating demands (by students, patients, or directors) while accomplishing their tasks. These actors welcome, indeed call for, greater certainty through laws or clear guidelines. At the same time they realize that rules never abolish ambiguity, nor do they wipe away ambivalence.

BIBLIOGRAPHY

Arborio, Anne-Marie. 2001. *Un personnel invisible. Les aides-soignantes à l'hôpital.* Paris: Anthropos.

Baubérot, Jean and Raphaël Liogier. 2010. *Sacrée médecine. Histoire et devenir d'un sanctuaire de la raison.* Paris: Entrelacs.

Belorgey, Nicolas. 2010. *L'hôpital sous pression. Enquête sur le "nouveau management public".* Paris: La Découverte.

Bowen, John R. 2007. *Why the French Don't Like Headscarves: Islam, the State, and Public Space.* Princeton, NJ: Princeton University Press.

Brenner, Emmanuel, ed. 2002. *Les territoires perdus de la République.* Paris: Éditions Mille et Une nuits.

Douglas, Mary. 1986. *How Institutions Think.* Syracuse, NY: Syracuse University Press.

Dubois, Vincent. 2003. *La vie de guichet. Relation administrative et traitement de la misère.* Paris: Economica.

Goffman, Erving. 1961. Asylum. *Essays on the Social Situation of Mental Patients and Other Inmates.* New York: Doubleday Anchor.

Haut Conseil à l'Intégration (HCI). 2007. *Charte de la laïcité dans les services publics et autres avis.* Paris: La documentation française.

Lévy, Isabelle. 2011. *Menaces religieuses sur l'hôpital.* Paris: Presses de la Renaissance.

Lipsky, Michael. 1977. *Street-Level Bureaucracy. Dilemmas of the Individual in Public Services.* New York: Russel Sage Foundation.

Mucchielli, Laurent. 2005. *Le scandale des "tournantes".* Paris : La Découverte.

Peneff, Jean. 1992. *L'hôpital en urgence. Etude par l'observation participante.* Paris: Métailié.

Pinto, Louis. 1975. L'armée, le contingent et les classes sociales. *Actes de la Recherche en Sciences Sociales* 1(3) : 18–40.

Sargent, Carolyn and Stéphanie Larchanché. 2007. The Muslim Body and the Politics of Immigration in France: Popular and Biomedical Representations of Malian Migrant Women. *Body and Society* **13**(3): 79–102.
Stasi, Bernard (Commission présidée par). 2003. *Laïcité et République. Rapport au Président de la République.* Paris: La documentation française.
Strauss, Anselm, Shizuko Fagerhaugh, Barbara Suczek, and Carolyn Wiener. 1982. The Work of Hospitalized Patients. *Social Science and Medicine* **16**(9): 977–986.

PART II

INSTITUTIONS AND NATIONAL POLITICAL IDEOLOGIES

6 Juridical Framings of Muslims and Islam in France and Germany

John R. Bowen and Mathias Rohe

Across the courtrooms and public venues of Western Europe, judges, jurists, and public figures routinely translate ideas about Muslims and Islam into legal forms. In what follows we consider ways in which these actors frame the actions and values of Muslims using discursive legal means. We argue here that judges face quite specific institutional constraints on how they decide and how they justify those decisions, a point we explore through a series of decisions and responses concerning marriage and religious freedom. We examine how judges draw on broadly distributed practical schemas concerning Muslims and Islam, and we do so by contrasting juridical reasoning in France and Germany, as well as between two higher courts in France. We argue that the contrasts are the result of different weightings of the same legal components, which we see as practical schemas for rendering decisions.

JUDGING ACROSS STATES AND COURTS

Across Western Europe, judges and jurists work with many of the same legal "building blocks." Among the imperatives they share are: preserving the stability of personal relationships as people move across national boundaries, guaranteeing equal rights to all adults and to all children, and defending societal interests, often couched in terms of *ordre public* (public [moral] order, public policy). These imperatives – family stability, equal rights, and public moral order – sometimes are seen to conflict among themselves, as when a polygamous family seeks recognition in a country for which monogamy is seen as part of public moral order. Family stability would imply recognizing the family's rights of residence, whereas *ordre public* might imply the need to deny such recognition. In those instances judges must weigh these conflicting norms in order to render a judgment.

We see these shared imperatives as building a sense of law as a cross-national social institution, in the form of practical schemas that allow judges in Britain to recognize commonalities with judges in Germany, despite drawing from different legal traditions and working in very different historical contexts. We see them as "schemas" in that they consist of ideas, evaluations, and ways of speaking that shift in their relative importance or weight as events occur in the social world. We see them as "practical" in that they are deployed without constant reference to theories of why they are important. They are quickly available as guides for living: "marriage ought to look like this or that," "this is how we do things here," "religion belongs in the private sphere," "we ought not to disrupt people's lives," and so forth.

When these schemas overlap, they make it possible to discuss law as a social institution that crosses national boundaries. John Meyer and his colleagues (Meyer and Rowan 1977) have claimed that many institutions (schools, courts, professions) replicate across national contexts for reasons that have to do with broader historical mechanisms, such as the rise of professional associations and cross-national treaties. Similarities in law across nations reflect the shifting relationships between nation-states and other political units. Nation-states emerged out of broader imperial and colonial contexts. Today judges and jurists draw from supranational repertoires that validate and shape the work of law within any one country. The problems that lead to many of the best-known cases reflect processes of international permanent and temporary migration, and the subsequent challenges of regulating a pluralistic society.

If many of these schemas are shared across countries, do judicial institutions show effects of national ideologies? They do, but less because national ideologies are translated into decisions, and more because they may shape how a judge weighs the conflicting imperatives mentioned earlier, both in arriving at decisions and in formulating explicit justifications of those decisions. Legal reasoning has its own logics, and these are institutional logics, even when they are inflected by national politics (Latour 2010).

Cross-national contrasts, explored in what follows, allow us to detect some of these national effects. For example, French judges give a particularly strong moral character to *ordre public* compared to those in Britain. Judgments about the "foreignness" of a person reflect differing ways of thinking about citizenship and belonging in Germany and in France. These distinctions have to do with relative weighting of legal schemas, not with incommensurable differences across national contexts. Complicating such distinctions is the increasing openness of national legal decisions to European decisions, a change that over time somewhat reduces these contrasts.

Of course, courts also differ in their general relationships to statutes. Legal systems forming part of the civil-law tradition, such as France, Germany, and Austria, start from the theorem that legislators make law and judges enforce it. They therefore tend to intensely regulate legal issues through legislation, restricting judicial power much more than in countries with the common-law tradition, such as Great Britain and the United States. Whereas the former start from the idea of an existing legal order already covering many legal problems, the latter rest on the notion that law is developed case by case, a process in which judges play an important role.[1] In addition, there are considerable differences among various civil-law systems as to the self-understanding of judges: The French judiciary traditionally was restricted to the role of the "mouth of the law," that is, only to "pronounce" the contents of the law. In Germany, the role of the (higher) judiciary goes far beyond that, because the legislator often expressly leaves clarifications and developments of the laws to the courts. Within the same country, moreover, specific institutions have their own sets of practical schemas and their own specific relationships to legislatures and executives, a point we make later in the chapter by contrasting the approach taken by the French State Council to that taken by the Constitutional Council on the issue of banning full-face veils.

Western European legal institutions also have specific and to a great extent shared modes of framing issues regarding religion. Judges, jurists, and legislators (who work in the shadow of the courts) must talk about the law in ways that remain neutral with respect to citizens' moral and religious convictions. Judges cannot target one religion over others lest they run afoul of national or supranational courts, such as the European Court of Human Rights. At the same time, these legal systems contain key conceptual operators that allow judges and legislators to translate cultural understandings into law. Civil law is assumed to be purely secular, and rarely do rules acknowledge religious specificities. Christian roots, with respect to monogamy and restrictions on divorce, for example, are rarely rendered explicit or referred to in legal texts. Laws often are based on relatively vague terms such as "the welfare of the child," "hardship," or "public order," thus leaving broad space for judicial interpretation. This is exactly the doorway through which broader understandings enter the legal arena, and through which such understandings can be translated into legal terms.

[1] Of course practice is more complex, as in the case of the highest administrative court in France, the State Council, which, unlike the Cassation Court and the rest of the civil and criminal law system, works in ways similar to an English court and also theorizes what it does in common-law terms (Latour 2010).

An example might help see how in different courts it is different *questions* that lead to a different results. A recent verdict of the British Immigration Tribunal concerned whether to recognize a temporary marriage as defined in Iranian law.[2] The Tribunal did not accord recognition, saying:

> Notions of marriage naturally vary between cultures, but we do not think that it would be wrong to regard permanence and exclusivity as essential features of the institution. … Rules allowing polygamy, and rules permitting divorce, are found in many societies. But it does not seem to us than an institution which by its nature is neither permanent nor exclusive can properly be regarded as marriage.

The Tribunal might have taken a different approach, one more likely to be followed in Germany (as discussed later), where the court looks at the concrete case in a consequentialist way. Under this logic, when examining a polygamous marriage, the judge would ask: If the marriage was concluded validly abroad under foreign law, and if this recognition would enable the second wife to claim maintenance from her husband, could the marriage then be recognized? Several European courts have argued that, even though polygamy does not fit into European laws, many (non-Muslim) Europeans do engage in what is in effect "serial monogamy," which creates analogous problems in distributing the family income among more than two spouses (or former spouses).

Courts also might weigh differently two meta-legal options that are particularly evident in the domains to be discussed here. On the one hand, law can be seen as "sending a message" about the shared values of the society, with an eye to encouraging or compelling people to act in particular ways. This function adheres especially to public law, but also to mandatory private law. On the other hand, law can be seen as mainly designed to regulate relationships among individuals, particularly in large parts of (optional) private law (e.g., contract law). These two emphases correspond to the forms of law that Émile Durkheim associated with "mechanical" and "organic" forms of solidarity, respectively. They dominate in certain legal domains: as Durkheim pointed out, they are most important, respectively, in criminal and civil law. But they also can emerge as alternative possibilities with respect to the same legal issue, an eventuality that we illustrate later in the chapter with respect to polygamy.

In what follows, we look at two sets of issues that indicate the different possible approaches within the broader European framework. In general, family law lies at the crossroads of the two functions of the law described earlier: while

[2] LS Mut'a or sighe Iran [2007] UKAIT 00072.

freedom of choice is granted to a broad extent, the state also takes account of differences in bargaining power within the families, so as to protect the weaker party from being deprived of rights. Here, conflicts may arise from different perceptions regarding the scope of "privacy" of family life. In many patriarchal cultures relying on extended family structures, family issues are taken to be solely private and family conflicts are supposed to be resolved "internally." In Europe, the threshold of state interference is relatively low, because state institutions have broadly replaced many functions of family structures, and the European welfare state feels responsible to protect the weak effectively. Nevertheless, the toleration or acceptance of difference varies considerably across European states and institutions.

The first issue concerns marriage and divorce, and more specifically, whether European judges will recognize effects in European countries of a Muslim marriage or divorce performed legally abroad. In particular, polygamous marriages and talaq divorces (pronounced by the husband and in Islamic terms bearing unilateral force) test the workings of private international law because they raise issues of the equality of men and women. In response to equality concerns, judges and jurists often invoke ideas of public moral order (*ordre public*) that can overrule the normal workings of international law. "Normal workings" in this sense means to stick to the core principle of private international law, which says that all private legal orders are equal in principle, and within the limits of *ordre public* should be recognized. To do otherwise would be to act contrary to the reasonable expectations that people who marry or divorce in one place remain married or divorced when they cross international borders. Invoking *ordre public* to thwart these expectations is considered to require special justification. When judges invoke public moral order considerations, they reframe social and moral perceptions of Islamic norms as legal issues, susceptible to legal solutions. They bring into play their own schemas about what Islam implies for gender equality and procedural fairness.

The second issue is really a bundle of claims made by judges and jurists concerning Islamic values and citizenship. One such claim concerns Islamic head and face coverings (*hijab* and *niqab*). Here again equality of women is at the forefront of debates. Those arguing for restrictions on the rights of women to wear head scarves or full veils argue that these items of clothing represent, and in some ways promote, the submission or the inequality of women, most notably in France. Here the legal questions are much broader than in the cases of marriage and divorce. In those cases, debates are limited to the treatment of foreign law. The debates are about legal procedures taking place elsewhere (recognition issues) or about cases to be decided under foreign law according to private international law rules because of their predominantly international aspects (e.g., concerning couples living abroad). But debates about women's clothing concern behavior and modes of thinking on the part of men and women residing in, and often citizens of, European countries. Those advocating laws against such practices condemn them as indicative of moral failings on the part of Islam or on the part of some Muslims residing in Europe. We note that the head scarf issues resembles others, such as the argument made by a German judge that because Islam permitted wife-beating, a Muslim wife was not due the same protections as her non-Muslim counterpart. In both French and German cases, these arguments rest on the assumption that Islam contains a set of agreed-on meanings that can be discerned by the state. They emerge at a time when public figures across Western Europe are denouncing Islam as a source of non-European values.

In seeking to unpack the cultural frameworks for legal decisions we often usefully have recourse to published, official legal justifications. These writings form a tightly constrained subset of a larger universe of legal commentary and public debate. Put another way, judges must couch a broad set of reasons and opinions in a way that is legally acceptable. They do not want their decisions to be overturned, or their careers to be retarded, by writing in ways that are legally unacceptable. At the same time, they draw on philosophical, political, and cultural frameworks that are broader than that of the current law. We know that we can benefit by distinguishing between judges' reasons for making decisions and their public justifications for those decisions: the latter generally are narrower than the former, and might be made in different ways to different audiences (Baum 2006).

Legal commentary provides an additional way to study reasoning processes and frameworks that are shared by members of the legal community but that do not appear explicitly in published legal decisions. They help us understand what otherwise appear as holes or lapses in the legal reasoning. Such is particularly the case in discursive traditions where published decisions are very concise, with little expansion and no debate. If we can derive much of judges' debates and broader concerns from published decisions of the U.S. Supreme Court or the German Supreme Court, we cannot do so from the French State Council or Court of Cassation. In the French cases, jurists writing in eminent commentaries such as the *Recueil Dalloz* expand and rationalize brief decisions. In building their particular interpretations, these jurists cite other jurists and decisions but they also cite public commentators and scholars who support their view. Public figures weigh in as well and may shape future decisions directly. Legal framing thus has both a narrow and broader range: narrow when judges are writing decisions, broader when commentators bring in the supplementary information necessary to understand those decisions.[3]

Each legal order follows its own particular traditions in that respect. In Germany, the superior courts are not restricted to quashing decisions of the lower courts and referring cases back to the lower courts, but have to ultimately decide the case if the facts are undisputed. They usually debate in a broad manner the arguments given by other courts as well as by scholars and publish these arguments. Even legislators repeatedly say that fundamental legal issues should be further developed by legal scholars and in the courts. Thus, debates among jurists play a much more important direct role in public life than in France.

Western courts share many institutional features, including practical schemas about religious freedom, preserving family stability, and *ordre public*, but judges and jurists give differing (and sometimes changing) weightings to each of these schemas, both from one country to another and across judicial institutions within any one country. These and other institutional features (forms of publication and justification, relationships of courts to legislatures) then shape the way judges and jurists draw on practical schemas concerning Muslims and Islam in making and justifying their judgments.

ISLAMIC MARRIAGE AND DIVORCE, AND *ORDRE PUBLIC*

We now turn to issues raised by practices of polygamy and divorce by Muslims, a discussion which requires providing some background concerning how the broad principles of private international law can and do enter into conflict with the considerations proceeding from a national notion of *ordre public*. *Ordre public* translates current perceptions and cultural judgments and evaluations into legal form. Although often translated as "public order" or "public policy" in English, in French and German contexts, *ordre public* has quite specific, sometimes strongly moral resonances. It refers both to the conditions of social order and to basic values, and it limits the range of laws that a legislator may pass and the decisions that a judge may make. It upsets normal judicial life and suspends the application of the usual rules.[4]

3 Even when judges do not themselves refer to these commentaries, they may be read by others in the legal, political, and social worlds as the only "official" justification for a decision; Latour notes the disdain expressed by members of France's State Council (Latour 2010: 16 n.22; 121n.19) for *la doctrine*, and yet those commentaries are what becomes recycled as establishing to others – most likely including a fair number of lower-level judges – as the law. The subject deserves further research.

4 See the recent collection of studies on *ordre public* in Europe and North Africa edited by Bernard-Maugiron and Dupret (2012).

When such cases concern judgments made by foreign courts, courts sometimes misunderstand the social norms invoked in the foreign court. In a 1980 German case from Cologne, the judges mistranslated the Islamic marriage gift paid by the husband to his wife, the *mahr*, as the price paid for "purchasing" his wife. Now, there are such institutions in some societies, such as the Turkish "başlık" that does indeed serve as a payment to the bride's family for her "loss" and is therefore unacceptable to European courts. However, the *mahr* has the opposite consequences, in that the bride receives it for her own needs and, in countries with high levels of *mahr*, can provide her with a bargaining chip.

Although judges in many countries use the idea of *ordre public*, the concept resists definition preciselybecause it is expected to provide judges and jurists with the means to translate the protected values of a society into law, and as these values change, so do the limits of the law. With respect to matters that touch on the family, *ordre public* may be invoked to reject an option or action that otherwise would satisfy legal requirements. These "exceptions due to *ordre public*" can evoke from jurists terms that reflect the basic moral and emotional levels of the objection.

In fact, the scope of *ordre public* clearly reflects different approaches of laws and courts toward legal diversity despite common general convictions concerning private international law (PIL). As mentioned earlier, PIL rests on the idea that legal relations between parties should remain stable even where the foreign legal norms in question considerably differ from domestic law. The limit to this stability is indicated by invoking *ordre public*, in order to safeguard fundamental convictions. For example, marriages might be concluded with brides as young as nine years of age in some jurisdictions where traditional Islamic law is applied, but in Europe such marriages are considered to violate *ordre public*. Other cases are less clear. Of special interest is a matter of what we could call secondary *ordre public* rules, namely whether the *ordre public* effect of accepting, say, a marriage concluded in another country would be a set of positive, concrete consequences for the parties, or would this positive outcome be offset by a broader and less welcome message sent by the judge concerning what is accepted and what is not in the host country. These decisions thus serve as a valuable litmus test for how far judges will go in accepting de facto diversity in the host country.

We should emphasize that the *ordre public* test is intended to solve the concrete conflict at stake and not to judge the foreign laws as such: PIL rests on the presumption of the equality of legal orders. That said, laws or actions that are judged to be contrary to *ordre public* may be seen as characteristic of another society and thus decisions can be taken to implicitly criticize that society. Moreover, as a commentator on the role of *ordre public* in international private law points out, "[P]ersonal status is the privileged domain for exceptions due to ordre public, because it is there where we are most likely to encounter institutions absolutely opposed to the values of civilization retained by the nation." The definition of what offends *ordre public* in what other people do thus not only reveals current French, German, or British notions about the limits of the morally acceptable, but also may be used to render concrete a general sense of a "clash of civilizations." It is with respect to Islam that this last function of *ordre public* emerges most notably in current jurisprudence.

Most legal systems rest on the principle – known as the theory of vested rights – that individuals ought to retain their private relationships (notably their marital status) when they cross borders. Nevertheless, a national legal community may decide that in certain matters the same law should apply to all people who reside within national borders. These decisions are made particularly with respect to family law, and hence this is where conflicts between legal systems and involving Muslims most often arise.

We see these two imperatives, to safeguard both private relationships and public moral order, as giving rise to distinct practical schemas used by judges. They also refer back to the two bodies of private (or civil) law and public law in Western Europe. The two bodies of law both seek to protect individual interests, but are conceived of in very different ways. Public law guards the collective interests and is intimately tied to state sovereignty. Debates over freedom of religion concern its limits vis-à-vis the interests of the public and the role of the state in ensuring those interests. It is here that considerations of public moral order enter, and these are held to apply to all citizens of a country in the same way. In Western European private law, concerning relationships among individuals, one cannot have some laws applying to citizens of one religion and other laws to other such bodies of citizens, as is the case in countries with "personal status" systems of family law such as in India, Morocco, and Indonesia. The European way of granting pluralism is to enable choice within the existing family law, for example, by way of marriage contracts.

Private law places utmost importance on the autonomy of the individual and the stability of legal relations among individuals. In the sphere of private law, religious norms and indeed foreign legal norms can play a role if they are seen to be serving those objectives. States certainly intervene into these matters, seeking to ensure equal treatment of men and women and the welfare of children. Private law does not mean that the state does not intrude.

When Muslims with foreign nationality approach the courts, a major determinant of the outcome, and indeed how the case is framed in legal terms, is how the country's legal system understands the connection between people and a legal order. Two broad possibilities are present: the parties to the case are thought to retain their strongest ties to the country of which they are a citizen, or rather to the country where they reside. This question has repercussions for how family law issues are judged and, at the level of extra-legal public framing, on how the broader public thinks about Muslims of foreign origin legally residing in the country. Answering this question gives greater weight either to the public schema or to the private one, which then has consequences for the legal decision.

One also finds considerable variation in the way judges interpret the scope of public order as they give different relative weight to each of two legitimate goals for the law, what we earlier called the meta-legal issues. One goal is to establish clear-cut legal norms based on broadly accepted cultural and social convictions. This goal can imply a total rejection of legal institutions that are validly used by parties in other parts of the world, for example polygamy. The other goal is to do justice for concrete individuals, whose relationships were created under those foreign legal institutions, recognizing that taking the first approach would be to deny them a just outcome.

Tacking between those two goals, different countries tend to go different ways. German courts tend to follow the second approach and to weigh the effects on the individuals concerned of accepting foreign law. The courts do not judge the acceptability of the foreign legal rules in general. They tend to accept those rules if the parties are of foreign nationality and to reject them if one of the parties is a German citizen. For German judges, accepting the result of foreign norms in a particular case for the sake of the individuals concerned does not mean in any way approving the laws in question.

By contrast, France and Britain tend to evaluate the acceptability of foreign legal institutions as such and to ban them from any kind of recognition if they are seen as contradicting French or British public moral order, sending a clear message to the public that these institutions are rejected under any circumstances by the law of the land. The price to be paid here is that individuals lose their vested rights merely by changing their residence.

The difference between the two positions can be illustrated by the examples of polygamous marriages and Islamic unilateral talaq. All Western European countries make it impossible to enter into a second, polygamous legal marriage within the territory of that country. They reject polygamy to the extent of declaring it punishable with various penalties if entered into within their jurisdiction by using the official form of marriage.[5] But they differ in their

[5] For example, a German federal administrative court approved a decision depriving a former Pakistani husband of a German wife from his German citizenship because he had concealed

treatment of polygamous families whose second or subsequent marriages were lawfully entered into outside of Europe.

German law, for example, differentiates between mainly private aspects of marriage and predominantly public ones, especially those relating to immigration law. A second marriage would not be recognized as the basis for applying for a privileged residence permit, for example (a public aspect). However, it would allow the second or third wife to receive the same social security benefits after her husband's death as would be due the first wife, provided that the marriages were legally recognized in the country where they were performed and that the payments are based on the husband's financial contributions during his lifetime (a private aspect). The reason – obviously based on equity considerations – is that it would not help all the wives beyond the first one to deprive them of their marital rights such as maintenance. Under these conditions, German second and subsequent wives may equally bring their claims of maintenance or inheritance successfully before the courts (Rohe 2011: 361).

By contrast, courts in England have rejected claims for a widow's pension from a widow who had lived in such a marriage, with the result that *none* of the wives received a payment. English courts prefer to clearly reject the institution of polygamy as such, whereas the German legislation and courts tend to protect the interests of the individual claimant (the second wife) who has relied on the continuous validity of her legal relations irrespective of the place of residence.

It is not easy to explain these differences in a broader perspective. British colonial rule accepted and even preserved Islamic legal institutions in the countries under British power. In contrast, Germany had few experience with such institutions in the past, except the relatively short rule over Zanzibar where polygamy was indeed legally permitted under German rule. A possible explanation could be drawn from the different origins of Muslims in the two countries. In Germany, most non-German Muslims (about 2 million) are of Turkish or Balkan origin, from states that have abolished polygamy several decades ago. Thus, polygamy cases in their traditional form are extremely rare, and thus the German decisions in favour of widows' claims do not have a very broad social impact. In contrast, the vast majority of British Muslims are still intensely linked to the Indian subcontinent (Pakistan and Bangladesh), where polygamy is still permissible and widespread. British courts likely are reluctant to allow polygamy on British soil because doing so would be widespread and the wrong message would be sent. The Law Commission (1971, p. 9 n. 23) had

an already existing marriage in Pakistan at the time of the (second) marriage performed in Germany.

stressed the need for regulating polygamy because of "immigration which has brought into permanent residence in this country large numbers of people from countries where polygamy is one of the normal forms of marriage." According to a parliamentary statement of July 19, 2012, it is official British government policy to prevent the formation of polygamous households in the country by various restrictive measures.

We see corresponding differences in the recognition of the unilateral divorce (talaq) pronounced by the husband according to Islamic family law, which in some countries only involves the action of the husband. (In others the approval of a judge is required.) Such divorce would not be valid if performed in any European state. Nevertheless, the question that arises is whether their effects should be recognized in Europe if they were performed in another country according to the laws of that country.

In Germany, a talaq that is valid under a foreign legal order may be accepted if the prerequisites for a divorce according to German law were fulfilled (Rohe 2011: 353) – for example, if the spouses had lived apart for more than a year and if the wife was adequately informed about the talaq. It also might be accepted if the wife herself asked for it to be recognized, for example, so she might remarry. A decision of the German local family court of Siegburg in an Iranian divorce case in November 2011 gained vast attention because of the fact that a mullah and a representative of the Iranian embassy were present in the courtroom to witness the husband's readiness to divorce. The court applied Iranian divorce law according to the relevant bilateral treaty between Iran and Germany. In addition, it enabled the Shiite informal witness procedure to help the wife in getting the divorce recognized in Iran. This recognition was important for her because she urgently wanted to visit her ill parents with her children and feared that the Iranian administration could refuse the recognition of the German decision if the husband's declaration were not witnessed according to Shiite divorce law. This case triggered considerable media interest, but most commentators understood that the court's procedure was aimed at supporting the wife's interests.

The tone of decisions often corresponds to the different ways of handling foreign talaq. The German courts typically state in a neutral tone that the norms regulating talaq are not in conformity with the German Constitution, but that German *ordre public* leads them to evaluate only what the concrete outcome of these norms would be. They then compare such outcome with the hypothetical result of the application of gender-neutral German laws and then decide whether the differences, if any, were tolerable given the international aspects of the case. Only a few courts in Germany have expressed a general refusal to accept talaq divorces irrespective of the concrete circumstances.

Usually, they claim an absence of a fair trial if the wife was not able to present her side of the matter. Among German legal scholars one finds a new tendency based on human rights approaches to reject gender-biased rules as such, whereas the majority still sticks to the more traditional concrete approach.

By contrast, Austrian judges generally follow the human rights approach. The Austrian Supreme Court has refused to accept any kind of talaq even in cases where the wife applied for or agreed to the recognition of the divorce, where there was thought to be an "inner connection" of the case to Austria because the parties were residents or citizens of Austria. This approach reflects the "message-giving" attitude of legal interpretation described earlier. Interestingly, the normative basis followed in Austria (art. 17 IPRG) is virtually identical to that applied in Germany (art. 6 EGBGB), clearly demonstrating the measure of pre-legal influences on the interpretation of given legal norms.

Throughout Europe, we find a clear and deep sentiment against Islamic norms in public debates, and these expressions certainly exercise psychological pressure on courts and scholars who are now constantly blamed for "accepting" or even "promoting" gender-biased rules within European legal orders. The aspect of granting security and stability for individuals in private matters irrespective of their residence, which counts among the basic principles of PIL, is by now mostly ignored. The abstract protection of human rights is then turned against the concrete "victims" of human rights violations even in cases where women want to claim their rights on the basis of polygamous marriages. If a foreign talaq is not recognized even if the divorced wife applies for it, she is forced into new divorce procedures, which are usually costly and time-consuming (it is difficult to start court procedures against a husband living in Islamic countries, perhaps even at an unknown place). French courts once argued in ways similar to the German line of reasoning, but have since shifted in tone and substance, as detailed in the next section.

French Frame Shifts

We now turn to a more detailed account of frame shifts in the French legal debates on recognizing Islamic marriage and divorce. In France (as elsewhere), marriage is not only a technical matter of registration and obligation but also a symbol of social and moral order. The divergence or convergence of rules for marriage can be taken as indicating a divergence or convergence of broader moral worlds. Thus, practices whereby Muslims marry in religious fashion but do not marry legally, which does not seem to differ essentially from the widespread practice of co-residence or concubinage, nonetheless has excited great passions and denunciations. Precisely for this reason, judicial decisions concerning marriage and divorces conducted in countries with Islamic legal institutions have taken a recent turn based on a shift in the meta-legal rules of thinking about *ordre public*.

References to *ordre public* are anchored in France's colonial history, and in particular in the critical role played by legal personal status in sorting out identities in the colonies, protectorates, and in French Algeria. In order to avoid essentializing racial or ethnic difference, and thereby to preserve the possibility of assimilating the colonized to civilized France, colonial officials, notably in Algeria, used the idea of local personal status to distinguish North Africans who remained governed by Muslim laws from those (few) who renounced that status for membership in the French legal domain. The clash between Islamic law and French law thereby came to encode (and in official discourse often substitute for) the clash between backward and evolved, or between less and more civilized peoples. The dividing lines could be crossed, and colonized subjects could become French nationals and, eventually, French citizens. But they did so by renouncing Islamic family law; for this reason, some Islamic authorities in Algeria declared that crossing this legal line was tantamount to leaving Islam entirely. Thus crossing the line between Islamic law and French civil law came to signify for French authorities and jurists the possibility of emancipation through legal change; maintaining that line came to signify for some Muslims the resistance to colonial domination by nonbelievers.

These legal distinctions, transformed in various ways by succeeding constitutions, associated personal status with degrees of civilization but separated it from the issue of legal domicile. French citizens living permanently in the colonies were governed by French law, and subjects who remained governed by the local legal regime retained that legal status even if they entered France. Stepping onto the soil of metropolitan France did not suddenly let them enjoy the benefits of French personal status law any more than it suddenly gave them full French citizenship rights. The bilateral treaties signed by France with each of the former North African possessions at independence prolonged those arrangements.

This historical background and the schemas about Muslims and France it created probably contribute to recent decisions taken by some French judges and jurists affirming that elements of Islamic marriage and divorce are contrary to French *ordre public* and thus justify setting aside the usual rules for resolving conflict of laws. These jurists argue that the institutions of unilateral repudiation (talaq), on the one hand, and polygamy, on the other, not only are prohibited in France but also violate the French (and European) commitment to the equality of women and men. They would disallow any legal effects produced in France by a talaq divorce or polygamous marriage carried out in another country, even when the marriage or divorce was legal and proper in that country.

Other jurists have pointed out that this position may be logical but that it creates practical problems. If a couple divorces in a country with Islamic tribunals, at which the husband pronounces the talaq, are they then to be considered still married in France? To say so would keep the wife from remarrying were she to reside in or settle in France. That hardly seems to be in the woman's interest. And if a husband married a second wife in a country permitting polygamy and in accord with its rules, and then were to bring her and their children to France, those children would be denied social welfare benefits because their presence could not be justified under rules of family reunification. Refusing to recognize a polygamous marriage thus would deny those children the rights enjoyed by other children of the same man, and could be held to deny the couple the "right to lead a normal family life," both of which are principles enforced by the European Court of Human Rights.

Through the mid-1980s, French court decisions affirmed the general principle of conflicts of laws jurisprudence, namely that if a couple of the same nationality marries, the effects that marriage might have in another country are governed by their own national law, and thus that a polygamous marriage enacted in a country permitting polygamy was valid in France. Moroccans marrying Moroccans, or Malians marrying Malians, in Morocco or Mali, could enter France. The wives and children of a man legally resident in France were thus allowed to join him under the rules governing family reunification and to receive residence permits. Thousands of women and children did so, coming mainly from Senegal, Mali, and Mauritius.

During the early Mitterrand years, the "right to a difference" reigned, and polygamous marriage practices were looked on as foreign customs to be respected, or at least to be tolerated. With the change in government (Mitterrand's "cohabitation" as president, with Jacques Chirac as prime minister), and especially during the second term of Charles Pasqua's service as interior minister (1993–1995), things shifted abruptly, on this as on all questions pertaining to immigration. A 1993 law forbade giving residence permits to second wives, but subsequent ministerial directives allowed such wives living in France prior to 1993 to renew their identity cards, and disallowed expulsions if the wives had French children and had resided in the country for ten years.

Judges might, and did for a time, engage in socially pragmatic reasoning. They could distinguish among the several elements of a proceeding and discover those that could be approved from the standpoint of French notions of *ordre public*. For example, judges have argued (in a manner similar to that discussed for Germany earlier) that the problem is "attenuated" if basic principles of fair treatment are observed: if the wife was present at the divorce hearing, presented her case, and received a reasonable compensation. During the last decade of the twentieth century, judges followed this line of reasoning. In decisions from 1999 and 2001, the Court of Cassation refused to declare the talaq intrinsically repugnant but looked to the degree to which the wife's interests were guaranteed by the divorce tribunal. Perhaps reflecting the gulf between theory and practice, the masters of doctrine – those jurists who write influential comments on decisions – rejected these decisions on grounds that the very institution of talaq was contrary to French and European principles of gender equality and thus of human rights. Influenced by these objections, in February 2004, the same chamber of the Court of Cassation reversed itself and pronounced unilateral repudiation intrinsically contrary to French *ordre public* and also to the European Convention on Human Rights.

In these cases, there are broad, cross-national differences in how judges and legislators interpret the demands of *ordre public*, but the German case shows us how different judges may weigh differently the various practical schemas, and the French case shows how these weightings may shift over time.

SCHEMAS OF CITIZENSHIP AND ISLAMIC VALUES

Here we consider two examples of schemas emerging from legal decisions that characterize Islam as containing doctrines or encouraging practices inimical to gender equality and women's rights. In this section the debates concern not specific institutions in foreign countries but properties of the religion itself. For judges and jurists the challenge becomes how to reframe a concern with Islam in terms that are neutral or secular, in order to avoid discriminating against Muslims.

Sharia and Wife-Beating

In a case brought before a Frankfurt court in 2007, a judge refused to grant legal aid to a wife of Moroccan origin who wanted to obtain an immediate divorce and who claimed that she had been severely beaten by her Moroccan husband. The judge said that, according to the Qur'ān (Sūrah 4: 34), beating wives was common in the culture of origin of the parties and therefore did not justify finding that the wife was in a state of hardship. This decision ignored both Moroccan law, which does not permit domestic violence (see art. 98 sect. 2, 99 of the Family law code 2004), and the German law of conflicts, which would refuse the application of any foreign provision that allowed domestic violence on grounds of *ordre public*.

The decision was nonetheless revelatory of a tendency to see in Islamic scripture simple blueprints for Muslims' actions. In the case of the verse in question, Muslim scholars disagree over how to interpret it today. Some say that, yes, the husband can, as a last resort, physically correct his wife (although few, if any, would countenance beating). Others would point to the fact that the Prophet Muhammad never did so and that the verse was an attempt to curtail a widespread practice of the time and thus is no longer relevant, akin to verses on slavery. Some say that the verbal root *daraba* should be interpreted as "to separate" (read: divorce) instead of "to beat." Others are ready to historicize it, declaring it to be invalid in present times.[6] The German decision, which was reversed shortly after it was made public, caused a heated debate in Germany about the "Islamization" of the German judiciary. Some anti-Muslim fanatics confused this decision with the legitimate exercise of religious rights according to European and German constitutional provisions granting freedom of religion, obviously ignoring the very constitutional order they pretend to defend. Thereafter, when Muslims have successfully claimed their rights to build mosques or to establish Islamic instruction in public schools according to the German legal order, or to perform their religious rites according to their personal convictions in situations where there were no important obstacles to doing so, their success has been attributed to a judicial "Islamization strategy." The Deutsche Islam Konferenz (German Islamic Conference) established by the federal ministry of the interior in 2006, has been accused of contributing to this Islamization of Germany. The critics range from right-wing parties and fundamentalist Christians, to feminist ideologists and ex-Muslim converts, to extreme secularists (Bahners 2011). Lawyers are accused of facilitating this process, and court presidents now often receive hate mail when they issue decisions in favor of Muslims.

This sort of attack on law benefits from attitudes in favor of restricting the rights of minorities. A majority of the population in Germany (58 percent in total; 75 percent in Eastern Germany where only few Muslims are living) condones the idea of considerably restricting the rights of Muslims in the country (Decker et al 2010: 134). The Swiss ban on minarets following a plebiscite held in 2009, which many believe violates article 9 of the European Convention of Human Rights, is but one example of this trend, and it was followed by the French president expressing his own rejection of minarets on French soil (De Royer 2011; Jaxel-Truer 2011).

[6] See the analyses in Idriz (2010: 148–152) and Zentrum für Islamische Frauenforschung und Frauenförderung (2005).

The German "wife-beating decision" has contributed to a broad shift across Europe in how people frame the issues regarding Muslims and Islam. In Germany, since the 1990s, the debate on "problems arising from migration" has shifted to a focus on "problems arising from Islam." Cases of domestic violence and honor crime increasingly are attributed to the Muslim religious orientation of the persons involved. The frame of "problems arising from Islam" is promoted even when religious values have nothing to do with the phenomenon in question, as when in 2010 newspapers reported on the "first Muslim rocker gang" in Bremen.[7] While the members had a Muslim background, their criminal interests and activities seemed to have little to do with practicing their religion.

In the German wife-beating case, law was confused with religion in a way that portrayed Islam as having an essential, and misogynist, meaning. One finds related schemas regarding Islam and democracy employed at the European level, notably in the 2003 judgment by the European Court of Human Rights regarding the Refah Party. In 1998, the Turkish Constitutional Court had dissolved the Refah Party as a "center of activities contrary to the principle of secularism" and banned six of its leaders from political party activities for five years. The party appealed, but the ECHR ruled that:

> [T]he Court considers that sharia, which faithfully reflects the dogmas and divine rules laid down by religion, is stable and invariable. Principles such as pluralism in the political sphere or the constant evolution of public freedoms have no place in it. … It is difficult to declare one's respect for democracy and human rights while at the same time supporting a regime based on sharia, which clearly diverges from Convention values, particularly with regard to its criminal law and criminal procedure, its rules on the legal status of women and the way it intervenes in all spheres of private and public life in accordance with religious precepts. (Refah Partisi, §123)[8]

Contrasting sharia with human rights in an abstract fashion ignores the importance of determining how different actors interpret the Islamic texts and traditions (Rohe, 2012) and specifying which area of life is in question: religious issues, for example, clearly fall under the freedom-of-religion clauses of human rights conventions and charters. But essentializing Muslims and

7 Cf. the report on the activities of a "Muslim migrant clan" from October 19, 2010 at http://www.spiegel.de/panorama/justiz/0,1518,731181,00.html (accessed May 4, 2011). Many members of this clan are indeed famous for engaging into various criminal activities, but never attributed their actions to Muslim faith.

8 [2]*Refah Partisi (The Welfare Party) and Others v. Turkey*, Judgment, Strasbourg, February 13, 2003 (includes a concurring opinion of Judges Ress and Rozakis [pp. 46–47] and a concurring opinion by Judge Kovler [p. 48]).

their religion is not the privilege of poorly informed courts. Experience shows that Muslim parties can actively play the religious or cultural card from time to time. In an English postmarital maintenance case decided by the Court of Appeal (*Al-Saffar v. Al-Saffar* [2012] EWCA Civ 1103), the Muslim husband claimed that such maintenance payments were "illegitimate and illegal according to Islamic culture" as far as they exceed the short period of three months according to traditional Islamic law. It was not only the court that did not accept that as a valid argument against the divorced wife's claim. The British Association of Muslim lawyers declared the former husband's allegations simply to be wrong. In a German case decided by the Federal Supreme Court (BGH NJW 1999, 135) concerning a Muslim couple of Turkish origin, the wife had given a financial guarantee in favor of her husband. When the guarantee was claimed, her lawyer tried to convince the court that the guarantee contract was void for being concluded under force, because as a "wife living in a typical Muslim marriage" she were not able to decide freely on such issues. This attempt to use widespread prejudice failed, because the court made clear that they cannot presume that a Muslim wife's rights are suppressed unless it is presented with concrete information about her *individual* situation. These two cases remind us that individuals may invoke religious or cultural normative arguments for very worldly financial purposes.

Face Veils and Women's Equality

We can also track changes in dominant justifications given for laws. Here we turn to a series of decisions regarding the hijab, coverings prescribed by Islam to be worn by women over their head or face. In March 2004, the French parliament passed a law prohibiting public school students from wearing "ostentatious" religious signs. Although the major arguments made for the law in public debates and political speeches centered on opposing political Islam and its subjugation of women, the public legal justifications given for the law after its passage emphasized its protective function. According to these justifications, the law had nothing to do with the meaning of the head scarf, or indeed with those girls who chose freely to wear the scarves. It was entirely motivated by the need to protect those girls who preferred not to wear the scarf from social pressures to do so.[9]

A new and more convoluted set of legal justifications accompanied a second legal step. In June 2008, the French State Council (Conseil d'État) refused

[9] On the debates surrounding the law, see Bowen (2007); the major writings explaining the law after its passage come from Patrick Weil (2009).

to grant French nationality to a woman from Morocco on grounds that her religious practices had led her to hold values that ran counter to the equality of men and women and that caused her to suffer from insufficient assimilation to become a French citizen: she had a *défaut d'assimilation*. The woman had married a French convert to Islam who had requested that she wear a full face covering (known as a *niqab* but generally, as here, mislabeled in France as a *burqa*). She was reported to stay at home and to have insufficient knowledge of the right to vote and of the basics of *laïcité*. She had met the formal conditions for citizenship, having waited the required period of time after marriage before requesting naturalization. The couple had three children born in France, a situation that normally strengthens a case for naturalization.

The State Council was careful to make women's equality the major grounds for rejecting her request for citizenship. Just as in the debate over the head scarf, the Council tried as much as possible to not make religion the issue, for clear constitutional reasons. But the jurists commenting on the decision pointed out that at issue was, as one put it, "the wearing of the burqa and the behavior to which it leads" (Chrestia 2008). Although the most visible organs of state policy tried to avoid stating so directly, the practical schema invoked by the decision was that certain kinds of head scarves implied a rejection of French sociability. Indeed, a 2000 interministerial circular (Circ. DPM no. 2000–254, 12 mai 2000) instructs immigration agents to indicate whether someone applying for naturalization wears the "traditional head scarf in use notably in the North African countries and Turkey," or the "hijab that covers the head and neck and that, as with the chador, is a sign of belonging to fundamentalist Islam. In these last cases one should tell the applicants what wearing these vestimentary signs means."

This decision had quick results, and these testify to the readiness with which French public figures could accept and adopt this schema about the meaning of different kinds of head covering. In July (one month after the State Council's judgment), a housing authority in Vénissieux, a suburb of Lyon with a large Muslim population, refused to allow a family to occupy the apartment officially allotted to them, because the wife wore a "burqa." The letter of refusal repeated the words of the State Council's decision: "Madame wears the burqa, which characterizes a radical practice of religion incompatible with the essential values of the French community and the principle of the equality of the sexes."[10] Then the Halde (*La Haute Autorité de lutte contre*

[10] *Le Monde*, August 4, 2009: "Madame revêt la burka, ce qui caractérise une pratique radicale de la religion incompatible avec les valeurs essentielles de la communauté française et le principe de l'égalité des sexes."

les discriminations et pour l'égalité 2008), France's public watchdog group on discrimination, ruled in October 2008 concerning an administrative decision that denied a woman wearing a burqa access to the French-language classes that were required for her to remain in France. The Halde ruled that the exclusion was not discriminatory in that "the burqa carries a meaning of the woman's submission who goes beyond its religious significance and could be considered to attack the Republican values that govern these teachings." Other than La Halde's use of the conditional, the ruling follows the State Council's phrasing precisely.

In 2010, the French government entered a third phase, one of outright condemnation of the practice of wearing the full face veil. In October, parliament passed a law forbidding anyone "in public space, [to] wear clothing meant to cover his/her face."[11] Public space was given a broad definition, including any space open to general use or controlled by public service. Before its passage, the State Council had rendered its own judgment on such a law, finding it disproportionate to any possible problem and thus in violation of article 9 of the European Convention on Human Rights (Conseil d'État 2010). Parliament passed the law nonetheless, but prior to the law's promulgation asked the Constitutional Council (Conseil Constitutionnel) to decide whether the law conformed to the Constitution. The Constitutional Council affirmed the law's constitutionality. In their judgment they underscored two justifications for the law (aside from a brief reference to public safety): first, that such practices "misrecognize the minimal requirements of living in society," and that those women who decide to wear a face veil are simply unaware that they "find themselves placed in a situation of exclusion and inferiority clearly incompatible with the constitutional principles of freedom and equality."[12]

Why did these two judicial bodies, the State Council and the Constitutional Council, give opposed answers to the same question? The answer lies in the very different compositions and tasks of the two Councils and reminds us that in studying law we are studying specific institutions, each with its own habits of working and of evaluating that work.

The State Council dates from 1799, but it had existed in a slightly different form since the time of Louis XIV. It acts as a review body for actions arising in public institutions such as schools or immigration offices. The State Council decides whether actions taken by such institutions conform to the law, including international commitments and the French constitution. Its writ is grander than this single role implies, however, for the State Council also issues reports

[11] Law 2010–1192 of 11 October 2010.

[12] Conseil Constitutionnel, Décision no, 2010–613 DC, par. 4.

on various matters and is routinely asked to inform parliament of the state of the law on questions of the day. State councilors also act as multipurpose agenda setters for a wide array of commissions and legal institutions, and they move back and forth between the Council and other organs of government and the private sector (Latour 2010: 107–126). In addition, as of 2010, the State Council can be asked to render an opinion on the constitutionality of a proposed law or to forward a request to decide constitutionality to the Constitutional Council. These two institutions thereby now overlap in their roles of judging the constitutionality of a law, as in the case at hand.

Now, since the first "head scarf affair" emerged in 1989 (and until the 2004 law banning head scarves), the State Council had maintained a consistent policy of upholding the rights of Muslim schoolgirls to wear head scarves, providing the girls did not disturb school routine. In the face of shifting political winds on the subject, they followed a single line of reasoning (Bowen 2007). The training of councilors makes them highly professionalized, marked by the shared passage of most of them through the elite National Administration School (École Nationale d'Administration, ENA) (Latour 2010: 112–113). The institution's practices and rewards are focused on maintaining a continuous line of jurisprudence, to the point of seeming to one observer as cut off from the outside world, relatively indifferent to external events or opinions (Latour 2010: 250–255).

By contrast, the Constitutional Council is a relatively recent institution, created by the 1958 Constitution. The men and women who sit on the Constitutional Council are not necessarily trained in the law. Former presidents may sit on it along with individuals from other, varying backgrounds. The body considers requests to issue a decision on the constitutionality of a law being considered in either chamber of parliament. Since 2010, it may also respond to demands brought by ordinary citizens to judge the constitutionality of a law already passed (on "priority questions of constitutionality"). Historically, however, the Constitutional Council has given an opinion concerning the constitutionality of a proposed law to the legislator at the legislator's request, a role that reflects French (and generally civil-law) theory that legislators pass laws and courts enforce them (Eolas 2010). As Alec Stone (1992: 4) put it, "French judicial politics are legislative politics by any other name," as Counselors intervene on behalf of one or another political element. For a long time the Council was seen as a weapon to protect the presidency against parliament (Stone 1992). The body still is generally seen as supporting presidential preferences. At the moment that the State Council said that the burqa ban would violate religious freedom, President Sarkozy was on record as opposing such a broad ban, but by the time the question was posed to the

Constitutional Council, he had changed his mind and supported the law, as did leaders of the major political parties. The Constitutional Council clearly found itself politically obliged to support the measure.

The precise challenge the Constitutional Council faced was how to justify their decision in a way that would allow the law to be promulgated but would not set a precedent that would be at odds with most readings of the Constitution and the European Convention on Human Rights.[13] They had to find a justification for restricting actions of religious self-expression. However, the European Court of Human Rights (ECHR) (2010) had recently ruled that simply appearing in public in a certain set of clothes could *not* be considered a menace to *ordre public* or a threat to anyone. Therefore, the Council could not base its ruling on usual conceptions of *ordre public*, which have to do with the interests of citizens taken as a whole. These interests can take on a nonmaterial form, such as moral order and the respect for human dignity. In France, *ordre public* really concerns "public moral order," with its Durkheimian sense that the law protects socially embedded moral conceptions (Bénabent 1996). But the State Council had just ruled that public moral order could not be used to ban burqas because these items of clothing did not present an "immoral" character in any sense of the term (Conseil d'État 2010: 25). What was the Constitutional Council to do?

Blocked by the ECHR and the State Council from invoking established notions of *ordre public*, the Constitutional Council decided to create a new judicial instrument but to conceal the fact of that invention so as to be able to claim to act in line with established laws and rulings. The instrument in question was in fact a new notion of *ordre public*. In the quasi-official review of administrative law, the AJDA (*Revue d'actualité juridique du droit administrative*), the commentator on the Constitutional Council decision focused on the half-visible steps taken by the Council (Verpeaux 2010). In his analysis, the Council needed to create a new juridical base to approve the law, which otherwise (without that new base) would have been found to infringe disproportionally on religious freedom (the previous finding of the State Council). The State Council had offered a loophole, if only to quickly close it – and the Constitutional Council appears to have tried to stealthily reopen it. The State Council (Conseil d'État 2010: 26) had said that one could conceive of *ordre public* as the basic elements of reciprocity needed to live together in

[13] See Stone (1992) for the overall history of decisions when the Council did oppose the government; these decisions were not in the face of such broad public support. I (JRB) also rely on conversations with two former members of the Constitutional Council, who wished to remain anonymous.

society – but then it emphasized that this view could not be found in judicial texts or in judges' writings, or in the jurisprudence of neighboring countries, and was thus a risky path to explore. This "risky path" was, however, precisely what the Constitutional Council followed by stating that burqa-wearing practices "misrecognize the minimal requirements of living in society." Public moral order was implicitly extended to include the conditions for social life, conditions violated when burqa wearers close themselves off from everyday social interaction.

If weak on jurisprudential grounds, the Council's claim echoes long-standing claims about ways in which Muslim "communalism" has hindered full civic participation. Following this particularly French political idea, normal citizens are presumed to be civil; they interact in the "shared life" of civic France. Sociologist Dominique Schnapper had just stepped down as a member of the Constitutional Council when she accounted for the burqa ban in July 2010: "France is the country where everyone says 'bonjour'."[14] One cannot really greet another from behind a veil. Here we have essentially the same claim about communication made by British minister, Jack Straw, a few years earlier. But where Straw made it on personal grounds – he would not speak with someone whose face was covered – Schnapper made it on grounds of a theory of civic life (and see Schnapper 1998).

The contrast between the "message-sending" approach and its consequentialist alternative appears when we consider the contrasting German case. Over the course of 2010–2011, Germans debated whether their country also should ban full face veils, and the population would have strongly backed such a measure: polls taken in April 2011 indicate that nearly two-thirds of the population supported a ban. Nevertheless, the political parties represented in the federal parliament as well as high-ranking officials and politicians from all democratic political camps including the president and the chancellor were unanimous in rejecting additional legislation on the topic. The main reason was simply the fact that very few women ever appeared in public wearing a full face covering.[15]

Deep-rooted differences in French and German attitudes toward state and religions also underpin these contrasts in judicial reasoning. During much of modern French history, the Catholic Church was treated as the enemy of the

[14] Personal communication to JRB, July 9, 2010. As a strong signal of such ideas, in 2010, a female French lawyer felt so offended by a young Muslim woman who wore a niqab in a shop that she ripped it off her (Allen 2010).

[15] From a legal point of view, there is a similarly broad common conviction that the existing laws on public security and regarding public officers, among others, are sufficient to tackle the issue. Given the fact that a burka or niqab severely obstruct the usual forms of communication, they can already be banned in situations where open communication is not only desirable but simply necessary, as in public offices for those in contact with the public, in schools or universities.

state, and the law of 1905 on church-state separation was intended to provide a relatively moderate way of restricting the power of the Church. In contrast, the German Nazi experience showed that the state itself can turn into an instrument of the grossest injustice. Religion and beliefs are perceived to have the potential of stabilizing society and guaranteeing human rights. Germans also see France as having a weaker tradition of the coexistence of religions on equal terms, with the exception of Protestantism during the relatively short period of toleration, whereas after centuries of bloodshed, Germany reached a system of mutual recognition of different Christian religions with the 1648 Westphalia peace treaty. In Germany, confessional religious belief is taught in public schools and, more to the current point, Islamic theological studies and chairs are currently established in a number of universities.

CONCLUSIONS

Law may be unusual as an institution in that it both designates particularly strongly constrained institutions – legal argument, courtroom procedure – and a particularly powerful set of justifications for public policy – the law of the land. This power of the law helps explain the coexistence of two meta-legal frames we have encountered time and again in the preceding analysis. As with more specific schemas, judges consider both the idea of law as sending a message and that of law as solving concrete problems to be quite legitimate views, but weigh them differently across particular courts, across countries, and as a function of shifting political and social environments. We thus find iterative relationships between judicial reasoning and culturally dominant schemas.[16] In cases regarding citizenship, dress, and marriage mentioned throughout

Besides that, they have to be removed for control or security reasons, for example, at airports. There was only one concrete case to be solved in Germany, when in the city of Frankfurt a Muslim woman employee of the municipality intended to wear the niqab when returning to her job after a "baby pause." There was a storm of indignation in the media, and the state government issued an administrative circular on the ban of niqabs for public officers, and shortly after that the woman agreed to terminate her contract. This merely restated the law and was intended to calm down the broad anger about the woman articulated in the public debate in Frankfurt. If legislation would ban the burka or the niqab beyond such situations, it is broadly feared that such legislation would violate the freedom of religion granted by article 4 of the German constitution and article 9 of the European Convention on Human Rights because of its lack of proportionality.

[16] In this sense we find that Bruno Latour's (2010) analysis of the State Council as relatively closed-off in its reasoning – although not in the circulation of its members (a paradox he underscores) – to be insufficient for generalizing about law in general, as he does (see especially 2012: 244–277). The interactions between political positions, cultural schemas, and judicial decisions described here, even for France, suggest a more polycentric world of law-politics-culture.

this chapter, legal readings using standard judicial frames were followed by cultural framings in which Islam was at issue as a set of values, which were in turn followed by new legal readings that took these cultural schemas into account.

Analyzing courts as institutions, in which judges and jurists pursue lines of legal reasoning and strive for coherence, all the while offering judgments that take into account politics, values, religion, and broader cultural traditions, is not reductive of law (*pace* Latour 2010). It recognizes that, as with all institutions, courts exist in a broader environment that includes other courts, legal commentators, politicians, and of course social life as judges see it. Nor is it formalistic, although we emphasize how despite differences in legal forms and traditions, judges in Germany, France, and other countries of Europe work from a similar set of schemas, including elements of *ordre public*, private autonomy, and the importance of safeguarding personal status. We also, however, include in our set of schemas used by judges broader ideas, more likely to diverge across countries, about (for example) the role of religion in public life. In making decisions concerning Islam and Muslims, they may reweight these elements to decide one way or the other.

Analyzing judicial institutions does not foreclose critiquing legal reasoning. We found particularly problematic, in France and Germany, judicial efforts to determine what Islam has to say in general on an issue: what "the meaning" of head scarves is, or what the Qur'an says about women and men (see also Bowen 2011). These schemas, which have become increasingly dominant in public life in Europe, sidestep both Muslims' own scholarly traditions and the main lines of Western European jurisprudence. The latter point is worth emphasizing, as when French courts shift from an emphasis on religious freedom and the consequences of recognizing religious practices (such as Islamic marriage and divorce) to a presumption that Islamic institutions are ipso facto arrayed against women. When the private lives of families are concerned, the well-anchored traditions of international private law that look to the practical outcomes of decisions are worth supporting. However, doing so involves appreciating that both judges in European civil courts and judges on Islamic tribunals work from rich traditions of jurisprudence, which contain resources supportive of gender equality and of assuring equity.

BIBLIOGRAPHY

Alaux, Jean-Pierre. 2001. "À la rue sous prétexte de polygamie," *Plein Droit* N. 51.
Allen, Peter. 2010. "France has first 'burka rage' incident," *The Telegraph*, May 10, at http://www.telegraph.co.uk/news/worldnews/europe/france/7735607/France-has-first-burka-rage- incident.html

The Association of Muslim Lawyers (UK). 2012. "AML backs court of appeal decision that Islamic tradition is no defence against divorce ruling," press release, June 30, at http://www.aml.org.uk/cms/news?id=18
Bahners, Patrick. 2011. *Die Panikmacher. Die deutsche Angst vor dem Islam*. München: C. H. Beck
Baum, Lawrence. 2006. *Judges and Their Audiences*. Princeton: Princeton University Press.
Begdache, Roula el-Husseini. 2002. *Le Droit international privé français et la repudiation Islamique*. Paris: L.G.D.J.
Bénabent, Alain. 1996. "L'Ordre public en droit de la famille," in Thierry Revet, ed., *L'Ordre public à la fin du XXème siècle*. Paris: Dalloz.
Bernard-Maugiron, Nathalie and Baudouin Dupret, eds. 2012. *Ordre public et droit musulman de la famille en Europe et Afrique du Nord*. Brussels: Éditions Bruylant.
Bowen, John R. 2007. *Why the French Don't Like Headscarves: Islam, the State, and Public Space*. Princeton: Princeton University Press.
——2011. "How the French State Justifies Controlling Muslim Bodies: From Harm-Based to Values-Based Reasoning." *Social Research* 78(2): 1–24.
Braman, Eileen. 2009. *Law, Politics and Perception: How Policy Preferences Influence Legal Reasoning*. Charlottesville: University of Virginia Press.
Brenner, Emmanuel, ed. 2002. *Les Territoires Perdus de la République*. Paris: Mille et Une Nuits.
Chrestia, Phillipe. 2008. Le burqa est incompatible avec la nationalité française. *Actualité Juridique Droit Administratif*: 2013.
Conseil d'État. 2010. Étude relative aux possibilités juridiques d'interdiction du port du voile intégral, March 25, at http://www.conseil-etat.fr/fr/rapports-et-etudes/possibilites-juridiques-d-interdiction-du-port-du-voile-integral.html, accessed May 20, 2013.
De Royer, Solenn. 2011. Sarkozy veut un débat sur le multiculturalisme. *Le Figaro*, February 14, at http://www.lefigaro.fr/politique/2011/02/14/01002–20110214ART-FIG00718-sarkozy-veut-un-debat-sur-le-multiculturalisme.php
Decker, Oliver, Marliese Weißmann, Johanna Kiess, Elmar Brähler,. 2010. Die Mitte in der Krise. *Rechtsextreme Einstellungen in Deutschland*, at http://library.fes.de/pdf-files/do/07504.pdf
Eolas. 2008. Faut-il être française pour porter la burqa? *Journal d'un avocat*, July 11, at http://www.maitre-eolas.fr/post/2008/07/11/1030-faut-il-etre-francaise-pour-porter-la-burqa
——2010. "Bienvenue à la Question Prioritaire de Constitutionalité." Journal d'unavocat, March 2, at: <http://www.maitre-eolas.fr/post/2010/03/02/Bienvenue-%C3%A0-la-Question-Prioritaire-de-Constitutionnalit%C3%A9>, accessed May 20, 2013.
European Court of Human Rights. 2010. Ahmet Arslan and Others v. Turkey. No. 41135/98, February 23, at: http://cmiskp.echr.coe.int/tkp197/view.asp?item=1&portal=hbkm&action=html&highlight=Ahmet%20%7C%20Arslan&sessionid=47760027&skin=hudoc-en, Accessed May 20, 2013.
Fulchiron, Hugues. 2006. "'Ne répudiez point ...': Pour une interpretation raisonée des arrêts du 17 février 2004." *Revue internationale de droit compare* 1: 7–26.
——2008. De la virginité dans le mariage. *Le Blog Dalloz (dalloz.fr)*, June 2.

La Haute Autorité de lutte contre les discriminations et pour l'égalité. 2008. Déliberation No. 2008–193 du 15 septembre 2008, at http://www.halde.fr/IMG/pdf/4085.pdf
House of Commons Library. 2012. Standard Note SN/HA/5015 Polygamy (Catherine Fairbairn), at http://www.parliament.uk/briefing-papers/SN05051
Idriz, Benjamin. 2010. *Grüß Gott Herr Imam*, Munich: Diederichs.
Jaxel-Truer, Pierre. 2011. "Après l'identité nationale, le chef de l'État lance le débat sur la place de l'Islam." *Le Monde*, February 17.
Kreisstadt Siegburg. 2011. Scheidung mit Mullah. Report from November 16, at http://www.siegburg.de/stadt/aktuell/lokales/nachrichten/scheidung-mit-mullah/index.html
Lahouri, Besma. 2004. "Polygamie: Cet interdit qui a le droit de cité," *L'Express*, January 15.
Latour, Bruno. 2010. *The Making of Law: An Ethnography of the Conseil d'État.* (Originally in French 2002). Cambridge: Polity Press.
The Law Commission (Law Com. No. 42). 1971. Family Law Report on Polygamous Marriages, London, at http://www.official-documents.gov.uk/document/hc7071/hc02/0227/0227.pdf
Le Bars, Stéphanie. 2009. "Vivre en France avec le niqab." *Le Monde*, June 23.
Libchaber, Rémy. 1996. "L'Exception d'ordre public en droit international privé," in Thierry Revet, ed., *L'Ordre public à la fin du XXème siècle* (pp. 65 – 81). Paris: Dalloz.
Meyer, John W., and Brian Rowan, 1977. "Institutionalized organizations: Formal structure as Myth and ceremony," *American Journal of Sociology*, **83**:340–63.
Monéger, Françoise. 2005. *Droit international privé*, 3rd ed. Paris: LexisNexis.
Pearl, David and Werner F. Menski. 1998. *Muslim Family Law*. 3rd ed. London: Sweet & Maxwell.
Rohe, Mathias. 1994. "Staatsangehörigkeit oder Lebensmittelpunkt? Anknüpfungsgerechtigkeit im Lichte neuerer Entwicklungen," in Christoph Engel/Helmut Weber (eds.), *Festschrift für Dietrich Rothoeft* (pp. 1–39). München: Jehle-Rehm.
——2003. "Islamic Law in German Courts," *Hawwa* **1**(1): 46–59.
——2007. *Muslim Minorities and the Law in Europe. Chances and Challenges*. New Delhi: Global Media Publications.
——2011. *Das islamische Recht. Geschichte und Gegenwart*, 3rd ed. München: C.H. Beck.
——2012. "On the Foundations of Human Rights. Religious and Secular Approaches in the West and in Islam," in J.A. van der Ven/C. Sterkens/J. van de Vyver/H.-G. Ziebertz (eds.), *Empirical Research in Religion and Human Rights* (pp. 67–93). Leiden/Boston: Brill.
Schnapper, Dominique. 1998. *Community of Citizens: On the Modern Idea of Nationality*. (Originally in French 1994). Sévérine Rosée, trans. New Brunswick: Transaction Publishers.
Stone, Alex. 1992. The Birth of Judicial Politics in France: The Constitutional Council in Comparative Perspective. New York: Oxford University Press.
Tichomirowa, Katja. 2011. "Keine Chance für die beamtinnen-Burka," *Frankfurter Rundschau*, February 4, at http://www.fr-online.de/politik/integrationsdebatte-keine-chance-fuer-die-beamtinnen-burka,1472596,7152736.html

Vallar, Christian. 2009. Le radicalisme religieux et le refus fondé d'acquisition de la nationalité. *Recueil Dalloz*: 345.

Verpeaux, Michel. 2010. "Dissimulation du visage, la délicate conciliation entre la liberté et un nouvel ordre public." *Actualité Jurisprudentielle Droit Administratif* 42 (December): 2373–2377.

Zentrum für Islamische Frauenforschung und Frauenförderung (ed.). 2005. *Ein einziges Wort und seine grosse Wirkung. Eine hermeneutische Betrachtungsweise zum Qur'an, Sure 4 Vers 34, mit Blick auf das Geschlechterverhältnis im Islam*, Köln.

7 Legitimizing Host Country Institutions

A Comparative Analysis of the Content of Civic Education Courses in France and Germany

Ines Michalowski

INTRODUCTION AND THEORETICAL FRAMEWORK

Since 9/11, Muslims have moved into the center of political and public debates about immigration and the integration of immigrants in Western Europe. European states have responded to these debates through generic antiviolence policies, repressing religious violence and integrating religious minorities through enabling and compelling integration strategies (Bleich 2009: 361–362). One example of such compelling integration strategies "calling for immigrants to … adopt 'European values'" (Bleich 2009: 372) are the different forms of integration measures and requirements addressed to (family) migrants that have proliferated in Western Europe over the past decade. Several authors have suggested that these integration measures target Muslims in a particular way (Ersbøll, Kostakopoulou, and Van Oers 2010; Orgad 2010). The present work is designed to contribute to this debate by analyzing whether Muslims are a special target group of integration measures and how citizenship is framed for immigrants in different national contexts.

What has come to be known as civic integration measures often has two components: host country language acquisition and civic education. Many scholarly debates have been lead about how to interpret these civic integration measures (e.g., Bauböck and Joppke 2010; Carrera 2006; de Hart and van Oers 2006; Entzinger 2003; Ersbøll, Kostakopoulou, and Van Oers 2010; Fermin 2001; Groenendijk 2006; Joppke 2007; Michalowski 2004, 2009; Wallace Goodman 2010). In particular, there is dissent about the goals these measures pursue: Are they set up by governments to make citizenship more meaningful and accessible for immigrants, or do they seek cultural assimilation? Do they pursue neoliberal goals by fostering immigrants' host-country-relevant human capital, or are they second-order instruments of immigration control aimed at selecting the most willing and able to integrate? One answer to these questions probably is that these interpretations apply to a different degree to different forms of civic integration measures. For example, whereas civic integration measures in the immigrants' countries of origin have a strong tie to immigration control policies, this tie is less relevant for the granting of a permanent residence permit because immigrants who fail civic integration tests and measures (and are thus refused a permanent residence permit) nonetheless have the right to remain in the country on a short-term residence permit.

The remainder of this paper looks at integration requirements for permanent residence and therefore largely disregards the immigration control dimension. Instead, civic integration courses and tests are analyzed as measures that seek to teach new immigrants how to be or become good citizens.

As such, integration measures and requirements are an instrument aimed at increasing the legitimacy of existing norms and an existing social order, among newly arrived immigrants. Or, to phrase it differently, they are meant to support the socialization of immigrants to existing host country institutions by increasing their acceptance of these institutions (on the safeguarding of institutions, see Esser 2000: 40). This seems to be particularly true for civic education courses that teach immigrants about their new host society, its history, political system, social life, and other institutions. Civic education courses are trying to promote an institutional order. This institutional order gains its normative power from the prestige of serving as a model for thinking, feeling, and acting in a given situation. It is believed to be right and just (Esser 2000: 98). Given that the courses are meant to increase the acceptance of host country institutions among newly arrived immigrants, one might expect them to present these institutions in the most favorable and ideal way. Because they are meant to promote the values of liberal democracies, these courses should also in themselves be role models of these liberal democratic principles and, for example, refrain from targeting one particular religious group. At the same time, these courses are also expected to respond to other prerogatives that might be deemed less liberal. For one, the courses might try to cater to immigrants' practical needs for information about cultural differences. If so, the courses have to make assumption about how (certain groups of) immigrants differ from the host society and what their special "deficits" of information are. Another important goal of these courses is to foster the knowledge about and acceptance of host country institutions among newly arrived immigrants. From this perspective, immigrants are seen as a potential threat to host country institutions because their previous socialization to home country institutions that – in particular in the case of Muslim countries – are deemed to diverge considerably from host country institutions is expected to lead to insufficient support for host country institutions, thereby jeopardizing the latter's existence.

Thus civic education courses are torn between different prerogatives that either favor a specific targeting of particular immigrant groups or the most general approach to immigrants as individuals whose potential ethnic or religious group affiliation is ignored by the state. This set of constraints makes up part of these courses as "institutions" to the extent that those devising them are aware of the dilemmas sketched out earlier.

In fact, teaching a country's institutions is not an easy task because one central characteristic of institutions is that they are the result of many unwritten and implicit expectations about how things should be done in society (Esser 2000: 11–12). Thus, when civic education courses try to teach immigrants about different forms of institutions that form the host society, they may have to render explicit some of the usually internalized norms that characterize institutions. This is why integration measures have been criticized for aiming at cultural assimilation (Bader 2007: 56; Entzinger 2005; Orgad 2010; Scholten 2008: 203–249; Vasta 2007), even though it has also been debated under what conditions the explicit discussion of norms and values may be acceptable for liberal democracies (Bauböck and Joppke 2010). Despite these debates and diverging opinions, there is a broad consensus that the specific targeting of Muslim immigrants is in breach with liberal principles because it amounts to the direct discrimination of a specific religious group. It is one aim of the present contribution to discuss whether Muslims are specifically targeted by civic education courses for newly arrived immigrants, and if so, what schemas are used to frame the questions of citizenship, identity, of common belonging, and of inclusion and exclusion.

The general expectation might be that liberal democracies refrain from such a targeting because they value and protect their own liberal principles of equal treatment. However, the current focus of public debates on the integration of Muslims into Western societies suggests that a certain number of these integration requirements have been designed with Muslim immigrants as the most important target group in mind. In fact, the introduction of certain integration measures and requirements has been legitimized by referring to illiberal cultural practices such as forced marriages that public and political debates have associated with Muslims (Ratia and Walter 2009). Still, it is difficult to prove that integration requirements specifically target Muslim immigrants.

One of the few exceptions where this relationship is perfectly clear is the infamous interview guideline for citizenship introduced in the German state of Baden-Wurttemberg in January 2006. In its original version, this

TABLE 7.1: *Thematic summary of 2006 Baden-Wurttemberg-guidelines for citizenship interviews*

Themes	Schemas	# of questions
Gender equality institutionalized by law, relationship between men and women, gender equality in the professional world	Gender equality	3
Opinions about homosexuality, medical treatment by doctor of opposite sex	Sexuality, homosexuality	3
Polygamy, control, and self-autonomy of children (especially girls) with regard to partner choice, profession, dress	Marriage, family, and individual liberty	7
Participation of daughter in swimming classes, participation of children in school trips	Education of children	2
Honor killings, corporal punishment of wife by her husband, state intervention in case of domestic violence, reactions to sexual harassment of girls of the family or insults against boys of the family	Violence and physical integrity	5
Religious freedom (freedom to change one's religion or to become an atheist), religion, and freedom of speech	Religion, religious freedom, and state-church relationship	3
Commitment to the democratic order, preference for democracy over other forms of governance, rejection of unconstitutional political activities, attitudes toward Muslim extremist terrorism, antisemitism, and discrimination against black Africans from Somalia	Democracy, political system	7

Source: the author's classification

guideline was only used for citizenship applicants from the "Islamic League".[1] It included thirty questions about different themes that can be regrouped into seven broader schemas (cf. Table 7.1). Because these schemas have been used explicitly to target Muslims, I consider the appearance of these schemas

[1] It is not certain which international organization was meant by the legal expert report on the guidelines (Wolfrum and Röben 2006) when talking about the "Islamic League": the Arabic League (twenty-one member states) or the Organization of the Islamic Conference (fifty-seven member states). The revised version of the interview guideline officially applied to any country of origin (Baden-Württemberg-Innenministerium 2007).

in civic education courses as proof that these courses also specifically target Muslims.

The interview guideline from Baden-Wurttemberg was the object of a legal expert report (Wolfrum and Röben 2006) declaring it in breach with German constitutional principles of nondiscrimination because of the explicit focus on candidates from particular (Muslim) countries. This, however, was not the only reason why the guideline has been cited as a particularly blunt example of illiberalism (Ersbøll, Kostakopoulou, and Van Oers 2010; Joppke 2010a; Orgad 2010). It is also the choice of subjects, placing a strong focus on moral issues, as well as the fact that the guideline openly asks the candidate for his or her opinions and "inner disposition" (Joppke 2010a; Wolfrum and Röben 2006: 4), which brought up the question of precisely what a liberal democracy may require of its citizens.

This is why, next to a thematic analysis of integration requirements, it is important to distinguish two ways in which citizenship and more specifically social unity among citizens can be framed: one is the *sociocultural-norms schema* suggesting that citizens are united around common sociocultural norms; the other one is the *juridico-political-norms schema* suggesting that citizens are united around a common political project with its specific legal and political norms. This means, for example, that under the sociocultural-norms schema, the attitude toward homosexuality can be presented as the litmus test for the acceptance of liberal values. Under the juridico-political-norms schema, however, individual opinions and attitudes are not an issue. The only legitimate question here could be whether or not homosexuality or the discrimination of homosexuals is prohibited by law. Thus, how topics are framed does not depend on the issue itself, but rather results from state decisions.

ANALYZING INTEGRATION REQUIREMENTS

It is important to distinguish at least three forms of integration requirements (Ersbøll, Kostakopoulou, and Van Oers 2010). These are requirements for naturalization, usually known as citizenship tests, requirements for newly arrived immigrants who eventually seek to acquire permanent residence, and requirements for potential family migrants who still reside in their country of origin. Whereas integration requirements for citizenship such as citizenship tests, language tests, or assimilation requirements have existed for a long time, requirements for family reunification and permanent residence only emerged in Europe since the late 1990s. Over the past twenty years, integration requirements on all three levels have been in constant evolution and spread across Europe. These integration requirements usually have two components: language teaching and civic education. The following analysis will concentrate on the civic education components of these programs because they systematically focus on what it means to be a citizen and live as a citizen in the respective host country.

A previous study (Michalowski 2011) has coded and compared the content of citizenship tests in five countries, namely the United States, Germany, Austria, the United Kingdom, and the Netherlands. This study has shown that the content of these tests is surprisingly "liberal" in the Rawlsian sense (Rawls 1993) because all tests (except for the Dutch one) focus the majority of their questions on topics related to basic civic rights and freedoms and to the political system that is supposed to guarantee these rights, and because they only ask questions about facts and the knowledge of "what is right" (Michalowski 2011: 752). With the exception of the Dutch case, social norms about "what is good" are not addressed in these tests.

This, however, does not mean that these citizenship tests completely disregard culturally sensitive topics. For example, 5 percent of the 300 federal German citizenship test questions relate to lifestyles, but they do so by referring questions about lifestyles to what is allowed or prohibited under German law (Michalowski 2011: 759). Hence, the question is not whether the candidate for German citizenship for example appreciates certain ways of child education, but whether German law allows corporal punishment. One of the reasons why the test might be set up in this particular way could be that citizenship tests are in the focus of public attention and that the publication of a new citizenship test usually triggers extensive media reaction. In this sense, one might assume that because of this increased media attention, public authorities vet citizenship tests more closely with regard to whether they respect liberal principles. By contrast, civic education courses for newly arrived immigrants are far less formalized than citizenship tests are, and their questions are more complex and usually more difficult to access than a succinct list of citizenship test questions available online. Citizenship test questions have to be as clear as possible, because there is no explanation delivered on how to understand each question. The room for individual interpretation of each question should be as narrow as possible. This is different in civic education courses where teacher and students spend (with a variability across host countries) many hours together. During course hours, it is easier for the teacher to explain delicate topics such as cultural differences, mention that these differences are not etched in stone, and discuss diverging individual behaviors. Civic education courses that prepare immigrants for citizenship tests are very rare.[2] Civic education courses,

[2] To my knowledge, Germany is one of the few countries to offer such courses, but still they are rare, because most candidates for citizenship prefer to prepare for the test on their own given that all questions and answers are publicly available.

however, are much more frequent for newly arrived immigrants who wish to acquire permanent residence. Because these courses mainly address immigrants who have just arrived from their countries of origin, it is also more likely that they will deal with issues of cultural and religious difference.

According to the most recent version of the Migrant Integration Policy Index (Migration Policy Group 2010), only fifteen out of twenty-seven EU Member States implement some form of an integration measure for immigrants who wish to acquire permanent residence. Yet, only ten of these countries offer some kind of support and among them only five countries have rendered participation in these integration measures obligatory. These five countries are Austria, Denmark, France, Germany, and the Netherlands. On closer inspection, the Austrian case is not suited for this analysis because civic education is taught during language course hours without a separate curriculum. In addition, the Dutch case[3] was already included in a previous analysis (Michalowski 2011), and the Danish case has to be excluded for a lack of language skills. I therefore suggest analyzing the French and the German material for civic education courses.

In both countries, newly arrived immigrants, in particular family migrants, have to participate in these programs if their language skills and knowledge of the receiving country prove to be insufficient. Both Germany and France have implemented the full range of integration requirements that are endorsed by the European directive on the right to family reunification (2003/86/EC of 22 September 2003) and the European directive on the rights of third-country nationals who are long-term residents (2003/109/EC of 25 November 2003): candidates for family reunification are required to acquire basic language skills in their country of origin, and newly arrived immigrants are required to participate in integration programs. After arrival in France, immigrants (*primo-arrivants*) have to sign an integration contract (*contrat d'accueil*). This contract regulates whether they have to participate in a language and/or civic education course. While the French state offers a maximum of 400 hours of language tuition free of charge, civic education is taught in one day (*journée de formation civique*) but is also free of charge. After arrival in Germany, most immigrants (*Neuzuwanderer*) have to participate in an integration course if their language skills prove to be insufficient.[4] They have to participate in a language course of

[3] In the Netherlands, the tests (and thus the curriculum) for permanent residence and for citizenship are identical.

[4] Like in France, many exemptions to this obligation exist, for example, for EU citizens, individuals who are working and do not have the time to participate (even part time) in the course, for individuals with mental illnesses, for those who are participating in the German educational system, etc.

up to 900 hours and a civic education course of 60 hours.[5] Since July 2012, integration course participants have to contribute 1.20 Euro to each course hour. In Germany and France, regular participation in these courses and, in Germany, the passing of final language and civic education exams are taken into consideration for the attribution of a permanent residence permit. For the time being, both France and Germany keep their integration measures for permanent residence separate from citizenship acquisition. However Germany plans to introduce a revised civic education test that will be recognized as proof of sufficient civic knowledge during the naturalization procedure.[6]

The present analysis focuses on the material for teaching the civic education courses in both countries. For France, this is a PowerPoint presentation created by the ministry of interior, oversea territories, regional administration, and immigration's directorate for integration and citizenship and by the French Office for immigration and integration (OFII). This is the new version that entered into force in January 2011. The political argument behind this most recent change was that the course should focus on teaching the Republic's fundamental values. In addition, it is interesting to note that for the first time since 1998 when the reception platforms (*plate-forme d'accueil*) with their short introduction to French civic education were set up, the French state has decided to set up country-of-origin and level-of-education homogeneous groups of learners.[7] Even though in the end only one version of the PowerPoint presentation was developed, Eric Besson, the former minister for immigration and integration, had suggested that depending on the group, more emphasis could be placed on teaching values that are not a reference in the country of origin.[8] The new presentation entitled "Civic education" (*formation civique*) is slightly shorter

5 This difference in the number of hours of civic education provided in France and Germany might be explained as an effect of path dependence. Whereas the French state in the late 1990s began to set up so-called *plate-forme d'accueil* (reception platforms for newcomers) where immigrants were to receive a one-day introduction to life in France (including a one- or two-hour civic education session) and slowly extended from this to one entire day of civic education, the German state introduced an integration program in 2005 that was copied on the Dutch integration programs for newcomers and on the previously existing program for ethnic Germans. Both programs were much more important in terms of course hours (Michalowski 2007).

6 Zweite Verordnung zur Änderung der Integrationskursverordnung vom 20. Februar 2012, Punkt 13.

7 Two things need to be taken into consideration here: in contrast to Germany, the French civic education takes place right after immigration to France and not after completion of the language course. This is why the French civic education classes cannot necessarily count on existing French language skills. In the past, however, origin-homogeneous groups have been rejected for being in breach with the French Republican ideal.

8 http://www.20minutes.fr/societe/618249-societe-formation-civique-etrangers-nouvelle-formule-des-2011

(seventy-eight instead of ninety slides) but also more complex in terms of visual effects than the previous version that had been developed with the help of the High Council on Integration (HCI). Participation in this course is obligatory for most immigrants, even if they have sufficient French language skills.

For the German case, the focus will be on the booklet "45 hours Germany" (*45 Stunden Deutschland*), which is recommended by the Federal Agency for Migration and Refugees (BAMF) as study material for the civic education course. Since February 2012, the number of hours for this course have been raised from forty-five to sixty as negotiated by the coalition agreement from October 2009 in order to have more time to discuss issues such as the political order of the German Federal Republic.[9] Participation in the course is obligatory for newly arrived immigrants from most non-EU countries. The booklet combines text, graphic material, and incitements to group discussions among the participants and is based on the federal curriculum for civic education published by the BAMF. This curriculum will also be taken into account to see if and where the booklet diverges from the curriculum.

Given that this material is very diverse in terms of the support used for transferring knowledge, it is necessary to develop a roughly standardized framework for analyzing and comparing its content. I suggest a content analysis based on the thematic schemas previously derived from the content analysis of the Baden-Wurttemberg interview guideline for citizenship (see Table 7.1). As already mentioned, this test was addressed explicitly to Muslims, and therefore when these thematic schemas are used in other civic education material, we can take this use as indicating that Muslims are explicitly targeted. Six of the schemas were directly taken over from the classification of that interview guideline. A seventh ("customs and manners") has been added to this list, not because it is particularly important for the framing of Muslims but because it is useful for determining whether the sociocultural or the juridico-political norms schema is dominant in a given program. On the contrary, the thematic schema of "support for democracy" has been dropped because it turned out to be too difficult to differentiate between a general education about democracy (that is a prominent topic in civic education courses) and a Muslim-specific schema of democracy. This leaves us with the following seven thematic categories:

9 The publisher Klett Verlag announces an updated version but it is unlikely that much information will be added to this revised version (see http://www.bamf.de/SharedDocs/Anlagen/DE/Downloads/Infothek/Themendossiers/Tagung-Deutscher-werden-2012/20120703-tagung-einbuergerung-6-stahr.pdf?__blob=publicationFile [last visited on August 7, 2012]).

TABLE 7.2: *Thematic categories used for civic education course content analysis*

	Thematic category
1.	Gender equality and women's rights
2.	Sexuality, homosexuality
3.	Marriage, family, and individual liberty
4.	Education of children
5.	Violence and physical integrity
6.	Religious freedom and state-church relationship
7.	Customs and manners

In addition, the analysis draws attention to the way in which these subjects are treated in the civic education programs – that is, do they refer to political and legal or to social and cultural norms?

The standardized content analysis suggested here largely ignores the diversity of the support material in the sense that it does not reflect how the information was transmitted. In fact, different forms of items have been coded: in the case of the French PowerPoint presentation, each bullet point and each image was treated as a single item. A few PowerPoint slides contain test questions. Here, each question has been treated as one item. In the case of the German booklet for civic education courses, each exercise and, if present, sub-exercise has been treated as a single item. Finally, the German civic education curriculum contains a list of single points, each of which has been treated as a single item. Yet, despite these efforts of rendering the material comparable, important differences persist. This is why the following presentation of the empirical analysis does not deliver the results of a mere "coding and counting" of the different items, but rather a detailed description along the previously mentioned set of themes and frames as well as a rough estimate of the importance of each theme and frame within each country. The cross-national difference in the general importance attached to this civic education course will be discussed in the conclusion: in fact, the German course is ten times longer than the French civic education course (sixty hours versus six) and thus offers much more time for discussing topics.

RESULTS OF CONTENT ANALYSIS

The descriptive comparative analysis of the civic education material concentrates first on the themes, then on the schemas used. It treats the two countries separately.

Topics Treated in France

The French PowerPoint presentation[10] follows a rather formal approach. It is divided into six sections: (1) the reception and integration contract (two slides), (2) French history (seven slides), (3) the values, principles, and symbols of the Republic (thirty-nine slides), (4) the institutions of the Republic (sixteen slides), (5) French nationality and citizenship (six slides), and (6) France in Europe and in the world (six slides).[11] As the numbers in brackets show, these six chapters are not of equal length, and the chapter on values, principles, and symbols of the Republic is by far the longest, representing half of the slides. The mention of the themes defined in Table 7.2 as targeting Muslims in a particular way occurs in this section. Beside information on tax paying, parents' responsibilities at school, and the citizenship application procedures, the presentation includes very little information on practical aspects of life in France such as education, labor market participation, housing, or health. This is because a second, optional course entitled "Living in France" (*Vivre en France*) is offered on these topics. Thus, contrary to the Netherlands, which has produced a civic education curriculum presenting the difficulties of "real life" in the Netherlands,[12] France has opted for an ideal definition of citizenship along the lines of French Republican assimilation. In this sense, French civic education for immigrants resembles the U.S. approach, also focusing on how citizenship ideally functions (Michalowski 2011). The difference between the French and U.S. approaches is that France, like other European countries, addresses topics that (at least indirectly) relate to values and cultural differences.

The following content analysis reviews in detail how many bullet points relate to each of the previously identified topics. Except for a few images, all information is presented in form of such bullet points. The three themes that are most spoken about in terms of single bullet points are religious freedom and state-church relationship (thirteen bullet points), marriage, family, and individual liberty (twelve bullet points), and gender equality and women's rights (at least eleven bullet points). Gender equality and women's rights turn out to be the most important topic (fifteen bullet points), if two additional mentions of equal voting rights for men and women, parity in elected offices,

[10] I thank the Direction de l'Accueil et de l'Intégration of the Office Français de l'Immigration et de l'Intégration for making this presentation available to me.

[11] Two additional slides represent the first and the final pages, contributing to a total of seventy-eight slides.

[12] The film "Naar Nederland" was produced in the framework of the new integration policies abroad for candidates for family reunification and clearly aims at deterring candidates unwilling to integrate into a Western liberal democracy.

as well as the possibility for fathers to go on parental leave are added to this list. Four slides explicitly refer to this topic in their title. With regard to this topic, the participants of the civic education course learn that in France, women can go out alone without being accompanied, that men and women both have full rights to possess property, and that women may work without their husband's consent. Participants are taught that in France, men and women have the same rights regarding social life, marriage, family, and professional life. The four slides focusing on gender equality state that men and women are equal with regard to parental authority, that women do not have to ask for their husband's consent when deciding on contraception or abortion, and repeat that women have the right to work without their husband's consent. It is also underlined that women may open a bank or postal account in their own name, drive a car (if they have a driver's license), and work for pay equal to that of men. Given that gender equality and women's rights play such an important role in French civic education, it comes as no surprise that Marianne, the symbol of the French Republic, is presented in all details.

The second most important topic relates to religious freedom and state-church relationship (thirteen bullet points and two slides exclusively dedicated to this topic). This topic is already introduced on the title page to the section "The values and principles of the Republic" by adding it to the famous motto of the French Republic: "*liberté, égalité, fraternité* ... *laïcité*." Course participants learn that everyone living in France is free to practice the religion of his or her choice, change religion, or not have a religion, that the state respects all believes if they do not disturb public order, and that state and church are independent from each other. In schools, it is prohibited to wear religious signs and in France, the religious marriage has no legal value. On a next slide, a small quiz asks participants to demonstrate that they understand the principle of *laïcité* and of religious liberty, that one does not have to change religion when becoming a French citizen but that law is superior to religion. In addition, the quiz requires participants to know that it is not possible to fully cover one's face during a marriage at the town hall. On a later slide entitled "Security is a fundamental right" that talks about the rule of law and the state monopoly on violence, the poster of the official French government campaign for the prohibition of concealing one's face (www.visage-decouvert.gouv.fr) is presented as well. This poster shows a bust of Marianne and the slogan "The Republic lives with face uncovered" (*La République se vit à visage découvert*). Finally, the quiz that follows asks what the applicant understands by religious liberty in France.

The subject of marriage, family, and individual liberty (twelve bullet points) is brought up at different moments of the PowerPoint presentation, but no slide is solely dedicated to this topic. On a slide entitled "Liberty means possibility" it is stated that in France, one can decide with whom to live, with whom to be friends, or where to live. A quiz on different forms of liberty asks at what age one is allowed to marry, whether parental authorization is necessary for marriage, or whether it is obligatory to inform the parents about the move if one is changing residences. On a later slide, it is repeated that the minimum marital age for men and women is eighteen years and that marriage requires the consent of both spouses and solely of both spouses. This consent is symbolized by the signature of both spouses of the register of births, deaths, and marriages. It is added that forced marriage is prohibited in France. The presentation underlines that the spouses owe each other mutual respect, fidelity, help, and assistance, and that it is prohibited to repudiate one's wife. Divorce exists and can be pronounced under four different scenarios. A slide entitled "A woman's rights" explains that women have the freedom to decide over their bodies. Contraception is legally permitted, which allows choosing the timing of a pregnancy and the number of children one would like to have. French law also allows abortion up to twelve weeks of pregnancy. The last slide is entitled "Equality: the law protects women." It lists a number of acts that are prohibited and sanctioned by the law, among them polygamy and honor crimes.

A fourth topic with which the French civic education program deals, albeit in a slightly less prominent way, relates to violence and physical integrity (five bullet points). On a slide talking about security as a fundamental right, it is mentioned that the right to vengeance is prohibited and that the state regulates conflict; the quiz that follows asks whether courts sanction domestic violence. An additional slide explains that the law prohibits and sanctions domestic violence, genital mutilation (female circumcision), including genital mutilation that is carried out abroad on minors of French nationality or permanent residents in France, as well as so-called honor crimes.

Finally, the presentation dedicates two bullet points to the education of children. A slide entitled "The state guarantees the equality of all" mentions the equality of all children, be they born in or out of wedlock, disregarding their gender or rank in birth order; the other slide is devoted entirely to the rights and obligations of parents at school (e.g., ensuring the children's school attendance, or the general liability of parents for their children) and asks course participants to explain what mixed schools are.

By contrast with the German civic education course, the French presentation does not include any information on customs and manners. Citizenship is defined in formal political ways and has little to do with intercultural dialogue. In addition, sexuality is not an explicit topic of the presentation, even though the Delacroix painting from 1830 "Liberty leading the people" that is used to introduce the section "Values, principles and symbols of the Republic" shows Marianne bare-breasted. Yet, one could argue, this is much more subtle than the previously mentioned Dutch movie preparing immigrants for the integration exam abroad, which films a bare-breasted woman walking out of the waves of the North Sea. On this topic, one might equally like to mention that Marianne's breasts chosen for the revised version of the PowerPoint presentation only show older and rather chaste representations, whereas the 2006 version prominently showed Marianne modeled on Brigitte Bardot. Homosexuality is not mentioned in the present version of civic education for immigrants, whereas the previous version mentioned that individual liberties in France comprise the freedom to live with whomever one chooses (heterosexual or homosexual couple). This explicit reference to the acceptance of homosexuality as what is sometimes regarded as one of the spearheads of Western liberalism has been deleted from the current version.

Another striking omission relates to the fact that the 2006 civic education presentation included a slide detailing what was meant by the French Republican contract:

> The Republic is founded on the consensus and adhesion of all to the social contract. This implies the integration of all citizens into an ensemble of indispensable and shared values. … This does not mean the negation of one's roots but the adoption of the political principles laid down by the Constitution: equality between men and women, *laïcité* etc. [sic] This is an untouchable core. No claim in the name of diversity may question human rights and human dignity.[13]

The 2011 version of the civic education course is formulated in a similar spirit but is less outspoken when it comes to defining an "untouchable core."

In general, it can be concluded that the updated 2011 version diverges in details rather than fundamentally from the predecessor version published in 2006.[14] Information on values, principles, and symbols of the Republic strongly resembles the previous version and sometimes even uses the same wording. In

[13] The author's translation of: "Cela revient à dire que la République est fondée sur le consentement et l'adhésion de tous à ce contrat social. Il s'agit de l'intégration de tous à un ensemble de valeurs incontournables et partagées … Cela ne revient pas à nier ses origines mais à adopter les principes politiques définis par la Constitution: l'égalité de l'homme et de la femme, la laïcité, etc. [sic] Il s'agit d'un noyau intangible. Aucune revendication au nom de la diversité culturelle ne peut remettre en question les droits de l'homme et la dignité de la personne."

[14] The 2006 version is itself the revision of a first document published in February 2005. Short films to present the French Republic – for example, during citizenship ceremonies – have existed since the late 1990s.

addition, as in the previous version, gender equality still is the most important topic, followed by religious freedom and state-church relationship as well as marriage, family, and individual liberty. Violence and physical integrity as well as the education of children had also been included in the 2006 version. Thus one of the main differences between the two versions remains on the layout level: the 2011 version uses modern PowerPoint facilities much more aptly than the previous version, and the content has been better structured and lightened.

In sum, as will be discussed in more detail later in the chapter, the different topics in the French civic education course are framed in very formal and even abstract terms. For example, rather than framing Muslim head scarves as an issue of women's control over their bodies, this practice is framed in terms of *laïcité* and security, whereas collective decision making on marriage is not framed in terms of cultural differences in family structure but rather in terms of (individual) liberties.

Topics Treated in Germany

The study book "45 hours Germany" (Kilimann, Kotas, and Skrodzki 2008) follows the official curriculum for the civic education course that was published by the German Federal Agency for Migration and Refugees (BAMF 2008). It consists of three different modules: politics in democracy, history and responsibility, and the individual and society. The first two modules contain few, if any, Muslim-specific topics, so this analysis focuses on the module "The individual and society" which consists of four thematic units. The introduction to the module is called "What is culture?" Four individual units follow. The first one is called "Living together in a family and other communities (*Lebensgemeinschaften*)" and deals with questions such as "What are the functions of a family?", "What do equality and equal treatment mean?", and "How do elderly people live in Germany?" The second unit is called "Child-raising and education in Germany" and is subdivided into the themes such as "What is important for the education of children?", "Which role play education and success at school?", and "What are the educational and professional chances of men and women?" The third unit is called "Intercultural living together" (*Interkulturelles Zusammenleben*) and deals with the themes such as "Which norms, values and rules exist in Germany?", "Which role does time play?", and "How can intercultural conflicts be resolved?" The fourth unit is called "Religious Diversity" and is divided into the following themes: "What role plays religion?" and "What is essential for the coexistence of religions in Germany?" Each of these subthemes is composed of several exercises. As mentioned earlier, for the purpose of this comparative analysis, one exercise will be treated as the basic unit of analysis and thus count as the relative equivalent of one French PowerPoint slide. In total, there are seventy-five exercises, some of which contain subtasks that will be analyzed separately. All of these exercises explicitly deal with cultural or religious differences in very general terms and rarely refer to Muslims in particular. However, the book uses pictures and short texts to trigger discussions among the participants of the civic education course. Some of these discussions are framed in a way that makes it very likely to touch on differences and conflicts between Muslims and other religious groups. In total there are about twenty exercises that address one of the aforementioned themes and hence seem to focus more particularly on Muslims.

The first one is in the introduction to the module and cannot be attributed to any specific subject. Civic education course participants are supposed to discuss how they perceive others and how they are perceived by others. For a group discussion, participants are asked to look at their culture and country of origin through the eyes of others. A small cartoon next to this exercise shows a woman in a pink burqa who exchanges eyeglasses with a blond woman in a green miniskirt.

Just like in the French presentation, marriage, family and individual liberty represent an important topic in the German civic education course. Like all other units, this one starts with a brainstorm followed by more detailed information. In this case, the more detailed information consists of sixteen small drawings showing not only what is called the "traditional family" but also "modernized families" (both parents working or the woman working), "singles," "weekend relations," as well as "new parents and communities" (including "single moms," "patchwork families," and "rainbow families"). In a following exercise the participants are supposed to learn that marriage has lost its importance for many couples, that ever more women work and pursue a career, that the principle of individualization is typical for German society, and that because of changing values, not everything that used to be accepted is still accepted today. Then the participants are asked to read article 3(3) of the German fundamental law on the nondiscrimination principle before discussing the limits of their own tolerance. Questions here are: What do participants think about a mother going to work while the father takes care of the child? About a woman aged fifty-five walking hand in hand with her boyfriend aged thirty-three? Or about a woman who wants to convert to another faith? Participants are also asked whether they would vote for an openly homosexual politician and what happened if their son wanted to marry his German girlfriend. Given that the debate is preceded by the reading of the German constitution, legal norms of nondiscrimination will probably play a strong normative role.

Customs and manners represent another important topic, offered as conditions for a successful intercultural dialogue in a intercultural society (*interkulturelles Zusammenleben*). A photo on this page shows a Muslim woman with a veil and the German flag painted on her cheek and draped around her shoulders. Otherwise, this unit is formulated in very general terms, asking the participants to discuss why norms, rules, and values are important and why they differ, who makes these rules, what happens if a person does not respect them, whether there are universal norms, rules, and values, and whether it is possible to change them. Again, participants are asked to compare the norms, rules, and values of their country of origin with those of Germany. One exercise asks what a German traveling to the immigrant's country of origin should know about that country, more specifically about greetings, invitations and visits, cleanliness and order, dress codes in public and private spheres, gifts, smoking, rest periods, alcohol consumption, and politeness. In addition, several exercises are devoted to different perceptions of time and the alleged importance of being punctual in Germany. Finally, this unit also deals with the question of how to resolve intercultural conflicts, how to develop intercultural competence, and the meaning of integration.

Another topic is religious diversity, which is presented in very general terms, displaying pictures of places of worship from the five big religions as well as a series of five pictures showing rites from the Christian faith. Participants are invited to reflect on religious groups in Germany and the general role of religion. A small quiz teaches that state and church are separated in Germany but that the Catholic and the Protestant church play a special role. It is also explained that children can opt out of the religious education classes at school, that members of the Christian churches have to pay church tax, and that a Christian kindergarden is open to children of other faith groups as well. Another exercise deals with article 4 of the German fundamental law, stressing the right to religious freedom including the right to be an atheist. The unit closes on a discussion of religious conflicts such as Islamic prayer during work hours, Christian crosses in Bavarian public schools, and the height of minarets.

Gender equality and education also play a role in the course. The unit on gender equality displays the photographs of a woman repairing a car, a man taking care of the laundry, and a woman firing a gun during a military training. Comments that go along with the photographs explain that 77 percent of all men want to share household tasks with their partner and – next to a picture of Angela Merkel – that the number of women in politics has increased dramatically over the past thirty years, currently reaching 32 percent. Again, participants are asked to discuss different individual cases (a woman with an academic career who does not want children, a traditional housewife and a houseman) and to compare these situations with those in their country of origin. This is thematically very close to another exercise showing that in Germany girls are more successful at school than boys and asking for a comparison with the situation in participants' country of origin. The theme of gender equality also plays a role in the following unit on child raising and education in Germany. An exercise called "What is important in child raising and education?" discusses strict versus tolerant forms of education and also mentions values that are cherished in Germany such as commitment, responsibility, and autonomy. Again, participants are asked to compare Germany to their country of origin in this regard.

As in France, sexuality plays a negligible role, but in contrast to France, homosexuality is mentioned as one form of lifestyle and living together. Another difference between French and German civic education for immigrants lies in the fact that the German civic education booklet does not mention physical integrity. This might be attributable to the fact that female genital mutilation is not a very common practice among immigrants in Germany. On the other hand, it is interesting that honor killings or domestic violence are not mentioned in the German civic education booklet given that these issues were dominant in public discussions about Islam and are also mentioned in the official curriculum for the civic education course the BAMF publishes. This curriculum in fact states that the participants should learn about the fundamental rights and that these fundamental rights should be linked to "everyday experiences of the participants and current debates such as forced marriages, domestic violence and honor killings."

The Framing of French and German Citizenship in Sociocultural or Juridico-Political Terms

The French civic education material analyzed here has made the very clear choice of using a juridico-political-norms schema for the entire content. The French PowerPoint slides are almost formalistic because they define citizenship as a bundle of principles, rights, and duties. Even elements that tackle the very specific group of Muslim immigrants are presented in the most general way. For example, the right of women to move about freely without being accompanied by a male is linked to the right of free movement, whereas the prohibition of personal vengeance (the state is in charge of regulating conflicts) is linked to the very general notion of security. Thus, rights and rules that the French state deemed necessary to underline when addressing (Muslim) immigrants are always linked to the most general principles that are relevant for all citizens such as *laïcité*, liberty, security and equality. The only time that the word "culture" is mentioned on one of the French slides is right at the beginning when the integration contract is presented. Here, one bullet point reads: "France and the Frenchmen are attached to a history, a culture and fundamental values. To live together, it is necessary to know them, understand them and respect them." Other than this, the French PowerPoint presentation never incites to debates among participants about cultural differences between their countries of origin and France.

Similarly, Germany included Muslim-specific topics into its civic education courses. In contrast to France, however, citizenship is not exclusively framed in juridico-political terms but also in sociocultural ones. It should be noted, however, that the booklet itself does not take a very normative stance on this topic. Instead it relies on discussions among the course participants to bring up a normative evaluation of cultural and religious differences. For instance, in a sub-exercise, the course participants are asked to comment on individual lifestyle choices that were presented in the previous exercise (divorce, partnership without marriage, preference for professional career over children and family life for men and women, etc.) and to compare such lifestyles to sociocultural norms in their respective country of origin. Participants are also invited to reflect on the relativity of sociocultural norms. In this respect the booklet clearly follows the guidelines of the federal curriculum (BAMF 2008) stipulating that the presentation of difference should prevail over the teaching of assumed cultural standards. Seen from this perspective, the sociocultural-norms frame in Germany is existent but weak. Yet, because it exists, some of the scholars in favor of political liberalism previously mentioned might prefer the French approach of engaging in the civic education of immigrants.

This view, however, seems to conflict with the participants' interest for topics of daily life (cf. Table 7.3). As a representative survey among civic education course participants in Germany showed (Schuller, Lochner, and Rother 2011), these were among the mostly liked topics.[15]

The overwhelming majority of the participants reported to have been pleased to participate in the course (only 5 percent reported no or little pleasure, 28 percent opted for the middle category, and 67 percent reported very much or much pleasure in the course).[16] Yet, it is interesting to note that

[15] Participants from Turkey were more interested in the topic of living together in a multicultural society than any other group (Schuller, Lochner, and Rother 2011: 112); immigrants from Russia were overrepresented in the group of participants interested in the topic "family and other lifestyles" (Schuller, Lochner, and Rother 2011: 116).

[16] Groups that liked the course considerably less than the average are EU 15 (only 49% took very much or much pleasure in the course) and immigrants from East and Southeast Asia (60.5%). Sixty-four percent of the participants from Turkey took very much or much pleasure in the course. Educational level and years of stay in Germany had no influence on this outcome.

TABLE 7.3: *Participants' interest in German civic education course topics*

Topic	
Fundamental rights and a citizen's duties	60.1%
Education and raising children in Germany	58.2%
Life in Germany after reunification	58.2%
Family and other forms of living together	54.8%
The welfare state, e.g., social security	52.8%
German history after 1945	50.3%
The democratic structure of the German state	44.8%
Intercultural living together	42.8%
Political parties, state symbols, the German upper and lower chambers, etc.	27.7%
National socialism and its consequences	23.1%
Religious diversity	21.2%
Political participation	18.5%

Source: Adapted from Schuller, Lochner and Rother (2011: 115).

German integration course participants take such pleasure in the (scholarly contested) teaching of social institutions. Unfortunately, no comparable evaluation of the French civic education courses exists, and the German evaluation did not ask the participants to explain their preferences. Thus, it can only be speculated that the greater imminent relevance of social institutions for immigrants' life in a new country could explain this preference.

SUMMARY AND DISCUSSION OF RESULTS: A SPECIAL FRAMING OF CITIZENSHIP?

First of all, this comparative analysis of the material used for the civic education of new immigrants in France and Germany has shown that cultural, social, and religious differences are picked up as a theme in both countries. Also, both countries have opted for schemas that are Muslim-specific according to the definition used in this chapter. In addition, France and Germany both emphasize the subjects of religious freedom and state-church separation as well as marriage, family, and individual liberty. In neither of the two countries is sexuality discussed openly.[17] That said, the descriptive analysis as summarized in Table 7.4 also reveals differences between the two countries.

[17] This is different from the Netherlands. In his analysis of Dutch political party manifestos, Thomas Spijkerboer (2007: 65, author's translation) notes: "Equality between men and women is mentioned over and over again, the liberating sexual morality as demonstrated by nudist beaches and same-sex-marriages, the shaking of hands."

TABLE 7.4: *Importance of topics in the field of cultural, social, and religious difference*

++ theme mentioned extensively + theme mentioned repeatedly / frequently – theme mentioned once / never	France	Germany
Religion, religious freedom, and state-church relationship	++	++
Marriage, family, and individual liberty	++	++
Gender equality and women's rights	++	+
Education of children	+	+
Customs and manners	–	++
Violence and physical integrity	+	–
Sexuality, homosexuality	–	–

The French course attaches more importance to gender equality than the German course, and it touches on the issue of violence and physical integrity that is not dealt with by the German course. The most striking difference between the two countries, however, relates to the fact that the German civic education course talks quite extensively about customs and manners whereas this issue is absent from the French course. In addition to these differences in number, there are differences in kind. Here, the most important difference relates to the way in which the topic of religion, religious freedom, and the relationship between church and state are dealt with in both countries: French civic education places an important focus on *laïcité*, the freedom to be atheist and the supremacy of state law over religious law; the German civic education course, on the other hand, informs about religious groups in Germany, the most important Christian holidays, different forms of cooperation between church and state, religious conflict, and religious freedom.

Thus it seems that even though Muslims are specifically targeted in both countries, this targeting takes place in slightly different ways: the French civic education course material takes a formalistic approach to citizenship in the sense that it does not contain information about customs and manners or employs a sociocultural-norms frame. However, it frames as politico-juridical such issues as gender equality and women's rights, religious freedom and state-church relationship, and marriage, family, and individual liberty – issues that also figured in the infamous Baden-Wurttemberg "Muslim test." Contrary to Germany, however, no direct or indirect references such as pictures of veiled women point to Muslims as a particular target group. At least theoretically, any immigrant could be targeted by the French information. This is different for the German civic integration course that also contains pictures of veiled women, thereby making explicit that Muslims are an important target group of the German civic education courses.

To some extent, these differences can be interpreted in light of more general cross-national differences between the two countries, such as greater gender equality in the French than in the German labor market (Luci 2011), a German citizenship regime that is slightly more open to defining citizens in terms of their cultural belonging than the French one (Banting and Kymlicka 2012; Koopmans, Michalowski, and Waibel 2012), and a state-church relationship that is marked by cooperation in Germany and separation in France (Fox 2008: 108). Seen from this perspective, the civic education courses slightly differ in their framing of citizenship for (Muslim) immigrants because the institutions they are seeking to legitimize differ as well. This is particularly striking in the field of state-church relationship but also with regard to the fact that the mentioning of one particular ethnic or religious group in public discourse is less of a taboo in Germany than in France.

In addition, different amounts of time are available for this teaching. As previously mentioned, the German civic education course is ten times longer than the French one, which fits into a one-day event totaling six-hours. Because it is so short, there is no time to bring up delicate and rather lengthy discussions about cultural differences between France and the participants' countries of origin. And, as it is rather risky for a liberal state to anticipate a discussion about cultural differences, the French state retreats to a more formal (and thus less attackable) manner of teaching civic education. This results in a strong focus on teaching political, rather than social, institutions.

This hypothesis is strengthened if we compare the content of the German civic education course with that of the German citizenship test. The citizenship test offers no time for explanations on how to understand a particular question. This is why these questions have to be without ambiguity. It comes as no surprise that the German federal citizenship test includes – with one exception – only questions that refer to juridico-political norms (Michalowski 2011), whereas the German civic education course also refers to sociocultural norms. Second, the citizenship test only asks questions about traditions and cultural specificities of the host country (2 percent of all questions) that mainly relate to how certain public holidays (e.g., Easter, carnival) are celebrated in Germany. The civic education course, in contrast, deals with customs and manners, even if it does so in a relatively undogmatic way. It only proposes general discussions about different values or rules of politeness and largely leaves it to the course participants to discuss their perceptions of specific differences. It tries to raise awareness of diversity and possible cultural differences rather than proposing specific cultural norms. Thus this provides support for the initially formulated hypothesis that civic education measures may be more open than citizenship tests to treat the delicate topic of cultural differences. Yet, this hypothesis may only be defended in situations where the civic education course actually does provide enough time for discussion and explanation.

Civic education courses seek to legitimize existing institutions among newly arrived immigrants. As the content analysis of the French and the German civic education courses showed, three forms of institutions are seen as being particularly vulnerable in light of Muslim immigration: the relationship between state and religion that is ideally marked by separation, freedom, and tolerance, the promise that women are equal to men, and the acceptance of the supremacy of individual liberties over collectivist claims. This contribution has argued that the particular focus on these institutions reveals that Muslims are, at least implicitly, a specific target group for civic education courses in France and Germany. Another question that this contribution has tried to answer is whether Muslims are also explicitly addressed as a specific target group. Here, civic education courses are confronted with the dilemma of responding to four different objectives: (1) deliver an ideal representation of these institutions to promote them among immigrants; (2) respect liberal principles in order to avoid accusations of discrimination; (3) cater to the practical needs of immigrants for information about cultural differences; and (4) defend host country institutions deemed to be threatened by immigration from culturally, politically, and religiously different countries. The first two objectives push the civic education courses in the direction of strictly respecting liberal principles of pluralism, equal treatment, and nondiscrimination and thus toward not addressing specific religious or cultural groups explicitly. The last two objectives, on the contrary, push for teaching social norms and cultural difference (that are potentially in conflict with liberal precepts), even with a special focus on the course participants' culture and/or religion.

As has been shown, the solutions implemented by the French and the German civic education courses differ on this point. The French course refrains from explicitly addressing any specific target group and presents questions of cultural and religious difference in terms of very general human rights. In contrast, the German civic education course explicitly talks about cultural differences and even hints at Muslims as a specific target group, but also underlines that cultural norms have no universal validity. Future research could test whether the increase in understanding or support for state-church relationship, gender equality, and individual self-determination among recently immigrated Muslims is greater among those who have participated in the French or in the German civic education course.

ACKNOWLEDGMENTS

I thank the editors of this book as well as the other contributors for their valuable comments on different versions of this text.

BIBLIOGRAPHY

Baden-Württemberg-Innenministerium. 2007. "Pressemitteilung 18.7.2007. Überarbeiteter Gesprächsleitfaden für die Einbürgerungsbehörden: Innenminister Heribert Rech: *Unser Konzept hat sich bewährt und ist absolut praxistauglich.*"

Bader, Veit. 2007. "Changements récents dans les discours et les politiques d'immigration et d'incorporation aux Pays-Bas." *éthique publique* 9(2): 51–69.

BAMF. 2008. *Curriculum für einen bundesweiten Orientierungskurs.* Nuremberg: Bundesamt für Migration und Flüchtlinge.

Banting, Keith, and Will Kymlicka. 2012. *Multiculturalism Policy Index.* http://www.queensu.ca/mcp/ (accessed August 27, 2012).

Bauböck, Rainer, and Christian Joppke (eds.). 2010. *How liberal are citizenship tests?* EUI Working Papers RSCAS 2010/41. Robert Schuman Centre for Advanced Studies, EUDO Citizenship Observatory.

Bleich, Erik. 2009. "State Responses to 'Muslim' Violence: A Comparison of Six West European Countries." *Journal of Ethnic and Migration Studies* **35**(3): 361–379.

Carrera, Sergio. 2006. "A Comparison of Integration Programmes in the EU. Trends and Weaknesses." in *Challenge Papers, no. 1* Brussels.

de Hart, Betty, and Ricky van Oers. 2006. "European Trends in Nationality Law." Pp. 317–357 in *Acquisition and Loss of Nationality. Volume 1: Comparative Analysis. Policies and Trends in 15 European Countries,* edited by Rainer Bauböck, Eva Ersboll, Kees Groenendijk, and Harald Waldrauch. Amsterdam: Amsterdam University Press.

Entzinger, Han. 2003. "The Rise and Fall of Multiculturalism: The Case of the Netherlands." Pp. 59–86 in *Toward Assimilation and Citizenship: Immigrants in Liberal Nation-States,* edited by Christian Joppke and Ewa Morawska. Houndmills: Basingstoke.

——2005. "Changing the Rules While the Game Is On: From Multiculturalism to Assimilation in the Netherlands." Pp. 121–144 in *Migration, Citizenship, Ethnos: Incorporation Regimes in Germany, Western Europe and North America.,* edited by Michael Bodemann and Gökçe Yurdakul. New York: Palgrave MacMillan.

Ersbøll, Eva, Dora Kostakopoulou, and Ricky Van Oers. 2010. *A Re-definition of Belonging? Language and Integration Tests in Europe.* Leiden: Brill Publisher.

Esser, Hartmut. 2000. *Soziologie. Spezielle Grundlagen. Band 5: Institutionen.* Frankfurt/Main: Campus.

Fermin, Alfons. 2001. *Verplichte Inburgering van Nieuwkomers.* Utrecht: Ercomer.

Fox, Jonathan. 2008. *A World Survey of Religion and the State.* New York: Cambridge University Press.

Groenendijk, Kees. 2006. "Die neue Integrationspolitik (NIP) in den Niederlanden seit 2002." Pp. 125–141 in *Paradigmenwechsel in Einwanderungsfragen? Überlegungen zum neuen Zuwanderungsgesetz,* edited by Ulrike Davy and Albrecht Weber. Baden-Baden: Nomos.

Joppke, Christian. 2007. "Beyond National Models: Civic Integration Policies for Immigrants in Western Europe." *West European Politics* 30(1):1–22.
——2010. *Citizenship and Immigration*. Cambridge: Polity Press.
Kilimann, Angela, Ondrej Kotas, and Johanna Skrodzki. 2008. *45 Stunden Deutschland. Orientierungskurs. Politik, Geschichte, Kultur.* Stuttgart: Klett Verlag.
Koopmans, Ruud, Ines Michalowski, and Stine Waibel. 2012. "Citizenship Rights for Immigrants: National Political Processes and Cross-National Convergence in Western Europe, 1980–2008." *American Journal of Sociology* **117**(4): 1202–1245.
Luci, Angela. 2011. *Frauen auf dem Arbeitsmarkt in Deutschland und Frankreich. Warum es Französinnen besser gelingt, Familie und Beruf zu vereinbaren*. Berlin: Friedrich Ebert Stiftung.
Michalowski, Ines. 2004. "Integration programs for newcomers – A Dutch model for Europe?" *IMIS Beiträge* **24**: 163–175.
——2007. *Integration als Staatsprogramm. Deutschland, Frankreich und die Niederlande im Vergleich*. Münster: Lit Verlag.
——2009. "Liberal States: Privatised Integration Policies?" Pp. 259–276 in *Illiberal Liberal States*, edited by Elspeth Guild, Kees Groenendijk, and Sergio Carrera. Farnham/Burlington, VT: Ashgate.
——2011. "Required to Assimilate? The Content of Citizenship Tests in Five Countries." *Citizenship Studies* **15**(6–7): 749–768.
Migration Policy Group. 2010. *Migrant Integration Policy Index*. http://www.mipex.eu.
Orgad, Liav. 2010. "Illiberal Liberalism. Cultural Restrictions on Migration and Access to Citizenship in Europe." *American Journal of Comparative Law* **58**(1): 53–105.
Ratia, Emma, and Anne Walter. 2009. *International Exploration on Forced Marriages. A Study on Legal Initiatives, Policies and Public Discussions in Belgium, France, Germany, the United Kingdom and Switzerland*. Nijmegen: Wolf Legal Publishers.
Rawls, John. 1993. *Political Liberalism*. New York: Columbia University Press.
Scholten, Peter. 2008. "Constructing Immigrant Policies. Research-Policy Relations and Immigrant Integration in the Netherlands, 1970–2004." PhD dissertation, University of Twente.
Schuller, Karin, Susanne Lochner, and Nina Rother. 2011. *Das Integrationspanel. Ergebnisse einer Längsschnittstudie zur Wirksamkeit und Nachhaltigkeit von Integrationskursen*. Nuremberg: Bundesamt für Migration und Flüchtlinge.
Spijkerboer, Thomas. 2007. *Zeker weten. Inburgering en de fundamenten van het Nederlandse politieke bestel*. Den Haag: SDU.
Vasta, Ellie. 2007. "From Ethnic Minorities to Ethnic Majority Policy: Multiculturalism and the Shift to Assimilationism in the Netherlands." *Ethnic and Racial Studies* **30**(5): 713–740.
Wallace Goodman, Sara. 2010. "Integration Requirements for Integration's Sake? Identifying, Categorizing, and Comparing Civic Integration Policies." *Journal of Ethnic & Migration Studies* **36**(5): 753–772.
Wolfrum, Rüdiger, and Volker Röben. 2006. "Gutachten zur Vereinbarkeit des Gesprächsleitfaden für die Einbürgerungsbehörden des Landes Baden-Württemberg mit Völkerrecht." Heidelberg.

8 Minorities in Electoral Politics

Gender, Race, and Political Inclusion in Sweden, France, and Britain

Mona Lena Krook

In recent decades, there has been growing interest across Western Europe concerning the political participation and representation of marginalized groups. All countries have witnessed debates and initiatives regarding the political incorporation of women, with political parties and legislatures across the region introducing candidate gender quota policies in the 1970s through 2000s (Krook 2009). Concerns about the political status of minorities, however, have been more recent and much more uneven. In other parts of the world, minority groups have been granted a range of institutional concessions ensuring participation and influence, including reserved seats, decentralization, federalism, and proportional representation (Hughes 2011; Norris 2004; Reynolds 2005). In Western Europe, however, such mechanisms may operate for linguistic communities (O'Neill 1998), but do not apply to groups based on race, ethnicity, or religion.

What explains the tendency across Western Europe to introduce measures to enhance the political representation of women – but not members of other marginalized groups, particularly racial, ethnic, and religious minorities? Contrary to the assumptions of some political theorists (cf. Williams 1998; Young 1990), global variations in political incorporation initiatives cast doubt on claims that there is something inherent about marginalized identities – like exclusion based on ascriptive characteristics – that requires their political inclusion. Rather, as comparative evidence suggests, group recognition emerges through active construction of "relevant" political identities. The result is that states around the world may extend guarantees to multiple groups, one group, or no groups at all (Krook and O'Brien 2010).

This chapter argues that these cross-national variations are the product of the institutional dynamics of electoral politics, an arena driven by a sectoral logic of democratic competition that may lead political actors – most often, political parties – to change course should this be viewed as a way to compete more effectively on the electoral market. Pressures to respond to citizen demands can come together with the inherent flexibility of candidate selection approaches to introduce new ways of recruiting political candidates. More specifically, while parties generally aim to put forward qualified aspirants, there are no clear qualifications needed to hold political office, beyond requirements like age and residency (Phillips 1995). Rather, opinions on the requisite "qualifications" may vary significantly, being linked to a host of different criteria (Hazan and Rahat 2010). As a consequence, advocacy groups – engaging a wide range of civil society, state, and international and transnational actors – may emerge to promote the political inclusion of identity-based groups, albeit with varying degrees of success.

These two factors – democratic responsiveness and the elasticity of candidate selection criteria – work together to shape the prospects (1) that advocacy coalitions, if they materialize, can pressure political elites to respond to group-based demands, and (2) that parties translate this response into changes in their candidate selection practices. In the European context, supporters of women's representation have continually highlighted the fact that women constitute roughly 50 percent of the population, actively framing women as a sizeable – if not the largest – voting bloc in the country (Harvey 1998; Lovenduski and Norris 1993). This strategy has made the task of mobilizing for enhanced minority representation much more difficult, especially one that can "travel" across national borders: the proportion of citizens with minority backgrounds is much smaller and highly variable, depending on which groups are included under the rubric of "minorities" (Bird et al 2010; Krook and O'Brien 2010; Reynolds 2006; Ruedin 2009). As a result, advocates typically cannot rely on arguments about numbers, leading them to emphasize dynamics of historical subordination as a reason for change (Mansbridge 1999; Williams 1998). Although empirically valid and morally compelling, such claims may be less compelling from an electoral perspective, relying more on principled commitments for inclusion.

Opportunities for change, however, are also shaped in important ways by elements of the national context. Cultural ideologies, in particular, provide "schemas" that shape how demands need to be articulated in order to be persuasive, as well as whether policy solutions introduced in response to those demands are perceived as legitimate by the public at large. Consequently, the rhetoric used to justify the adoption of gender quotas, as well as the measures themselves that are introduced, vary significantly across Western Europe (Krook, Lovenduski, and Squires 2009). To the degree that debates over extending similar provisions to minority groups have emerged, moreover, these have developed in distinct ways. These patterns suggest that, while features of the electoral arena provide opportunities to reshape candidate selection processes in ways that give greater consideration to identity groups, how these discussions proceed – and their prospects for success – are refracted by key disparities across national contexts.

Two elements of the national landscape that appear to constrain or facilitate these efforts include prevailing repertoires of belonging and exclusion and the legal status of targeted policies for identity groups. Together, these affect the possibilities for affirmative action, as well as the range of groups that are deemed "deserving" of political representation. Focusing on ideas concerning citizenship and discrimination reveals that states have historically privileged some identities over others. As such, there is some "stickiness" with regard to the range of identities recognized as central to political life, affecting which groups are recognized. Evidence suggests, nonetheless, that while these cultural and legal legacies can guide or influence the course of a campaign for increased representation, they can also be manipulated strategically by actors in ways beneficial to their group.

To this end, this chapter compares debates and policy developments in three countries – Sweden, the United Kingdom, and France – to explore how such demands emerge, take form, and succeed (or not) in altering group access to electoral politics. The analysis focuses on these three cases to probe the relative importance of – and relationship between – national repertoires, discrimination law, and the logic of the electoral arena. On balance, the case studies reveal that particular framing strategies can be more persuasive in some contexts than in others, making distinct use of cultural schemas related to how concepts like equality, representation, and identity are broadly understood. At the same time, however, dynamics in the electoral arena – and political life more generally – appear to have a more immediate impact on the identities that are recognized as having a legitimate claim, introducing flexibility into the types of discursive strategies that are constructed.

Important long-term legal differences across discrimination laws in each country, in particular, shape how advocates have been able to present their claims for the increased election of ethnic minorities. In the United Kingom, where race discrimination was outlawed before sex discrimination, rates of success in altering candidate selection rules for minorities have been most extensive. In comparison, they have been more muted but present in Sweden, where sex discrimination was prohibited by law long before race discrimination, and almost totally absent in France, where sex is recognized as a legitimate category but race is not. Frames thus emerge from multiple sources, presenting actors with important tools that may also enable them to transform existing schemas in the course of pursuing social and political change.

DEFINING GROUPS: "MUSLIMS" AND "MINORITIES"

In Western Europe and beyond, the topic of women in politics has drawn greater political and scholarly attention than the electoral status of minority groups. Comparative research on the latter has been restricted to some extent by the fact that the concept of "minority" varies across countries, and as a result, identifying the salient groups and devising yardsticks for participation involve a more complex set of analytical considerations (Bird et al 2010; Ruedin 2009). Further, as noted in the introduction to this volume, the same group may be labeled in numerous ways: "Muslims" may be named as such, or as a group, they may be subsumed under or conflated with other headings like "immigrants" or "blacks." It is thus not always clear semantically which more specific groups are included under these labels. However, a closer examination of debates in Sweden, the United Kingsom, and France reveals that stereotypes about Muslims underlie, at least to some extent, concerns expressed about race- and immigrant-based groups and the reasons given as to why they should – or should not – be the focus of policies for enhanced representation.

Electoral dynamics open up the possibilities for change in patterns of representation, but practical schemas – including country-specific concepts and legitimate discourses regarding equality, representation, and identity – shape how these groups have been defined, as well as their prospects for political integration. Citizenship repertoires provide a starting point around which advocates may mobilize for change, affecting the tools at the disposal of campaigners – as well as the nature of the barriers they may need to overcome and their broader prospects for success.

Prevailing understandings of equality may tend toward *equal opportunities*, focusing on individual rights, or *equal outcomes*, recognizing that inequalities may derive from broader structures and are best altered through group-based solutions. Notions of representation may emphasize *substantive representation*, or a principal-agent conception of representation, which views representation as occurring when one person acts on behalf of another in the second person's interests. Alternatively, they may tend toward *descriptive representation*, an approach that sees representation as happening when one person acts on behalf of another by reflecting their various ascribed characteristics. Finally, owing to their histories of antidiscrimination laws, countries may differ with regard to their recognition of salient political *identities* (Krook, Lovenduski, and Squires 2009).

The power of these hegemonic discourses – as well as their tendency to vary across countries – is well illustrated across the three case studies with regard to how "Muslims" and "minorities" have been defined. In Sweden, initiatives to overcome exclusion have been directed toward "foreigners," a term that was later replaced with "immigrants," categories that encompass those from nearby countries to as far away as Africa and Latin America. Nonetheless, the term "immigrant" tends to be more closely associated with those with foreign-sounding names and darker skin colors. Although the country is often thought of as being relatively homogeneous, it has experienced several distinct waves of immigration: the 1940s, when immigrants arrived mainly from neighboring countries; the 1950s and 1960s, when they came primarily from Finland and Southern Europe; the 1970s and 1980s, when refugee immigration from the third world, especially from Latin America and the Middle East, increased, as did the need for family reunification; and the 1990s, when asylum seekers from ex-Yugoslavia constituted the vast majority of immigrants (Westin 1996).

As the country elaborated its immigration policy across these waves, it adopted a dual approach that sought to enable individuals to preserve their cultural heritage while also becoming integrated into Swedish society. A major landmark to this end was the extension of the right to vote and run for office to immigrants in local elections beginning in 1975, provided that they had resided in Sweden for at least three years. However, whereas sex discrimination in employment was banned in 1980, a similar law on ethnicity was not passed until 1999, at the same time as laws concerning disability and sexual orientation. These laws were brought together, updated, and expanded to realms beyond employment in 2003, 2005, and 2008. In recent years, the proportion of "immigrants" has grown to more than 10 percent of the overall population, whether this is measured in terms of being foreign-born (12 percent), being foreign-born or having two parents who were foreign-born (15.5 percent), or being foreign-born or having at least one parent who was foreign-born (21.8 percent) (Göransson 2005: 15). While immigrant representation in parliament is higher than in France and Britain, the figure does not approximate this share of the population: it stood at 6.6 percent after both the 2006 and 2010 elections. This compares favorably, however, with the proportion of those with immigrant backgrounds – 7.3 percent – among those who turned out to vote.[1] Discrepancies among population and voter statistics are rooted in the fact that one must become a Swedish citizen in order to run for and vote in national elections.

These patterns are different in the United Kingdom, which experienced an influx of economic migrants following World War II, many from the

[1] See http://www.immi.se/politik/riksdagen2006 and http://www.immi.se/politik/riksdagen2010, accessed December 7, 2010.

Commonwealth countries. These individuals were initially described as "black," but are now referred to as "black and minority ethnic" (BME). This group encompasses both Caribbean and South Asian populations, which, despite being lumped together, diverge greatly in terms of their language, origins, culture, and religion. This plural definition of race can be seen in the first Race Relations Act passed in 1965, outlawing discrimination in services on the grounds of "colour, race, ethnic or national origins." The Act was extended to cover employment and housing in 1968 and was repealed in 1976 by a more comprehensive Race Relations Act (RRA), prohibiting discrimination on grounds of race, color, nationality, ethnicity, and national origin in the fields of employment, the provision of goods and services, and education and public functions. It was amended in 2000 to incorporate a statutory duty on public bodies to promote race equality and was further revised in 2003 to add religious belief to the list of grounds for nondiscrimination.

This legislation preceded similar provisions for women, passed in 1970 as the Equal Pay Act and 1975 as the Sex Discrimination Act. The Equality Act passed in 2010 consolidates more than 100 pieces of antidiscrimination legislation to require equal treatment in employment, as well as public and private services, regardless of age, disability, gender reassignment, marriage and civil partnership, race, religion or believe, sex, and sexual orientation. Debates over this bill took place alongside a Speaker's Conference set up by the House of Commons in 2008 to study and make recommendations for rectifying the underrepresentation of women, ethnic minorities, and disabled people. Concluding its work one year later, the conference supported an extension to an act allowing the use of electoral quotas for women, and urged that similar legislation be enacted to allow parties to use similar strategies to increase the proportion of BME candidates (House of Commons 2010). Efforts by parties to select more BME candidates in the run-up to the 2010 elections led to growth in the proportion of BME members of parliament, from 2 percent in 2005 to 4 percent in 2010, which is nonetheless still below the 7.9 percent BME share of the UK population (Government Equalities Office 2010; Hinsliff 2008).

In France, campaigns for increasing minority representation have been constrained by discourses of universalism. According to this ideal, "equality is achieved ... by making one's social, religious, ethnic, and other origins irrelevant in the public sphere; it is as an abstract individual that one becomes a French citizen" (Scott 2007: 11). To this end, Article 1 of the Constitution states that "France ... shall ensure the equality of all citizens before the law, without distinction of origin, race or religion." Concerns to combat racism are further elaborated in two laws, one passed in 1972 banning discrimination and racist acts in public and private life, and the other approved in 1990 (known as the Gayssot Law) strengthening penalties against racists and adding to the list of crimes classified as racist. Laws on sex discrimination, in contrast, did not appear until 1983, with reforms to Article 1 to promote equal access of women and men to all elected posts occurring in 1999. However, whereas sex-based statistics have been collected since at least 1901,[2] a 1978 law on information storage and freedom includes a clause on computerized storage, which essentially bans the collection of race-based statistics. The upshot of the latter is that no systematic data has been collected on racial patterns in the French population.

The motivation behind race-based laws, as Erik Bleich (2004) notes, has been to punish racists committing bigoted acts motivated by racist intent. The goal has not been to foster racial equality per se or to compensate a class of victims defined by race. This approach is further illustrated by the decision by the Constitutional Council to strike down the act ratifying the European Charter for Regional or Minority Languages in 1999. The court justified its action on the grounds that, under French law, "collective rights" may never be granted to "any kind of group defined by shared origin, culture, language, or belief." The collective effect of these regulations is that more positive uses of race – for example the use of affirmative action to improve the status of minority groups – are equated with more invidious ones, both being viewed as illegitimate on their face (Calvès 2004). In France, therefore, questions of race and religion have been excluded from ideal visions of the nation, even as there has been sustained and highly publicized attention to problems of "Muslim" integration into French society (Bowen 2007; Scott 2007). In addition, the lack of official statistics on race makes it difficult to compare the proportion of minority citizens in the population with their numbers in parliament. Estimates as to the total number of non-European foreigners, immigrants and their descendants, and migrants from overseas departments living in the French "hexagon" place this figure around 7 million, about 12 percent of the population. However, until the 2007 elections, when three minority deputies were elected (0.5 percent), there had only ever been one minority elected to the French National Assembly. Similarly, there were four minority senators elected in 2004 (1.3 percent), prior to which there had been none (Bird 2005; Brothers 2009).[3]

[2] http://www.ined.fr/en/pop_figures/france/population_structure/ages_sex_final/, accessed December 7, 2010.

[3] These figures do not include representatives of French overseas departments, territories, and collectivities. In 2004, fifteen of the twenty-two members from these constituencies could be considered racial or ethnic minorities, but citizens of indigenous origin account for more than 90 percent of these districts' populations (Bird 2005).

Across these three countries, therefore, there have been recent notable shifts in levels of minority representation, but in none do these figures correspond with the proportion of minorities within the population at large. These changes are linked in many ways to campaigns to increase the percentage of women in political office, which have created both barriers and opportunities for mobilization on behalf of minority groups. Trends in Sweden appear disproportional, with women gaining nearly half of all seats in parliament and immigrant representation remaining below 10 percent. However, those members of parliament (MPs) brought in as replacements for cabinet ministers have led to the greater representation of immigrant groups, especially women of minority backgrounds, because of increased attention to questions of diversity by political parties.

Although women have received earlier and firmer equal guarantees in the United Kingdom, steps have been taken across the parties to extend similar provisions to BME candidates, albeit in a less strict form. Finally, gaining constitutional and legal reforms for the equal representation of women and men in public life in France have come at the expense of efforts to improve access for racial and ethnic minorities. Public debates over identity and representation have, however, enhanced the recruitment of ethnic minority women in several instances. These patterns indicate that the sectoral logic of the electoral sphere has created opportunities for marginalized groups to lobby for enhanced levels of political representation, dynamics that in Western Europe have ultimately favored women over minority groups. All the same, the specific form these debates and proposals have taken – both within and across national contexts – vary considerably, shaped by framing strategies in light of existing schemas of citizenship and discrimination law.

SWEDEN: VOTING RIGHTS AND IMMIGRANT CANDIDATES

Trends in Sweden reflect a middle position between developments in France and the United Kingdom, integrating commitments to individualism, universalism, and social partnership and consensus through direct relations between states and individuals and universalistic, redistributive welfare state policies. The centrality of individuals to Swedish citizenship leans toward a preference for equal opportunities, but recognition of the various structural factors that might get in the way of "natural" change simultaneously facilitates sympathy for equal outcomes. Similarly, an emphasis on universalism tends toward substantive over descriptive representation, but coexists – owing to the importance of social solidarity – with acceptance of some degree of group representation. In the early years of Swedish social democracy, "class" emerged as the main social cleavage that was intended to be reduced through the vehicle of social policy. The emergence of the "sex role debate" in the early 1960s, however, while largely initiated by academics, succeeded in placing gender equality on the political agenda and led to explicit acknowledgment of sex discrimination as a problem in Swedish politics and society (Hirdman 1990).

In contrast, legal and political strategies attended to minorities much later, constructing an implicit hierarchy among these groups. The result has been the adoption of distinct measures aimed at facilitating the participation of women and immigrants, with differing levels of political commitment. These outcomes are shaped to some extent by the nature of these two groups, but are also linked fundamentally to the tactics of their advocates. Consequently, the fact that women have tended to receive much stronger guarantees than immigrants stems from a combination of two factors: "immigrants" as they are defined in Sweden are not always citizens, meaning that their opportunities to vote and run for office at the national level are necessarily truncated; and women have organized longer and over time have increasingly radicalized their demands. While there have been conscious efforts to nominate more candidates with immigrant backgrounds, these pale in comparison to provisions made to women, which have since the 1990s amounted to the introduction of 50 percent quotas across almost all political parties.

This approach did not spring from an early recognition that women constituted half the population (Sainsbury 2004), but rather was the result of decades of ongoing mobilization by Swedish women. After bitter struggles in the 1930s and 1940s to gain the nomination and better placement of female candidates, activities to bring more women into politics waned in the 1950s but gained new life in the late 1960s, with new campaigns by women both inside and outside the parties to get more women in electable positions on party lists (Palme 1969). While all parties remained opposed to quotas, these demands led several parties – including the Liberal Party, the Left Party, the Social Democratic Party (SAP), and the Green Party – to adopt recommendations and targets for selecting female candidates, leading to growing differences in the numbers of women elected (Freidenvall 2006; Krook 2009).

Although quotas were highly controversial in all parties, over time, women inside the SAP eventually began to call for gender quotas in the form that neither sex could occupy more than 60 percent of seats. They stressed that quotas would not entail promoting "incompetent" women over "competent" men, but rather aimed to foster a more representative democracy that included members of various social and economic backgrounds (Sainsbury 2004). These varied efforts led to substantial increases in the proportion of women elected to parliament, which surpassed 30 percent by the mid-1980s.

These jumps, however, were not matched by similar increases in the number of women nominated by parties to local and national committee, leading to appointment of an expert commission, which ultimately endorsed a strategy they dubbed *varannan damernas* (every other one for the ladies), referring to a custom at countryside dances where every other song was women's turn to invite the men, a tradition also known as "democratic dancing."

Although these discussions revolved around women's status in appointed committees, they resurfaced and became relevant for elected positions several years later, when the number of women in parliament decreased for the first time since 1928 (Eduards 1992: 86). Women began to meet across party lines, triggering debates across the political spectrum on the need to adopt stronger measures to ensure equal representation. The group took the name Support Stockings,[4] and although its original intent was to serve as a pressure group on the existing parties, rumors soon circulated in the media that women might form an entirely new political party. Over the next several years, women pressed the parties to revisit their existing policies to incorporate the principle of *varannan damernas*, which many argued was not a quota, but rather a method for achieving gender balance. These efforts met with great success; by the late 1990s, most parties agreed to alternate between women and men, although parties differed to the degree that they characterized this policy as a "recommendation" or as a "quota," reflecting their commitment to gender balance but also their beliefs regarding the legitimacy of positive action (cf. Freidenvall 2005). The impact of these measures was palpable, setting a new world record with the election of 41 percent women in 1994 (Wängnerud 1999, 35).

In comparison to these decades of mobilization by women, immigrants have rarely organized collectively around the issue of political representation. In the face of increased rates of immigration from a more diverse range of countries in the 1970s, a parliamentary inquiry was organized in 1974 to focus on dealing with the social and cultural differences that immigration had brought, as well as how to promote immigrant adaptation to Swedish society. From these discussions emerged a new Immigrant and Minority Policy in 1975, which accompanied a shift in official policy from using the term *utlänning* (foreigner) to using *invandrare* (immigrant) (Bäck and Soininen 1998: 32). This approach, however, further evolved over time. In the 1970s, the situation

[4] The word in Swedish, *Stödstrumporna*, is a play on words in several senses. Although its primary meaning refers to the fact that the Support Stockings were a support network for women in politics, the term rhymes with *Rödstrumporna* (Redstockings), the radical feminist movements in Scandinavia in the 1970s, and literally means support hosiery, an allusion to the fact that many of the women involved tended to be middle-aged and older.

of "immigrants" and "ethnic minorities" were viewed as one and the same. Equality in this context entailed a combination of social and cultural rights to help immigrants maintain their own linguistic cultural identities, as well as political rights to enable them to build their own organizations and get more involved in Swedish politics and trade union affairs.

In the 1980s, "immigrants" and "ethnic minorities" were separated out as political categories, with groups like the Saami and Tornedal Finns of northern Sweden having a special constitutional entitlement to group-based rights. In contrast, "immigrant policy" moved to a more neutral position that did not promote but also did not oppose a move toward greater cultural assimilation. This approach shifted again in the 1990s, when closer attention was paid to making immigrants self-sufficient and self-supporting during their first years in Sweden, as well as a need to preserve the Swedish cultural heritage, through "integration policy" (Soininen 1999). The Swedish state has clearly experienced some ambivalence over the best way to deal with increased cultural diversity as a result of growing rates of immigration. Nonetheless, the overall policy approach used in recent decades has been characterized by relatively liberal citizenship legislation, including a more recent right to dual citizenship, and the granting of extensive civil, social, and political rights to resident aliens.

The aim of both sets of policies is to provide immigrants with full membership of society and promote integration of new arrivals. One of the most dramatic reforms, in international comparison, was the decision in 1975 to grant foreign citizens living in Sweden for at least three years the right to vote and run for office in local elections. This reform intended to open up political and trade union participation for these groups, as well as to help immigrants get their questions onto the local political agenda (Soininen 1999). Although first introduced in 1968, passage of this proposal was delayed by differing opinions regarding the relationship between local and national elections. This issue was taken up again in 1983, when a proposal was made to extend similar rights to national elections, starting first with citizens of other Nordic countries along the same principles as regulated local elections, and then slowly expanding this to other immigrants over time. The committee charged with developing this proposal, however, was split and such a bill never reached parliament for consideration. On one side, the conservative parties argued that the right to vote and run in national elections should be reserved exclusively for citizens. On the other, parties on far left did not want this right restricted to Nordic citizens (Dahlström and Möller 2004).

The impact of the local voting rights reform has been somewhat mixed. Electoral participation among immigrants reached 60 percent in 1976, but it fell to 40 percent by 1994 and to 35 percent in 2002, when the average level of participation for the electorate as a whole is around 80 percent (Bäck and Soininen 1998: 34–35; Dahlström and Möller 2004: 149). This disparity extends to naturalized citizens as well: in the 2002 parliamentary elections, turnout among this group was 67 percent compared to 83 percent in the electorate overall. In an effort to overcome these patterns, state agencies were given the task of tackling factors specific to immigrants that might hinder their political participation, like lack of information, language problems, difficulties with voting technicalities, lack of knowledge about political parties and Swedish politics, and feeling of not belonging in Swedish society (Bäck and Soininen 1998). To this end, across various elections, the State Immigration Office, the Swedish Tax Agency, and the Integration Office have sought to stimulate participation by producing and distribution information, using a wide range of media outlets and making materials available in more than ten languages, with more work being done by local authorities and parties over time (Dahlström and Möller 2004).

A second trend has been the increased recruitment of immigrant candidates for municipal elections (Soininen 2011), as well as of naturalized citizens for parliamentary office. Whereas the foreign-born accounted for approximately 10 percent of the population in the 1990s, they occupied only 4.6 percent and 4.4 percent of elected representatives in local and county councils, respectively (Bäck and Soininen 1998: 40). Over time, however, these numbers have increased to 11.8 percent as compared to 6.5 percent and 6.9 percent by 2002 (Dahlstedt 2004: 50). Evidence from these various levels, however, points to some uneven trends with the very diverse category of "immigrants," which may also include those that are foreign-born as well as those who are the children of one or more foreign-born parent.

At the local level, for example, one study finds that there appears to be an ethnic hierarchy among immigrant groups related to their ability to access numbers of municipal offices, as well as the relative the status of the offices achieved. Candidates born in the Nordic countries, Western Europe, and North America are more successful than other groups, followed by people born in Eastern Europe, Southern Europe, and Latin America, and then candidates from Asia and Africa (Blomqvist 2005). Similar trends emerge at the national level as well, where most politicians of immigrant background come from Scandinavia and other parts of Europe, with only 14 percent of immigrant politicians come from elsewhere in the world (Niklasson 2005: 123). Interviews with minority elites reveal that these patterns may be related to how "non-Swedish" an individual appears. They may also be attributable to a group's position in the waves of immigration: most immigrant politicians are often those who have been Swedish citizens for decades (Niklasson 2005). Still others express concerns that immigrant politicians serve as mere window dressing, who may risk not being nominated if they are perceived as being too vocal or provocative in their opinions on racism and discrimination (Dahlstedt 2004).

In 2000, there was some discussion in Sweden regarding the possibility of introducing quotas for immigrants, but there was little public support for such a proposal (Jarstad 2004). After elections in 2002, however, there was increased attention to questions of diversity in Swedish party life. In particular, the SAP government was criticized for not doing enough to promote "immigrant representation." In fact, some in the party stated publicly that inside SAP there is "a circle of friends and colleagues who block new groups and people in politics," and that "people with immigrant backgrounds continue to be discriminated against and don't receive the same chances to become politicians and elected officials" (*Dagens Nyheter*, January 16, 2003). Nonetheless, these elections resulted in a more than doubling in the numbers of immigrant representatives, from thirteen in 1994 to thirty-one by 2010.

Among these, the majority are women, even if the exact proportion varies over time: women made up 69 percent of immigrant representatives in 1994, 53 percent in 1998, 74 percent in 2002, 55 percent in 2006, and 52 percent in 2010.[5] Further, the kinds of immigrants elected have also diversified in recent elections, with individuals tracing their ancestry to Egypt, Eritrea, Ghana, Congo, Turkey, and Chile being elected in 2002 (Richburg 2005). This variety remaining relatively stable through the 2006 elections, but grew more diverse in 2010 to include Kurdish candidates, as well as those with origins in Somalia and Iran (Amin 2010; Hussein 2010; *Iran Times* 2010). The Swedish case, placing emphasis on practical schemas of solidarity and inclusion, has thus served as a resource for both women and minorities in their quest for political representation, albeit in distinct ways and with differing levels of political commitment.

UNITED KINGDOM: ALL-BLACK SHORTLISTS

The British case reflecting liberal ideals, in contrast, is marked by a commitment to individualism. Equal opportunities are valued above other principles,

[5] Author's calculations based on data available at http://www.immi.se/politik/1998/riksdag.htm, http://www.immi.se/politik/index.htm, http://www.immi.se/politik/2002/riksdagen-valda.htm, all accessed September 15, 2009, and http://www.immi.se/politik/riksdagen2010, accessed on December 7, 2010. With the addition of replacements – all male – for those appointed as cabinet ministers, the overall proportion of women dropped to 45 percent.

attributing responsibility for unequal outcomes to individuals themselves. The configuration of values also emphasizes substantive representation but does not offer any expectations about the desired direction of policy outputs. Consistent with these goals, equality legislation in the United Kingdom is focused on outlawing discrimination in three key areas: employment, the provision of goods and services, and education and public functions. These groundings have generated extensive debates over the legal status of strategies to combat discrimination in candidate selection processes. The main question concerns the issue of whether standing as a candidate constitutes "qualification for employment" (that is, whether serving as an MP is like any other job). Legal precedents resulting from court challenges pursued by male and minority party members, respectively, have resulted in opposite outcomes, creating distinct opportunities for devising positive action strategies for increasing the proportion of female and minority MPs.

Legal ambiguities were clarified in the case of women by a government-initiated reform to the Sex Discrimination Act (SDA) in 2002. The legislation was due to expire in 2015, but was extended in 2010 until 2030. This reform excludes from the purview of the SDA any act taken by a party to reduce inequality in the numbers of women and men elected. Consequently, it permits parties to adopt strategies, like the policy of "all-women shortlists" (AWS) approved by the Labour Party in 1993, to ensure the selection of female candidates. In contrast, the law is less clear in the case of race discrimination, casting doubt on the legality – and broader desirability – of "all-black shortlists" (ABS), even among minority MPs themselves. The early recognition of race discrimination in the United Kingdom might lead to an expectation that provisions on the grounds of race may be better developed than those for sex, which was indeed the case as it concerns government bureaucracies: before they were merged as the Equality and Human Rights Commission in 2007, the Commission for Racial Equality enjoyed far greater resources than those on Disability Rights and Equal Opportunities (EOC). However, more contingent events related to nature of the cases brought before the employment tribunals led the two groups down different paths, such that positive action in candidate selection is permitted for women but forbidden for BME candidates.

In both instances, however, group-specific measures introduced in the two main parties have met with a great deal of controversy, being framed as "unfair" and "discriminatory" to men and majority populations, consistent with the broad contours of the British liberal model. All the same, when viewed alongside other cases in Europe, debates in the United Kingdom have come the closest to demands for minority group quotas in the form of ABS, a proposal directly inspired by attempts to increase women's representation via AWS. The focus on shortlists stems from institutional constraints in ensuring the selection of female candidates in a first-past-the-post electoral system, where only one person is elected per district. This structural feature renders impossible the usual strategy of applying quotas to party lists, used in countries with proportional representation. Gender quotas in the British Labour Party thus require that final lists of candidates – or "shortlists" – in certain constituencies be composed entirely of women.

The AWS policy was passed by the 1993 party conference as part of a broader package of proposed changes to the party constitution. The adoption of ABS was also briefly debated, but the National Executive Committee (NEC) decided to take time to consider this proposal (Norris 1997). The approval of AWS met with some negative reactions inside the party, but the most vehement critiques came from the opposition, which described them as a superficial solution that would have a perverse effect on women's status by privileging "special treatment" over "equal treatment" (Squires 1996). The Labour Party was forced to abandon the policy in 1996 as a result of a successful court challenge in 1996 by two male party members, who argued that their exclusion from the process of candidate selection in districts designated for AWS violated the employment provisions of the SDA. The party responded that parliamentary candidates were officeholders, not employees, and that another article of the SDA allowed parties to make special provisions for one sex, but the tribunal decided in favor of the men (Russell 2000). Female candidates selected via AWS before the decision were permitted to stay on, and in large part owing to this policy, the proportion of women in parliament doubled from 9 percent in 1992 to 18 percent in 1997.

Legal ambiguities regarding this decision led to further debates as to the permissibility of positive action, but no steps were taken until the numbers of female MPs decreased in the 2001 elections, at which point the Labour government submitted the Sex Discrimination (Election Candidates) Bill for debate in the newly elected House of Commons (Krook 2009). This bill did not compel parties to adopt positive action, but sought to exclude from the purview of the SDA any act taken by a political party to reduce inequality in the numbers of women and men elected. In spite of the bitter controversies that had emerged over the earlier policy of AWS, opposition parties decided not to object to the reform, enabling the proposal to pass all stages without a vote (Childs 2003). The Labour Party has since reinstituted AWS, and the Conservatives, seeking to achieve electoral victory after three consecutive defeats, have experimented with a variety of methods to ensure the selection of at least 50 percent women and a "significant" proportion of black, minority ethnic, and disabled candidates in Conservative-held and target constituencies (Campbell, Childs, and Lovenduski 2006; Krook 2009).

In contrast to the campaigns waged by women inside the Labour Party, black activists faced an uphill battle by the mid-1980s in getting black candidates selected. On the one hand, black sections were associated with the radical left-wing of the party, which was largely marginalized by 1987. On the other hand, few Labour MPs have retired in black target seats (Norris, Geddes, and Lovenduski 1992). Nonetheless, the number of BME MPs began to grow slowly after 1987, with the vast majority being elected for Labour (Ali and O'Cinneide 2002). Inside the party, other Labour candidates tended to blame underrepresentation of members of these groups on the party for not providing opportunities for black people (Norris, Geddes, and Lovenduski 1992: 105–106). Similar to the Jepson decision, the party was eventually challenged on this point, although via a very different set of circumstances.

Between 1991 and 1998, a man named Raghib Ahsan from Pakistan was a Labour Party councilor for the Sparkhill Ward of Birmingham, a ward with a large Pakistani population. As the 1998 local government elections approached, he hoped he would be reselected. However, by that time, the Sparkhill branch had been suspended for nearly three years by the central Labour party leadership. The reason was that, in early 1995, newspaper articles appeared in which it was alleged that local councilors associated with the Pakistani community were helping Pakistani residents jump the queue for housing grants. The reaction of Labour Party NEC was to suspend four constituency parties, including Sparkhill, which also happened to be the wards with the highest concentration of ethnic minority groups. In the event, after an inquiry, no evidence was found of any impropriety on the part of Ahsan or any other Pakistani councilors. Although Ahsan was interviewed, the candidate ultimately chosen for Sparkhill was a white man. In 1998, Ahsan took his complaint to court, alleging a violation of the RRA on the grounds that being a councilor is a profession. Over the next several years, he launched several court cases against the party for race discrimination in candidate selection.

One of these challenges eventually reached the House of Lords, which, like the original employment tribunal, found that the Labour Party had engaged in discrimination (for other examples, see Solomos and Back 1995). The Court of Appeals had deemed the party's wish not to have a candidate identified with the Pakistani community to be a "legitimate objective … provided that the perception that the problem was predominantly a Pakistani one was itself legitimate" and was illegitimate if "the judgment that the problems were particularly associated with the Pakistani community had been influenced at least in part to the racial make-up of that community." The Lords did not accept this distinction, as racial makeup is what enables it to be described as a Pakistani community. For these reason, the House of Lords allowed the appeal and restored the earlier decision. Although these disputes were resolved in the case of Ahsan, substantial legal ambiguity still surrounds the use of ABS as a measure to promote BME representation. Unlike the decision regarding AWS, which found for the overrepresented group (men), the Ahsan decision interpreted the RRA from the perspective of the underrepresented group (blacks/Asians/Muslims).

Crucially, as had occurred earlier with passage of AWS, there were brief discussions of including race when the SDA was being reformed, but this intention was later dropped. All the same, Labour changed its selection rules after 1997 to ensure that minority candidates were reaching final shortlists. The new rules required that in parliamentary selections, if no BME candidates received a nomination by a branch to the shortlisting stages, and where one or more black or Asian members expressed an interest in selection, the constituency executive was required to interview and nominate from among the applicants to ensure that at least one was shortlisted. However, this new provision did not lead to a major increase in number of minority candidates selected and elected in 2001 (Ali and O'Cinneide 2002). In 2005, concerns that AWS would "all-white women shortlists" (*Muslim News*, April 25, 2003) were confirmed: no BME women were selected as Labour Party candidates via AWS. However, a BME woman was still elected to parliament, because while she had been unsuccessful in contesting an AWS in one district, she was successful in another district that used an ABS by default. In the aftermath of the election, suggestions were made that it was time for hybrid "woman and BME shortlists" to ensure greater numbers of BME women in parliament (Childs 2005: 155).

To remedy this situation, in 2007, the government held talks with a leading black pressure group, Operation Black Vote, to explore whether future change in the law to let parties choose parliamentary candidates from ABS could work in practice. There were also calls for legislation on ABS voiced among several prominent Labour politicians (Woodward 2007). In 2008, a report was commissioned by Labour's deputy leader, Harriet Harman, and written by Simon Woolley, the director of Operation Black Vote, making a case for ABS. Woolley proposed that the reform of the RRA be along similar lines to the SDA reform, in that it would not force parties to apply ABS. The report also identified 100 constituencies with large ethnic minority communities as prime targets for shortlists (Hinsliff 2008). A week before, however, former minister Keith Vaz introduced a backbench bill proposing the introduction of ABS, which was instantly condemned by a Tory backbencher as "politically correct" and "divisive" (Hinsliff 2008).

Despite these initiatives, the interim report of the Speakers' Conference established in late 2008 reaffirmed the earlier bifurcation between women and minorities, recommending that parties commit themselves to nominating at least 50 percent female candidates, including via AWS, and ensure that a significantly greater proportion of BME candidates be selected. Along similar lines, the Equality Act 2010 extends the period for which AWS may be used until 2030 by exempting women as a group from restrictions on drawing up shortlists of people with a particular protected characteristic. In comparison, it allows parties to reserve places on shortlists for people on the grounds of race or disability, but shortlists comprised solely of people selected on these grounds are not permitted (Kelly and White 2009). However, as previously noted, the final report of the Speakers' Conference took a more generous view, urging reform of the RRA to allow parties to use strategies to promote the representation of BME candidates similar to those in effect for women. Practical schemas informing British politics have thus created important obstacles to efforts to increase female and minority representation that, together with distinct trajectories with regard to the law, affect the basis on which parties may take steps on behalf of each group.

FRANCE: INDIVIDUALIZED RECRUITMENT OF DIVERSITY CANDIDATES

French debates on minority representation have been shaped by both the French citizenship repertoires and the framing strategies developed by women's groups in response to these constraints. French republicanism is characterized by a philosophical commitment to the principle of universalism. As such, it privileges equal opportunities among all citizens but also enjoins them to transcend individual specificities. Republican values also embrace a generic view of substantive representation, arguing that elected officials must not represent any group-based interests but instead the nation as a whole. Consequently, individuals are framed in these practical schemas as abstract subjects with no group identities or memberships. This tendency toward erasing difference is evident, above all, in the legal approach to race discrimination pursued in France, which equates any mention of "race" to be harmful and retrograde. However, following a constitutional amendment in 1999 and electoral reform in 2000, France became the first country in the world to promulgate a 50 percent gender quota law, known as *parité*.[6]

6 Belgium and Spain today have similar parity laws. Most other quota laws require a smaller proportion of female candidates, usually 30% (Krook 2009).

This provision introduced a sharp distinction between the provisions made to women and minorities in electoral politics. Understanding how this occurred requires careful attention to the arguments developed by parity advocates, who astutely theorized and popularized the concept of "parity" as a means to overcome legal obstacles to the use of "quotas" in elections. This solution required, in large part, silencing – and delegitimizing – the claims of other groups, especially racial and ethnic minorities, but also gays and lesbians. It has its roots in a more contingent set of events, namely efforts by various female politicians in the late 1970s and early 1980s to establish a 25 percent quota for women in municipal elections. The law was approved unanimously by both houses of parliament in 1982, but was overturned several months later by the Constitutional Council. The court argued that the law violated Article 3 of the Constitution and Article 6 of the Declaration of the Rights of Man and the Citizen, which together affirmed a principle of equality before the law, which precluded all types of division of voters and candidates into categories for all types of political voting.[7]

The verdict affirmed the importance of equal opportunities and cast doubt on legal means to compel parties to promote women's access to political office. Over the next decade, supporters found a new strategy, inspired by work in the Council of Europe as well as the Green movement focused on the promotion of "parity democracy" (Krook 2007). The term "parity" quickly garnered a broad base of support among different sectors following the publication in 1992 of *Au pouvoir citoyennes! Liberté, égalité, parité*,[8] a self-proclaimed manifesto of the parity movement. This was possible in light of the nature of the parity solution, which sought to redefine the principles used by the Constitutional Council to reject quotas – equality before the law and representation of the whole, rather than its parts – to devise a new normative justification for gender quotas consistent with the broader framework of French republicanism.

To accomplish this, advocates strategically argued that reigning understandings of equality and representation – as well as their subject, the universal citizen – were originally deemed to apply only to men. Rather than abandon these concepts entirely, however, they proposed reforming the constitution to recognize explicitly the "two sexes" of the abstract universal citizen. Instituting parity was crucial, they claimed, because "sex" was the "universal" difference among human beings, a division that cut across all other groups, categories,

7 Décision no. 82–146 DC du 18 novembre 1982.

8 The title of this book (Gaspard, Servan-Schreiber, and Le Gall 1992) reconfigures two central slogans of the French Revolution: *aux armes citoyens* (to arms, citizens), the refrain of the French national anthem, and *liberté, égalité, fratenité* (liberty, equality, fraternity), the motto of French republicanism.

and communities (Halimi 1997; cf. Bereni and Lépinard 2004). This policy differed fundamentally from establishing "quotas," they suggested, because quotas implied special rights for minorities, whereas parity simply called for equitable sharing of power between the "two halves of the human race" (Agacinski 2001). They argued, therefore, that adding parity to the constitution would not reverse the accomplishments of the French Revolution, but rather would finally fully realize them (Guigou 1998).

The argument that sex is the universal difference presented advocates with a means to justify their focus on women while reducing the impact of criticism that recognizing parity would escalate claim-making by other underrepresented groups (Scott 2005). There was skepticism toward this solution among both feminist and nonfeminist critics, who felt that recognizing sexual difference was "reactionary" and that a concession to women would spur "differentialism" and "communitarianism" among other groups, with fatal consequences for the secular and universal republic (Badinter 1996; Ozouf 1995; Varikas 1995). However, in the end, parity received high-profile support from President Jacques Chirac and Prime Minister Lionel Jospin. While agreeing to water down the amendment language from "guarantees parity" to "promotes equal access" (Giraud and Jenson 2001), the two achieved nearly unanimous passage of the constitutional reform and a later revision to the electoral law to require equal numbers of male and female candidates, with the state funding of political parties reduced in proportion to their rates of noncompliance. Although the law has been successful at the local level, loopholes for national elections have led to small changes in the numbers of women elected, from 10.9 percent in 1997 to 12.2 percent in 2002, 18.2 percent in 2007, and 26.9 percent in 2012 (Inter-Parliamentary Union 2013).[9]

Despite the modest achievements of the parity law at the national level, recent years have witnessed attempts by some minority activists to extend these provisions to a wider range of groups, contrary to the assurances of parity advocates. One of the groups that have sought to promote ethnic diversity in political life is *Le conseil represéntatif des Associations Noires* (the Representative Council of Black Associations, or CRAN), which has worked to raise public consciousness concerning the absence of ethnic minorities at all levels of French politics. It has also lobbied for legislative changes that would correct the invisibility of black people in France more generally by authorizing the collection of data on ethnic and racial backgrounds in the national census. Crucially, CRAN frames its goals in relation to republican principles, in an effort to call attention to the fact that discourses of "universalism" in fact

9 This compares to a world average of 21.3 percent (Inter-Parliamentary Union 2013).

conceal "a symbolic male, white, bourgeois, Catholic political order."[10] To enact a shift in focus from "parity" to "diversity," the association argues that only through the explicit recognition of difference can the principles of republican democracy be truly realized (Bird 2008).

These demands have found less resonance than those for parity, however. Some scholars argue, indeed, that the framing strategies employed successfully by the gender parity campaign have had strong "silencing effects" on efforts to promote the political presentation of racial and ethnic minorities (Lloyd and Bassel 2008: 100), given tendencies to downplay differences among women along lines of class, race, and ethnicity (Lépinard 2007). The exclusionary nature of the parity argument, moreover, extends to additional groups: some parity advocates have explicitly used arguments for parity as a way of stressing more traditional views of gender and family relations, thereby undercutting the claims of gays and lesbians who do not fit the "natural order" of the heterosexual couple (cf. Agacinski 2001). Yet, as several researchers point out, the tenets of French republicanism are not just gendered, but also racialized (Ducoulombier 2002).

These discursive obstacles are exacerbated by the fact that feminist and antiracist groups in France have rarely cooperated, or even referred to one another's initiatives, despite the central emphasis that antiracists place on areas of intervention that implicitly involve women. As a result, there is been a general lack of communication and coordination between the campaigning and claims-making by majority French women and women of migrant origin (Lloyd and Bassel 2008). This can be explained in part by the absence of "race" and questions of "intersectionality" – how class, race, or sexuality intersect with and shape gender relations – more generally in French feminist theory (Ducoulombier 2002; Lépinard 2007). It may also be attributed to a strategic decision on the part of parity supporters, who drew inspiration from the way in which the Beur movement of 1980s challenged the abstract universalism of French republicanism (Scott 2005), but were required – as a result of this discursive strategy – to overlook potential alliances with ethnic minorities by rejecting the ideal that women were a minority at all. As a consequence, the parity campaign "opened the system to women, but ... did not challenge whiteness or universality as pillars of national identity" (Lloyd and Bassel 2008: 107).

Observations such as these, perhaps not surprisingly, have generated expectations among ethnic minority women that the parity law does not have any substantial positive effect on their lives, but instead mainly benefits the elite

[10] http://www.lecran.org

and white women who were its strongest advocates (Bird 2001; Ducoulombier 2002). Nonetheless, a set of interviews conducted with French women of immigrant origin, who were active in associations promoting the rights of immigrant women and French women of immigrant origin, reveals that three of the six interviewed were at the time candidates for municipal elections and that a further two had been asked to run but had declined (Bird 2001: 281). While not definitive evidence of a new trend, this pattern speaks to the recent "fast-tracking" of minority ethnic women to prominent political positions in France and other European countries like Belgium and the Netherlands in recent years (Achin and Lévêque 2009; Hughes 2008).

The first cabinet of Nicolas Sarkozy upon his election as French president in 2007, for example, was notable not only in its high proportion of women, but also with regard to its inclusion of three minority women, two of whom were full ministers: Rachida Dati as Minister of Justice, Fadela Amara as Minister for Urban Renewal, and Rama Yade as Secretary of State in charge of human rights, within the Foreign Ministry. While these nominations constitute crucial steps forward for women, these and similar developments have also met with skepticism from feminists as well as ethnic minority women themselves. Some fear that incumbent white women rather than men are being replaced with "candidates of diversity" as a way to maintain white male privilege: when gender difference and diversity are reflected in the same candidate, there is no need to make room for two newcomers. Among minority groups, an additional concern is that diversity candidates are political tokens used to attract voter support, but with little commitment or capacity to address issues related to social exclusion of minorities (Bird 2008). Others worry that minority women are "there just to add color" (Bird 2001: 284). These patterns highlight the ways in which measures for one group may come at the cost of another, owing to the practical schemas provided by existing value repertoires that, in combination with the strategizing of activists, may provide differential opportunities for women and minorities in their struggles for political access.

CONCLUSIONS: FRAMING CITIZENSHIP MODELS AND LEGAL LEGACIES

Comparing debates within and across countries on strategies for increasing the political representation of women and minorities reveals that the institutional arena of electoral politics can create possibilities for many different kinds of marginalized groups to make claims for increased political representation. Despite tendencies to draw parallels among these groups, however, basic demographic features appear to have shaped argumentative strategies, as well as favored responses to claims made by women, as opposed to those put forward by members of minority groups. The relationship between these groups is not necessarily a zero-sum game, with one advancing at the expense of the other, but simultaneous debates may even enhance opportunities for minority women to be the focus of increased political recruitment (cf. Hughes 2011). Rather, the analysis here suggests that elements of both structure and agency are important for making sense of variations across cases, and thus the degree to which one or both groups are recognized – and in what fashion.

More specifically, citizenship repertoires, together with antidiscrimination laws, provide a set of practical schemas for judging such claims to be legitimate or illegitimate, thereby shaping the possibilities for reform. In France, discourses of universalism have influenced the rhetorical strategies of parity advocates, which they translated into a strategic decision to privilege sex above all other differences. In Sweden, concerns about individualism and solidarity have produced tensions in the application of quota strategies, with a preference for softer measures to improve the status of underrepresented groups giving way to stricter policies only in the case of women. In the case of the United Kingdom, efforts to preserve an equal-opportunities notion of equality have undercut opportunities to pursue positive action in candidate selection, except in very circumscribed circumstances subject to time limits. Yet, as all these case studies also show, the decisions made by various actors – often contingent, but almost always without a full appreciation of the implications – shape the nature and outcome of these framing processes. These possibilities emerge from institutional features of the electoral realm, which permit great fluidity in the characteristics required to hold political office, as well as decisions in the past and present to give legal precedence to some identities over others.

BIBLIOGRAPHY

Achin, Catherine and Sandrine Lévêque. 2009. "Parity Context in France." Paper presented at the European Conference on Politics and Gender, Queen's University Belfast, Northern Ireland, January 21–23.

Agacinski, Sylviane. 2001. *Parity of the Sexes*. New York: Columbia University Press.

Ali, Rushanara and Colm O'Cinneide. 2002. *Our House? Race and Representation in British Politics*. London: Institute for Public Policy Research.

Amin, Kawa. 2010. "Five Kurds Enter Swedish Parliament." Online at: http://www.rudaw.net/english/world/3178.html (accessed December 7, 2010).

Bäck, Henry and Maritta Soininen. 1998. "Immigrants in the Political Process." *Scandinavian Political Studies* **21** (1): 29–50.

Badinter, Élisabeth. 1996. "Non aux Quotas de Femmes." *Le Monde*, June 12.

Bereni, Laure and Éléonore Lépinard. 2004. "'Les femmes ne sont pas une catégorie': les stratégies de légitimation de la parité en France." *Revue française de science politique* 54(1): 71–98.

Bird, Karen. 2001. "Liberté, Égalité, Fraternité ... and Diversité? The Difficult Question of Ethnic Difference in the French Parity Debate." *Contemporary French Civilization* 25 (2): 271–292.

—— 2005. "The Political Representation of Visible Minorities in Electoral Democracies." *Nationalism and Ethnic Politics* 11 (4): 425–465.

——2008. "Assessing the Multiple Impacts of Parity in France." Paper presented at the Annual Meeting of the Midwest Political Science Association, Chicago, April 3–6.

Bird, Karen, Thomas Saalfeld, and Andreas M. Wüst, eds. 2010. *The Political Representation of Immigrants and Minorities*. New York: Routledge.

Bleich, Erik. 2004. "Anti-Racism without Races." In *Race in France*, ed. Herrick Chapman and Laura L. Frader. New York: Berghahn, 162–188.

Blomqvist, Paula Rodrigo. 2005. *Närvaros politik och det mångetniska Sverige. Om att ta plats I demokratin*. PhD Dissertation, Gothenburg University.

Bowen, John. 2007. *Why the French Don't Like Headscarves: Islam, the State, and Public Space*. Princeton: Princeton University Press.

Brothers, Caroline. 2009. "French Minorities Have Doubts on Political Success." *New York Times*, April 12.

Calvès, Gwénaële. 2004. "Color-Blindness at a Crossroads in Contemporary France." In *Race in France: Interdisciplinary Perspectives on the Politics of Difference*, ed. Herrick Chapman and Laura L. Frader. New York: Berghahn, 219–226.

Campbell, Rosie, Sarah Childs, and Joni Lovenduski. 2006. "Women's Equality Guarantees and the Conservative Party." *Political Quarterly* 77 (1): 18–27.

Childs, Sarah. 2003. "The Sex Discrimination (Election Candidates) Act and Its Implications." *Representation* 39 (2): 83–92.

——2005. "Feminising Politics: Sex and Gender in the Election." In *Britain Decides: The UK General Election 2005*, ed. Andrew Geddes and Jonathan Tonge. New York: Palgrave, 149–169.

Dahlstedt, Magnus. 2004. "'En av 1,8 miljoner!': Röster från ett monokulturellt partiliv." In In *Engagemang, mångfald och integration*, ed. Anders Westholm, Karin Borevi, and Per Strömblad. Stockholm: Statens Offentiliga Utredningar, 49–86.

Dahlström, Carl and Ulrika Möller. 2004. "Statens väljarskola – strategin för att öka valdeltagandet bland utländska medborgare i Sverige, 1976–2002." In *Engagemang, mångfald och integration*, ed. Anders Westholm, Karin Borevi, and Per Strömblad. Stockholm: Statens Offentiliga Utredningar, 149–176.

Ducoulombier, Audrey. 2002. "Parity Is About 'Race': French Republican Citizenship and the French Caribbean." *Modern & Contemporary France* 10 (1): 75–87.

Eduards, Maud L. 1992. "Against the Rules of the Game: On the Importance of Women's Collective Actions." In *Rethinking Change: Current Swedish Feminist Research*, ed. Maud L. Eduards et al. Uppsala: Swedish Science Press, 83–104.

Freidenvall, Lenita. 2005. "A Discursive Struggle – The Swedish National Federation of Social Democratic Women and Gender Quotas." *NORA: Nordic Journal of Women's Studies* 13 (3): 175–186.

——2006. *Vägen till Varannan Damernas: om kvinnorepresentation, kvotering och kandidaturval i svensk politik 1970–2002*. PhD Dissertation, Stockholm University.

Gaspard, Françoise, Claude Servan-Schreiber, and Anne Le Gall. 1992. *Au pouvoir, citoyennes!: liberté, égalité, parité*. Paris: Éditions du Seuil.

Giraud, Isabelle and Jane Jenson. 2001. "Constitutionalizing Equal Access." In *Has Liberalism Failed Women?*, ed. Jytte Klausen and Charles S. Maier. New York: Palgrave, 69–88.

Göransson, Anita. 2005. "Utländsk bakgrund – tillgång eller hinder på vägen mot makt?" In *Makten och mångfalden: Eliter och etnicitet I Sverige*, ed. Anders Westholm, Karin Borevi, and Per Strömblad. Stockholm: Justitiedepartementet, 7–39.

Government Equalities Office. 2010. "Representation in Public Life." At: http://www.equalities.gov.uk/what_we_do/representation_in_public_life.aspx (accessed 4 November 2010).

Guigou, Élisabeth. 1998. "Projet de Loi Constitutionelle Relatif à L'égalité Entre les Femmes et les Homes." Speech to the French National Assembly, December 15.

Halimi, Gisèle. 1997. *La nouvelle cause des femmes*. Paris: Seuil.

Harvey, Anna. 1998. *Votes Without Leverage: Women in American Electoral Politics, 1920–1970*. New York: Cambridge University Press.

Hazan, Reuven Y. and Gideon Rahat. 2010. *Democracy within Parties: Candidate Selection Methods and their Political Consequences*. New York: Oxford University Press.

Hinsliff, Gaby. 2008. "Labour Report Backs All-Black Shortlists." *Observer*, February 10.

Hirdman, Yvonne. 1990. "Genussystemet." In *Demokrati och makt i Sverige*. Stockholm: Statens offentliga utredningar, 73–116.

House of Commons. 2010. *Speaker's Conference (On Parliamentary Representation): Final Report*. London: House of Commons.

Hughes, Melanie M. 2008. *Politics at the Intersection: A Cross-National Analysis of Minority Women's Legislative Representation*. PhD Dissertation, Ohio State University.

——2011. "Intersectionality, Quotas, and Minority Women's Political Representation Worldwide." *American Political Science Review* **105** (3): 604–620.

Hussein, Abdi Hajji. 2010. "For First Time, Somalis Elected MPs at Swedish Parliament." Online at: http://beforeitsnews.org/story/210/653/For_First_Time,_Somalis_Elected_MPs_At_Swedish_Parliament.html (accessed December 7, 2010).

Inter-Parliamentary Union. 2013. "Women in National Parliaments: Situation as of 1 July 2013." At: http://www.ipu.org/wmn-e/classif.htm (accessed 9 July 2013).

Jarstad, Anna. 2004. "Ur askan i elden? Om etnisk kvotering som medel för politisk integration." In *Engagemang, mångfald och integration: Om möjligheter för politisk jämlikhet*, ed. Anders Westholm, Karin Borevi, and Per Strömblad. Stockholm: Statens Offentiliga Utredningar, 177–205.

Kelly, Richard and Isobel White. 2009. "*All-Women Shortlists*." London: House of Commons.

Krook, Mona Lena. 2007. "National Solution or Model from Abroad? Analyzing International Influences on the Parity Movement in France." *French Politics* 5 (1): 3–19.

——2009. *Quotas for Women in Politics: Gender and Candidate Selection Reform Worldwide*. New York: Oxford University Press.

Krook, Mona Lena and Diana Z. O'Brien. 2010. "The Politics of Group Representation: Quotas for Women and Minorities Worldwide." *Comparative Politics* **42** (3): 253–272.

Krook, Mona Lena, Joni Lovenduski, and Judith Squires. 2009. "Gender Quotas and Models of Political Citizenship." *British Journal of Political Science* **39** (4): 781–803.

Lépinard, Eléonore. 2007. "The Contentious Subject of Feminism: Defining Women in France from the Second Wave to Parity." *Signs* **32** (2): 375–403.

Lloyd, Catherine and Leah Bassel. 2008. "Bridging Differences or Building Silences? Parité and the Representation of 'Women' in French Political Life." *Journal of Contemporary European Studies* **16** (1): 99–110.

Lovenduski, Joni and Pippa Norris, eds. 1993. *Gender and Party Politics*. London: Sage.

Mansbridge, Jane. 1999. "Should Blacks Represent Blacks and Women Represent Women? A Contingent 'Yes.'" *Journal of Politics* **61** (3): 628–657.

Niklasson, Birgitta. 2005. "Enstaka öar av framgång: Etnicitet och invandrarrepresentation I den politiska eliten." In *Makten och mångfalden: Eliter och etnicitet i Sverige*, ed. Anders Westholm, Karin Borevi, and Per Strömblad. Stockholm: Justitiedepartementet, 117–137.

Norris, Pippa. 1997. "Equality Strategies and Political Representation." In *Sex Equality Policy in Western Europe*, ed. Frances Gardiner. New York: Routledge, 46–59.

——2004. *Electoral Engineering: Voting Rules and Political Behavior*. New York: Cambridge University Press.

Norris, Pippa, Andrew Geddes, and Joni Lovenduski. 1992. "Race and Parliamentary Representation." *Journal of Elections, Public Opinion, & Parties* **2** (1): 92–110.

O'Neill, Michael. 1998. "Re-imagining Belgium: New Federalism and the Political Management of Cultural Diversity." *Parliamentary Affairs* **51** (2): 241–258.

Ozouf, Mona. 1995. *Les Mots des Femmes*. Paris: Fayard.

Palme, Sven Ulric. 1969. "Vid valurnan och i riksdagen under femtio år." In *Kvinnors röst och rätt*, ed. Ruth Hamrin-Thorell, Ulla Lindström, and Gunvor Stenberg. Stockholm: AB Allmänna Förlaget, 41–110.

Phillips, Anne. 1995. *The Politics of Presence*. Oxford: Oxford University Press.

Reynolds, Andrew. 2005. "Reserved Seats in National Legislatures: A Research Note." *Legislative Studies Quarterly* **30** (2): 301–310.

——2006. *Electoral Systems and the Protection and Participation of Minorities*. London: Minority Rights Group International.

Richburg, Keith B. 2005. "Europe's Minority Politicians in Short Supply." *Washington Post*, April 24.

Ruedin, Didier. 2009. "Ethnic Group Representation in a Cross-National Comparison." *Journal of Legislative Studies* **15** (4): 335–354.

Russell, Meg. 2000. *The Women's Representation Bill: Making It Happen*. London: Constitution Unit.

Sainsbury, Diane. 2004. "Women's Political Representation in Sweden: Discursive Politics and Institutional Presence." *Scandinavian Political Studies* **27** (1): 65–87.

Scott, Joan Wallach. 2005. *Parité! Sexual Equality and the Crisis of French Universalism*. Chicago: University of Chicago Press.
——2007. *The Politics of the Veil*. Princeton: Princeton University Press.
Soininen, Maritta. 1999. "The 'Swedish Model' as an Institutional Framework for Immigrant Membership Rights." *Journal of Ethnic and Migration Studies* **25** (4): 685–702.
——2011. "Ethnic Inclusion or Exclusion in Representation? Local Candidate Selection in Sweden." In *The Political Representation of Immigrants and Minorities*, ed. Karen Bird, Thomas Saalfeld, and Andreas M. Wüst. New York: Routledge.
Soininen, Maritta and Henry Bäck. 1999. "Invandrarkanditaterna i personvalet." *Premiär för personval*, ed. Sören Holmberg and Tommy Möller. Stockholm: Statens offentliga utredningar, 165–196.
Solomos, John and Les Back. 1995. *Race, Politics, and Social Change*. New York: Routledge.
Squires, Judith. 1996. "Quotas for Women: Fair Representation?" *Parliamentary Affairs* **49** (1): 71–88.
"Swedes Elect Four Iranian Legislators." 2010. *Iran Times*, October 8. Online at: http://www.iran-times.com/ (accessed December 7, 2010).
Varikas, Eleni. 1995. "Une répresentation en tant que femme? Réflexions critiques sur la demande de la parité des sexes." *Nouvelles questions féministes* **16** (2): 81–127.
Wängnerud, Lena. 1999. *Kvinnorepresentation. Makt och möjligheter i Sveriges riksdag*. Lund: Studentlitteratur.
Westin, Charles. 1996. *Immigration to Sweden: An Overview*. Stockholm: Centrum för invandringsforskning.
Williams, Melissa S. 1998. *Voice, Trust, and Memory: Marginalized Groups and the Failings of Liberal Representation*. Princeton: Princeton University Press.
Woodward, Will. 2007. "Harman Tests Ground to Let Parties Draft All-Black Shortlists of Would-Be MPs." *Guardian*, September 25.
Young, Iris Marion. 1990. *Justice and the Politics of Difference*. Princeton: Princeton University Press.

9 How Institutional Context Shapes Head Scarf Debates across Scandinavia

Birte Siim

INTRODUCTION

In this chapter, I place debates over Islamic head scarves in specific institutional contexts by making two contrasts: (1) between public and private institutions, and (2) across three Scandinavian countries. The chapter thereby situates the justifications advanced for particular policies in their national and their occupational contexts. I begin with regulations and justifications occurring in Danish and Norwegian labour markets and then contrast the Swedish, Danish and Norwegian debates about the right of employees or students to wear a head scarf within public institutions. I argue that justifications are shaped by the kinds of authority actors possess in each setting, as well as broader principles. Migration and cultural diversity have posed new challenges to European countries on issues of welfare, democracy and citizenship. These concerns are reflected in research emphases on the relation between gender equality and diversity (Squires 2007) and on "intersectionality", or how gender intersects with ethnic, racial, religious and other kinds of diversity and inequality (Yuval-Davis, 2007; Verloo 2006). In this chapter I draw on these concerns to show how institutional and national contexts matter in debates about Muslim women's head scarves in Scandinavia. Important to my approach have been two European research projects[1] on these broad issues (Kilic, Saharso and

[1] The VEIL project, *Values, Equality and Differences in Liberal Democracies: Debates about Muslim Women's Headscarves in Europe* (2006–2009), has analyzed the head scarf issue in eight European countries: Austria, Denmark, France, Germany, Greece, the Netherlands, Turkey and the United Kingdom: http://www.veil-project.eu/. The findings from the VEIL-project have been published in KIlic, Saharso and Sauer, eds. (2008). *Social Politics International Studies in Gender, State and Society.* Special Issue. Debating Citizenship, Gender and Religious Diversity. No. 4, and Sieglinde Rosenberger and Birgit Sauer, eds. (2012). *Politics, Religion and Gender. Regulating the Muslim Headscarf*, New York: Routledge. The EUROSPHERE project, *Diversity and the European Public Sphere* (2007–2012), has analyzed gender and diversity in fourteen EU countries as well as Norway and Turkey: http://www.eurospheres.org. The

Sauer 2008; Rolandsen Agustin and Siim 2010). They found that new conflicts about accommodating religious and ethnocultural diversity occur within and between specific institutions as well as across national and transnational levels. They pointed to the crucial role actors play as advocates for competing and conflicting perceptions of gender and religion. The studies also underscored the limitations of national models as primary explanatory factor for how particular sets of actors, in specific institutions, framed the head scarf "problem" (Kilic, Saharso and Sauer 2008: 403).[2]

The present chapter takes these studies one step further by comparing how these debates are framed in three Scandinavian countries: Sweden, Denmark and Norway. It focuses on the variations in the practical schemas actors use in selected public and private settings in these countries. The three countries are worth comparing because they have taken relatively accommodating approaches to veiling in public institutions, in spite of differences in migration and integration policies. Sweden is the only Scandinavian country that at some point embraced multicultural policies, whereas Denmark in 2001 adopted one of the most restrictive migration policies in Europe, with Norway positioned somewhere in between (Brochmann and Hagelund 2012).

The Danish and Norwegian comparisons concern highly visible and politicized cases with specific interactions of actors and institutions. One of the key debates involved the principle of religious discrimination of private employees weighed against the employer's authority to decide about company regulations. Another involved the neutrality of legal judges and police officers vis-à-vis the right of public employees to express their religious beliefs (Siim and Skjeie, 2008). The politicization of the two cases contrasts with the depoliticized Swedish debates, which concerned veiling for students and student within educational institutions. In these cases the justifications referred to "the primacy of religion" against one school's decision to forbid veiling (Lanefelt 2010). This case suggests that arguments that give primacy to religion may have unintended negative consequences for Muslim women.

The chapter thus provides a detailed comparison of different justifications in Scandinavian head scarf debates in public and private settings. The first two cases compare regulations and justifications in head scarf debates in Danish

findings from the EUROSPHERE project concerning interactions of gender and diversity is published in Birte Siim and Monika Mokre, eds. (3). *Negotiating Gender and Diversity in and Emergent European Public Sphere*. London: Palgrave/Macmillan.

2 Denmark was the only Nordic country included in the VEIL project, and the EUROSPHERE project included research on gender and diversity in Denmark, Norway and Finland – but not in Sweden. The analysis of gender and religious diversity includes findings from other research projects (see Siim and Skjeie 2008; Lanefelt 2010, 2012).

and Norwegian labour markets (see Siim and Skjeie 2008). Both cases involved claims by female employees about the right to wear the Muslim head scarf to work for religious reasons against private employers who demanded the authority to dismiss employees who did not adhere to the company's dress code. The detailed analysis discloses, however, that the justifications, public involvement and rulings in the two cases were quite different (Siim and Skjeie 2008).

The second set of cases compares the Danish and Norwegian debates about the right of employees to wear a head scarf within public institutions. This concerns legal judges in Denmark and police officers in Norway. In these two highly visible and politicized cases within strategic public institutions, the justifications included claims for religious freedom against demands to defend the neutrality of the state. The last section contrasts the Danish and Norwegian approaches with the similar but depoliticized Swedish conflict about veiling in public schools, where the Swedish board of education successfully defended the freedom-of-religion principle (Lanefelt 2010).

In contrast to cross-national comparisons based on the notion of national models, this chapter proposes comparisons that focus on variations in the justifications of actors in public and private arenas, within specific institutions and in particular sites. It argues that head scarf regulations and debates concern the authority of actors to decide on these issues within particular public and private institutions, as well as the reference to underlying principles, reasoning and justifications. Finally it indicates that the mobilization of public and private actors play a crucial role in debates on various sites and thus influences the construction of identities of religious minorities.

HEAD SCARF DEBATES IN PUBLIC VERSUS PRIVATE INSTITUTIONS

Here I examine how actors framed the wearing of head scarves in private and public arenas in Denmark, Norway and Sweden. I draw on theoretical and methodological debates of the VEIL-project,[3] which addressed the right to wear religious symbols in liberal democracies. Muslim women are the bearers and representatives of these symbols, and these public debates about Muslim

[3] The VEIL project combined a critical frame analysis of documents with historical-institutional analysis. This approach is briefly presented by Kilic, Saharso and Sauer in the introduction to the special issue of Social Politics on the Veil: *Debating Citizenship, Gender and Religious Diversity*. Here a frame is defined as an "interpretative schemata that signifies and condenses the "world out there" by selectively punctuating and encoding objects, situations, events, experiences and sequences of actions in one's present or past environment" (Kilic, Saharso and Sauer 2008: 402).

head scarves illustrate the tensions and conflicts around gender and religious diversity occurring across Europe. They disclose how political forces on the left and right employ similar schemas and arguments, and that they depend on conceptions of gender equality and Islam that often have exclusionary meanings and effects (Rosenberger and Sauer 2012).

The three Scandinavian countries have many similarities in terms of citizenship, immigration and gender legislation and are said to belong to the same Scandinavian welfare, citizenship and gender model, but they have recently chosen different approaches to migration (Siim and Skjeie 2008). They do not fit any of the classical citizenship models: the ethnocultural model, the civic-assimilationist or republican model, or the multicultural model (Kilic, Saharso and Sauer 2008). Sweden is perceived as the only multicultural Nordic country because it accepted dual citizenship and in 2001 separated state and church. Norway has recently decided to separate state and church, while Denmark has preserved a state church. In spite of these differences, research has documented that all three countries have had similar problems with integrating immigrants on equal terms in the labour market, in public institutions and in society more generally (Brochmann and Hagelund 2010).

The detailed analyses across public and private sectors reveal both similarities and differences in the framing processes of Muslim head scarves between and within the three countries, between the public and private arenas and between specific public institutions. The first section compares articulations of veiling by different actors in the Danish and Norwegian debates about veiling in private companies. The second section addresses conflicts about veiling in selected public institutions using examples from Denmark, Norway and Sweden.

Debates in Private Companies in Denmark and Norway

This section focuses on the process of various framings of veiling in private companies by public and private actors, and the arguments of these various actors involved in this process. It is worth noticing that contrary to events in France and Germany, the first Danish and Norwegian debates on this topic did not concern public institutions, but addressed employees' right to wear the hijab to work and thus concerned the role of religion in private companies. The debates illustrate that in spite of the similarities in the political and discursive opportunity structures of the two countries, there are also important differences, especially in the role of public actors. They show that differences in the mobilization and identities of public and private actors had implications for Muslim women's ability to influence the framing process.

In the Danish case, there were a number of conflicts about veiling in private companies around 2000 between the Danish Trade Union, acting on behalf of employees, and the Employers' Union. There were at least four court cases, of which two ended with reconciliation among the labour market organizations involved in the dispute.[4]

The two best-known court cases were the *Magasin* case and the *Føtex* case. In the *Magasin* case, a department store rejected a young woman wearing the hijab applying to work as a trainee. The hijab was presented as a problem because it would be repulsive for clients. This case was decided by the High Court in 2000 in favour of a Muslim employee, and Magasin was sentenced to pay a fine of 10,000 Dkr (about 1,330 euros). The court reasoned that a ban on the hijab for employees would be *indirect discrimination* against a religious minority according to the 1996 Law on Antidiscrimination in the Labour Market. Following this case, some employers (a major example being COOP) decided to give up the ban against the hijab, while other employers (for example, Dansk Supermarked) decided to change their strategy and adopt the ban as part of a general clothing regulation.

In the second and most important case, the *Føtex* case, the conflict was framed as the right to wear a head scarf to work for religious reasons against the employer's right to decide the dress code of the employees. The trade union, Handel og Kontor (HK), took court action on behalf of an employee, Najla Ainuz, who had been dismissed because she wore the hijab to work, against her employer, Føtex, which is part of the big Danish concern, Dansk Supermarked. The trade union argued on behalf of the employee, who began wearing the hijab after working for five years as a full-time bakery manager, stating that dismissal of the employee made her the victim of indirect religious discrimination. Dansk Supermarked argued that as a private company they had the power to dismiss an employee who did not live up to the general dress code of the supermarket, which demanded that employees had to be "professionally and nicely dressed."

The legal aspects of the case were relatively complex, and the trade union took the case to court twice. The case was first decided by the High Court in

[4] The first case was the *Magasin* case, which was decided in court. The second case was about veiling at Tom's Chocolate Factory, which ended in a settlement. The Danish trade union, Handel og Kontor (HK), has led two cases: the *Aldi* case, which was settled in 2003 with the employee being awarded 30,000 Dkr according to the Danish discrimination law; and the *Føtex*-case, which HK lost. The analysis of the Danish court cases is based on empirical material and research findings from the VEIL project (see Andreassen and Siim 2007; Andreassen, Lund and Siim 2009), and the Norwegian case is based on empirical material and research findings provided by Hege Skjeie (see Siim and Skjeie 2008).

2003 in favour of the employer, who was allowed to ban the hijab provided this was part of a general dress code. The High Court ruled that the company's dismissal of veiled employees would be legal if they had already instituted a general ban that prohibited all visible political, religious and cultural symbols. The important point was that a ban must be universal and should not be directed towards a specific religious group.

Dansk Supermarked is a powerful concern; it owns the large food chains Føtex, Netto and Bilka. The concern had already introduced new clothing regulations in August 2000 as a result of the previous court case, which sentenced the department store Magasin to a fine for not accepting an employee wearing the hijab. These clothing regulations prohibited veiling for employees who were in contact with costumers, but allowed veiling for employees working in the store room. They were directed towards all religious groups and also prohibited caps, Jewish skullcaps (kippas) and large Christian crosses as well as visible piercings or unnatural hair colors. These regulations had been written down and distributed among all Dansk Supermarked's staff during the fall of 2000, and from August 2000 onwards all new employees had been receiving a pamphlet describing the clothing regulations.

On this basis the legal judges ruled that Føtex's veil prohibition was not a question of discrimination but rather a question of employees' obligation to adapt to a general clothing uniform. According to Najla Ainouz's contract dating from March 1, 2001 (when she was hired full time in the bakery), she had accepted that her employment included "the rules and duties described in the staff regulations." The argument was that when signing her contract she had also accepted to obey the staff regulations. The clothing regulations from August 2000 state: "In all areas where there is not a demand for a certain head covering it is a part of our uniform demands that employees do not wear headgear." The trade union appealed the court's decision, arguing that the dismissal on religious grounds was a violation of the Danish Antidiscrimination Law. The case was then taken to the Supreme Court, which finally confirmed the decision in January 2005 (Andreassen and Siim 2007).

We now move to the Norwegian debate, which contrasts with that in Denmark in terms of the institutions involved, their arguments, and the reasoning followed in the final decision. Individual cases of veil discrimination were brought before the Norwegian Equality Ombudsman, but no decision was reached until 2004. At the origin were complaints by a number of employees who were not allowed to wear head scarves to work. The Ombudsman ruled in favour of the employees, stating that prohibitions of veil in work places were a violation of the prohibition against religious discrimination and an expression of "indirect gender discrimination."

In reaching this decision, the Ombudsman compared restrictions of Muslim head scarves in private companies with the uniform regulations within the military services, for example those regarding turbans. The Ombudsman reasoned that many Muslim women wear the veil for religious reasons and she found that situations could occur where "they could not accept to work if they could not wear the head scarf." A prohibition would thus entail significant disadvantage for these women. In more recent decisions the Ombudsman has upheld this general line of reasoning. A ban of the veil was later tried both according to the Gender Equality Act and the later Act against Ethnic and Religious Discrimination, and found to be a violation on both grounds (Siim and Skjeie 2008).

In the two cases, the judges framed the problem in differing ways. In the Danish case, the main conflict was formulated as a struggle between the principles of religious discrimination against the liberal principle of private employers' power to decide without interference from the state. Here the concern for religious rights found in the Danish Constitution and European Human Rights Convention lost out. The Norwegian Ombudsman used concepts of religious discrimination and indirect gender discrimination, stated that it is women who wear the scarves, and on those grounds supported women's right to wear the scarves to work (see Skjeie 2007). Siim and Skjeie (2008) suggest that the Ombudsman's arguments rests on "inclusionary framing" because it recognizes the intersections of different categories that, when combined in situations of religious diversity, promote inequality.

One key factor differentiating these two ways of framing the cases were differences in the interface between various actors and particular institutions involved. First there were two different types of institutions involved, because the Norwegian Equality Ombudsman is a specific institution with the authority to decide the hijab cases, whereas in Denmark the hijab cases were resolved by the ordinary court system. The Ombudsman is known to be more receptive to the arguments and activities of public actors than are legal judges within the normal court system (Siim and Skjeie 2008: 329–334). Another equally important factor in the Norwegian case was the high degree of mobilization of public actors around the women's right to wear head scarves for religious reasons. For example, the MIRA-centre, the National Union of Muslim Women's Organizations and the Organization against Ethnic Discrimination (SMED) formed an alliance in support of those rights. On this basis it seems reasonable to conclude that the differences in interactions between particular institutions and public actors were decisive in shaping the outcomes. Important similarities across the two countries exist in the sense that both Norway and Denmark have strong anti-Muslim political parties with much electoral support and a highly politicized debate about Muslim head scarves. In addition, both countries have witnessed intense public debates about Muslim head scarves in the public and private sectors. In spite of these similarities we found different framing dynamics in the private arena, which resulted in different regulations of veiling.

CONFLICTS ABOUT VEILING IN PUBLIC INSTITUTIONS IN SCANDINAVIA

The following section compares Scandinavian debates about veiling of public employees within different institutional settings. The focus is on two controversial cases within particular public institutions: the Danish debate about judges[5] and the Norwegian debate about police officers. These debates are then contrasted with the Swedish debate about veiling in educational institutions, which received relatively little media attention. As mentioned earlier, the three countries combine similar welfare systems, labelled "welfare nationalism" (Brochmann and Hagelund 2010), with different approaches to migration and integration. On this basis, this section asks to what extent the different national policies towards migration and integration influenced how the debates over veiling were framed.

During the last twenty-five years, the meanings of "Danishness" and "Danish values" have become a controversial public issue, and debates about national and religious belongings have intensified. After the general election in November 2001, a government coalition between the Liberal and Conservative Parties came to power with parliamentary support of the far-right Danish Peoples' Party (DPP, *Dansk Folkeparti*), which is a populist anti-immigration party that aims to limit social policies to Danish citizens. As a result, the Danish migration policies and discourses shifted from relatively liberal towards more restrictive between 2001 and 2011. Government policies were influenced by demands from the DPP to adopt restrictive policies, including restrictions on family unification, as a way to combat forced marriage; the adoption of the infamous twenty-four-year rule was one of the most illustrative examples (Borchorst and Siim 2008; Siim and Skjeie 2008).

In spite of the general shift in migration and integration policies followed by intensive debates and negative framings of the Muslim head scarf in

[5] The results from the VEIL project showed that in the Danish case, the six most important sites for the head scarf debates were the media, the employer/workplace, the courts, parliament/legislative, parties and women's groups. Voices from "public intellectual" and from "Muslim women's organizations" were marginal in the Danish debates (see Andreassen, *Denmark: Executive summary on qualitative analysis*, October 2007).

the media (Andreassen 2005), there has been a relatively accommodating Danish approach to regulation of veiling in public institutions (Hadj-Abdou, Rosenberger, Saharso and Siim 2012). The two cases presented in this section illustrate recent shifts as well as variations within the Danish approach to veiling in two crucial public institutions: the courts and parliament.

The first case concerns the debate about the right of elected members of parliament with a head scarf to speak from the rostrum. The case was provoked by the election of Asmaa Abdol-Hamid, who wears a head scarf, as a substitute deputy for the Red-Green Alliance in 2007. The DPP proposed that parliament should adopt a law to prohibit members with head scarves to speak in parliament. The case ended with a statement issued by the presidium of parliament in the spring of 2008, supported by all political parties except the DPP. It confirmed the relatively accommodative approach by making it legal for an elected member of a political party wearing a head scarf to speak from the rostrum providing the face was visible and the person could be identified. The formulation stated that a legally elected politician has *a democratic right* to be represented in parliament as well as *a constitutional right* to speak from the rostrum no matter what their religious affiliation.

The second case, from the spring of 2008, indicates a shift in the accommodating Danish approach to veiling in public institutions (see Hadj-Abdou, Rosenberger, Saharso and Siim, 2012). This case was inspired by a statement by the Independent Board of Judges declaring that there was nothing that prohibited judges from wearing head scarves in courtrooms. The government proposed to prohibit all religious and political dress or attire for judges, and their bill was adopted by a large majority on May 29, 2009, after a long and heated public and political debate. The bill states: "A judge must not in court sessions appear in a way that could be interpreted as an expression of the person's religious or political affiliation or of the person's attitude to religious or political questions in other respects." The government's main arguments referred to "the neutrality and impartiality" of legal judges vis-à-vis all religions. The government (Liberals and Conservatives) argued that a fair and equal treatment of the accused would not be possible if the judge were wearing visible religious attire.

The analysis shows that the two most important schemas employed here to support the liberal approach to veiling for judges were (1) a nonintervention frame in legal matters, which argues that the bill intervenes in the separation of the legislative and the judicial power and thus challenges fundamental elements of the Danish democracy; and (2) a rights frame, which argues that the bill violates the rights guaranteed by the Danish Constitution, especially (§70) and the European Convention on Human Rights (§ 9) regarding principles of religious freedom and nondiscrimination (Siim 2011).

The case ended with the adoption of a law prohibiting religious and political dress or attire for judges that is restricted to legal judges and framed as a universal ban on all religious and political symbols based on the principle of "court neutrality." This regulation represents a discursive shift in the Danish approach to veiling in public institution. It was only a half-victory, however, for the DPP, which had initiated the parliamentary debate. The party had proposed a ban that would be limited to the Muslim head scarf and not a general ban on all religious symbols because it considers a Muslim judge incapable of judging in accordance with Danish legislation and traditions.

The DPP played a crucial role in the public political debate about a ban against veiling of judges. The party circulated an ad titled SUBMISSION, which linked the debate about the right of the judges to wear head scarves with the opposition against women wearing a burka. The text of the ad read:

> The Islamic head scarf is a symbol of women's submission. The Islamists use it as a strong and visible sign of the belief system that dominates man and women, Muslims and non-Muslims. It is not only about "30 grams of cloth." It is about tyranny and submission! A majority in Parliament is willing to accept this in Parliament, and the Independent Board of Judges has decided that you as a citizen in the future must accept that you in the courtroom can meet a judge clocked in the tyranny of the veil.

The ad ends with an emotional call to national feelings of belonging: "Give us back Denmark."

The party's political campaign presents a forceful illustration of how the populist right frames the notion of national belonging in its use of strong rhetoric that constructs a borderline between "us" and "the others." With its negative rhetoric, the text of the ad aims to construct all Muslims as different "from us" who do not cloak our women and therefore as outside the dominant schemas of "Danishness." The ad thus constructs all Muslims as being outside the national Danish community because Islam is based on a belief system that dominates women, and this framing is premised on an underlying notion about ethnic Danish women's gender equality. The example illustrates how the Danish People's Party cleverly uses "politics of belonging" as a political project to define who is "in" and who is "out" in terms of the national community. In both cases the constructions link gender, ethnicity and national belongings, and the text demonstrates how a negative framing of these categories can be instrumentalized to exclude immigrant minorities.

The two cases demonstrate the complex processes of framing regarding a ban on the veiling in public institutions and illustrate the different arguments and justifications proposed by public actors in legal debates compared to media debates. In the first case the main actor was the presidium, which decided to allow elected deputes to wear the hijab for democratic reasons. This relative accommodating approach to veiling in public institutions was later confirmed when the government in January 2010 rejected the proposal to ban or limit the burka or niqab in public institutions. The government's framing in the second case, which prohibited veiling for legal judges with reference to "the neutrality of the court," represents a remarkable shift in the arguments of the political elite towards framing in public institutions from both the left and the right of the political spectrum. One can only speculate to what extent the negative rhetoric against judges with head scarves was able to influence the outcome.

The Norwegian Debate about Hijab in the Police[6]

The framings of the Norwegian and Danish debates about the right for public employees to wear head scarves in public institutions concern different processes and institutions, and to some extent the public actors also presented different arguments. The Norwegian case, to which we now turn, started when, on February 4 2009, the police issued a dress code for police officers that banned religious head scarves as part of their uniform. The debate was sparked by an announcement by the minister of justice, Knut Storberget, who stated on his Web page that hijab should be allowed as part of the police uniform in Norway. This decision was followed by a media debate and political resistance, and the government's decision to allow the hijab in the police was withdrawn on February 20.

In the Norwegian debate, the main argument for preventing public employees from wearing the hijab as part of the police uniform directly linked the hijab to the police as the representatives of the Norwegian state. The main justification was the reference to "police neutrality": the police should wear a neutral uniform in order to be trusted by the public. According to Døving (2010: 16), the actors in the public and political debate defined the hijab as a religious and political symbol and as a direct challenge to police neutrality.

One example of a more negative framing was presented by Siv Jensen, the leader of the Progress Party, who launched the term "*snikislamisering*" ("sneak-islamization," a gradual Islamization process, which indicates that

6 The summary of the debate is based on the work by Døvling (2010) and Skjeie (2010). These articles do not analyze the arguments in terms of policy frames and the analysis is not as detailed as in the Danish case.

"Islam is coming through the backdoor"). In this justification presented by the populist right, the hijab is not just presented as a threat to state neutrality but becomes a political symbol of an Islamic state. This raised questions about Muslim immigrants and their loyalty to Norway. The gender equality frame was also presented in the political debate, where gender equality was used as an argument both for and against the hijab (Thun 2010).

The Equality and Anti-Discrimination Ombudsman brought the case before the Equality and Anti-Discrimination Tribunal because the government would not change its decision prohibiting the hijab in the police. In August 2010, the Tribunal decided that it would be a violation of the right to religious freedom according to the Anti-Discrimination Act and an indirect violation of the Gender Equality Act to prohibit the hijab in the police. This argument for allowing the hijab in the police is thus another example of practical schemas that combine gender and religion in thinking about discrimination.[7] This time, however, the minister of justice did not accept the Ombudsman's reasoning and did not change his decision to ban the hijab in the police. In this case, the tribunal has no authority to suspend or alter resolutions made by other administrative bodies, nor can it stipulate how the authority to make decisions is exercised (Døving 2010: 17; Skjeie 2010).

Researchers have identified three competing sets of practical schemas, which are reified and labelled as policy frames in the Norwegian debate about whether to allow hijab as part of the police uniform. The dominant justification is the neutrality frame, which refers to the argument presented by the minister of justice against allowing the hijab as part of the uniform. In the minority frame, the justification refers to the hijab as "a political symbol of an Islamic state," presented by the Norwegian Progress Party. These two policy frames thus resemble the Danish arguments for prohibiting religious and political symbols for legal judges. The third justification, the discrimination frame, presented by the tribunal, would allow the hijab as part of the uniform. It is worth noticing that this framing is different from the Danish arguments for allowing legal judges to wear religious symbols. While the Danish legal community refers only to a violation of religious discrimination according to Danish, EU and international law, the Norwegian tribunal refers to multiple discriminations violating both the Norwegian Antidiscrimination and the Gender Equality Act. In both cases the populist right played an important role in the negative framings in the media

[7] For a summary of the Ombudsman's arguments for allowing hijab in the police, see http://www.ldo.no/no/Aktuelt/Nyheter/Arkiv/Nyheter-i-2010/JA-til-religiose-hodeplagg-i-politiet/

debates, but we do not know to what extent the two parties were able to influence the outcomes.

The Swedish Debates about Veiling in Educational Institutions

The Swedish case can contribute to illuminating the dynamic and framings of the two previous cases concerning veiling in public institutions. The comparison demonstrates that in issues of veiling, in the Swedish case the dynamic of the debates and the public actors involved were different from those in the other two countries. In the Swedish case, the issue addressed a conflict within specific educational sites, and here public actors used religion to justify positions for and against allowing the hijab. According to Lanefelt (2010), there was virtually no media debate or any political debate about head scarves in public institutions in Sweden.

Lanefelt's (2010; 2012) analysis of the Swedish approach to Muslim head scarves in public educational institutions includes four different cases:[8] (1) the Burgården high-school case, where two female students wanted to attend classes dressed in a burka; (2) the Minerva elementary school, where the school ordered a student to take off her veil on the school premises; (3) a case concerning two students at the Swedish Institute of Education who wanted to attend classes dressed in niqab; and (4) the Västerort Adult High School case, where a woman who was not allowed to wear a niqab reported the school for discrimination.

These cases were decided by different institutional instances: the first two by the Swedish Board of Education, the third locally at the University of Stockholm, and the last by the Swedish Equality Ombudsman (*diskrimineringsombud*). In the first case, the board upheld the school's decision to forbid wearing the burka for several reasons including pedagogical arguments, practical arguments and the freedom-of-religion argument. In the Minerva, case the board went against the schools' argument for a ban of the veil to allow the wearing of the veil in the specific school. The board mentioned several justifications but the main reason was one of freedom of religion (Lanefelt 2010: 6). The third case is the only case where freedom of religion was not given as the main reasons for allowing the veiled girls to follow classes. Instead the justification refers to equal treatment and to the fact that discrimination should not

[8] The description of the Swedish cases is based on Lanefelt's analysis in "Regulating the veil in Swedish style: Tolerance and the absence of intersectionality in public reasoning on the issue of veil", presented at the Second DEMDI Conference in Oslo on January 28–29, and her chapter "Women's freedom of choice and the issue of the veil", in L. Freidenvall and M. Micheletti (eds.) *Comparisons, Quotas and Critical Change*, Stockholm: Stockholm University Press.

occur at University of Stockholm (SU). In the last case, the argument given for exclusion of a female student who wanted to follow an adult education program wearing the niqab was the aim of fulfilment of education. The student brought the case to the Equality Ombudsman who in 2010 decided to annul the exclusion of a female student from education based on two arguments: (1) the democratic principle of the individual's free will to express, or not express, her religious beliefs, here combined with (2) the principle of equal treatment, since the case concerned citizens' equal rights to education (Lanefelt 2012: 160–161).

Lanefelt concludes that the primary justification in the Swedish case is the freedom-of-religion argument. She finds that this framing may have unintended negative consequences for moral reasoning, because "a policy of the veil that bases the rationale of non-exclusion of female veiling practices from education on the right of freedom of religion can tend to embrace the negative connotations that religion is assigned when contrasted with reason" (Lanefelt 2010: 14). This policy runs the risk of labelling women carrying the veil as *being unreasonable.* Female veiling is assigned only one meaning as a religious symbol, and thus the policy neglects the intersectionality of meanings that veiling represents for women wearing the veil but also the different interpretations that second parties make of veiling traditions.

Lanefelt's reading of the Swedish approach to veiling focuses on the negative implications that depoliticize veiling, because she finds that this reasoning tends to hide that it is a controversial normative issue both for veiled women and for second parties. She suggests that an alternative reasoning would be to acknowledge the intersectional aspects of veiling practices. This interpretation raises interesting questions about the implications of politicization versus depoliticization of veiling for the inclusion/exclusion of minority groups, which should be explored by further studies.

CONCLUSION

The chapter has compared debates about Muslim head scarves in private and public settings in Denmark, Norway and Sweden. It has addressed the various justifications for banning or allowing Muslim women to wear the hijab in particular institutions comparing intersections of justifications, locations, authority and mobilizations of public and private actors.

The comparisons illustrate that Scandinavian debates about the Muslim head scarf concern different articulations of gender and religion in private and public arenas and within particular institutions. The public and private actors presented different justifications for allowing or banning veiling in particular locations, often referring to competing principles and schemas about law or about Muslims. The comparisons suggest that political and legal debates are different from media debates. In the former, justifications often refer to universal principles like the freedom of religion or the neutrality of the state. This contrasts with public media debates, which tend to claim simply on the basis of gender equality that veils should be banned, or allowed. The Danish and Norwegian cases illustrate that actors articulate competing sets of schemas to justify regulations of the Muslim head scarves on the private labour market. The dominant policy frame competes with alternative minority frames, and the outcome depends on the power of public actors, political institutions and social movements to mobilize their resources. The comparison of the arguments for the banning of veiling on the private labour market illustrated that although the justifications of employers and employees were similar in the two cases, the outcome was different. In Norway, the right of private employees to express their religion prevailed, whereas the employers' right to determine the dress code of their employees prevailed in Denmark.

The Norwegian case represents an exception to the ungendered justification for allowing veiling in private institutions. Here the Equality Ombudsman did not reason primarily with reference to the principle of "religious rights" but linked two competing principles: gender equality and religious diversity. The Anti-Discrimination Tribunal used the same reasoning in the arguments to allow hijab in the police, but in this case it did not have the power to determine the outcome. This articulation was interpreted as a multidimensional approach to equality, which interprets relations between gender, religion and nationality as multiple intersecting forms of discrimination, not as contradictory or competing equality claims. From a democratic perspective this seems like a promising strategy.

The Danish case clearly illustrates variations in the framings of gender and religious diversity by public actors in public and private settings, as well as discursive shifts in the framings in public institutions. Here the DPP's proposal to ban the head scarf for legal judges was interpreted as an example of an exclusionary discourse that frames the head scarf as "oppressive to women," excluding the Muslim culture and religion from the dominant Danish culture. This justification contrasts with the ungendered arguments on the political and legal sites, which referred to the principle of "democratic right" in the parliamentary setting as justification for allowing the Muslim head scarf; to the principle of the "neutrality of the court" as a justification for prohibiting religious and political symbols for legal judges in the courts; and finally to "the power of employers to determine the dress-code" on the labour market site.

The comparisons of the three Scandinavian countries illustrate that head scarf debates and regulations of veiling concern questions of authority to decide the issues, the mobilization, empowerment or disempowerment of public and private actors, as well as conflicts and negotiations between public actors and particular institutions about principles, reasoning and interests. The Danish case suggests that there are limits to the politicization of Muslim head scarves by the far right, even at a time where the anti-migration party represented the parliamentary support for the government. The Norwegian case suggests that there are positive implications of an accommodating approach to Muslim head scarves that can recognize the intersections of gender and religious diversity. Arguably the framing of a ban of the hijab as an issue that concerns multidimensional discrimination became a favourable discursive opportunity structure for the mobilization and alliances between human rights activists addressing the discrimination of *religious minorities* and the activities of women's networks addressing the discrimination of Muslim women. This contrasts with the Swedish and Danish cases, where a ban against the hijab was framed solely as an expression of religious discrimination. This indicates that there may also be unintended negative implications of depoliticizing the Muslim head scarf if it is articulated solely as a religious and not as an intersectional issue, which involves (Muslim) women.

This analysis demonstrates that the similarities in state-church models cannot explain the justifications for banning or allowing veiling in specific settings. The Scandinavian cases have illuminated the specific justifications for allowing or banning the head scarf in particular institutional settings. They show that public and private actors justify head scarf claims with reference to universal principles like the right to practice your religion versus the neutrality of the state and gender equality versus oppression of women. The three cases suggest that the outcomes are influenced by the interface between the struggles, conflicts and uneven power relations of public actors and organizations on the one hand and particular institutional settings on the other hand.

The reasoning and rulings of the Norwegian Gender Equality Ombudsman, which from 2006 became the Gender Equality and Anti-discrimination Ombudsman, can be seen as an example of the European trend towards acknowledging and addressing multidimensional discrimination. This was first expressed in the prohibition of discrimination on the basis "sex, racial and ethnic origin, age, religion or belief, disability age or sexual orientation" in the Amsterdam Treaty (1997) and later expanded as part of the fundamental rights with the adoption of the Lisbon Treaty (1999). Research has documented that this was followed by institutional changes in the tackling of multiple discrimination in the member states, where Denmark, Norway and Sweden has chosen different institutional solutions, Norway being the only Scandinavian country that has opted for institutional solutions able to address multiple and interwoven grounds for discrimination (see Krizan, Skjeie and Squires 2012).

BIBLIOGRAPHY

Agustin, Rolandsen L. (2009). "'It is all about the women': Intertwining discourses on gender equality, ethno national diversity and identity constructions among Danish politicians". *Eurosphere Working Paper*, No. 22, University of Bergen.

Agustin, Rolandsen Lise and Birte Siim. "Intersectionality, diversity and gender identity: National and European belongings", in Peter Madsen (ed.) *Challenging Identities. The European Sphere* (forthcoming).

Andreassen, Rikke (2005). The Mass Media's Construction of Gender, Race, Sexuality and Nationality. An Analysis of the Danish News Media's Communication about Visible Minorities from 1971–2004. Department of History, University of Toronto.

——with Birte Siim. (2007). *Country Report Denmark*, unpublished paper, January.

Andreassen, Rikke, Linda Lund Pedersen, and Birte Siim (2008). Cross National Comparisons Denmark, unpublished notes, September.

Bellamy, Richard, Dario Castiglione, and Emilio Santoro, eds. (2003). *Lineages of European Citizenship. Rights, Belonging and Participation in Eleven Nation-States*. Basingstoke: Palgrave/Macmillan.

Borchorst, Anette and Birte Siim (2008). "Women-friendly policies and state feminism. Theorizing Scandinavian gender equality". *Feminist Theory* 9(2): 207–224.

Brochmann, Grete, and Anniken Hagelund, ed. (2012). *Immigration policy and the Scandinavian welfare state 1945–2010*. Houndmills, Basingstoke, Hampshire: Palgrave Macmillan.

Christensen, Ann-Dorte and Birte Siim (2010). "Citizenship and politics of belonging – inclusionary and exclusionary framings of gender and ethnicity". *Kvinder, Køn and Forskning. Special Issue: Intersevtionality at Work: Concepts and Cases.* 2–3: 8–17.

Døving, Cora Alexa (2010). *Religionspluralisme. Religion, migrasjon og integrering.* [Religious Pluralism. Religion, Migration and Integration]. Oslo: Norges forskningsråd.

Hadj-Abdou L., S. Rosenberger, S. Saharso, and B. Siim (2012). "The limits of populism. Accommodative headscarf policies in Austria, Denmark, and the Netherlands", in Sieglinde Rosenberger and Birgit Sauer (eds.) *Politics, Religion and Gender. Regulating the Muslim Headscarf.* New York: Routledge.

Kilic, Sevgi, Sawitri Saharso, and Birgit Sauer (2008). "Introduction: The VEIL: Debating citizenship, gender and religious diversity". *Social Politics. International Studies in Gender, State and Society.* Special Issue: The Veil: Debating Citizenship, Gender and Religious Diversity 4: 397–410.

Krizan, A., H. Skjeie, and J. Squires (2012). *European Equality Regimes. Institutional Change and Political Intersectionality.* Basingstoke: Palgrave/Macmillan.

Lanefelt, Lily (2012). "Women's freedom of choice and the issue of the veil", in L. Freidenvall and M. Micheletti (eds.) *Comparisons, Quotas and Critical Change*. Stockholm: Stockholm University.
——(2010). "Regulating the veil in Swedish-style: Tolerance and the absence of intersectionality in public reasoning on the issue of veil", unpublished paper presented at the DEMDI Conference, Oslo, January 28–29.
Lettinga, Doutje and Rikke Andreassen (2008). "Gender equality as a tool in European national narratives", unpublished paper presented at the International VEIL Conference, Vienna, November 20–21.
Lister, Ruth et al. (2007). *Gendering Citizenship in Western Europe. New Challenges for Citizenship Research in a Cross-National Context*. Bristol: Policy Press.
Lombardo, Emanuela and Lise Rolandsen Agustin (2008). *Framing intersectionality in the European Union gender equality policies: What implication for the quality of policies?* Unpublished Paper.
Lombardo, Emanuela, Petra Meier, and Mieke Verloo, eds. (2009). *The Discursive Politics of Gender Equality*. London: Routledge.
Rosenberger, Sieglinde and Birgit Sauer, eds. (2012). *Politics, Religion and Gender. Regulating the Muslim Headscarf*. New York: Routledge.
Sawitri, Saharso (2007). "Headscarves: A comparison of public thought and public policy in Germany and the Netherlands". *Critical Revue of International Social and Political Philosophy* 10(4): 513–530.
Sawitri, Saharso and Doutje Lettinga (2008). "Contentious citizenship: Policies and debates on the veil in the Netherlands", *Social Politics. International Studies in Gender, State and Society*. Special Issue: The Veil: Debating Citizenship, Gender and Religious Diversity, 4: 455–481.
Siim, Birte (2009). "Gender and Diversity in the European Public Sphere", *EUROSPHERE Working Paper Series*, No. 17, March.
Siim, B. "Gender, Diversity and Migration – Challenges to Nordic Welfare, Gender Politics and Research", *Equality, Diversity and Inclusion* (EDI) (forthcoming).
Siim, Birte (2011). "Det muslimske tørklæde som udfordring til demokratisk ligestilling" [The Muslim Headscarf as a challenge for democratic equality], in Inge Degn and Kirsten Molly Sørensen (eds.) *Tørklædet som tegn. Tilsløring og demokrati i en globaliseret verden*. Århus: Aarhus University Press.
Siim, Birte and Monika Mokre, eds. (2013). *Negotiating Gender and Diversity in an Emergent European Public Sphere*. Basingstoke: Palgrave/Macmillan.
Siim, Birte and Hege Skjeie (2008). "Tracks, intersections and dead ends. State feminism and multicultural retreats in Denmark and Norway". *Ethnicities* 8(3): 322–344.
Skjeie, Hege (2007). "Religious exemptions to equality", *Critical Revue of International Social and Political Philosophy (CRISPP)* 10(4): 471–490.
——(2010). "Rettsrespekt. Kan 'det politiske Norge' velge hvilke lover det vil følge?"[Respect for the law. Can the "political Norway" chose what laws it wants to follow?] *Dagens Næringsliv*, September 18. Available at: http://kilden.forskningsradet.no/artikkel/vis.html?tid=73498
Squires, Judith (2007). *The New Politics of Gender Equality*. Basingstoke: Palgrave/Macmillan.
Thun, Cecilie (2010). Norwegian feminist in a hijab? – Intersections between feminism, ethnicity and religion, unpublished paper.

Verloo, Mieke, ed. (2007). *Multiple Meanings of Gender Equality. A Critical Frame Analysis of Gender Policies in Europe*. Budapest and New York: Central European University Press.

Verloo, Mieke (2006). "Multiple inequalities, intersectionality and the European Union". *European Journal of Women's Studies* **13**(3): 211–228.

Yuval-Davis, Nira (2007). "Intersectionality, citizenship and contemporary politics of belonging". *Critical Review of International, Social and Political Philosophy* **2007**(4): 561–574.

Internet sites: http://www.ldo.no/no/Aktuelt/Nyheter/Arkiv/Nyheter-i-2010/JA-til-religiose-hodeplagg-i-politiet/

http://kilden.forskningsradet.no/artikkel/vis.html?tid=73498

10 Populism, Sexual Politics, and the Exclusion of Muslims in the Netherlands

Justus Uitermark, Paul Mepschen, and
Jan Willem Duyvendak

The discourses framing Islam as deviant and problematic for Europe described in Chapter 1 have had a loud expression in the Netherlands, where political leaders and public figures have reconfigured what had been values of universal liberal citizenship into national values of cultural distinctiveness: "Dutch values" versus "Islamic values." Some analysts join these public figures in arguing that "multiculturalism" was once the Dutch national model and is responsible for weakening Dutch values by adopting a soft position on Muslims and Islam.

In this chapter we examine the Dutch case as a particularly visible instance of a European exclusivist "neocultural" framing of migrants as outsiders who must either completely assimilate into or be actively excluded from the "modern" moral universe.[1] We use the term "neoculturalism" to identify a form of cultural protectionism, representing the world as divided into different, inimical cultures, and to distinguish this way of thinking from forms of cultural relativism.[2] Muslim citizens have become the most conspicuous objects of this neoculturalist discourse, portrayed as backward, intolerant, and incongruous with European secular modernity.

1 Other notions for more or less the same discourses used in the context of the Netherlands include "culturism," which Willem Schinkel (2007) conceptualizes as the functional equivalent of racism. Schinkel prefers the term above – "culturalism" – used by Uitermark (2012), as it can be easily confused with culturalist traditions in American anthropology and sociology. While American culturalists tend to believe in the equality of cultures, contemporary culturalist ideologies emphasize hierarchies. We propose the term "neoculturalism" to distinguish contemporary discourses from the cultural relativism of past culturalist traditions.

2 Movements for cultural protectionism have proliferated in recent years throughout many parts of the world. In countries as diverse as Cameroon and Belgium, discourses of inclusion and exclusion have pitted autochthonous communities against outsiders with, allegedly, aberrant morals and devious intentions (cf. Geschiere 2009).

Preceding chapters have explored ways that schemas and boundaries concerning Muslims arise in particular institutional settings and how they articulate with more broadly national ideologies. Focusing on the Dutch case permits us to analyze the creation and manipulation of ideological elements as part of everyday politics. In particular, we show how the neocultural schemas that were introduced by politicians in the 1990s simultaneously referred to Muslims and to the liberal Dutch elite; this linking gave a political potency to a neoculturalist framing. In short, the rise of these specific schemas about Muslims and Islam was part of an intense struggle among Dutch political leaders. Ideologies grow out of specific institutional contexts – in this case, the complex context of local and national politics.

In our analysis, we identify two central schemas in neoculturalist discourse. First, neoculturalists employ a populist schema to challenge the political establishment in general and allegedly multicultural or leftist elites in particular. Dutch neoculturalists have used a transposed class discourse that pits the white working class against a state-entrenched progressive elite (Uitermark 2012; Mepschen 2012). The second neoculturalist schema targets Muslims in the name of progress and sexual emancipation.[3] As we will show by zooming in on Dutch debates on gay rights, sexual freedom, and the alleged intolerance of Muslim citizens, European identities and nationalisms have become reimagined as progressive and tolerant while Muslims have become framed as homophobic, sexually backward, and stuck in traditional family and religious values. Although particularly evident in the Netherlands, this framing is Europe-wide.[4]

Analysts of neoculturalism and populism in Europe often overlook the extent to which cultural protectionists have appropriated feminist achievements and the discourse of sexual progress to frame Muslims as conservative and intolerant and as the "constitutive outside" of secular, modern, and "progressive" European national projects. The rise of neoculturalist populism in Western Europe is mistakenly analyzed as a shift toward conservatism. Instead, we argue that neoculturalists combine the discourse of sexual progress with anti-Muslim and anti-immigration perspectives. This logic has become increasingly hegemonic because it has salience beyond the populist, nationalist right. Even critics of neoculturalism can only show their commitment to progressive

3 The Netherlands are far from unique in this respect. In various European countries, discourses of sexual democracy (Fassin 2010) have come to play a prominent role in framing Europe as "the avatar of both freedom and modernity" (Butler 2008: 2), while depicting Muslims as backward, devious, and intolerant in terms of sexual freedom and gender equality (cf. Ewing 2008; Fassin 2010; Guenif-Souilamas 2006; Haritaworn 2008; Puar 2007; Scott 2009).

4 Among others, see Buijs et al. (2011); Butler (2008); Ewing (2008); Fassin (2010); Ghorashi (2003); Haritaworn (2008); Jusová (2008); Mepschen et al. (2010); Puar (2007); Sabsay (2012); Van der Berg and Schinkel (2009); Wekker (2009).

values by distancing themselves from Muslims' and migrants' alleged sexual conservatism.

In this chapter we first examine the populist challenge of neoculturalism, after which we analyze the sexual politics undergirding neoculturalist discourse. Subsequently, we address the progressive dilemmas arising from neoculturalist sexual politics, to conclude with an examination of the implications of our approach for the study of perceptions and boundaries related to Islam and Muslims in the Dutch context.

THE POPULIST POLITICS OF NEOCULTURALISM

The progressive movements and idea dominant during the period of state expansion of the 1960s and 1970s had a lasting effect on the forms and functions of the Dutch state (cf. Duyvendak 1999). This is particularly true for policies related to minorities, which have traditionally been the province of left-leaning administrators, professionals, and civil associations (Uitermark 2012). However, in this context, leftist or progressive should not be equated with multiculturalist.[5] While commentators in and of the Netherlands have spoken of a dramatic shift away from multiculturalism toward policies aimed at assimilation, the Netherlands never pursued a multiculturalist policy. Few intellectuals espoused multiculturalist principles, nor were policies justified in terms of multiculturalsm. Specifically, the protection and preservation of minority cultures – a central component of any coherent multiculturalist discourse – was never a goal of policy in itself. The aim of the Dutch "minorities policy," and of the "integration policy" following it, was precisely to prevent the process of minority formation, routinely conceptualized as the formation of an ethnic underclass (cf. Van Amersfoort 1974; Penninx 1988; Scholten, 2007). Policies thus exclusively targeted stigmatized ethnic groups in lower class positions. By incorporating minority representatives and associations into governance networks, it was hoped that minority groups would find it easier to integrate into Dutch society.

[5] Policies were not simply "multiculturalist" but also did not become "assimilationist." Although it is certainly true that, after the emergence of Fortuyn, there were more administrators who wanted to force migrants to integrate, at the same time there was an intensification of efforts to assist or force minorities, and especially Muslims, to identify, organize, and express themselves. It is understandable that researchers have used the lingua franca of international comparative research to categorize the Netherlands, but when we examine the Dutch case (and probably any other case), it becomes apparent that that these concepts tend to reify what is better understood as a dynamic field where different actors push in different directions.

It is essential to understand this prehistory of integration politics to appreciate what is new about neoculturalist schemas. Those who use these schemas did not introduce the idea that migration causes problems, that migration had to be curtailed, that migrants had to become autonomous citizens, that unemployed and unskilled labor migrants had to become productive workers, or that some cultural practices (such as forced marriages or domestic abuse) had to be ended. All of these ideas were well established by the late 1980s and the early 1990s.[6] The designers and defenders of the minorities policy and integration policy sought to put these ideas into practice through a combination of paternalism and "poldering" (the term denoting the "Dutch tradition" of social conflict resolution by means of dialogue and cooperation, invoking ways of collectively draining lands). Because they want to deal with integration issues as practically and efficiently as possible, we refer to these actors as pragmatists. While multiculturalists would view diversity as something to be valued and preserved, pragmatists view it as something that needs to be carefully managed to prevent problems. Consequently, they have put in place an extensive infrastructure to monitor and intervene in ethnic and religious relations. Researchers, advisors, and managers within this field have emphasized the need for policy development on the basis of careful research and dialogue with stakeholders. Their discourses are characterized by technical sophistication, and they argue there is a need for moderation and management rather than passion and drama.

Pragmatist discourse has been formulated to have maximum effect in the policy field, not in public debate. This is what neoculturalists primarily challenged: the pragmatist way of conducting politics with its focus on consultation, moderation, and expertise – in short, the polder model itself. While parliamentary elites and their associates in civil society were firmly committed to pragmatism, actors on the margins were sowing the seeds of the symbolic revolution that would occur after 1991. Intellectuals attacked discursive moderation (redefined as political correctness), radical-right politicians played into xenophobia, and far-left politicians argued that the influx of foreign workers merely served to strengthen the position of capitalists vis-à-vis workers. However, for a long time these were marginal and disunited discourses. The breakthrough of neoculturalism came in 1991, when Frits Bolkestein, at the time the parliamentary leader of the right-wing liberals, argued that Western civilization was fundamentally different from – and vastly superior to – Islamic civilization. He unfolded his vision at a meeting of European Liberal parties in the Swiss city of Luzern on September 6, but his opinion article in De

[6] Tijdelijke Commissie Onderzoek Integratiebeleid, 2004, pp. 436–445.

Volkskrant (Bolkestein 1991) became the debate's focal point (cf. Bracke 2011; Prins 2002). Its central message was that the government should take robust measures to prevent or reduce the formidable problems arising from migration. He also argued Islam is a source of backwardness:

> Islam is not just a religion; it is a way of life. And as such it is at odds with the liberal division between church and state. Many Islamic countries have hardly any freedom of speech. The Salman Rushdie affair is perhaps an extreme case but it shows how much we differ from one another in these matters. (Bolkestein 1991)[7]

Bolkestein saw himself as an exponent of the Enlightenment and Western civilization, praising the achievements of intellectual icons like Goethe and Plato. But he also presented himself as belonging to the "ordinary people" – those who had to shoulder the consequences of mass migration (Prins 2002). Bolkestein observed that Dutch natives were developing a popular counter discourse, outside of the realm of public discourse:

> There is an informal national debate that is not held in public. Voters feel that politicians are not sufficiently aware of their problems. The minority issue is constantly discussed in places like bars and churches. If this is not sufficiently represented in The Hague [the seat of parliament] people will say: why should I vote anyway? (Bolkestein, cited in Prins 2004: 28)

Bolkestein himself was from the elite, but nevertheless presented himself as a redeemer of unjustly marginalized working-class voices: "a representative who ignores the people's concerns is worth nothing" (ibid.). He thus enlisted "the people" in a critique of accommodation and consensus politics. "The people" here specifically refers to Dutch natives living in disadvantaged neighborhoods: people with experience, forms of knowledge and discourses that were not sufficiently valued in public and political arenas. Far from being the perpetrators of racism, Bolkestein presented these people as victims – the "autochthonous [native] minorities in poor neighborhoods in the big cities who are living in the midst of an allochthonous [foreign] majority" (ibid.).[8] In his assessment of

7 All translations from Dutch to English by the authors.

8 The Netherlands does not have an explicit race discourse, but the state and statisticians do categorize people along ethnic lines. The categories currently employed are: "autochthonous," used for people whose parents and grandparents were born in the Netherlands; "allochthonous" (used for people not from the Netherlands, but from Western countries; and "non-Western allochthonous" (people with a relatively recent genealogy in non-Western countries like Turkey, Morocco, and the former Dutch colonies). For an extensive analysis and critique

the transformation of Dutch society and politics, Ian Buruma (2006: 58) quotes Bolkestein saying: "You should never underestimate how deeply Moroccan and Turkish immigrants are hated by the Dutch. My political success rests upon the fact that I have listened to these feelings."

This transposed class discourse frames the autochthonous, Dutch working class as a victim of cultural rather than economic liberalism and consequently espouses cultural rather than economic protectionism. Bolkestein appealed to the populace in a strategy to challenge his political competitors. The state, in his view, should not accommodate a diversity of interests through extensive consultative structures but rather discipline migrants into the moral-cultural universe of the nation.

Bolkestein's attack on the minorities policy paralleled his critique of the "Rhineland model," a corporatist model for socioeconomic regulation that was prevalent in Northwest Europe and that afforded a larger welfare state and more leeway for state intervention than the "Anglo-Saxon model." According to Bolkestein (1996), this model lacked flexibility and was burdened by too many consultative and regulatory structures. More generally, neoculturalists' discursive assaults were, as a rule, not just aimed at minorities but also at the political culture and institutions of consociational corporatism, a political model based on bringing together different blocks for shared governance (Lijphart 1988). In neoculturalist views, an expansive and complex network of interest groups and stakeholders had smothered political debate. They had cultivated a political culture where conflicts were managed among elites rather than sharply debated in public. Especially in the field of integration, neoculturalists would employ their critique of migrants and minority cultures to target the entrenched elites who had grown accustomed to working out differences without causing public consternation.

Bolkestein was the first to successfully challenge his competitors through a provocative integration discourse, but he was surely not the last. The populist politician Pim Fortuyn and the parliamentarian Ayaan Hirsi Ali also incorporated schemas of a divide between "the West" and Islam into their political rhetoric. And they, too, did not just discursively assault minorities but also the political culture and institutions of consociational corporatism. Fortuyn and Hirsi Ali shared an antipathy toward Islam and a strong drive to challenge the culture of consensus. As Hirsi Ali (2003) argued: "I ... realized that Fortuyn had not only been correct about Islam but also with respect to the condition of established politics. We are still going round in the same little circles. Still.

of the use of these categories and the production of populations that are part and parcel to them, see Geschiere (2009); Yanow and Van der Haar (forthcoming).

We avoid any risk, we do not want to offend or upset anyone. Everything is in the service of harmony.".

Hirsi Ali sought to break with a consensus-based integration policy and extract Dutch politicians from the slumber of the polder model. These examples illustrate that when central players in politics articulate positions in opposition to Muslims or Islam, they also position themselves in relation to their political adversaries, who are usually not Muslims. When Bolkestein claimed that he was realistic and frank on Islam, he positioned himself in relation to an entrenched liberal elite that inherited and embodied a style of politics characterized by discursive moderation, especially toward minorities (often referred to as political correctness). The framing of Islam has become a battleground where an ascendant coalition of cultural protectionists confronts entrenched pragmatist elites and consensus politics.

Geert Wilders, the leader of the populist right Freedom Party, is the most recent and most extreme reincarnation of a politician who dissociates himself from the entrenched and "corrupted" liberal elite by drawing a dividing line between the West and Islam and by voicing a fear of mass immigration. He argues that the differentiation between the "two Netherlands" is most apparent in this field:

> The difference between the beliefs of the Dutch people and of the elites are nowhere more glaring than when it comes to mass migration. Almost sixty percent of the Dutch people view Islam as the greatest threat to our identity. Another sixty percent view mass migration as the biggest mistake since the [Second World] War. But here, in parliament, no more than six percent holds these views.[9]

While Wilders has been part of parliamentary life for more than two decades, he stokes a populist hatred against the elite, a rhetoric that appeals to sections of the electorate who have grown disenchanted with liberal elites and their policies (cf. Mouffe 2005).

THE SEXUAL POLITICS OF NEOCULTURALISM

The preceding section has shown that the entrenchment of liberalism – in the field of integration politics and in the state generally – has created the conditions in which populist cultural protectionists attempt, with considerable success, to mobilize disenchanted voters against established political culture,

[9] Wilders, Geert (2008) Parliamentary debate 2009. Available at: http://www.pvv.nl/index.php?option=com_content&task=view&id=1288.

its institutions, and its dignitaries. Neoculturalists challenge an entrenched liberal tradition of pragmatist policy and moderate language by marshaling and organizing audiences through affect, focusing on a fear of Islam and distaste with mass immigration. In the Netherlands, and in Europe in general, sexual liberties and feminist achievements have come to play increasingly pivotal roles in these dynamics. As Francisco Panizza (2005: 11) argues, there can be "no populist leadership unless there is a successful constitution of new identities and of a representative link with those identities." As we shall show, neoculturalist and populist leaders in the Netherlands have depended on and have reinforced the proliferation of discourses of sexual progress to constitute new identities, establish a "representative link" with them, and thus make a new kind of populist imagination and politics possible. To come to a closer understanding of this dynamic, we turn our attention to the sexual politics of Dutch neoculturalist populism.

Discourses of feminist and sexual progress have been pivotal to the ascent and growing entrenchment of neoculturalist perspectives in the Netherlands.[10] Muslim immigration is delineated as a threat to the stability of the Dutch progressive moral order, and cultural protectionists have set out to guard Dutch cultural and sexual liberties against the dangers allegedly posed by Muslim immigrants (Van der Veer 2006; Verkaaik and Spronk 2011). Gay rights and gender equality have thus offered a normative framework and a set of specific schemas to shape the critique of Islam and multiculturalism. This framework renders Muslim citizens "knowable" and makes them objects of critique. The central tropes of this discourse – individualism versus the lack thereof; "tolerance" versus "fundamentalism" – frame an imagined modern self against an imagined traditional (Muslim) other. Such tropes are especially powerful because they put progressives and pragmatists who oppose neoculturalist discourse, but who are, on the other hand, attached to the achievements of sexual and feminist progressive politics, in a rather serious bind. Taking up the defense of lesbian and gay rights comes to be associated with anti-Muslim cultural protectionism, while solidarity with Muslims against Islamophobic rhetoric is represented as trivializing homophobia of conservative Muslim communities.

The power of discourses of sexual progress to create a wedge between allegedly conservative Muslim and migrant minorities and supposedly progressive Dutch people came into full effect in May 2001, when a conservative imam in Rotterdam, Khalil El-Moumni, caused a commotion in a television interview in which he commented on the introduction of gay marriage laws in the

[10] See the analyses in Bracke (2012); Ghorashi (2003, 2010); Josuvá (2008); Mepschen et al. (2010); Schinkel (2011); Van den Berg and Schinkel (2009).

Netherlands. "What Islam says about homosexuality," the imam argued, "is known among all Muslims. It is a sin." The Dutch reporter responded by asking El-Moumni if Islam was capable of accommodating to "the Dutch mentality." The imam responded:

> Islam forces us to integrate in every society, as long as we don't act in discordance with our faith, culture and morality. I agree with integration at the level of science, education and work .... Homosexuality is harmful to society in general and in particular for the Dutch, I think. If this phenomenon is spreading among the young, both among boys and girls, this will lead to extinction. As far as I know, there are more elderly than young people in the Netherlands. When elderly are no longer active in reproduction, who will make children when men and women can marry each other?

Homosexuality, argued El-Moumni, was a contagious disease that had to be contained, although he condemned violence against gays – an important part of the interview that was omitted from the television broadcast. A moral panic followed the broadcast (Hekma 2002; Mepschen et al. 2010). El-Moumni had tread on one of the cornerstones of Dutch cultural self-representation. He was at the center of media attention for weeks. The debate showed a broad consensus about the incompatibility of the imam's views with Dutch society. The sociologist Gert Hekma recalls, for instance, that even the prime minister used "the full 10 minutes of his weekly interview ... to tell Muslims to respect the Dutch tolerance of homosexuality," although he was clearly uncomfortable speaking about the issue in public (Hekma 2002: 242). The Dutch minister responsible for integration, Rogier van Boxtel, invited El-Moumni for a session in which Dutch values were explained. The liberal daily NRC Handelsblad rhetorically asked: "Homosexuality is tolerated in the Netherlands. Shouldn't the role of imams be to promote tolerance and acceptance?"[11] A poll on the Web site of a mainstream gay and lesbian monthly showed that 91 percent of respondents agreed that "newcomers should tolerate our tolerance or should leave" (Prins 2002: 15). The Amsterdam branch of the leading free-market liberal party (VVD) published a pamphlet titled "We also want to live in freedom and without fear" in the Amsterdam newspaper *Het Parool*:

> As in other centuries, our society is still being enriched by new cultures and religions. However, this should not be a one-way process. Moreover, the principles of the liberal free state, equality, tolerance and non-discrimination, are elements of a culture that newcomers can be enriched by. The comments

[11] *NRC Handelsblad*, May 9, 2001.

> of the imams are an active call for intolerance and discrimination against gay men and lesbians. This is blatantly ignoring the basic values of Dutch society.[12]

A commentator in the tabloid *De Telegraaf* argued that El-Moumni's views could only be found in "the medieval deserts of North Africa."[13]

One reason for the performative power of El Moumni's remarks is the wide support among the Dutch of lesbian and gay rights (see discussion later in the chapter). This contributed strongly to the framing of El-Moumni as a backward bigot. But perhaps more important was the fact that El-Moumni could be construed as a religious and cultural outsider, a framing move that played a key role in inciting a moral panic concerning the nation's sexual boundaries (compare Fassin 2010). Some native Dutch commentators had spoken out against public homosexuality in much the same way as El-Moumni, but their words had not elicited a similar societal response. Three years before the El-Moumni-affair, in 1998, a rather harsh debate about public homosexuality accompanied the Gay Games in Amsterdam, a large sporting and cultural event organized by and for international lesbian and gay communities. In that debate, Muslims had not been vocal and had also not been construed as uniquely homophobic. White Dutch conservatives were, on the other hand, very vocal about their antipathy toward gays (cf. Mepschen et al. 2010). In fact, the conservative critic Gerry van der List was fired as a columnist for one of largest Dutch broadsheets after writing a column in which he spoke of "an Amsterdam orgy" and argued that gay men were "obsessed with sex," led "a horrendous lifestyle," and should return to "their darkrooms" and "orgies of sperm": "Good riddance!" (Van der List 1998). Some years later, Van der List (2004) had embraced gay rights as exemplary of "Western achievements and ideals." Similarly, the columnist Sylvain Ephimenco in 1998 wrote an article in which he defended Van der List's right to express his "deep disgust of male-to-male-love." But in 2001, Ephimenco responded to El Moumni's similar homophobic excesses by publishing an "open letter" in which he called Islam a sickness (Mepschen et al. 2010). Now that Muslims became identified with conservative views on sexual freedom and gay rights, formerly conservative commentators suddenly embraced progressive values.

The successful populist politician Pim Fortuyn, who emerged on the political scene in 2001, capitalized on the trope of sexual progress as essentially Dutch and managed to ingrain it deeper into the Dutch self-image. Fortuyn

[12] *Het Parool*, May 12, 2001.
[13] *De Telegraaf*, May 8, 2001.

was openly and flamboyantly gay, and spoke of Muslims as backward and rural. In the slipstream of the El Moumni affair and, more dramatically, of 9/11 and the ascent of the "war on terror," he argued that he saw his sexually expressive lifestyle and his liberties and joys as a gay man threatened by backward Muslims (cf. Van der Veer 2006). Fortuyn managed to reframe the Dutch political landscape by entangling traditionally "new left" themes – secularism, gender equality, and gay liberation – with a neoliberal and anti-immigration, populist agenda. Fortuyn thus successfully entangled antipathy toward Islam with a politics of sexual freedom (cf. Pels 2003; Van der Veer 2006). His party won almost 35 percent of the vote in his hometown of Rotterdam in the March 2002 municipal elections (see Uitermark and Duyvendak 2008), and 17 percent nationally in May of that year in elections held only days after his assassination. Fortuyn attacked the established political right for not heeding the widespread frustration with refugees and immigrants. He proposed to close the borders to most asylum seekers and promoted a tough approach toward the Muslim community (Van der Veer 2006). Unlike Islam, Fortuyn argued, Judaism and Christianity had been transformed by "the Enlightenment," during which essential "Western" values had developed: individual responsibility, the separation of church and state, and the equality of men and women: "I refuse to start all over again with the emancipation of women and gays."[14]

Framing Muslims in terms of gender and sexual equality has remained publicly salient since Fortuyn was dramatically shot dead in May 2002. Ayaan Hirsi Ali (2005) pointed out frequently that Islam constituted a violation of the rights of women, homosexuals, and children. Neoculturalist political leader Geert Wilders has repeatedly evoked the number of violent antigay incidents in large, multicultural cities in the Netherlands to score points against Muslims, Dutch-Moroccan young men, and cultural diversity. It has become almost impossible to discuss lesbian and gay emancipation without it being associated with migration and the "problem" of multiculturalism. Indeed, this practical schema is so well entrenched that it has become "common sense" in the Netherlands to represent homophobia, even homophobic violence, as alien to white Dutch culture and society and as the unique possession of young Dutch-Moroccan men and Muslims. Whereas lesbian and gay rights have a rather short history in the Netherlands, they are nonetheless now mobilized as exemplary of a Dutch "tradition of tolerance" (Mepschen et al. 2010; cf. Bracke 2012; Jivraj and De Jong 2011; Wekker 2009).

[14] Pim Fortuyn in the Dutch newspaper *de Volkskrant*, February 9, 2002. Available at: http://www.volkskrant.nl/vk/nl/2824/Politiek/article/detail/611698/2002/02/09/De-islam-is-een-achterlijke-cultuur.dhtml

This entwinement of sexual freedom with neoculturalist discourse has deep roots in the structural transformation of Dutch society since the 1960s. The Netherlands changed from one of the most religious societies in the world to one of its most secular (Van Rooden 2004). Discourses of sexual freedom have played cardinal roles in these transformations. As shown in surveys, large segments of the Dutch population after the 1960s distanced themselves from moral traditionalism (cf. SCP 1998; Uitterhoeve 2000; Arts et al. 2003; Duyvendak 2004; Halman et al. 2005). The percentage of Dutch citizens who now agree with the proposition that "homosexuality is normal" and who support gay marriage exceeds that in other countries (cf. Gerhards 2010). More than most other Europeans (not to mention Americans), the Dutch disagree with conservative survey items such as: "women must have children to be happy"; "a child should respect its parents"; or "we would be better off if we returned to a traditional way of life." Surveys show that the Dutch are among the most ardent supporters in Europe of the right to freedom of speech and expression (Inglehart and Baker, 2000; Inglehart and Welzel, 2005) and civil rights for sexual minorities and gender equality. These opinions differ little by level of education. When it comes to ideas about sexual freedom and gender equality, the Netherlands are now among the three least-polarized countries in Europe (Achterberg 2006, 55). Polarization at the level of cultural values declined as a progressive consensus came into being, in which people distanced themselves from moral – sexual, family, and gender – traditionalism (Duyvendak 2004; Houtman and Duyvendak, 2009).

Dutch migrants – especially Muslims – form a tangible, visible "constitutive outside" (Panizza 2005; Mouffe 2005) of this Dutch majority and as such play a key role in constituting and reinforcing the Dutch self-image of cultural and sexual progressiveness. Moreover, the discourse of Dutch sexual tolerance plays a central role in transposing homophobia onto the migrant and religious other; a transposition that successfully erases the recent homophobic past and the continuous heteronormativity of Dutch society from the national imagination. Recent research of the Netherlands Institute for Social Research has nonetheless shown that homophobia remains virulent. Young Dutch lesbians and gays struggle, disproportionally, with exclusion, bullying, and depression (SCP 2010). When, in early 2011, a popular soap opera staged a sex scene between two men, the response on social network sites like Twitter was overwhelmingly homophobic. And research in the province of North Holland has recently shown that half of young people there considered homosexuality "abnormal." The discourse pitting Dutch progressives against Muslim conservatives has rendered these difficult facts and developments increasingly obscure. Once the schemas become deeply held, contrary evidence makes little headway.

Many Dutch citizens now demand that migrants adjust to an official discourse of sexual and moral "progressiveness." In this respect, the Netherlands is characteristically similar to Denmark. In other words, when it comes to issues of public morality and personal values, citizens in liberal countries do not always value diversity in opinions and cultural repertoires (e.g., Lægaard 2007; Wikan 2002). Indeed, sexual progressiveness and tolerance may be employed as discourses of power (cf. Brown 2006; Butler 2008; Puar 2007), producing migrants and religious minorities as cultural others and excluding them by redrawing the contours of the national community.

THE PRAGMATIST PROBLEMATIC

Framing homophobia (and antigay violence) as a migrant or Muslim problem places pragmatists in a difficult situation. Pragmatists need to avoid accusations of not caring enough about antigay violence and homophobia, but they also wish to avoid stigmatizing ethnic or religious minorities. Pragmatists want to convey that they care as much for the safety and rights of gays as do neoculturalists, but their castigation of migrant perpetrators of violence is necessarily more nuanced and less uncompromising. Neoculturalists renounce such pragmatist efforts as attempts to create understanding where only passionate rejection is morally legitimate. Pragmatists have thus been forced into a defensive position and have not yet found a way out. By way of their commitment to feminist achievements and sexual progress, pragmatist politicians and public intellectuals have been "drawn into" neoculturalism.

That said, it must be emphasized that the critique of cultural appeasement has not been limited to the new right, but in fact also has a genealogy in the social-democratic wing of Dutch politics. In 2000, the prominent social-democrat Paul Scheffer published a landmark article in which he argued that the Netherlands were in the midst of a multicultural drama, and which contained a strong plea for acknowledging and promoting Dutch national identity as a first step toward a more strict integration policy targeting migrant communities (Scheffer 2000; cf. Uitermark 2012: 66–67). Lodewijk Asscher, a very prominent member of the Labor Party, recently remarked that Geert Wilders should be seen as "the bad consciousness of the Labor Party. He points to the things that we have neglected."[15] With this remark, Asscher followed up on an older, already established trope within social-democracy and demonstrated that neoculturalist representations extend far beyond the populist right.

[15] 'Geert Wilders is het slechte geweten van de PvdA . . . Hij wijst op de dingen die wij hebben verwaarloosd.' *De Volkskrant*, January 21, 2012.

After Paul Scheffer's article in 2000, the good consciousness of the Labor Party has most conspicuously, albeit not uniquely, been voiced by social-democrats with a migrant and Muslim background, like Ahmed Aboutaleb (the Labor Party mayor of Rotterdam) and Ahmed Marcouch (Labor Party MP). These Labor Party leaders have been particularly vocal about the need to defend tolerance, gay rights, and sexual progress, even if that means being critical of Muslim and migrant communities. Ahmed Marcouch, formerly the district chairman of the Amsterdam borough Slotervaart and currently a member of parliament, has developed a discourse that serves as an alternative to neoculturalist discourse without negating its central premise that sexual and gender intolerance are mostly Muslim or migrant problems. Marcouch argues that neoculturalists are right when they maintain that a large taboo rests on sexuality in general and lesbian and gay sexuality in particular in Dutch Muslim communities. In an interview on Amsterdam's local television station he pointed out: "Take into account that there is hardly a positive vocabulary to speak about lesbians and gays in Dutch Muslim circles. I was recently at a school and I asked kids there what would happen if they would talk about gayness at home. They said: 'The first thing that would happen is that we would get slapped.' It is a dirty word that you are not supposed to use in public."[16]

Marcouch combines a defense of Islam against neoculturalist attacks with a politics of (sexual and gender) emancipation, and as such attempts to bridge the gap between pragmatists and neoculturalists. Like neoculturalists, Marcouch posits that homophobia among Muslims should be passionately and uncompromisingly countered. His political agenda is rooted in a belief in the necessity of a moral and strong state:

> When it comes to rights of women and gays and lesbians, the reality in many Muslim families and communities is far from ideal. The political sphere, government and society must be unequivocal about this and speak clearly about this. When laws are being broken, we need to act. Muslim women and Muslim gays and lesbians who want to emancipate and fight for their rights must be morally and practically supported. (Marcouch 2008)

Marcouch thereby bridges classic social-democratic passions – a moral state, emancipation – with important elements of neoculturalist discourse. But at the same time, he and others destabilize the secularist imperative in Dutch neoculturalist integration discourse by transcending the taken-for-granted contradiction between religious (Muslim) subjectivity and ideals of

[16] AT5, February 21, 2009. Available at: http://www.at5.nl/artikelen/13152/uitgebreid-interview-met-marcouch-over-homobeleid-in-slotervaart (accessed February 28, 2011).

sexual progress. For Marcouch, defending gay rights is a question of being a good Muslim in the contemporary Dutch context. He says: "We as Muslims are not barbarians, we can talk about homosexuality. The right of a Muslim to be Muslim is the right of a homosexual to be a homosexual."[17] The debate over sexual emancipation and gender equality thus has had a strong impact on how Muslims have framed their own situation in the Netherlands. First of all, pragmatists are drawn into the logic of neoculturalism, which represents Dutch society in terms of an opposition between sexual progress and Muslim moralities. The investments of pragmatists and social-democrats in the discourse of sexual and feminist progress have made it increasingly difficult for pragmatists to find a language to negate neoculturalist framings of Muslims as traditional and intolerant. Second, the position of lesbians, gays, bisexuals, and transgenders and women within Muslim communities has become a rallying point of self-proclaimed progressive Muslims, like Ahmed Marcouch, who reinforce the framing of Muslims as sexually conservative as a way of relating politically to the hegemony of the neoculturalist framework.

CONCLUSION: POLITICAL CULTURE AND NEOCULTURALIST POLITICS

We have shown how discourses about and policies toward ethnic and religious minorities in the Netherlands have changed in recent decades. While in the past cultural differences were settled through a politics of accommodation, more recently the integration of minorities has become a political and cultural battleground (Uitermark 2012). These changes in discourses and balances of power raise important questions, not least with respect to the ways in which framing contests are analyzed. It is often assumed that the framing of Muslims emanates from "national models." Those who analyze Dutch policies and actions as reflecting a national model of "multiculturalism" argue that the Dutch state applied its long-term tendency to institutionalize cultural pluralism, believing that the cultural emancipation of immigrant minorities was the key to their integration into Dutch society (Duyvendak and Scholten 2011).

These analysts often make a connection between claims about "multiculturalism" and the peculiar Dutch history of "pillarization," referring to the period from the 1920s to 1960s when most of Dutch society was structured according to specific religious (Protestant, Catholic) or sociocultural (socialist, liberal)

[17] Speech during a public meeting, 'Jezelf kunnen zijn in Slotervaart'. Amsterdam, May 31, 2010.

pillars (Lijphart 1968). Sniderman and Hagendoorn (2007), for example, claim that the multiculturalist labeling of collective identities inadvertently deepened sociocultural cleavages in society rather than bridging these differences. They trace the presumed Dutch approach back to the history of pillarization: "The Netherlands has always been a country of minorities thanks to the power of religion to divide as well as unite" (Sniderman and Hagendoorn 2007: 13). Joppke adds that the Dutch changed their policies because they found that previous multicultural policies had been a failure: "Civic integration is a response to the obvious failure of one of Europe's most pronounced policies of multiculturalism to further the socioeconomic integration of immigrants and their offspring." If multiculturalism tended to "lock migrant ethnics into their separate worlds, the goal of civic integration is migrants' participation in mainstream institutions" (Joppke 2007: 249). Koopmans (2005) makes the additional claim that strong path dependency is at work, leading the Dutch to continue the policies of pillarization as multiculturalism, and even today, despite apparent policy shifts, to continue to base policy on ethnic identity.

As these quotes suggest, some scholars and politicians use the phrase "multicultural model" to normatively disqualify certain past and present policies that they think have failed. However, it turns out that Dutch policies were not developed to celebrate cultural differences, as is often assumed. Preserving cultural identities of some minorities was thought to be useful for instrumental reasons. Those pointing to path dependency are correct – but in a more limited way than they sometimes claim. Pillarization did indeed shape responses to Muslims, but these new minorities never achieved the level of organization and separation that national minorities achieved in the early twentieth century. Jan Rath (1999: 59) states that "in terms of institutional arrangements, there is no question of an Islamic pillar in the Netherlands, or at least one that is in any way comparable to the Roman Catholic or Protestant pillars in the past." Integration policy was never oriented toward the construction of minority groups as pillars, nor was there ever a "national multicultural model."

The key assumption informing our analysis is that framing contests over Muslims have to be understood as part of more fundamental and encompassing discursive conflicts occurring at the cultural fault line of contemporary politics. Like their counterparts in the United States (Teles 2007), cultural protectionists in Western Europe claim that they represent the "authentic" voice of "ordinary people," protecting the cultural traditions of their country against liberal elites, who – supported by state institutions – try to impose their agenda from above. This cleavage is culturally defined but has strong class undertones: cultural protectionists suggest that "limousine liberals" or "the leftist elite" favor migrants and betray the autochthonous working-class people who are simultaneously construed as more deserving than either the unassimilated migrants or the hypocritical elites. This populism attacks a political culture that is considered deeply elitist and cosmopolitan. As Kriesi et al. (2008: 164) note for Fortuyn: "[He] attacked the consensual Dutch politics .... He wanted to free the people from paternalistic governance structures and elite cartels. ... He criticized the paternalistic culture of the Dutch elite ... with its autistic elements, with its very special world view, and even with a jargon of its own that is hardly comprehensible for outsiders."

The populism and transposed class politics of Dutch cultural protectionists resembles the rhetoric of the neoconservatives in the United States in many ways. Like cultural protectionists in Europe, Tea Party Republicans rebelled against the political culture of an entrenched liberal elite, portrayed as betraying and threatening hardworking, ordinary people who comprise the nation's cultural heartland. However, whereas American neoconservatives oppose progressive values, neoculturalists propagate lesbian and gay rights and gender equality.

In recent analyses of new political cleavages in Western Europe, the pivotal role played by the propagation of sexual and gender progress is often overlooked. In fact, the rise of neoculturalist populism in Western Europe is often mistakenly analyzed as a shift toward conservatism, as if protectionists at both sides of the Atlantic want to conserve the same "culture."[18] This misunderstanding is caused by a conflation of progressiveness and pro-immigration viewpoints. Our analysis shows, however, that neoculturalists combine the framing of Dutch national culture as morally progressive with a virulent anti-immigration agenda. When Kriesi et al. (2008: 171) conclude that the "cultural liberalism of the most educated has declined quite considerably ... [it] probably reflects ... the general hardening of the Dutch attitude to immigration," they miss the cardinal point that Dutch anti-immigration discourse goes hand in glove with a rhetoric of sexual emancipation and gender equality. The rhetoric of sexual progress plays a key role in the representation of migrant and Muslim communities as culturally other. Progressive values are espoused these days from the far left to the populist right, making the Netherlands into one of the most homogeneous countries in terms of expressed values and attitudes on sexual and moral issues. Dutch neoculturalism should thus not be equated with cultural, ethical, and moral conservatism.

The irony is that Dutch Muslims are framed as if they were American conservatives – as averse to sexual freedom and prone to censorship. A further

[18] For instance: "The whole configuration of the Dutch party system shifted in a culturally conservative direction" (Kriesi et al. 2008: 181).

irony is that the populists' electorate have been treated somewhat like minorities. Neoculturalists often claim that left-wing elites shy away from criticizing minorities because of a deeply entrenched yet misplaced sympathy for the underdog. The argument may have validity for pragmatists' relationship to migrants but it may also hold for their relationship to the supporters of new Dutch populism. Pragmatists'·nominal commitment to inclusion and equality constrains is holding them back from speaking out against the xenophobia and Islamophobia of populists and their supporters. Pragmatists' nominal commitment to inclusion and equality prohibits them from speaking out against the xenophobia and Islamophobia of populists and their supporters. Rather than passionately countering the ideological claims of their opponents, pragmatists seek to accommodate conflicts through dialogue and understanding. It appears they have not been doing very well. Neoculturalists have dominated the debate, and pragmatists have internalized many of the criticisms directed against them, thereby implicitly recognizing neoculturalists as the consciousness of the nation and the people.

BIBLIOGRAPHY

Achterberg, Peter. (2006) *Considering Cultural Conflict. Class Politics and Cultural Politics in Western Societies.* Maastricht: Shaker.

Arts, W., J. Hagenaars en L. Halman, (eds.). (2003) *The Cultural Diversity of European Unity. Findings, Explanations and Reflections from the European Values Study.* Leiden: Brill Academic Publishers.

Bolkestein, F. (1991) Integratie van minderheden moet met lef worden aangepakt. *De Volkskrant*, 12 September.

Bolkestein, F. (1996) Vrijheid schept verantwoordelijkheid. *De Volkskrant*, 9 February.

Bracke, Sarah (2011) Subjects of debate: Secular and sexual exceptionalism, and Muslim women in the Netherlands. *Feminist Review* 98: 28–46.

——(2012) From "saving women" to "saving gays": Rescue narratives and their dis/continuities. *European Journal of Women's Studies* 19 (2): 237–252.

Brown, Wendy. (2006) *Regulating Aversion. Tolerance in the Age of Identity and Empire.* Princeton, NJ: Princeton University Press.

Buijs, Laurens, Jan Willem Duyvendak, and Gert Hekma (2011) "As long as they keep away from me": The paradox of antigay violence in a gay-friendly country. *Sexualities* 14: 632–652.

Buruma, Ian. (2006) *Murder in Amsterdam.* New York: Penguin Press.

Butler, Judith. (2008) Sexual politics, torture, and secular time. *British Journal of Sociology* 59 (1): 1–23.

Duyvendak, JanWillem (2011) *The Politics of Home. Nostalgia and Belonging in Western Europe and the US.* London: Palgrave.

Duyvendak, J. W. (1999) De Planning van ontplooiing. Wetenschap, politiek en de maakbare samenleving. The Hague, SDU.

——(2004) *Een eensgezinde, vooruitstrevende natie. Over de mythe van 'de' invidualisering en de toekomst van de sociologie*. Amsterdam, Vossiuspers.

Ewing, Katherine Pratt (2008) *Stolen Honor. Stigmatizing Muslim Men in Berlin*. Stanford, CA: Stanford University Press.

Fassin, Éric (2010) National identities and transnational intimacies: Sexual democracy and the politics of immigration in Europe. *Public Culture* **22** (3): 507–529.

Gerhards, Jürgen (2010) Non-discrimination towards homosexuality. The European Union's policy and citizens. *Attitudes towards Homosexuality in 27 European Countries. International Sociology* **25**(1): 5–28.

Geschiere, Peter (2009) *The Perils of Belonging. Autochthony, Citizenship, and Exclusion in Africa and Europe*. Chicago: The University of Chicago Press.

Ghorashi, Halleh (2003) *Ayaan Hirsi Ali: Daring or dogmatic?* Debates on multiculturalism and emancipation in the Netherlands, in T. van Meijl and Driessen, Henk (eds.) *Multiple Identifications and the Self*. Utrecht: Stichting Focaal.

Guenif-Souilamas, N. (2006) The other French exception. Virtuous racism and the war of the sexes in postcolonial France. *French Politics, Culture & Society* **24** (3): 23–41.

Halman, L., R. Luijkx and M. van Zundert (2005) *Atlas of European Values*. Leiden: Brill Acade.

Haritaworn, Jinthana (2008) Loyal repetitions of the nation. Gay assimilation and the "war on terror". DarkMatter 3, http://www.darkmatter101.org (accessed February 2010).

Hekma, G. (2002) Imams and homosexuality. A post-gay debate in the Netherlands. *Sexualities* **5** (2): 237–48.

Hirsi Ali, A. (2003: 13) Het gelijk van Fortuyn. *De Volkskrant*, 12 December.

——(2005). Fundamentalisme is niet af te kopen met diplomatie. Maandag een half jaar geleden werd Theo vermoord. Critici van de islam treft het verwijt van huisvredebreuk. *De Volkskrant*, 4 May.

Houtman, Dick and Jan Willem Duyvendak (2009) Boerka's, Boerkini's en Belastingcenten. Culturele en Politieke Polarisatie in een Post-Christelijke Samenleving. in *Raad voor Maatschappelijke Ontwikkeling* (ed.) Polarisatie. Bedreigend en Verrijkend. Amsterdam: Uitgeverij SWP.

Inglehart, R. & W. Baker, (2000) Modernization, cultural change and the persistence of traditional values. In: American Sociological Review 65 (February), p. 19–51.

Inglehart, R. and C. Welzel (2005). Modernization, Cultural Change, and Democracy: The Human Development Sequence. New York: Cambridge University Press.

Joppke, C. (2007). "Beyond national models: Civic integration policies for immigrants in Western Europe." West European Politics 30(1): 1–22.

Joppke, Christian (2004) The retreat of multiculturalism in the liberal state: Theory and policy. *British Journal of Sociology* **55**: 237–257.

Jusová, Iveta (2008) Hirsi Ali and Van Gogh's submission: Reinforcing the Islam vs. women binary. *Women's Studies International Forum* **31**: 148–155.

Koopmans, R., Statham, P., Giugni, M. and Passy, F. (2005) *Contested Citizenship: Political Contention Over Migration and Ethnic Relations in Western Europe*. Minneapolis: University of Minnesota Press.

Lægaard, Suzanne (2007) Liberal nationalism and the nationalisation of liberal values. *Nations and Nationalisms* **13** (1): 37–55.

Li, Tanya Murray (2000) Articulating indigenous identities in Indonesia. Resource politics and the tribal slot. *Comparative Studies in Society and History* **42**: 149–179.

Lijphart, Arend (1968) *The Politics of Accommodation. Pluralism and Democracy in the Netherlands*. Berkeley: University of California Press.
Lijphart, A. (1988). *Verzuiling, pacificatie en kentering in de Nederlandse politiek*. Haarlem, Becht.
Marcouch, Ahmed (2008) *Mijn vader kwam te voet*. Amsterdam: Waterlandstichting.
Mepschen, Paul (2012) Gewone mensen. Populisme en het discours van verdringing in Amsterdam Nieuw West. Sociologie 8 (1): 66–83.
Mepschen, Paul, Jan Willem Duyvendak, and Evelien Tonkens (2010) Sexual politics, orientalism and multicultural citizenship in the Netherlands. *Sociology* 44 (5): 962–979.
Mouffe, Chantal (2005) The "end of politics" and the challenge of right-wing populism, in Franco Panizza (ed) *Populism and the Mirror of Democracy*. London and New York: Verso.
Panizza, Francisco (2005) *Introduction: Populism and the mirror of democracy, in Francisco Panizza (ed) Populism and the Mirror of Democracy*. London and New York: Verso Books.
Pels, Dick (2003) *De geest van Pim Fortuyn. Het gedachtengoed van een politieke dandy*. Amsterdam: Anthos.
Penninx, R. (1988) *Minderheidsvorming en emancipatie. Balans van kennisverwerving ten aanzien van immigranten en woonwagenbewoners*. Alphen aan de Rijn, Samson.
Prins, B. (2004) *Voorbij de onschuld. Het debat over integratie in Nederland*. Amsterdam, Van Gennep.
Prins, Baukje (2002) The nerve to break taboos. New realism in the Dutch discourse on multiculturalism. *Journal of International Migration and Integration*: 363–379.
Puar, Jasbir K. (2007) *Terrorist Assemblages. Homonationalism in Queer Times*. Durham, NC: Duke University Press.
Rath, J. (1999) The Netherlands. A Dutch treat for anti-social families and immigrant ethnic minorities. In M. Cole and G. Dale *The European Union and Migrant Labour*. Oxford, Berg Publishers.
Sabsay, Leticia (2012) The emergence of the other sexual citizen: Orientalism and the modernisation of sexuality. *Citizenship Studies* 16 (5–6):.
SCP (Netherlands Institute for Social Research) (1998) Sociaal en Cultureel Rapport 1998. 25 Jaar Sociale Verandering [The Social and Cultural Report 1998. 25 Years of Social Change]. The Hague: Sociaal en Cultureel Planbureau.
——(2010) *Gewoon anders. Acceptatie van homoseksualiteit in Nederland*. The Hague: Sociaal en Cultureel Planbureau.
Scheffer, Paul (2000) *Het multiculturele drama*. NRC Handelsblad, January 29.
Sniderman, P. M. and L. Hagendoorn (2007) *When Ways of Life Collide: Multiculturalism and Its Discontents in the Netherlands*. Princeton, NY, Princeton University Press.
Teles, Steven M. (2007) *Conservative mobilization against entrenched elites*, in, Pierson, Paul and Theda Stocpol (eds) *The Transformation of American Politics. Activist Government and the Rise of Conservatism*. Princeton: Princeton University Press.
Uitermark, Justus (2012) *Dynamics of Power in Dutch Integration Politics. From Accommodation to Confrontation*. Amsterdam: University of Amsterdam Press.

Uitermark, Justus and Jan Willem Duyvendak (2008) Civilizing the city: populism and revanchist urbanism in Rotterdam. *Urban Studies* **45** (7): 1485–1503.

Uitterhoeve, Wilfried (2000) *Nederland en de Anderen. Europese Vergelijkingen uit het Sociaal en Cultureel Rapport 2000 [The Netherlands and the Others. European Comparisons from the Social and Cultural Report 2000]*. Nijmegen: Uitgeverij SUN.

Van Amersfoort, J. M. M. (1974) *Immigratie en minderheidsvorming. Een analyse van de Nederlandse situatie 1945–1973*. Alphen aan den Rijn: Samson.

Van den Berg, Marguerite and Willem Schinkel (2009) "Women from the Catacombs of the City", Gender Notions in Dutch Culturalist Discourse. *Innovation* **22** (4): 293–410.

Van der List, G. (1998) Een Amsterdamse orgie. *De Volkskrant*, 14 augustus

——(2004). *Islamitische uitdaging*. Elsevier, 7 augustus.

Van der Veer, Peter (2006) Pim Fortuyn, Theo van Gogh, and the politics of tolerance in the Netherlands. *Public Culture* **18** (1): 111–124.

Van der Waal, Jeroen, Peter Achterberg, and Dick Houtman (2007) Class is not dead – it has been buried alive: Class voting and cultural voting in postwar Western societies (1956–1990). *Politics and Society* **35**(3): 403–426.

Van Rooden, Peter (2004) Oral History en het Vreemde Sterven van het Nederlands Christendom. *Bijdragen en Mededelingen betreffende de Geschiedenis der Nederlanden* **119**: 524–551.

Verkaaik, Oskar (2010) The Cachet Dilemma: Ritual and Agency in New Dutch Nationalism. *American Ethnologist* **37** (1): 69–82.

Verkaaik, Oskar and Rachel Spronk (2011) Sexular practice: Notes on an ethnography of secularism. *Focaal 2011* (59): 83–88.

Wekker, G. (2009) *Van homo nostalgie en betere tijden. Multiculturaliteit en postkolonialiteit*. George Mosse Lecture: Amsterdam.

Wikan, Unni (2002) *Generous Betrayal. Politics of Culture in the New Europe*. Chicago: University of Chicago Press.

Yanow, Dvora and Marleen van der Haar (2011) People out of place: Allochthony and autochthony in Netherlands identity discourse – metaphors and categories in action. *Journal of International Relations and Development* **16**(2), 227–261.

11 Conclusion

John R. Bowen, Christophe Bertossi, Jan Willem Duyvendak, and Mona Lena Krook

In this volume on European states and "their" Muslims, we have presented a way to understand how actors, situated in particular institutions and at specific times and places, draw on practical schemas regarding others in their midst who are often categorized as "Muslims". We see institutional life as the central space in this story. Looking "downward," we see actors who face varied and shifting demands and who in response reformulate and reweight the schemas that shape their practices – schemas that classify persons, erect boundaries, and inform practices. Looking "upward," we see certain of these actors as empowered to circulate schemas in broader spheres, and thereby inflect national ideological discourses.

Of the chapters assembled in this volume, some focus on how institutional programs articulate with the day-to-day life of actors; others analyze the articulation of key institutional actors with national political ideologies. Bertossi analyzes the schemas and moral boundaries that arise out of everyday social interactions in the French army, for which he relied on extended interviews and observations, as did Sargent and Erikson in their study of French and German hospitals. Both works show how the practical and moral exigencies that define each institution – what armies, or hospitals, generally do – interact in spatially and temporally varying ways with national ideologies. Sunier studies a similar institution, the public school, and gives examples of everyday interactions, but his comparative approach leads him to also analyze how schools respond differently to student diversity and demands across four countries. These chapters focus on everyday life in their respective institutions, as does Bertossi and Bowen's contrastive study of social location and conjunctures across hospitals and schools.

Taken together, these analyses emphasize the internal variation and historical contingency in the practical schemas actors use in each institution. These particular institutions – army, hospital, school – are particularly susceptible to ideological confrontations. On the one hand, they are charged with performing a specific practical and moral duty, which has relatively strong shaping effects on how personnel carry out their tasks of policing, teaching, or healing. On the other hand, for diverse sociohistorical reasons, they are burdened with considerable "representational baggage" in that they are seen as standing for, or saying something about, the nature of public life in each of these countries. The tension thereby produced leads to considerable variation in which schemas are deployed by which actors (and at which historical moments), and also to often intense public debate about whether each institution is internally acting in a morally and socially correct way. Boundary maintenance is of great concern, aimed at ensuring that the purity and the mission of the institution can be maintained.

The second group of chapters links institutional specificities to judicial decisions, policy outputs, or political rhetoric, all elements that shape and are shaped by national political and cultural ideologies. Krook builds a contrastive model to provide explanations of different policy approaches to the political representation of various kinds of groups. Siim accounts for divergent responses across Scandinavian countries to legal challenges about discrimination and religious freedom. Both works show how analyses of cultural contrasts must be combined with analyses of the constraints faced by specific legal or political bodies in order to explain legal and political decisions. Both also illustrate tensions internal to any one country's ideas about political representation, complicating ideas of a national "model." In similar fashion, Bowen and Rohe start from schemas shared by much of Europe concerning international private law and religious freedom; they then show how (1) these schemas are differently weighted in different countries and how (2) particular institutional constraints and national pathways together explain that variation. Michalowski analyzes the internal tensions in citizenship course materials between universalistic principles and Islam-specific targets, a tension redolent of that pointed out by Bertossi for the French army. Uitermark, Mepschen, and Duyvendak link current Dutch framing of Muslims to intense political and electoral struggles against the background of the post-1960s public expression of progressive cultural values.

The essays in this second category trace diverse pathways along which institutions complicate or disrupt allegedly consistent national ideologies. In particular, universalistic principles encounter specific complicating factors in specific institutional settings: *ordre public* exemptions are taken to broadly accepted legal principles by judges, and conflicts emerge between nationalist ideologies and nondiscrimination principles in electoral or judicial spaces. It is in such moments of departure from general principles that we can discern the operation of schemas concerning Muslims.

SEX AND ISLAMIC CULTURE

With all these sources of variation – in countries, institutions, and analytical perspectives – are there major themes? Does each institution just "do its job," or does each country just "apply its model"? As we assembled the results of these research projects, we found that the practical schemas we studied shared two major elements or themes across institution and country: anxiety over gender and sexuality and – relatedly – worries about Islam as "culturally backward".

Concerns about gender and sexuality surface consistently as a central theme in these practical schemas. Often the debates give particular emotional urgency to claims that moral boundaries must be maintained. It is striking, for example, that many of the religious practices in question – the wearing of head scarves, social norms regarding marriage and reproduction, and conflicts arising from women's increased participation in the public arenas of politics and the judiciary – closely map onto issues related to women's bodies and to the broader social control of women. Such observations have previously been made by scholars exploring tensions between goals of feminism and multiculturalism (Okin 1999; cf. Phillips 2007).

Yet, the case studies in this book go further than existing debates in at least two ways.

First, the cases reveal that such debates take place in a wider array of institutional settings than has been previously recognized. While head scarves, for instance, have been of particular concern in French schools, their use has also raised questions in the labor market and in coutrooms in Denmark and Norway, as Siim describes. Similarly, while a great deal of activist and scholarly attention has focused on the practice of female genital mutilation, Sargent and Erikson indicate that women's reproductive health more generally has been the subject of contestation between competing logics, as illustrated in their case by patient-doctor interactions. Not only do these cases draw attention to additional arenas of interest, but they also reveal how closely questions of female sexuality tie into dynamics of assimilation and cultural mistrust.

Second, the book underscores how, partly in reaction to such debates, "gender equality" has emerged as a new trope used by those who oppose the further integration of Muslims into European societies. This concern manifests itself in a number of different ways. The citizenship training modules Michalowski analyzes in her contribution to this volume include a specific component on the equality of women and men – implying that Muslims and immigrants more generally need to be "taught" this value, which is assumed not to exist in their own communities. Representations of the threat that veiled judges pose to Danish conceptions of justice play out in a similar manner, the underlying suggestion being that the veil is truly "foreign" to Danish ways of life. Yet, as Krook shows, the status of Muslim women need not always been viewed negatively: in countries like France and Sweden, the desire to appear modern and inclusive on the part of certain political parties has led to enhanced opportunities for minority female candidates to be nominated and elected.

A related set of tropes can also be seen with respect to sexual orientation. Gay rights are now put forward, even sometimes instrumentalized, in public criticism of Islam and in arguments about the supposed backwardness of European Muslims. This leads to portrayals of gay rights and identity as if they had been the foundation of European culture for centuries, with the suggested contrast that Muslims are, for this reason, fundamental enemies of European culture. Cases involving homophobia among citizens from Muslim communities are highlighted, epitomized as archetypal, and cast within narratives that underwrite the superiority of European secular modernity. Similar to what occurs with gender equality narratives, the making of homosexuality into a weapon to be used against Islam puts gay rights advocates in a difficult bind, placing them on one or the other side of the divide – defending gay rights or defending Muslims – with those they see as holding unsavory views. An example of these dynamics can be seen in the Netherlands, as detailed by Uitermark, Mepschen, and Duyvendak.

The use of sexuality as an anti-Islam trope is closely connected with the second theme we found across countries and institutions in Western Europe: namely, Islam is increasingly criticized as a religion that carries certain immutable values, that these are attached to the religion (rather than to particular country traditions), and that they are inimical to Western European or nation-specific values.[1] Although some politicians already voiced these critiques of Islam in the 1980s and 1990s, they were part of a larger set of critiques and schemas concerning the problem of integrating immigrants into specific European nation-states. These schemas appeared in specific national forms, such as the notion of *Gastarbeiter* (guest worker) in Germany, the immigration of non-white Commonwealth members to Britain, or the broader French category of *immigrés*. By the 2000s, however, we see the emergence of a pan-European set of schemas that bring together earlier, nationally-specific schemas to focus on the question of Islam. If the problems used to be framed in terms of multiple schemas of immigrants, racial minorities, and Muslims, increasingly they have been framed in terms of Islam.

[1] Anti-Islam discourse is not necessarily pro-European, as Geert Wilders's positions in the early 2010s illustrate.

This shift is well documented for the Netherlands in the previous chapter, where the authors show how the values-based critique of Islam emerged in a particular social and political context, producing a striking configuration of progressivism and anti-Islam. We saw this shift particularly clearly within one set of institutions in the case of the evolution of judicial rulings in France analyzed by Bowen and Rohe in this volume. If in the 1980s and 1990s the highest courts used harm to individuals and religious freedom as the principal standards for judgment on cases about Islamic dress, citizenship, or personal status (marriage and divorce), by the late 2000s those same courts had mounted a systematic critique of "Islamic values". This trend converged with changes in the schemas used to criticize wearing Islamic dress in schools as well. Civic education course materials also reflect implicit schemas about Islamic values.

On a broader level, this shift can be traced to the development of several distinct yet converging discourses: the arguments for officially recognizing Europe's Christian tradition in a new European constitution; the parallel debates about the effects of admitting a large Muslim-majority country, Turkey, into the European Union; the "clash of civilizations" thesis; and the less well-bounded but telling increase in denunciations of Islam as such by former Muslims, in which Ayaan Hirsi Ali is only the most prominent figure.[2]

However, we should also note the limits of this theme. Even if it appears in popular media, political debates, and best sellers, the cultural critique of Islam does not generate the schemas that we have discovered in the everyday life of major institutions. Hospital workers develop quite particular ideas about how to deal with religious demands (halal food, head coverings) or with particular patient behaviors. These ideas may invoke ethnic and racial stereotypes about "Africans" or "Turks" alongside or instead of stereotypes about Muslims Teachers start from classroom diversity and explore, in relatively pragmatic fashion, the limits of reasonable accommodations. Soldiers seem to continue an older anti-immigrant way of talking while their leaders think quite differently. Institutional logics drive much, perhaps most, of what occurs in institutional life.

INSTITUTIONS AND CULTURAL ANALYSIS

In Chapter 1, we placed our approach in the context of institutionalist and cultural approaches to social life. Now we ask how our findings can contribute to analytical work in those fields.

[2] For the abundance of French-language examples, see Bowen (2010: 4).

Institutionalist approaches in political science and sociology developed against older alternatives that had failed to analytically seize the implicit and yet powerful sets of norms and values that shape institutional life: what a school is supposed to do, how people should discuss things, how companies should make decisions. The sociologist John Meyer and his colleagues (Meyer and Rowan 1977) called these norms and values "myth" in the sense of normatively powerful ideas that are not part of a bureaucratic blueprint and have their own forms of reproduction. Although these early formulations imputed clarity to institutional contours, others pointed to the improvised nature of everyday life (Goffman 1983) and to the flexibility or ambiguity of rules; both features of institutions can help explain endogenously driven change (Mahoney and Thelen 2010). Others contributed to a "cognitive turn" in the study of institutions, arguing that actors internalized schemas and scripts that guided them in everyday social life (DiMaggio 1997; DiMaggio and Powell 1991).

We agree with much of this literature and draw from our studies to augment it, especially regarding the issues of variation and change. Our studies illustrate internal variation in institutions that derives from two processes. First, actors do not follow institution-wide rules or scripts but respond to specific challenges and perceptions. These vary with the roles and tasks faced by a particular actor within an institution, and with the specific constraints and opportunities appearing at any one moment: what we have called social location and conjunctures. Secondly, actors may hold multiple practical schemas, each of which receives greater or lesser weight in response to events; the *combinatoire* of schemas is what translates shifting environments into ideas and practices (Bowen 2006).

These two dimensions of internal variation mean that we do not need to find ambiguities or looseness in rules in order to indicate mechanisms that allow for change. *Variation and change are built into institutions.* Let us return to the case of the hospital to see how this works out. In examining the French and German cases, we noted ideas about the neutrality of the hospital, about the importance of serving patients, and about particular behavioral features associated with particular categories of people. Personnel in a hospital may "subscribe" to each of these ideas to some extent, but the weight given to each will be a function of the social location of the actor, her or his particular biography, messages sent or pressures exerted by hospital leaders, and other factors, and these weightings may shift over time in response to external events. By contrasting the French and German hospitals, we were able to see how different histories of the broader political and demographic contexts also shape the ways personnel in each country see their various clients. Indeed, the way German hospital staff "encode" identities appears to vary by region of the country, for example, regarding the relative prevalence of ethnic/geographical versus religious encoding. The schemas concerning "typical Turks" as un-German and alien are further complicated by the dyad of former West Germans and East Germans, as well as the category of *Aussiedler* (resettler) patient.

In the French hospitals reported on earlier in the book, personnel work from two sets of practical schemas that can exist in tension. One categorizes African patients in terms of myriad features, among them difficulties with French and with keeping appointments, practices of polygamy and specific patterns of male-female interactions, and beliefs in sorcery. These schemas may shape treatment and lead some personnel to speak of Africans' general difficulty integrating into French society. However, these same hospital actors also hold to universalistic normative ideas, especially, in this context, ideas about gender equality and religious neutrality, which emphasize the importance of giving all patients the same information. These second set of ideas may keep personnel from acting on the first set by, for example, developing more effective ways of dealing with difficulties in communication or with differences in idea of illness, as they see their own practices as color-, language-, and religion-blind. Moreover, this type of conflict or interference is more likely to be found among some personnel than others. Midwives may dispense prescriptions for contraception without telling the new mothers; here they are giving more weight to schemas concerning the excessive high fertility of these women in general than to schemas concerning the full disclosure of information.

It is telling to contrast the way in which hospital staff Sargent interviewed denied the relevance of religion for hospital interaction with North or West African women, with the way certain hospital directors were widely reported by French newspapers in 2003–2004 as denouncing the impact of Islam on their ability to do their job. They only did so at a particular moment, probably because they followed the example of earlier public statements by school officials (Bertossi and Bowen, Chapter 5 in this volume). How a particular hospital staff person will frame her or his interactions with a patient from, say, West Africa is thus dependent on social location and conjuncture, and will involve (re)weighting the elements involved in that actor's repertoire of schemas. It is less that actors change attitudes than that they draw on a repertoire that is continually inflected by all that is happening around them.

Cultural approaches to moral boundaries and social hierarchies developed in reaction to what some perceived as overly deterministic theories of social causation. In France, this reaction (in part to the work of Pierre Bourdieu) took the form of an empirical program for studying morality in the form of the sociology of judgments and justification (Boltanski andThévenot 2006). Implicitly building on the empirical-normative articulation developed earlier by Michael Walzer (1983), this approach was also *pragmatic* in that it located morality in the reflections individuals make on their social lives as they live them. Closely related has been the sociology of moral boundary-making (Lamont 1992; Lamont and Fournier 1992), which sought to place Bourdieu's (1984 [1979]) analysis of taste and hierarchy on firmer, and more inductive, comparative grounds.

These approaches start from the notion that ideas and practices are shaped by broadly distributed cultural premises concerning justice, morality, and value (Lamont and Thévenot 2000). This may seem at first to be close to the "explanation from national models" approach that we have critiqued in Chapter 1, but it must be seen in a dialectical relationship with earlier Marxist or functionalist approaches. If functionalist approaches treated institutions as "churches" or "schools," cultural sociology approaches them as forms of social life in which the actors draw on nationally specific schemas concerning justice, morality, order, and so forth. Consonant with this approach, in the study of German and French courts, Bowen and Rohe found judges to draw on similar background notions of the functions of law and to justify their judgments in terms of the techniques of law, but also to exhibit deeply rooted national differences regarding the place of moral judgments and religious diversity in law. A corresponding contrast emerged in Michalowski's analysis of differences between German and French citizenship courses. Cross-national differences emerge from studying cultural forms that emerge from highly specified institutions: national tribunals of a particular composition; instruments designed to limit the attribution of permanent residence permits.

Although in this respect we align ourselves with pragmatic and cultural sociology, we propose that the properties of institutions play a more explicit role in explaining the construction of practical schemas than is clear from much of the work shaped by those approaches. In particular, we suggest making more variegated the national backdrop for cultural analysis, such that the properties of institutions gain their relative autonomy vis-à-vis moral boundaries and social hierarchies. We propose this change precisely because we find actors constructing boundaries, representations, and hierarchies in specific institutional contexts. In our view, an actor is to be studied not only as a member of a certain class and nation, but also as, for example, a nurse in a public hospital with an urban clientele, or the head of a rural school, or a judge on an administrative tribunal. If we extract these actors from their institutional contexts, they can then stand as representatives of their class and nation (and perhaps region), and their statements as directly indicative of national-level boundary-making. And yet when seen in their workplaces, their social locations and institutional constraints come to the fore. What the foregoing analysis adds to these cultural approaches is – among other things – a greater attention to institutions as capable of generating and inflecting broad, national ideas.[3] Adding this element ensures that cross-national sociologies of institutions will not collapse back onto "national models" approaches and will not assume that a key set of values are directly internalized by actors.

CHANGE, VARIATION, AND MUSLIMS

We have argued for greater attention to how institutions doubly articulate with actor-specific schemas and with national-level ideologies. We examined how actors see others (and their own institutions) by employing schemas; we looked at change and variation across different tokens of the same institutional type; and we analyzed internal differences into the perceptions and constraints characteristic of distinct social locations in an institution. Actors give differential and shifting weightings to the several ideas and images they hold concerning Muslims as a function of biographical differences, conjunctural shifts, social locations, and other factors. We take these dynamic interfaces as integral to each institution, and thus we assume no particular stable equilibrium.

Recall some of these cases. One might take international private law to be a particularly difficult field for studying variation and change, because jurists strive for cross-national uniformity in order to avoid disrupting the stability of families as they pass across international borders. But Bowen and Rohe found contrasts across countries and changes within one country (France) regarding the status to be accorded Islamic divorces (in Islamic-law countries). They analyzed these differences into differential and shifting weightings of two generally held yet conflicting schemas: one concerned with underscoring general principles of gender equality and the other concerned with maximizing the welfare of particular individuals. Shifts and contrasts in weighting of these schemas are no less to be expected than are uniform and stable results. They

[3] For example, the insightful contrastive study of environmental policies in France and the United States developed by Thévenot, Moody, and Lafaye (2000) severely underappreciates the important role exercised by U.S. regulatory agencies, which have their own highly path-dependant norms and procedures. We thank John Inazu for this observation. The contrast between a more or less explicit attention to institutions within cultural sociology – for we see ourselves as within that tradition – becomes even more striking when contrasted to the analysis of worlds of justification (Boltanski and Thévenot 2006 [1991]).

have to do with relative weighting of legal schemas, not with incommensurable differences across national contexts.

Siim offered a similar analysis of Scandinavian court decisions about discrimination and religious freedom. Differences in judgments are attributable to ways in which each tribunal's mandate privileged some considerations over others. Krook's account of different outcomes of debates about minority electoral representations linked electoral strategizing to the differential strength of schemas about race discrimination across different countries, leading to greater success in Britain than in Sweden, for example.

In Chapter 1, we used these and other examples to argue against the idea that a national model concerning religion-state relation exists and can explain everyday practical schemas and policy outcomes. These cases also suggest that we invert the frequently assumed priority of stability over change. Variation and change appear not as a problem to require further explanation, but as built into the very idea of institutions. Even in the most "uniformizing" environments, such as French schools, the ways teachers and school heads perceive and practice matters of ethnic and religious diversity will of course be highly sensitive to differing student populations, parent demands, disruptive events, and the biographic experience of a school head.[4] Our interest is at least as much in variation as in change, because our central questions include that of the relationship between aggregate national ideologies, on the one hand, and the practical schemas drawn on by actors working in specific institutions (and in particular roles within those institutions), on the other. We are thus most interested in tracing effects of intra-institutional specificity on these schemas.

If variation and change in European institutions is the "normal" condition, then we do not need to conceive of institutions in terms of equilibrium states, to be guarded against challenges and collective mobilizations.[5] Here we enter an ongoing debate among rational choice, historical, and sociological institutionalists (Schmidt 2008; Thelen 1999; Hall and Taylor 1996), and side

4 The "anecdotal" literature written in recent years by secondary school teachers is replete with examples of working through tensions between top-down demands for uniformity and school-specific demands to address the specific populations of students, with regard to questions about religion and science, history, and everyday school comportment; see, for example, Butaud and Kovacs (2008) and Goyet (2003).

5 To return to the topic of this volume, starting from institutional equilibria as part of "normal" politics implies that institutions are successful when they resist the pressures of their social and political environment. Or, to put it differently, normal functioning means resisting dysfunctional claims (Dubet 2005), including those stemming from collective mobilizations involving Muslims (see Koopmans and Statham 2005; Joppke 2009). We see a danger here in thinking of institutional change as a matter of a cultural (and even moral) crisis of an otherwise seemingly successful institutional order.

with those who insert institutions in broader social processes. Rather than conceiving of institutions as "holding together" a particular pattern of politics, historical institutionalists argue that institutions emerge from features of the broader political and social context (Thelen 1999: 384). This perspective thereby questions the notion of an overarching, consistent, and coherent institutional order. Within the "cognitive turn" stream of institutionalist sociology, this issue emerges with respect to the idea of cultural scripts, which could be seen as a subtype of what we have called practical schemas, but also could be seen as a way of translating norms into cognitive elements (see Dobbin 1994; Heimer 1999). As Stark (2009) observes, one danger is that the older assumptions about an "over-socialized man" are revived in a new garb.

SCHEMAS, TASKS, AND NATIONAL IDEOLOGIES

What, then, can be said at a more general level about "European states and their Muslims" from the perspective we have set out? We have argued that it is through *public institutions* that citizens experience the state. As public institutions, those we have studied have a particular sensitivity to fields of state power and national ideologies. But they also have specific tasks that define and legitimate them: healing patients, defending the country, and so on. These institutions thus already harbor in their midst the broadest tensions that we have been addressing: between the functional tasks, structures and schemas particular to an institution, and more broadly distributed national structures and schemas regarding issues of diversity, religion, and citizenship. Our critiques of national models and of functionalist analyses can all be reconceived as appeals to seize this tension rather than as settling on one of its terms as an analytical foundation.

In our analyses we have approached this tension from two directions. The first is to ask how practical schemas about Muslims *bear on an institution's principle tasks*. How do actors perceive the relationship between those tasks and the presence of religious and ethnic diversity? To what extent does this relationship differ across particular instances of an institution, and across countries? We saw this articulation most clearly in the study of the French army, where the military leadership saw recruitment of Muslims as important both for accomplishing practical tasks, such as policing in poor areas, and for representing the army as reflecting all of France. However, we also saw that such a position translated neither into general acceptance of Muslims by other soldiers nor into Muslims' acceptance of their imputed difference. For many soldiers, recruits from North African backgrounds were inferior; for many of those recruits, being seen as "Muslim" ran counter to their own desire for acceptance as fully French. Hospitals presented the inverted case: directors spoke of the neutral and secular hospital, whereas other personnel dealt in practical ways with differing ideas about gender and sexuality (although there, too, often with schemas that denigrated Muslim or African patients).

From this first direction, then, the issue revolves around the relationship between definitions of the institution's main tasks and the diversity of ideas and practices associated with Muslims. It is perhaps in schools where this issue has been given the sharpest scrutiny, and also where we find the greatest degree of cross-national difference, because of the tendency to see in the school the aspirations of the society. But this "reflexivity" itself varies in degree. Reporting on his four-country study, Sunier (Chapter 3 in this volume) says that "the main differences between the four schools with regard to frames of teaching concerned the extent to which the schools consider themselves as a reflection of (civil) society." Even if British schools do not find ethnic diversity to facilitate their tasks of educating students, they do incorporate such diversity into the school's public image of itself and into the way in which the smooth functioning of the school is understood. Problems of discipline, which in the French and German schools were seen as resulting from a breakdown in the vertical social order, were in the British school attributed to the student's "lack of respect for the normative multicultural mosaic." British students understood this moral order, and would "ethnicize" issues in framing them and mobilize on ethnic lines – a practice unacceptable to French, Dutch, or German school directors. The greatest contrast to the British school is found in France, where the mere presence of tokens of Islamic religious affiliation are seen by many teachers and directors as interfering with the accomplishment of the school's mission.

Institutions differ, then, by type and also by country in the way that the everyday experience of religious or ethnic diversity is seen as supporting or endangering the performance of their task. This is also the case for those institutions in our second grouping, where we focused on their policies or justifications. Debates over electoral representation, examined by Krook, turn on the very concept of the requirements of a representative and the divisibility of the electorate. Does religious or ethnic diversity among citizens argue for corresponding diversities among elected representatives? This question is indeed task-based, and the cross-national differences reflect different historical discussions about difference and society, where the British history of debating matters of race contrasts with a Swedish focus on class and gender (and a French tension between universalism and electoral opportunism).

Our second point of departure in analyzing the function-ideology tension within institutions emerges when we ask about the reciprocal relationships between schemas and practices specific to an institution and *schemas that circulate nationally*. This question allows us to ask (1) whether some institutions provide material that is then recuperated for cross-institutional discursive production, and (2) whether some institutions are particularly susceptible to shaping by top-down pressures. (Further development of these questions brings in the dimensions of social location and conjuncture, or space and time, already discussed.)

As we have seen in the chapters, the army, school, and hospital are particularly likely to be inspected to see whether they accurately reflect national values and principles. The degree of this mirror function varies for specific historical reasons: the French school as the site of Church-Republic battles contrasts with the pluralist idea of church-dependent English schools and with somewhat similar Dutch ideas; the decentralized character of German schools probably reduces the potential of such national mirroring. The reasons for each specific configuration lie in past battles and current anxieties. However, these different potentials require mobilization. For example, only in the mid-2000s did certain French national actors call on school heads to complain about the presence of religion in the schools, with a particular policy goal in mind, namely banning the Islamic head scarf. Krook documents the quite diverse reasons that led actors to mobilize around ethnic representation in Sweden, Britain, and France.

Other institutions produce statements that can be justified wholly in terms of institutional reasoning but have a reciprocal relationship with national political and cultural ideologies. Legal reasoning is always justified in purely legal terms, as the application of legal principles, statutes, or jurisprudence. But the schemas judges have available to them are multiple and conflicting: assuring a beneficial outcome, emphasizing national principles, and agreeing with a past decision are among them. The open-ended nature of this assortment of schemas contrasts with a juridical ideology of closed continuity, well documented by Latour (2010) for the French State Council. This ideology enables judges to translate broader values or political exigencies into juridical terms, because they can justify decisions ex post facto in the sole terms of the juridical field: as simple applications of the law. We saw this most clearly in the contorted justification given by the French Constitutional Council to the law banning face-covering, where the reasoning had been explicitly rejected by the State Council but allowed the Constitutional Council to provide juridical cover to what had by that time become a political inevitability. It is the specific set of constraints and opportunities afforded to each of these two judicial bodies that explains their divergent reasons. At the same time, however, *both* bodies had begun to take account of mounting critiques of Islam as harboring values incompatible with the Republic, leading to a series of decisions that associated female dress with radical Islam and "assimilation defects" (Bowen and Rohe, Chapter 6 in this volume).

These judicial decisions created moral boundaries that were now defined in cultural terms rather than in immigration terms. The same boundary schemas emerge in less obvious form in the civic education materials examined by Michalowski; her analysis reveals the implicit assumption that the problem immigrants are Muslims, and the consequent need to highlight behavioral issues they are assumed to have.

Institutions differ, then, by token (one hospital is not identical to another), by functions (hospitals do different tasks than do elections or tribunals), and by the particular national and regional contexts in which they develop and transform. Some have, by their very nature, more to do directly with national debates; others enjoy a greater degree of autonomy. The actors who spend much of their lives working in them have their own private lives and their specific social locations in the institution itself. They draw on the repertoires of ideas, emotions, and memories that we have analyzed as practical schemas: as multiple and often conflicting sources of orientation and justification. Outside events and internal pressures shape and reshape these schemas, sometimes leading one or another idea to carry the day and influence practices. We have looked at this complex world of institutions, national ideologies, and particular actors only as it shed light on how those women and men often seen as Muslims encounter particular faces and facets of the state as they go about their lives, seeking help and legitimacy as new citizens of a fast-changing Europe. These encounters, perceptions and boundaries will continue to have much to do with shaping the new Europe.

BIBLIOGRAPHY

Boltanski, Luc, and Laurent Thévenot. 2006. *On Justification: Economies of Worth*. Princeton: Princeton University Press. (Orig. French 1991).

Bourdieu, Pierre. 1984. *Distinction: A Social Critique of the Judgement of Taste*. Cambridge, MA: Harvard University Press. (Orig. French 1979).

Bowen, John R. 2006. "*Anti-Americanism as Schemas and Diacritics in France and Indonesia*", in Peter Katzenstein and Robert Keohane (eds.), *Anti-Americanisms in World Politics*, pp. 227–50. Ithaca: Cornell University Press.

——2010. *Can Islam Be French?: Pluralism and Pragmatism in a Secularist State*. Princeton: Princeton University Press.

Butaud, Nadia, and Marie-Céclie Kovacs. 2008. *Rapports de Classe*. Paris: Éditions de L'Olivier.

Cefaï, Daniel. 2009. "Looking (desperately?) for cultural sociology in France," http://www.ibiblio.org/culture/?q=node/21.

DiMaggio, Paul. 1997. "Culture and Cognition." *Annual Review of Sociology* 23: 263–87.
DiMaggio, Paul. and Walter W. Powell, eds. 1991. *The New Institutionalism in Organizational Analysis*. Chicago: University of Chicago Press.
Dobbin, Franck. 1994. *Forging Industrial Policy: The United States, Britain and France in the Railway Age*. New York: Cambridge University Press.
Dubet, François. 2005. *Le déclin de l'institution*. Paris: Seuil.
Goffman, Erving. 1983. "The Interaction Order", *American Sociological Review* 48: 1–17.
Goyet, Mara. 2003. *Collèges de France*. Paris: Gallimard.
Hall, Peter A. and Rosemary C. R. Taylor. 1996. "Political Science the Three New Institutionalisms." *Political Studies* 44 (5): 936–57.
Heimer, Carol A. 1999. "Law, Medicine, and Family in Neonatal Intensive Care", *Law & Society Review* 33 (1): 17–66.
Joppke, Christian. 2009. "Limits of Integration Policy: Britain and her Muslims", *Journal of Ethnic and Migration Studies* 25 (3): 453–472.
Koopmans, Ruud and Paul Statham. 2005. "Multiculturalisme, citoyenneté et conflits culturels: le défi posé par les revendications des groupes musulmans en Grande-Bretagne et aux Pays-Bas", in Lionel Arnaud (ed), Les minorités ethniques dans l'Union européenne. Paris: La Découverte, p. 139–163.
Lamont, Michèle. 1992. *Money, Morals and Manners: The Culture of the French and the American Upper-Middle Class*. Chicago: University of Chicago Press.
Lamont, Michèle, and Marcel Fournier, eds. 1992. *Cultivating Differences: Symbolic Boundaries and the Making of Inequality*. Chicago: University of Chicago Press.
Lamont, Michèle, and Laurent Thévenot, eds. 2000. *Rethinking Comparative Cultural Sociology: Repertoires of Evaluation in France and the United States*. Cambridge: Cambridge University Press.
Latour, Bruno. 2010. *The Making of Law: An Ethnography of the Conseil d'État*. Cambridge: Polity Press. (Orig. French 2002).
Mahoney, James and Kathleen Thelen, eds. 2010. *Explaining Institutional Change: Ambiguity, Agency, and Power*. New York: Cambridge University Press.
Meyer, John W., and Brian Rowan, 1977. "Institutionalized Organizations: Formal Structure as Myth and Ceremony", *American Journal of Sociology* 83: 340–363
Okin, Susan Moller. 1999. *Is Multiculturalism Bad for Women?* Princeton: Princeton University Press.
Orren, Karen and Stephen Skowronek. 1994. "Beyond the Iconography of Order: Notes for a 'New' Institutionalism." In Lawrence C. Dodd and Calvin Jillson (eds.) *The Dynamics of American Politics*, Boulder, CO: Westview, pp.311–30.
Phillips, Anne. 2007. *Multiculturalism without Culture*. Princeton: Princeton University Press.
Schmidt, Vivien A. 2008. "Discursive Institutionalism: The Explanatory Power of Ideas and Discourse." *Annual Review of Political Science* 11: 303–26.
Stark, David, 2009. *The Sense of Dissonance: Accounts of Worth in Economic Life*. Princeton: Princeton University Press.
Thelen, Kathleen. 1999. "Historical Institutionalism in Comparative Politics." *Annual Review of Political Science* 2: 369–404.

——2009. "Institutional Change in Advanced Political Economies", *British Journal Of Industrial Relations* 47(3): 471–498.

Thévenot, Laurent, Michael Moody, and Claudette Lafaye, 2000. "Forms of valuing nature: arguments and modes of justification in French and American environmental disputes", in Lamont and Thévenot (eds.), *Rethinking Comparative Cultural Sociology: Repertoires of Evaluation in France and the United States*. Cambridge: Cambridge University Press, pp. 229–272.

Walzer, Michael. 1983. *Spheres of Justice: A Defense of Pluralism and Equality*. New York: Basic Books.

Index

Abdol-Hamid, Asmaa, 224
Abortion, civic education in France regarding, 175–176
Aboutaleb, Ahmed, 248
Ahsan, Raghib, 204–205
Ainuz, Najla, 220–221
Alcohol, civic education in Germany regarding, 180
Alford, R., 15
Algeria
  French military, Algerians in (*see* Military in France)
  Islamic Salvation Front, 106
  "local personal status" in, 148
Amara, Fadela, 210
Amsterdam Treaty 1997, 231
Anderson, B., 57
Anti-Semitism in France, 107
Armed forces in France. *see* Military in France
Asscher, Lodewijk, 247
Austria
  civic education in, 170
  civil law tradition in, 137
  Supreme Court, 147
  talaq (unilateral divorce) in, 147

Baumann, G., 55
Bellil, Samira, 115
Bensoussan, Georges, 107, 108
Berlin Wall, 106
Bertossi, Christophe, 8, 18–19, 256
Billig, M., 57
Birth control
  civic education regarding in France, 175–176
  in French hospitals, 36–38
  "rule of forty days," 38
von Bismarck, Otto, 46
Bleich, Eric, 195
Bolkestein, Frits, 238–240, 241
Bouchaud, Olivier, 33
Bourdieu, Pierre, 263
Bowen, John R., 19–20, 256, 257, 263, 264
van Boxtel, Rogier, 243
Breivik, Anders Behring, 7
Brenner, Emmanuel, 107, 108
British Association of Muslim Lawyers, 153
Burqas. *see* Headscarves
Buruma, Ian, 240

Çağlar, Ayşe, 4
Candidates. *see* Electoral politics
Castañeda, Heide, 49
Chadors. *see* Headscarves
Chérifi, Hanifa, 113–114
Children, education of, civic education regarding
  in France, 176
  in Germany, 181
Chirac, Jacques, 106, 108, 115, 149, 208
Church of England, 60
Church-state relationship
  civic education regarding
    comparative analysis, 186
    in France, 175
    in Germany, 180
  headscarves and, 231
  practical schemas regarding, 265
Citizenship
  defining, 4
  in Denmark, headscarves and, 219

Citizenship (*cont.*)
electoral politics and, 210–211
framing of, 181–186, 210–211
in France
civic education and, 174, 176–177, 181
headscarves and, 153–154
military and, 74–75, 97
in Germany
citizenship law, 39, 45–46
civic education and, 180, 181
integration requirements, 183–186
national imaginaries and, 2, 7
in Norway, headscarves and, 219
in Sweden, headscarves and, 219
tests, civic education compared, 169–170, 185–186
Civic education
analytical framework, 172–173
in Austria, 170
children, education of
in France, 176
in Germany, 181
citizenship and
framing of, 181–186
in France, 174, 176–177, 181
in Germany, 180, 181
integration requirements, 183–186
overview, 164–168
tests compared, 169–170, 185–186
comparative analysis, 183–186
conflicting goals of, 164–165, 166
corporal punishment, 169
cross-national differences, 185
customs and manners
comparative analysis, 184
in France, 176–177
in Germany, 180
in Denmark, 170
difficulties in, 166
in France, 174–178
children, education of, 176
customs and manners, 176–177
gender equality and women's rights, 174–175
homosexuality, 176–177
importance of topics, 184
mandatory nature of, 170–171
marriage, family and individual liberty, 175–176
overview, 20, 171–172, 173, 174, 177–178
religious freedom and church-state relationship, 175
"untouchable core" of French Republicanism, 177
violence and physical integrity, 176
gender equality and women's rights
comparative analysis, 186
in France, 174–175
in Germany, 180–181
in Germany, 178–181
Baden-Wurttemberg interview guideline, 166–168, 184
children, education of, 181
corporal punishment, 169
customs and manners, 180
45 *Stunden Deutschland* (435 hours Germany), 172, 178
gender equality and women's rights, 180–181
homosexuality, 181
importance of topics, 184
mandatory nature of, 170–171
marriage, family and individual liberty, 179
overview, 20, 172, 173, 178–179
participants' interest, 183
perceptions, 179
religious freedom and church-state relationship, 180
violence and physical integrity, 181
homosexuality
in France, 176–177
in Germany, 181
immigration and
framing of, 181–186
in France, 174, 176–177, 181
in Germany, 180, 181
integration requirements, 183–186
overview, 164–168
integration requirements generally, 168–169
language skills compared, 164–165
liberal nature of, 169
mandatory nature of
in France, 170–171
in Germany, 170–171
marriage, family and individual liberty
in France, 175–176
in Germany, 179
Muslims, special targeting of, 166–168, 186
in Netherlands, 170
overview, 20, 164–168
religious freedom and church-state relationship
comparative analysis, 186

in France, 175
in Germany, 180
social order, and legitimacy of, 165–166
sociocultural versus juridico-political norms, 168
in France, 181–182
in Germany, 182–183
standardized content analysis, 173
thematic categories, 173
time spent on, 185
violence and physical integrity
in France, 176
in Germany, 181
Civil competence, 57–58
Civil culture, 56–57
Civil enculturation, 57
Civilizing agents, schools as, 56–58
Communalism
assimilation versus, 77–78
in hospitals, 122
in military, 77–78
religious freedom versus, 106–109
Conflicts of law jurisprudence, 149
Constitutional Council. *see* France
Constitutional Council (France)
electoral quotas and, 207
European Charter for Regional or Minority Languages and, 195
headscarves and, 137, 153–158
historical background, 157
legal reasoning in, 268
Contraception
civic education regarding in France, 175–176
in French hospitals, 36–38
"rule of forty days," 38
Corporal punishment, civic education regarding, 169
Courts
Denmark, judges wearing headscarves in, 224–225
juridical framing (*see* Juridical framing)
Cultural analysis, 260–264
Customs and manners, civic education regarding
comparative analysis, 184
in France, 176–177
in Germany, 180

Dans l'Enfer des tournantes (Bellil), 115
Dati, Rachida, 210
David, Matthias, 44
Delacroix, Eugène, 176–177
Denmark
civic education in, 170
Conservative Party, 223
Constitution, 222, 224
Danish Trade Union, 220
"Danish values," 223
Dansk Folkeparti (Danish People's Party), 223, 224, 225, 230
Dansk Supermarked stores, 220–221
Employers' Union, 220
Føtex stores, 220–221
Handel og Kontor (trade union), 220
headscarves in (*see* Headscarves)
High Court, 220
Independent Board of Judges, 224, 225
Law on Antidiscrimination in the Labour Market, 220, 221
Liberal Party, 223
Magasin stores, 220
national imaginaries in, 7, 8
Red-Green Alliance, 224
sexual politics, Netherlands compared, 247
Supreme Court, 221
Deutsche Islam Konferenz, 151
DiMaggio, Paul J., 14
Divorce
civic education in France regarding, 175–176
talaq (unilateral divorce), 146–147
in Austria, 147
in Germany, 146–147
overview, 139
Døving, Cora Alexa, 226
Durkheim, Emile, 138
Duyvendak, Jan Willem, 21, 257, 259

ECHR. *see* European Convention on Human Rights; European Court of Human Rights
Education
civic education (*see* Civic education)
schools (*see* Schools)
Egalité, Laïcité, Anxiété (French television program), 110
Electoral politics
advocacy groups, prospects for, 190
citizenship and, 210–211
cross-national differences, 191
elasticity of candidacy requirements, 189–190
electoral trends

Electoral politics (*cont.*)
in France, 196
overview, 196
in Sweden, 196, 200–201
in UK, 196
equal opportunities versus equal outcomes, 192
in France, 206–210
conflict between feminist and anti-racist movements, 209
electoral trends, 196
ethnic minority women and, 209–210
homosexuality and, 207, 209
immigrants, 210
overview, 20–21
"parity democracy," 206–210
quotas, 206–210
race, focus on, 194–195, 208–210
universalism and, 194–195
women versus other groups, 206–210
identities, recognition of, 192
Muslims, defining as group, 192
national context, 190–191
overview, 20–21, 189–191, 210–211
practical schemas, 192
substantive representation versus descriptive representation, 192
in Sweden, 196–201
electoral trends, 196, 200–201
ethnic minorities as separate category, 199
foreigners, focus on, 5, 192–193
immigrants, focus on, 5, 192–193, 198–201
non-European immigrants, 196, 197, 201
overview, 20–21
quotas, 197–198, 201
women versus other groups, 196–198
in UK, 201–206
"all-black shortlists" (ABS), 204–206
"all-women shortlists" (AWS), 202–204, 205, 206
black and minority ethnics (BMEs), focus on, 193–194, 204–206
electoral trends, 196
overview, 20–21
women versus other groups, 202–204
women versus other groups
in France, 206–210
overview, 189, 190
in Sweden, 196–198
in UK, 202–204
El-Moumi, Khalil, 242–244
Employment, wearing headscarves in. *see* Workplace, wearing headscarves in
England. *see* United Kingdom (UK)
Ephimenco, Sylvain, 244
Erikson, Susan L., 4, 17–18, 256, 258
European Charter for Regional or Minority Languages, 195
European Convention on Human Rights
French anti-head scarf law, 117, 155, 157
headscarves, 222, 224
minarets, 151
talaq (unilateral divorce), 150
European Court of Human Rights
freedom of religion and, 137
French anti-head scarf law in, 157
polygamy in, 149
Turkish Refah Party in, 152

Family, civic education regarding
in France, 175–176
in Germany, 179
Ferree, Myra Marx, 39
Ferry, Luc, 108–109
Fortuyn, Pim, 1, 240–241, 244–245, 251
Framing
of citizenship, 181–186, 210–211
in civic education (*see* Civic education)
in courts (*see* Juridical framing)
in electoral politics (*see* Electoral politics)
headscarves and (*see also* Headscarves)
in Denmark, 225–226, 230
in Norway, 226–228, 231
in private institutions, 219–223
in Sweden, 228–229
in hospitals (*see also* Hospitals)
in France, 31–33
in Germany, 40
institutional approach to (*see* Institutional approach to framing)
laïcité and, 109–112 *see also* (*Laïcité* (Secularism))
in military *see also* (Military in France)
overview, 75–79
professional military and, 79–84
routine military interactions, 90–97
universalism and, 84–90
national imaginaries and (*see* National imaginaries and framing)
neoculturalism and (*see* Neoculturalism in Netherlands)

in schools (*see* Schools)
France
anti-Semitism in, 107
Beur movement, 209
Catholic Church in, 158–159
Catholic schools in, 109–110, 129
Charte de la personne hospitalisée: des droits pour tous (The patient's charter: rights for all), 32–33, 120
"citizen-soldier" concept, 74–75, 79–80
civic education in, 174–178 *see also* (Civic education)
Code de la Santé Publique (Public Health Code), 120
conflict between feminist and anti-racist movements in, 209
conscription in, 76
Constitution
anti-head scarf law and, 117, 157
electoral quotas, 207
race and, 194
Constitutional Council (*see* Constitutional Council (France))
Court of Cassation
legal commentary and, 140
talaq (unilateral divorce) in, 149–150
Declaration of the Rights of Man and the Citizen, 207
Defense Information and Communication Bureau, 80
École Nationale d'Administration (National Administration School), 156
electoral politics in, 206–210
see also (Electoral politics)
Foreign Ministry, 210
Front National, 94
Gendarmerie, 82–83, 84, 89–90, 100
Haut conseil à l'intégration (High Council for Integration), 120, 171–172
headscarves in (*see* Headscarves)
hospitals in (*see* Hospitals)
immigration policy in, 35
juridical framing in (*see* Juridical framing)
La Haute Autorité de lutte contre les discriminations et pour l'egalité (La Halde), 154–155
laïcité (secularism) (*see Laïcité* (Secularism))
Le conseil representatif des Associations Noires (Representative Council of Black Associations), 208–209
Malian population in, 34
military in *see* (Military in France)
Military School of Intelligence and Linguistic Studies, 84
Ministry for Urban Renewal, 210
Ministry of Education, 111–112, 113–114
Ministry of Health, 32, 36
Ministry of Interior, 171
Ministry of Justice, 210
Muslim population in, 34
National Council of Gynecologists and Obstetricians (CNGOF), 118
national imaginaries in, 7, 8, 9
see also (*Laïcité* (Secularism))
Ni Putes ni Soumises (Neither Whores nor Doormats) movement, 115
Office for Immigration and Integration (OFII), 171
professional military in, 79–84
Revue d'actualité juridique du droit administrative (AJDA), 157
schools in
discipline and social order and, 62–63
headscarves, 105–117
see also (Headscarves)
laïcité and, 109–112
overview, 18
Stasi Commission (*see* Stasi Commission (France))
State Council (*see* State Council (France))
volunteer military in, 76–77
Friedland, R., 15

Gay Games, 244
Gays. *see* Homosexuality
Gender equality
civic education regarding
comparative analysis, 186
in France, 174–175
in Germany, 180–181
in electoral politics
in France, 206–210
overview, 189, 190
in Sweden, 196–198
in UK, 202–204
practical schemas and, 258–259
Genital mutilation, 176, 258
Germany
Ausländerfeindlichkeit (negative attitude toward foreigners), 63–65
Aussiedler (resettlers), 40, 49
"belonging," 47–49

Germany (*cont.*)
citizenship law in, 39, 45–46
civic education in, 178–181 *see also* (Civic education)
decentralization of education in, 61
destabilized national identity in, 49–50
East Germans versus West Germans, 40, 47–49
ethnic population in, 41
Federal Agency for Migration and Refugees (BAMF), 172, 178, 181
headscarves in, 10, 39, 180
health care in, 46
hospitals in (*see* Hospitals)
juridical framing in (*see* Juridical framing)
Ministry of Interior, 151
Muslim population in, 40
national imaginaries in, 7, 9
Nazi period in, 159
Residence Act (2005), 46–47
right to reside laws
health care and, 46
Residence Act (2005), 46–47
schools in (*see* Schools)
Supreme Court, 140
"teachers of confidence" in, 63–65
Turkish population in
labor shortage and, 45
statistics, 40
Gilroy, Paul, 44
von Goethe, Johann Wolfgang, 44, 239
Goffman, Erving, 15
Great Britain. *see* United Kingdom (UK)
Guéant, Claude, 118
Guldbrandsen, Thaddeus C., 4

Hagendoorn, Louk, 250
Hall, Peter, 11
Harman, Harriet, 205
Headscarves
church-state relationship and, 231
citizenship and
in Denmark, 219
in France, 153–154
civic education in Germany, 180
in Denmark
accommodating approach, 223–224
citizenship and, 219
framing and, 225–226, 230
immigration and, 219
judges wearing, 224–225, 226
overview, 21, 216–218, 230, 231
Parliament members wearing, 224, 225–226
in private institutions, 219–223
public versus private institutions, 218–219
workplace, 220–221, 222–223
framing and
in Denmark, 225–226, 230
in Norway, 226–228, 231
in private institutions, 219–223
in Sweden, 228–229
in French hospitals
hygiene and, 125–126
nurses wearing, 124–128
in French schools
anti-woman nature of, 116–117
Catholic schools compared, 109–110, 129
conflicting schemas, 112–117
Constitutional Council and, 153–158
laïcité and, 109–112
overview, 10, 19, 104–105
religious freedom versus communalism, 106–109
tournantes (collective rapes) and, 114–115
in Germany, 10, 39, 180
juridical framing and
in France, 153–158
in Germany, 158–159
overview, 139–140
in Norway
citizenship and, 219
framing and, 226–228, 231
immigration and, 219
overview, 21, 216–218, 230, 231–232
police wearing, 226–228
in private institutions, 219–223
public versus private institutions, 218–219
workplace, 221–223
overview, 21
practical schemas and, 258
in Sweden
citizenship and, 219
framing and, 228–229
immigration and, 219
overview, 21, 216–218, 231
in private institutions, 219–223
public versus private institutions, 218–219
schools, 228–229
in UK, 10
VEIL-project, 218
in workplace (*see* Workplace, wearing headscarves in)
Health care. *see* Hospitals

Hegel, G.W.F., 44
Hekma, Gert, 243
Het Parool (Dutch newspaper), 243–244
Hijabs. *see* Headscarves
Hirsi Ali, Ayaan, 240–241, 245, 260
Homosexuality
civic education regarding
in France, 176–177
in Germany, 181
electoral politics in France, 207, 209
neoculturalism in Netherlands and, 236, 241–247, 251
practical schemas and, 259
"Honor killings," civic education in Germany regarding, 181
Hospitals
framing and
in France, 31–33
in Germany, 40
in France
accommodative practices, 122–124
Charte de la personne hospitalisée: des droits pour tous (The patient's charter: rights for all), 32–33, 120
Code de la Santé Publique (Public Health Code), 120
communalism and, 122
contraception and, 36–38
food, 122
framing and, 31–33
framing of difference, 31–33
Germany compared, 50–51
Groupe de Reflexion sur la Prise en Charge des Migrants de l'Hôpital Avicenne, 33
hygiene and headscarves, 125–126
immigration policy and, 35
integration, 33–36
Islam and, 37–38
language skills and, 35, 38
midwives, perceptions by, 36–39
nurses wearing headscarves, 124–128
overview, 4–5, 17–18
religious neutrality, 119–122
women, perceptions of, 35–36
in Germany
Aussiedler (resettlers), 40, 49
"belonging," 47–49
in *Besprechung* (daily conference), 41–44
citizenship law and, 39, 45–46
destabilized national identity and, 49–50
East Germans versus West Germans, 40, 47–49
ethnicity versus religion, 41
exclusionary incorporation, 39, 41–44
framing and, 40
France compared, 50–51
overview, 5, 17–18
Turks versus Muslims, 39–40
Typische Turk (typical Turk) stereotype, 41–44
globalization and, 30–31
overview, 17–18, 29–31
Hudson, Ghislaine, 111
Hugo, Victor, 79

Ideologies. *see* National imaginaries and framing
Imaginaries. *see* National imaginaries and framing
Immigration
in Denmark, headscarves and, 219
in France
civic education and, 174, 176–177, 181
electoral politics, 210
immigration policy, 35
military and, 80
Office for Immigration and Integration (OFII), 171
in Germany, civic education and, 180, 181
integration requirements, 183–186
in Netherlands, neoculturalism and, 242
in Norway, headscarves and, 219
in Sweden
electoral politics, 5, 192–193, 196, 197, 198–201
headscarves and, 219
Immigrant and Minority Policy, 198
UK Immigration Tribunal, 138
Individual liberty, civic education regarding
in France, 175–176
in Germany, 179
Institutional approach to framing
change and variation in, 261–262, 264–266
civic education (*see* Civic education)
courts (*see* Juridical framing)
cross-national differences and, 263, 267
cultural analysis, 260–264
cultural differences and institutional diversity, 10–14
electoral politics (*see* Electoral politics)
experience of state through public institutions, 266

Institutional approach to framing (*cont.*)
functionalist approach compared, 263
historical development of, 261
hospitals (*see* Hospitals)
Marxist approach compared, 263
military (*see* Military in France)
national imaginaries, role of, 7–9, 257
overview, 1–3
political science compared, 5–6
practical schemas and institutional structures, 14–17, 256–257
schools (*see* Schools)
sociology compared, 6–7
study of institutions, 3–7
workplace, wearing headscarves in (*see* Workplace, wearing headscarves in)
Integration
civic education, integration requirements generally, 168–169
in France
hospitals, 33–36
military, opposition to integration in, 85–86, 93
International Classification of Diseases, 31
Italy, national imaginaries in, 9

Jensen, Stiv, 226–227
Joppke, Christian, 250
Jospin, Lionel, 208
Judges wearing headscarves in Denmark, 224–225
Juridical framing
in Austria
civil law tradition, 137
talaq (unilateral divorce), 147
civil law tradition, 137
common law tradition, 137
cross-national contrasts, 136–137
in France
civil law tradition, 136–137
conflicts of law jurisprudence, 149
headscarves, 153–158
historical background, 147–148
ordre public (public order) and, 144
overview, 19–20
polygamy, 148–150
practical schemas and, 149
"right to a difference," 149
talaq (unilateral divorce), 148–150
in Germany
civil law tradition, 136–137
headscarves, 158–159
ordre public (public order) and, 144
overview, 19–20
polygamy, 145–146
talaq (unilateral divorce), 146–147
headscarves and
in France, 153–158
in Germany, 158–159
overview, 139–140
legal commentary, role of, 140–141
maintenance payments, 152–153
meta-legal options, 138, 144
minarets, 151
ordre public (public order) and, 141–144
in France, 144
in Germany, 144
meta-legal options, 144
people versus legal order, 143–144
private international law versus, 142–143
in UK, 144
vested rights theory and, 143
overview, 19–20, 135, 159–160
polygamy and, 144–146
in France, 148–150
in Germany, 145–146
overview, 139
in UK, 145–146
published opinions, role of, 140
religion and, 137–138, 158–159
shared imperatives, 135–136
sharia and, 150–153
talaq (unilateral divorce), 146–147
in Austria, 147
in Germany, 146–147
overview, 139
in UK
common law tradition, 136–137
ordre public (public order) and, 144
polygamy, 145–146
wife-beating, 150–153

Kabtane, Kamel, 113
Kelkal, Khaled, 112
Khomeini, Ruhollah, 106
Klemperer, Victor, 44–45
Koopmans, Ruud, 78, 250
Kotobi, Laurence, 31–32
Kriesi, Hanspeter, 251, 251
Krook, Mona Lena, 5–6, 20–21, 257, 259, 265, 267, 268

Lafaye, Claudette, 11
Laïcité (Secularism)
  headscarves and
    in hospitals, nurses wearing, 124–128
    hygiene and, 125–126
    overview, 19, 104–105
    in schools, 109–112 *see also* (Headscarves)
  in hospitals
    accommodative practices, 122–124
    communalism and, 122
    food, 122
    headscarves, nurses wearing, 124–128
    overview, 19, 117–119, 128–130
    religious neutrality, 119–122
  military, role in, 95–97, 99
  overview, 2
Lamont, Michèle, 11, 15
Lanefelt, Lily, 228, 229
Language skills
  civic education compared, 164–165
  in French hospitals, 35, 38
Latour, Bruno, 268
Le Pen, Jean-Marie, 94
Lesbians. *see* Homosexuality
Les Soldats de l'An II (Hugo), 79
L'Express, 109
Liberty, civic education regarding
  in France, 175–176
  in Germany, 179
Lisbon Treaty 1999, 231
The Lost Territories of the Republic (Brenner), 107, 108, 109, 117–118, 123
Louis XIV (France), 155

Mahr (marriage gift), 142
Maintenance payments, 152–153
Mali
  French hospitals, Malians in (*see* Hospitals)
  Malian population in France, 34
Mandel, Ruth, 44
Marcouch, Ahmed, 248–249
Marianne (symbol of France), 175, 176–177
Marriage
  civic education regarding
    in France, 175–176
    in Germany, 179
  mahr (marriage gift), 142
  polygamy
    in France, 148–150
    in Germany, 145–146
    overview, 139
    in UK, 145–146
  practical schemas and, 258
Mepschen, Paul, 21, 257, 259
Mestre, Claire, 31
Meyer, John, 9, 136, 261
Michalowski, Ines, 20, 257, 258, 263, 269
Michelet, Jules, 79
Migrant Integration Policy Index, 170
Military in France
  assimilation versus communalism, 77–78
  citizenship and, 74–75, 97
  "citizen-soldier" concept, 74–75, 79–80
  conflict resolution, 97–100
  conscription and, 76
  demographics of military, 75–76
  diversity in recruitment, 80
  expectations of Muslim soldiers, 87
  framing and
    overview, 75–79
    professional military and, 79–84
    routine military interactions, 90–97
    universalism and, 84–90
  Gendarmerie, 82–83, 84, 89–90, 100
  harassment of Muslims, 94
  immigration and, 80
  insubordination toward Muslim superiors, 94–95
  laïcité, role of, 95–97, 99
  leaving military, 99–100
  motivation for joining military, 86–87
  opposition to integration, 85–86, 93
  overview, 18–19, 73–75
  passive agency, Muslim soldiers as, 78–79
  practical schemas, 97–100
  professional military and, 79–84
  questioning allegiance, 92–93
  recruitment, 79–84
  religion, role of, 78, 88–89, 95–97
  routine military interactions, 90–97
  shortcomings of military service, 87–88
  "social representation" concept, 81–82, 83–84
  stereotypes, 92
  UK compared, 80–82
  universalism, 84–90
  US compared, 80–81
  volunteer military and, 76–77
Miller, P., 54
Minarets, 151
Mitterrand, François, 149

Moody, Michael, 11
Moro, Marie Rose, 31, 37
Mucchielli, Laurent, 115
Muhammad (Prophet), 151
Multiculturalism
in Netherlands, neoculturalism versus, 2, 237, 249–250
in UK, 2

National imaginaries and framing
citizenship and, 2, 7
civic education (*see* Civic education)
courts (*see* Juridical framing)
in Denmark, 7, 8
electoral politics (*see* Electoral politics)
in France, 7, 8, 9 *see also* (*Laïcité* (Secularism))
in Germany, 7, 9
institutional approach to framing, role in, 7–9, 257
in Italy, 9
multiculturalism (*see* Multiculturalism)
neoculturalism in Netherlands (*see* Netherlands)
in Netherlands, 7
in Norway, 7, 8
in Québec, 9
in Sweden, 8, 9
in UK, 7, 9
Neoculturalism in Netherlands
Anglo-Saxon model, 240
historical background, 238, 246
homosexuality and, 236, 241–247, 251
immigration and, 242
Islam and, 239, 240–241
left-wing politics and, 247, 251–252
multiculturalism versus, 2, 237, 249–250
overview, 21, 235–237, 249–252
populism and, 236, 237–241
pragmatism versus, 238, 247–249
Rhineland model, 240
US compared, 251
working class and, 239–240
Netherlands
"black schools" in, 61
civic education in, 170
Constitution Article 23, 60
Freedom Party, 241
homophobia in, 246
homosexuality and neoculturalism in, 236, 241–247, 251
Islamic schools in, 60–61
Labor Party, 247–248
national imaginaries in, 7
neoculturalism in (*see* Neoculturalism in Netherlands)
Netherlands Institute for Social Research, 246
"pillarization," 249–250, 250
"poldering," 241
populism and neoculturalism in, 236, 237–241
schools in
conflict resolution and, 67–70
discipline and social order and, 63
overview, 18
religion and, 60–61
religious dietary issues, 67–70
sexual politics, Denmark compared, 247
Norway
Act against Ethnic and Religious Discrimination, 222
Anti-Discrimination Act, 227
Equality and Anti-Discrimination Ombudsman, 221–222, 227, 230
Equality and Anti-Discrimination Tribunal, 227, 230
Gender Equality Act, 222, 227
Gender Equality and Anti-Discrimination Ombudsman, 231
headscarves in (*see* Headscarves)
Ministry of Justice, 227
MIRA-centre, 222
national imaginaries in, 7, 8
National Union of Muslim Women's Organizations, 222
Organization against Ethnic Discrimination (SMED), 222
Progress Party, 226–227
NRC Handelsblad (Dutch newspaper), 243
Nurses wearing headscarves in France, 124–128

Ordre public (public order), juridical framing and, 141–144
in France, 144
in Germany, 144
meta-legal options, 144
people versus legal order, 143–144
private international law versus, 142–143
in UK, 144
vested rights theory and, 143

Panizza, Francisco, 242
Parliament members in Denmark wearing headscarves, 224

Partridge, Damani, 39
Pasqua, Charles, 149
Physical integrity, civic education regarding
  in France, 176
  in Germany, 181
Plato, 239
Police wearing headscarves in Norway, 226–228
Politics. *see* Electoral politics
Polygamy, 144–146
  in France, 148–150
  in Germany, 145–146
  overview, 139
  in UK, 145–146
Populism and neoculturalism in Netherlands, 236, 237–241
Practical schemas, institutions and
  church-state relationship, regarding, 265
  electoral politics, 192
  gender equality and, 258–259
  headscarves and, 258
  homosexuality and, 259
  hospitals (*see* Hospitals)
  institutional approach to framing and, 14–17, 256–257
  institutional tasks, effect on, 266–267
  juridical framing in France and, 149
  legal reasoning and, 268–269
  marriage and, 258
  military (*see* Military in France)
  national circulation of, 267–268
  overview, 269
  schools (*see* Schools)
  workplace, wearing headscarves in (*see* Workplace, wearing headscarves in)
Pragmatism versus neoculturalism in Netherlands, 238, 247–249
Private international law, *ordre public* (public order) versus, 142–143
Public order. *see Ordre public* (public order), juridical framing and

Québec, national imaginaries in, 9
Qur'an, 150

Raffarin, Jean-Pierre, 109
Rath, Jan, 250
Reime, Birgit, 44
Religious freedom, civic education regarding
  comparative analysis, 186
  in France, 175
  in Germany, 180

Rohe, Mathias, 19–20, 257, 263, 264
Rose, N., 54
Rottmann, Susan B., 39
"Rule of forty days," 38
Rushdie, Salmon, 106, 239S

Santana, Jean-Claude, 112, 114, 119
Sargent, Carolyn, 4, 17–18, 256, 258, 262
Sarkozy, Nicolas, 35, 109, 156–157, 210
Scheffer, Paul, 247
Schemas. *see* Practical schemas, institutions and
Schiller, Glick, 4
von Schiller, Johann Christoph Friedrich, 44
Schnapper, Dominique, 158
Schools
  civic education (*see* Civic education)
  civil competence, 57–58
  civil culture, 56–57
  civil enculturation, 57
  civilizing agents, schools as, 56–58
  conflict resolution and, 63–70
  discipline and, 62–63
  in formal curricula, 58–59
  in France
    discipline and social order and, 62–63
    headscarves, 105–117
      see also (Headscarves)
    laïcité and, 109–112
    overview, 18
  in Germany
    Ausländerfeindlichkeit (negative attitude toward foreigners), 63–65
    conflict resolution and, 63–65
    discipline and social order and, 62
    overview, 18
    religion and, 61–62
    "teachers of confidence," 63–65
  in Netherlands
    conflict resolution and, 67–70
    discipline and social order and, 63
    overview, 18
    religion and, 60–61
    religious dietary issues, 67–70
  overview, 18, 54–55, 70–71
  religion and, 59–62
  schools as part of civil society versus instruments of state, 59–60
  social order and, 62–63
  in UK
    assaults, 66–67
    conflict resolution and, 65–67
    discipline and social order and, 63

Schools (*cont.*)
insensitivity, 65–66
overview, 18
religion and, 60
Schwarts, Remy, 116
Scott, Joan, 1
Secularism. *see Laïcité* (Secularism)
Seksig, Alan, 110
Sexual politics
abortion, civic education in France regarding, 175–176
contraception
civic education regarding in France, 175–176
in French hospitals, 36–38
"rule of forty days," 38
gender equality (*see* Gender equality)
genital mutilation, 176, 258
homosexuality (*see* Homosexuality)
Islam and sexuality, 258–260
Sharia, wife-beating and, 150–153
Siim, Birte, 8, 21, 222, 257, 258, 265
Skjeie, Hege, 222
Sniderman, Paul M., 250
La Squale (French film), 115
Stark, David, 266
Stasi, Bernard, 106
Stasi Commission (France)
headscarves in schools and, 10, 106, 109, 110, 111, 115–116
hospitals and, 117, 120, 122, 125
schools, primacy of, 59
State-church relationship
civic education regarding
comparative analysis, 186
in France, 175
in Germany, 180
headscarves and, 231
practical schemas regarding, 265
State Council (France)
headscarves and, 107, 109, 113, 114, 117, 137, 153–158
historical background, 155–156
legal commentary and, 140
legal reasoning in, 268
Stone, Alec, 156
Storberget, Knut, 226
Straw, Jack, 158
Sunier, Thijl, 5, 18, 256
Sweden
Board of Education, 228
electoral politics in, 196–201
see also (Electoral politics)
Equality Ombudsman, 229
Green Party, 197
headscarves in (*see* Headscarves)
Immigrant and Minority Policy, 198
Integration Office, 200
Left Party, 197
Liberal Party, 197
national imaginaries in, 8, 9
Social Democratic Party, 197
State Immigration Office, 200
Support Stockings, 198
Tax Agency, 200
Switzerland, ban on minarets in, 151

Talaq (unilateral divorce), 146–147
in Austria, 147
in Germany, 146–147
overview, 139
De Telegraf (Dutch newspaper), 244
Thévenot, Laurent, 11, 15
Tournantes (collective rapes), 114–115
Treaty of Westphalia, 159
Turkey
Constitutional Court, 152
in European Union, 260
German hospitals, Turks in (*see* Hospitals)
Refah Party, 152
Turkish population in Germany
labor shortage and, 45
statistics, 40

Uitermark, Justus, 21, 257, 259
Unilateral divorce *(Talaq)*, 146–147
in Austria, 147
in Germany, 146–147
overview, 139
United Kingdom (UK)
British Association of Muslim Lawyers, 153
Church of England, 60
Commission for Racial Equality, 202
Conservative Party, 203–204
Court of Appeal, 153
Disability Rights Commission, 202
Education Reform Act 1988, 60
electoral politics in (*see* Electoral politics)
Equality Act 2010, 194, 206
Equality and Human Rights Commission, 202
Equal Opportunities Commission, 202

Equal Pay Act 1970, 194
headscarves in, 10
Home Office, 83
Immigration Tribunal, 138
juridical framing in
common law tradition, 136–137
ordre public (public order) and, 144
polygamy, 145–146
Labour Party, 202, 203–205
Law Commission, 145–146
military, France compared, 80–82
multiculturalism in, 2
national imaginaries in, 7, 9
Operation Black Vote, 205
Race Relations Act 1965, 194, 204, 205, 206
schools in (*see* Schools)
Sex Discrimination Act 1975, 194, 202, 203, 205
United States (US)
common law tradition in, 137
military, France compared, 80–81
neoculturalism in, Netherlands compared, 251
Supreme Court, 140
Tea Party Republicans, 251
University of Stockholm, 228

Van der List, Gerry, 244
Vaz, Keith, 205
VEIL-project, 218
Veils. *see* Headscarves
Vested rights theory, 143
Violence, civic education regarding
in France, 176
in Germany, 181
Voting. *see* Electoral politics

Walzer, Michael, 263
Weber, Eugen, 81, 98–99
Weil, Patrick, 116
White, Jenny, 48
Wife-beating, 150–153
Wilders, Geert, 241, 245, 247
Women's rights. *see* Gender equality
Woolley, Simon, 205
Workplace, wearing headscarves in
in Denmark
judges, 224–225
overview, 220–221, 222–223
Parliament members wearing, 224, 225–226
France, nurses in, 124–128
in Norway
overview, 221–223
police, 226–228
World on Trial (French television program), 116

Yade, Rama, 210

Other Books in the Series (*continued from page iii*)

The Invention of the Passport: Surveillance, Citizenship and the State
John Torpey

Governing Morals: A Social History of Moral Regulation
Alan Hunt

The Colonies of Law: Colonialism, Zionism and Law in Early Mandate Palestine
Ronen Shamir

Law and Nature
David Delaney

Social Citizenship and Workfare in the United States and Western Europe: The Paradox of Inclusion
Joel F. Handler

Law, Anthropology and the Constitution of the Social: Making Persons and Things
Edited by Alain Pottage and Martha Mundy

Judicial Review and Bureaucratic Impact: International and Interdisciplinary Perspectives
Edited by Marc Hertogh and Simon Halliday

Immigrants at the Margins: Law, Race, and Exclusion in Southern Europe
Kitty Calavita

Lawyers and Regulation: The Politics of the Administrative Process
Patrick Schmidt

Law and Globalization from Below: Toward a Cosmopolitan Legality
Edited by Boaventura de Sousa Santos and Cesar A. Rodriguez-Garavito

Public Accountability: Designs, Dilemmas and Experiences
Edited by Michael W. Dowdle

Law, Violence and Sovereignty among West Bank Palestinians
Tobias Kelly

Legal Reform and Administrative Detention Powers in China
Sarah Biddulph

The Practice of Human Rights: Tracking Law Between the Global and the Local
Edited by Mark Goodale and Sally Engle Merry

Judges Beyond Politics in Democracy and Dictatorship: Lessons from Chile
Lisa Hilbink

Paths to International Justice: Social and Legal Perspectives
Edited by Marie-Bénédicte Dembour and Tobias Kelly

Law and Society in Vietnam: The Transition from Socialism in Comparative Perspective
Mark Sidel

Constitutionalizing Economic Globalization: Investment Rules and Democracy's Promise
David Schneiderman

The New World Trade Organization Knowledge Agreements: 2nd Edition
Christopher Arup

Justice and Reconciliation in Post-Apartheid South Africa
Edited by François du Bois and Antje du Bois-Pedain

Militarization and Violence against Women in Conflict Zones in the Middle East: A Palestinian Case-Study
Nadera Shalhoub-Kevorkian

Child Pornography and Sexual Grooming: Legal and Societal Responses
Suzanne Ost

Darfur and the Crime of Genocide
John Hagan and Wenona Rymond-Richmond

Fictions of Justice: The International Criminal Court and the Challenge of Legal Pluralism in Sub-Saharan Africa
Kamari Maxine Clarke

Conducting Law and Society Research: Reflections on Methods and Practices
Simon Halliday and Patrick Schmidt

Planted Flags: Trees, Land, and Law in Israel/Palestine
Irus Braverman

Culture under Cross-Examination: International Justice and the Special Court for Sierra Leone
Tim Kelsall

Cultures of Legality: Judicialization and Political Activism in Latin America
Javier Couso, Alexandra Huneeus, and Rachel Sieder

Courting Democracy in Bosnia and Herzegovina: The Hague Tribunal's Impact in a Postwar State
Lara J. Nettelfield

The Gacaca Courts and Post-Genocide Justice and Reconciliation in Rwanda: Justice without Lawyers
Phil Clark

Law, Society, and History: Themes in the Legal Sociology and Legal History of Lawrence M. Friedman
Robert W. Gordon and Morton J. Horwitz

After Abu Ghraib: Exploring Human Rights in America and the Middle East
Shadi Mokhtari

Adjudication in Religious Family Laws: Cultural Accommodation, Legal Pluralism, and Gender Equality in India
Gopika Solanki

Water on Tap: Rights and Regulation in the Transnational Governance of Urban Water Services
Bronwen Morgan

Elements of Moral Cognition: Rawls' Linguistic Analogy and the Cognitive Science of Moral and Legal Judgment
John Mikhail

A Sociology of Constitutions: Constitutions and State Legitimacy in Historical-Sociological Perspective
Chris Thornhill

Mitigation and Aggravation at Sentencing

Edited by Julian Roberts

Institutional Inequality and the Mobilization of the Family and Medical Leave Act: Rights on Leave
Catherine R. Albiston

Authoritarian Rule of Law: Legislation, Discourse and Legitimacy in Singapore
Jothie Rajah

Law and Development and the Global Discourses of Legal Transfers

Edited by John Gillespie and Pip Nicholson

Law Against the State: Ethnographic Forays into Law's Transformations

Edited by Julia Eckert, Brian Donahoe, Christian Strümpell, and Zerrin Özlem Biner

Transnational Legal Process and State Change

Edited by Gregory C. Shaffer

Legal Mobilization under Authoritarianism: The Case of Post-Colonial Hong Kong

Edited by Waikeung Tam

Environmental Litigation in China: A Study in Political Ambivalence
Rachel E. Stern

The Politics of Law and Development in Sudan: Who Rules the Law?
Mark Fathi Massoud

Pakistan's Experience with Formal Law: An Alien Justice
Osama Siddique

Political and Legal Transformations of an Indonesian Polity: The Nagari from Colonisation to Decentralisation
Edited by Franz von Benda-Beckmann and Keebet von Benda-Beckmann

Why Prison?
Edited by David Scott

Human Rights under State-Enforced Religious Family Laws in Israel, Egypt, and India
Yüksel Sezgin

Complementarity in the Line of Fire: The Catalysing Effect of the International Criminal Court in Uganda and Sudan
Sarah M. H. Nouwen

European States and Their Muslim Citizens: The Impact of Institutions on Perceptions and Boundaries
Edited by John R. Bowen, Christophe Bertossi, Jan Willem Duyvendak, and Mona Lena Krook